BLACK EUROPE
AND THE
AFRICAN DIASPORA

THE NEW BLACK STUDIES SERIES

Edited by Darlene Clark Hine
and Dwight A. McBride

A list of books in the series appears at the end of this book.

BLACK EUROPE AND THE AFRICAN DIASPORA

EDITED BY

DARLENE CLARK HINE,

TRICA DANIELLE KEATON,

AND STEPHEN SMALL

UNIVERSITY OF ILLINOIS PRESS

Urbana and Chicago

Manufactured in the United States of America
1 2 3 4 5 C P 5 4 3 2 1
∞ This book is printed on acid-free paper.

Library of Congress Cataloging-in-Publication Data
Hine, Darlene Clark.
Black Europe and the African diaspora / edited by Darlene Clark Hine, Trica Danielle Keaton, and Stephen Small.
p. cm. — (New black studies series)
Includes bibliographical references and index.
ISBN 978-0-252-03467-1 (cloth: alk. paper) —
ISBN 978-0-252-07657-2 (pbk.: alk. paper)
1. Blacks—Europe. 2. Blacks—Race identity—Europe.
3. Blacks—Europe—Social conditions. 4. Europe—Civilization—African influences. 5. Europe—Race relations. 6. African diaspora.
I. Keaton, Trica Danielle. II. Small, Stephen. III. Title.
D1056.2.B55H56 2009
305.896'04—dc22 2009000570

CONTENTS

FOREWORD

PHILOMENA ESSED

Black Europe is an anthology about being black in Europe and Europe turning black. It is also about the (historical) quality of life in Europe for those identified as or identifying as "black European." The persistence of "Othering" and the denial of racism form a red thread throughout the volume. Over the past decades, there has been ample finger wagging among European Union members about the spread of racism in Europe. But when it comes to accountability, each and every member state looks the other way: racism might be out *there,* somewhere else, but never *here,* not in their own country. Frequently used, but misleading, arguments include the following: You do not understand "our" culture; "our" history is very special; racism is an American thing; we do not have the word "race" in our language, therefore there is no racism; we used to send immigrants to other countries, therefore we would never discriminate; "our" country is the most tolerant in Europe, therefore our traditions preclude racism; we fought against the Holocaust, therefore "we" are above sentiments such as racism. The lived reality for black Europe is different. Being European and being brown, black, and/or Muslim are perceived as mutually exclusive categories. A case in point was the assassination of the Dutch columnist and filmmaker Theo van Gogh. I wrote in my virtual notebook:

> The evening of the assassination the air is thick with emotion. The country is in a state of shock: a ritual murder by an Islamic fundamentalist in defense of Islam and the prophet Mohammed! Van Gogh had made no secret of his anti-Islamic feelings: he had ridiculed and humiliated Muslims, Allah and the prophet Mohammed in the name of freedom of expression. In the center of Amsterdam 40 to 50,000 people flock together in grief and rage on the Dam Square. "Keep your hands off! Freedom-of-the-word!" The crowd is overwhelmingly white, but certainly not exclusively so: young, old, men, women, scarf, no scarf, public

> figures, and ordinary people. The TV camera zooms in on a scene, a verbal fight: Whites surrounding a brown man, probably Hindustan-Surinamese-Dutch:
>
> White [firm and hostile]: "Why don't you go back to your country?"
>
> Brown [angry and hurt]: "What do you mean? This *is* my country!"
>
> Pushing and shoving. . . . the camera moves on . . .
>
> The following days, commentators, politicians, public intellectuals, talk shows, and people in the street debate the assassination. How could this have happened? Fingers point to the direction of the Moroccan community, the assassin identified as "their son": "You should come out and openly condemn this brutal slaughter!" (which they do the next days in demonstrations). "You should control your youngsters!" (more difficult . . .)
>
> Then there is Fatima Mernissi, professor of sociology at Mohamed V University in Rabat, Morocco, and an internationally recognized authority on feminism and Islam, whose wise words bring some relief in the midst of emotional turmoil inside, madness outside, and volatile tension everywhere. She happens to be in the Netherlands that week in order to receive the Dutch Erasmus prize for her contribution to a better understanding of religion and modernization. She comments about the assassin: "He grew up in the Netherlands. He is a product of the Netherlands. What you want to explore is: what has happened in his life, in his environment to isolate him to the extent that he felt the only way forward to be this gruesome violence?"

It took a woman of color, a feminist, an intellectual leader and activist with a race and gender critical perspective to shift the discussion into another direction—at least for a brief moment: from problematizing Islamic Netherlands to questioning the Dutch environment; from attributing violence to Moroccan identity to identifying the Netherlands as cocreator, consciously or unconsciously. *Black Europe and the African Diaspora* can have a similar function: to critique, inspire, lead the way, to offer a different framework, a different lens for understanding "race" in Europe, as a concept, as symbol, as experience. It can also inform, educate, document, and detail many dimensions of the black presence in Europe.

As an intellectual product, a debate on black Europe, between American- and European-based scholars, would not have been possible if not for black European resistance expressed in seminal publications largely but not exclusively from the 1980s. Two particular volumes come to mind: *The Empire Strikes Back: Race and Racism in '70s Britain* (UK, 1982), and *Farbe Bekennen* (Germany, 1986). The fact that these publications are from different countries than my own is not surprising: race critical work in (mainland) Europe developed profoundly in relation to and inspired by transnational identifications. These publications relate to three significant moments in the conceptual making of "black Europe": *publishing* from a black perspective, *institutionalizing* race critical research and teaching, and *grounding* black experiences and redefinitions of the social.

The *Empire Strikes Back* is generally seen as the first collective *publication* featuring complex theories on race in Europe, from a "black European" perspective. Whether it is true that it is the first, it is the kind of decisive text that created a sense of "before" and "after," or "where were you when you first read it?" I still remember the excitement when I discovered it in "my" bookshop in Amsterdam. At the time, I was writing *Everyday Racism* (1990; first issued in Dutch in 1984) and I bought any publication on race and racism that I could afford to. The Dutch university libraries were no use; studies of racism were rare in their collections. A regular visitor of secondhand bookstores, I made many bike rides through the city of Amsterdam, a balancing act, plastic bags filled to the top with old-smelling American and British books, sometimes falling apart. To me these books were the most precious possession, an extension of identity, a lifeline connecting me to an outside world where racism could be mentioned. Occasional trips to London and the United States ended with boxes of books being sent to the Netherlands. My story is not unique. Intellectual isolation is and has been the experience of many scholars of color in Europe. From my experiences in the 1980s, I learned that if there is no pain, no anger, there is no struggle, no change. Isolation was not just a disadvantage. It has also nurtured the ability among us to identify across boarders, to understand the relativity of our own experience compared to the United States, the United Kingdom, and other European countries.

A second significant moment was an attempt towards *institutionalizing* racism studies with the establishment of the Centre for Race and Ethnic Studies (CRES) at the University of Amsterdam (1984), headed by Chris Mullard, a black professor from Britain, the first black ethnic studies professor in Europe.[1] Similar institutes had already been set up in Britain, for example, the Centre for Research in Ethnic Relations Warwick University (preceded by research units at the Universities of Bristol and Aston), not to mention the more radical Race Today Collective and the Institute of Race Relations in London. For me, too, a dream could come true: to be part of the creation of the first antiracism academic unit on the European mainland, CRES. Initially, the curriculum consisted foremost of English-language publications. *The Empire Strikes Back* was "hot." It helped us to understand Dutch racism and to legitimate local resistance. But tolerance had its limits. Attracting many students of all colors, antiracism became too much to bear for mainstream academia and media. The closure of CRES in 1991 sent the Netherlands from a potentially leading position in race critical research to the bottom of the canal. The end of CRES was one episode in a larger Western European scene throughout the 1980s and 1990s: the rise and fall of antiracism (studies).

Race critical work never develops in complete isolation. Put in general terms, one can observe an interesting chain connecting emergent black European critical writings throughout Europe from French anticolonialism and liberation writings of the 1950s and 1960s (Fanon), to antiracism and multiculturalism: in Great Britain (late 1960s onwards), the Netherlands (early 1980s to 1990s), France (1980s), Germany (late 1980s), Belgium (late 1980s), Sweden, Norway, Italy, Spain (early 1990s), Portugal (late 1990s), and Finland (2000). In the new millennium, critical studies of race are being developed in Eastern Europe: Russia, former Yugoslavia, Latvia, Romania, Turkey . . .

Who are these black Europeans? I am not sure. "Black Europe" is a descriptive category, an identity category, an unsatisfactory identity, no doubt to be contested by readers now and into the next generation. Europe created "Other" in order to find a common identity. "Other"—whether color, culture, religion, or ethnicity—became organic to European white identities, but nonwhite is not organic to the identities of those who are not native to Europe. Black is an adopted category with essentialist undertones (color) but flexible boundaries (any color and ethnicity has been included in its particular context and location, from Irish to Chinese, Indian, and African). It has been rejected by brown Ethiopians (I am not black) and embraced by ivory-colored Chinese-Indonesian-Dutch (I am black too). The search for and defense of a black European identity is not a new phenomenon. This introduces the third significant development: *grounding*. More precisely, I mean grounding "black" experiences and definitions of reality in national stories—past and present. Crucial in this process are and have been cross-European networks, in particular among women.

Early 1980s: This is one of the first *black women's* workshops on the European mainland. "Black" was always capitalized at the time. Many more would follow throughout the 1980s and 1990s. It is important to understand the significance of women's groups in European antiracism and ethnic emancipation movements. Many of the women's groups consisted of feminists who had been part of the larger white-dominated women's movement. From questioning the "we" of the "we women's movement" emerged antiracist organizations among women. Solidarity across ethnic and national borders led to the formation of numerous black women's groups, which in some countries, such as the Netherlands, renamed themselves *black and migrant women* (immigrants in the context of decolonization and labor migration) and then *black, migrant, and refugee women*. This points to the nonessentialist inclusiveness of women's groups. Throughout the 1980s and 1990s, activist conferences were organized in all of the Western European countries. Academic women, those aspiring to a career as university teachers and professors, were scarce. Most, if not all, shared the experience of isolation, marginalization, absence of institutional possibilities and virtual absence of any local or national support for racism studies.

Around the table, at that first meeting, were women of diverse colors and ethnic backgrounds. A professional translator switched effortlessly between French, German, and English. If I thought I felt vulnerable after I had publicly taken an unpopular position with my first Dutch article on *Racism and Feminism* (1982),[2] I had not seen anything yet. Black women born in Germany—the name Afro-German had yet to be invented—told their stories. Invariably, it was about growing up as the only *Farbige* (colored) in white, intensely racist, environments; no black community, no ethnic communities, only white German communities. And then to be rejected by the community of Germans. A chill went through me, still does. From their pains and struggles emerged in 1986 the women's collection *Farbe Bekennen: Afro-deutsche Frauen auf den Spuren ihrer Geschichte*,[3] unique, but as a political statement reminiscent of the black British publication *The Heart of the Race: Black Women's Lives in Britain* (1985).[4]

Where the outstanding *Empire Strikes Back* had followed academic convention by making all but invisible the persons behind the scholars, *Farbe Bekennen* was all about the lived experiences, racialized women as human beings with emotion, intellect, and dignity embedded in a historical and social context. *Farbe Bekennen* was a courageous political act, the racial unveiling of Germany, the birth of a common identity as Afro-Germans.

Without an understanding of national and cross-national struggles to claim *the right to be*, one cannot understand the significance and depth of another initiative, twenty years after the publication of *Farbe Bekennen*, namely, the BEST—Black European Studies—conference in Germany, November 2005, a (black) German initiative. This event was significant because the backlash of the 1990s, all over Europe, which went together with the unification and Europeanization of (white) Europe, had subdued many race critical voices. Black identity politics and antiracism had been criticized if not ridiculed from various sides. Personally, I have written and will continue to write critically about one-dimensional identities.[5] At the same time, in the 1990s, it had become shamefully easy and fashionable to join the bandwagon of antiracism bashing.

Participants at the BEST conference included "old timers" from the 1980s and new generation black European experts, young and upcoming scholars who, as could be expected, contested the notion of *black* emotionally and intellectually. Also not surprising were tensions resulting from the illusion called "imagined hierarchies of suffering": between visible and less visible minorities in Europe, between different gendered experiences of racism. New were (some) tensions between black U.S. participants and black European participants.

In the new millennium, I joined the black European exodus to the United States. This recent cross-Atlantic migration was not nearly as dramatic as earlier ones. Between 1950 and 1970, my family moved back and forth between the Netherlands, where I was born, and Suriname, then still a Dutch colony. In the 2000s, no one-way ticket, no "waiving white handkerchiefs," no "goodbyes for ever," and no three-minute phone calls with family left behind, where both parties would shout simultaneously "can you hear me?" Rather, continuous virtual connections. Whether in the United States or back in Amsterdam for a short visit, who would know where my e-mails came from? In the age of the virtual, illusions sometimes count as real. I might be in the ideal position to compare the racial-ethnic United States to the European versions. But I find myself resisting comparisons, fascinated by the forces of the contextual. The racial-ethnic structures of location immediately pull, push, squeeze, oppress, catch, imprison, or liberate any *body* entering its territory. So does the notion of *black Europe:* liberating, yet boxing; proactive, yet responsive; innovatively clichéd; new, yet addressing an old problem.

Black Europe is in the air. This volume, the result of a U.S.-based initiative, is a timely publication, a statement of ownership, of redefining Europe. The theories, analyses, concepts, images, and memories illuminate black Europe as [an] intellectual body and as embodiment of the intellectual. The black European project is also a product of our times, no national or disciplinary parochialisms. Contributors, a heterogeneous group in terms of gender, nationality, citizenship, or first language, offer smaller and larger pieces of the black European puzzle, the completion of which still has a long journey to go. These joint critical voices offer a different framework of thinking about Europe. The language of the volume, English, is not coincidental. It points to global power differences and to the historical influence of U.S. and British publications on the emergence of race critical publications. As some of the chapters will show, there is a thin line between feeling supported and feeling encroached upon by hands reaching out to black Europe from sisters and brothers located in the United States. Contributors have managed to address the issue with sensibility, but it remains a sensitive spot to be handled with care. That holds for me personally, too, located mostly in the United States but academically and emotionally grounded in Europe.

Notes

1. For a more detailed account of the Centre for Race and Ethnic Studies and its relation to Dutch academia, see Philomena Essed and Kwame Nimako, "Designs and (Co)Incidents: Cultures of Scholarship and Public Policy on Immigrants/Minorities in the Netherlands," *International Journal of Comparative Sociology* 47, nos. 3–4 (2006): 281–312.

2. Published as "Racisme en feminisme" in the main Dutch feminist scholarly journal at the time, *Socialisties Feministiese Teksten* no. 7 (1982): 9–40.

3. Katharina Oguntoye, May Opitz, and Dagmar Schultz, eds., *Farbe Bekennen: Afrodeutsche Frauen auf den Spuren ihrer Geschichte* (Berlin: Orlanda Verlag, 1986). English translation, *Showing Our Colors: Afro-German Women Speak Out* (Amherst: University of Massachusetts Press, 1992).

4. Beverly Bryan, Stella Dadzie, and Suzanne Scafe, *The Heart of the Race: Black Women's Lives in Britain* (London: Virago, 1985).

5. Among others, in my book *Diversity: Gender, Color, and Culture,* trans. Rita Gircour (Amherst: University of Massachusetts Press, 1996); and my articles "Multi-Identifications and Transformations: Reaching Beyond Racial and Ethnic Reductionisms," *Social Identities* 7, no. 4 (2001): 493–509; and "Gendered Normativities in Racialized Spaces: Cloning the Physician," in John Solomos and Karim Murji, eds., *Racialization: Studies in Theory and Practice* (Oxford: Oxford University Press, 2005), 229–49.

PREFACE

DARLENE CLARK HINE

This anthology is the product of the Black Europe and the African Diaspora symposium held at Northwestern University in April 2006. However, this journey actually began in 2004 in Paris, France, at the W. E. B. Du Bois Institute's conference at the Sorbonne on African American and Diasporic Research in Europe where I chaired a panel and later heard Trica Keaton deliver a superb paper that would prompt me to invite her to co-convene a conference on several of the issues that she raised. Owing to the superlative work that he has produced on Blacks in Europe and the United States, I invited Stephen Small to coedit this volume with me and Trica. Stephen gave the symposium's closing address for which he deservedly received a standing ovation.

This volume brings together authors from a range of multidisciplinary and interdisciplinary backgrounds whose study of the global and European African diaspora complicates how we apprehend notions of race, common experiences, identities, and desires relative to ever-evolving notions of blackness. This volume appears, then, at the precise moment when the notion of diaspora itself risks drifting into vacuity, owing to its overdetermination or application to any and all ethno-racial migrations. The unsettling and marginalizing responses of European nation-states to Black populations warrant sustained study, as the brilliant papers in this anthology well demonstrate. Indeed, questions relating to the historical origins and the significance of the African diaspora in Europe today command greater attention of students, scholars, and policy makers than at any previous moment. Collectively the contributions in this anthology underscore the complex theoretical and conceptual issues that animate the larger project of African diaspora studies. The essays will provoke new assessments and challenges, as the illuminating foreword by Philomena Essed and the incisive epilogue by Barnor Hesse well evince. In short, these essays underscore the imperative to engage multiple perspectives and contexts about the political economy of race, sexuality, and gender with critical emphasis on theoretical and conceptual issues emerging from these dynamics.

The Northwestern symposium and this volume additionally demonstrate that scholars of Black studies, however broadly or narrowly defined, have a great deal to learn not only *from* one another but also *about* one another and the respective challenges that we face in U.S. and European academies. To illustrate this, at one point during the symposium a heated exchange erupted concerning what some participants deemed as "African American hegemony" and the structural privilege that U.S. scholars in African diaspora studies appear to enjoy vis-à-vis their European counterparts. The very convening of such a stellar group of scholars in the United States to discuss Blacks in Europe seemed to suggest as much, even as it concealed the historical and present Black labor that goes into the making of such events. And while African American perspectives have tended to exert overwhelming influence on discourses about the global experiences of African-descended peoples, that tense moment serves as a reminder that power asymmetries operate on Black bodies and minds in faculties neither controlled nor owned by Blacks in Europe and the United States. Ultimately, African American scholars defended the hard-won resources at their command, while recognizing that it is important to think deeply and critically about the social construction of race and the destructive powers of racism in myriad historical and contemporary contexts. In short, whether in the United States, France, Britain, the Netherlands, Italy, or Germany, race issues possess continuing significance. Indeed, the modern migrations of former subjects to European cities and suburbs invites comparative analysis with the history of segregation, urban migration, and freedom struggles in the United States.

This collection of essays offers telling portraits of multifaceted dimensions of Black experiences in diverse European societies. Together they deepen our understanding of a much wider world of Black striving. They add fuel to the larger project of African American and African diaspora studies to engage and embrace the Black presence globally. As readers will note, several chapters focus on France, one of those rare sites in Europe of long-standing and complicated African, African American, and Afro-Caribbean migration. As one reviewer of the volume shared, "Another major contribution of the manuscript is related to the many European societies that are dealt with, although France appears many times, but not in a repetitious way at all because there are so many different probing approaches to even one state and also the general problem of the plight of people of African descent in Europe. Scholars who study such matters in the USA will have much to think about reading through the manuscript, and I predict that in general the chapters on Europe will lead to more refined analysis and interpretation of the many meanings and dimensions of the African diaspora globally." We concur, and thank our anonymous reviewers for their glowing praise of this volume.

The global politics of race and blackness have become increasingly salient, evidenced by the watershed election of President Barack Hussein Obama. When 69 million American voters responded so powerfully to Obama's inspirational message of hope, diverse populations across the globe took note. The call for change and the exhortation to hope resonated across Black Europe, even as many observers found it difficult to imagine, indeed hope for, an Obama in their own countries. *Black Europe and the African Diaspora* offers sophisticated treatments of important issues and themes of citizenship and belonging, and in so doing, the authors facilitate the production of even more refined and timely discourses about the meanings and hopes of the global African diaspora.

ACKNOWLEDGMENTS

Collected works such as this anthology always require the combined efforts of a range of individuals, and, when such works are based on conference proceedings, as in this case, the effort usually involves a multitude of people over an extended period of time. We wish, then, to take this opportunity to thank all of those who were involved in every aspects of this anthology from its inception to its publication. Our heartfelt thanks include everyone involved in the planning and implementation of the "Black Europe and the African Diaspora" symposium that took place at Northwestern University on April 21–22, 2006, and without whose insights and advice that event and this volume would not be possible. In particular, we wish to acknowledge the members of the conference steering committee, specifically: Martha Biondi (Northwestern University), Sherwin K. Bryant (Northwestern University), Barnor Hesse (Northwestern University), Richard Iton (Northwestern University), Aldon D. Morris (Northwestern University), Tyler Stovall (University of California, Berkeley), and Erin Winkler (University of Wisconsin, Milwaukee), and we offer specific thanks to Dwight D. McBride, former Chair of the Department of African American Studies at Northwestern University and now Dean of Arts and Sciences at the University of Illinois, Chicago. We also wish to thank the wealth of brilliant scholars who participated in the "Black Europe" symposium, in particular our keynote speaker Hortense Spillers, Manthia Diawara, Bennetta Jules-Rosette, Simon Njami, Kate Lowe, Bachir Diagne, Jennifer Brody, and Didier Gondola, as well as the graduate students who, collectively, made this such an intellectually enriching and stimulating gathering. Indeed, we thank them all for their tremendous contribution and faith in our mission that made this event such a huge success.

We extend our deep thanks and appreciation to the contributors of this anthology for their outstanding scholarship and sustained commitment to this project, not to mention their great forbearance during this protracted and complex process. They have responded with great warmth to all our requests and we are deeply grateful to them. We have gained invaluable insights from their work, and we hope that they gain some reward from seeing their scholarship finally in print.

Finally, we wish to extend our thanks to the sponsors of the "Black Europe" symposium, specifically, the Center for African American History, the Department of African American Studies, the Department of History, the Institute for Diaspora Studies, the Office of the Provost, the Weinberg College of Arts and Sciences Program in African Studies, and the Center for International and Comparative Studies, all at Northwestern University. We also greatly thank the Department of African American Studies at the University of California, Berkeley, for its support, especially in making Stephen Small's contributions to this anthology possible. And, we would be remiss in not acknowledging Henry Louis Gates Jr., Director of the W. E. B. Du Bois Institute for African and African American Research at Harvard University, whose conference in Paris, France, in 2004 proved fertile ground for the fortuitous meeting of Darlene Clark Hine and Trica Danielle Keaton. Many thanks to Anne Youmans and Angela Lintz for their thoughtful and thorough edit of the manuscript. We also thank everyone who provided administrative and technical support, in particular Kulsum Jaffer, Marshanda Smith, and Lisa Yamanishi (one of our graphic artists). We also greatly appreciate the patient and thoughtful editors at the University of Illinois Press, including Rebecca McNulty and Tad Ringo, whom we wish to thank for their diligence and hard work.

INTRODUCTION

The Empire Strikes Back

STEPHEN SMALL

In this anthology, we explore multidisciplinary approaches to the documentation, interpretation, and understanding of the Black diaspora in Europe. We examine the geographical, political, ideological, and imaginative parameters of Europe and the European Union, and the persistent paradoxes that the Black presence presents for such definitions. And we explore the ways in which diaspora is conceptualized, imagined, embraced, and negotiated. Who is included in diaspora? And who is excluded? Our interest is with the connective tissue of collective belonging—individual, family, and community—in what we call the Black diaspora in Europe. Our concern is with the hard facts of migration and settlement, citizenship and nationality, both historically and at present; with the harsh facts of poverty, inequality, and economic well-being; with the subtle nuances of representations across the media; and with the shifting terrains of blackness and the diaspora.[1] In this anthology, we have urged contributors to take up some of the most salient issues, especially those that transcend geographic and disciplinary specificity. We are confident that readers of the anthology will agree that the contributors have provided engaging, insightful, and provocative responses.

Before I continue, let me tell you a fact. Although I was born and bred in Liverpool, England, the largest slave port of the largest empire to ransack the continent of Africa, and home of the nation's longest-standing Black population; and although I lived in England until the age of twenty-five, I didn't know that I was a European until I stepped off a plane in San Francisco airport in 1984. Why? I'll get back to that.[2]

The Decline of the British Empire

The title of this chapter is, of course, adapted from the title of a book published in Britain in 1982.[3] Jointly published under the name of the Centre for Contemporary Cultural Studies (CCCS), at that time directed by Professor Stuart Hall, it included contributions from several young scholars who have gone on to make a name for themselves on both sides of the Atlantic, including Paul Gilroy, Hazel Carby, and John Solomos. It is a powerful, insightful and compelling piece of work, which I urge you to consult. Many of the issues they raised are as compelling today as they were twenty-five years ago, and I want to highlight several of them.

First, they highlighted the need to put race, racism, and British-born Black people at the forefront of any analysis of the crisis of British capitalism. They were insistent that British-born and -raised Blacks, and other children of Britain's former colonies, should be at the forefront of any analysis and solutions to the crisis of capitalism, as they saw it, reflected in the enduring problems of "race relations."[4] This idea was particularly reflected in a slogan common among trade union strikers, especially Asian women—in response to the British query—"Why are you here? And why don't you go back to where you came from?" The answer is, "We are here because you were there!"[5]

Second, they insisted on the need for a collaborative, multidisciplinary enterprise, difficult as it was and is, to address the myriad issues confronting Black people in Britain, as a diasporic site, and Britain's relationship with Europe, Africa, and the world. Third, the primary focus of the book was consideration of how race, and the presence of Black people in Britain, reflected the crisis of capitalism and highlighted the role of the state apparatus in resolving race relations—"never trust the state," they told us—as it negotiated the nation's economy in an increasing globalized world dominated by multinational companies. They looked at immigration and migration, at employment and education, at law and order, and at the myriad negative images of Blacks, especially women, in the media. They also reprimanded British cultural studies for ignoring the central role of race and empire in British imperial cultural formation—high culture and low culture, from European classical music to cricket.

Fourth, they brought gender analysis to the foreground by articulating the role of gender and gender ideologies in the formation of state policies, insisting on the need to document the particular experiences of Black and Asian women in all aspects of their diasporic settlement and, importantly, the need to question the limitations and racism of white feminist analysis. In that volume, Hazel Carby's much-cited essay "White Women Listen?" and Pratibha Parmar's essay on Asian women's struggles was joined two years later by an article "Challenging Imperial Feminism" by Valerie Amos and Pratibha Parmar.[6] Valerie Amos, by the way, is now Baroness Amos in the House of Lords, and is currently the Labor Party's leader of the House of Lords.[7] A solitary Black woman, and a salutary reminder that high office awaits all of us who would join the state. Gilroy, who wrote the introduction, reminded us that the final draft of the book was done in a context of massive street riots across Britain—some called them "race riots"—in 1981, including that of Brixton.

After rereading the book in the summer of 2006, my own conclusion is that much of what they called for in the analysis of these issues is in progress—not enough overall, of course, but enough, I suspect, to suggest that we are working in the right direction. But don't take my word for it—Carby, Gilroy, Parmar, and Solomos are still alive and kicking, so you can consult their work.[8] Of course times have changed, and here I take up some of the issues that they raised, relate them to the context of the twenty-first century, and to Europe and the Black diaspora more generally. I then introduce the chapters that comprise this book, and the themes and issues raised in them.

Conceptualizing "Black Europeans" and "Black Europe"

As I said above, I didn't know that I was a European until I stepped off a plane in San Francisco International Airport in 1984. People in Liverpool who looked like me grew up with various names, but "European" was not one of them. We called ourselves "West Indians" or "half-caste" or "Black British" or later, "Liverpool-born Blacks."[9] We might have called ourselves British, but we were never English (that was too white) and, from our point of view, like most people in England at that time, Europe was always over there. "Where are you going on holiday?" someone might ask. "I'm going to Europe," we might say. The European Union (EU) did not exist at that time—it was still the Common Market—and in Britain our monetary system was not even decimal—pounds, shillings, and pence, it was (12 pennies in a shilling, 24 shillings in a pound), all designed, no doubt, to confuse and perplex foreigners. Besides, for many in Britain, there was another reason not to call ourselves European. Europe was the place all the diseases came from: French pox, German measles, Spanish flu, Dutch disease . . . and rabies! But when I got to California, I found out that I was a European. People asked me, "What is it like in Europe?" "I don't know," I said, "but I can tell you about England."

So who is a Black European and what is Black Europe? Contributors to this anthology pose this question several times, and it is one we must confront from the start. Are "Black European" and "Black Europe" American constructions to classify Europe? Or do they reflect a sense of identity indigenous to Europe? They are, of course, not just questions of legal definition, but of individual and collective definition, of belonging and yearning—even of status and attainment. I for one have never called myself a Black European, and I have never met anyone who called themselves a Black European.

And if we ask who is a Black European, we must also ask, who is Black in Europe? In this volume, Allison Blakely shares with us statistics on Blacks in

Europe; Nimako and Small comment on the high concentrations of Blacks in certain nations, cities, and neighborhoods. These data provide us with a necessary and useful point of departure. But census definitions probably don't correlate with the way most people define themselves in practice. Tina Campt's essay in this anthology of the young German of Algerian descent is a case in point. Blackness is not just, or even, about African ancestry. It's about racialization and the ascription of blackness—which reminds us, once again, you don't have to be Black to be racialized as Black. For example, at a conference in England that I attended in the 1980s, I asked a woman where she was from. "I'm Moroccan," she said. "So you're an African?" "Yes," she said. "So are you Black?" "You know what is funny? In Morocco I'm never Black, and in England I'm never white." This is not just a matter for Moroccans, as any one familiar with the construction of race in the British census will tell you. Britain introduced race into the census in 1991—in which Blacks were divided into Black-African, Black-Caribbean, and Black-other; and Asians into Asian-Indian, Asian-Pakistani, Asian-Bangladesh, and Asian-other. And then to crown it all off, "other-other" is a category.[10]

As most readers of this anthology already know, definitions of race vary with gender and class. For example, the number of Blacks in Liverpool has decreased dramatically in recent decades—from an estimated high of 17,900 in 1981 to less than 7,000 in 1992. The change is not only because people like me left the city for economic reasons and because of racial hostility, but also because white mothers of kids of mixed origins, after family breakups, moved to areas of the city with almost no blacks, and then raised their children to define themselves as white.[11]

My own phenotype allows me to pass—at least in the eyes of others—for many things. Growing up in Liverpool in the 1960s and 1970s, I was often called "half-caste"; in England in the 1980s, I was never anything but Black. When I lived in Amsterdam in 1980, I was called a Surinamer or a Turk, and people spoke to me in Dutch or Surinamese. After moving to northern California, people called me English, Latino, or Black, depending on what clothes I was wearing, what music I was listening to, and whether the people I was with spoke English or Spanish. When I taught at Leicester University in 1992–1995—the city with the largest proportion of what we in Britain call "East African Asians"—people spoke to me in Gujerati or Panjabi.[12] When I lived in Bordeaux in 2002–2004, people thought I was Algerian and spoke to me in French and Arabic. Variations are in the eye of the beholder, but they are shaped by localities, prevailing understandings and subjectivities, themselves reflecting the particular histories of nations and cities. So who is Black is not something we should take for granted. And in our empirical research, as is exemplified in several chapters in this anthology, we must examine the precise empirical referents to the language and terminology that we use.

And what is Europe, when we talk about the Black diaspora in Europe? What are its geographic, its political, and its imaginative boundaries? What is at stake in the struggle over such definitions? Europe constructed itself in its dealings with the world in the fractures and frictions of the European enterprises known as empires. But how European is Europe?[13] And who will decide? And if we take the case just of the European Union, it is constantly expanding. This association of nations began in 1951 with six members; by 2006 it had twenty-five members and a total population over 450 million.[14] As Nimako and Small remind us in this anthology, over 70 percent of Blacks live in six nations. For those studying the Black diaspora in Europe, it is highly likely that these nations will be the main focus of our attention. In the chapters in this anthology the following nations are discussed in some detail: Great Britain, France, the Netherlands, Germany, Italy, and Portugal. Others are also discussed, including Spain, Russia, Switzerland, and Greece. But as Sharpley-Whiting and Patterson, among others, point out, we must pay attention to thousands of Blacks, thousands of miles outside the immediate geographical boundaries of Europe if we want to come to terms with the conundrums of identification that the notion of Black Europe conjures up.

Class, Inequality, and the State

Discussion of class, inequality, and the state is implicit, sometimes explicit, in most of the chapters in this anthology. The state regulates immigration, manages policies around discrimination and integration, collects and distributes data on racial demographics, and arbitrates the resources for education, employment, and unemployment. It is also the site for so much protest and negotiation, all the more so in a context of increasing international migration and the attendant aspects of globalization. Though it is self-evident, it nevertheless merits mentioning that power and powerlessness, from citizenship, the right to vote, employment and wealth—around gender, class, and race/blackness—is a central organizing theme in Europe that shapes what happens to Black people and what Blacks can do.

As we examine Blacks in Europe, so much of our work would benefit from consideration of questions of capitalism and the state, of class and class inequality—in immigration and citizenship, in asylum seekers and illegal residents. There is tremendously important work and it is substantial—from Stuart Hall and Chris Mullard to Valerie Amos and Hazel Carby. Much of Paul Gilroy's work before he moved to the United States was on class and politics in Britain and Europe. One of the most consistent analyses of class and race and gender is to be found in the work of Robert Miles and Annie Phizacklea. A prominent issue here of course has to do with the international division of labor and its analogue the international division of reproductive labor. Phizacklea, Nira Yuval-Davis, Philomena Essed, and others focus centrally on these issues.

Gender Ideologies and the Experiences of Black Women

As is evident in many of the chapters in this anthology, one does not and cannot define, conceptualize, theorize, or research the Black diaspora in Europe without bringing gender ideologies and the experiences of Black women to the foreground. Collectively the chapters remind us that in terms of diaspora our concern is to explore the ways in which blackness and race are created and constituted through gender. Carby's agenda in 1982 focused on absences and visibilities—the absence of the experiences of Black women in the work of white feminism or in the documentation of the lives and agency of immigrants, migrants to postwar Britain. The roles of women as family makers in reproductive labor, as activists in trade unions and in the schools whose racist education stifled Black children's ambitions. She highlighted the consistent failure to document Black women as initiators of migration. And in terms of visibilities, she highlighted stereotypes and caricatures of Black women in film, television, and advertising and as savages in children's schoolbooks. What we need, she urged us, was more Black herstory to complicate and detail the real history of Black migration as more than that of man. We see much more of this in this anthology.

Carby also called for gender analysis more generally in the racial formation of the British state. Her call has been taken up, not only in Britain but elsewhere in Europe.[15] A new generation is in action and well represented in this anthology in the chapters by Keaton, Di Maio, Campt, Wright, Wekker, and Brown.[16] Work continues on a wide range of issues—gender in the implementation of state racism and discrimination in employment—from unequal wages in women's work and domestic violence to overrepresentation of Black women and children in poverty. But more needs to be done—international division of reproductive labor through globalized networks—from farm and factory in the so-called third world, to hospitals and public transport. There is increasing involvement of Black women, many from Africa, as drug mules and as sex workers—from Brazilians in Lisbon and Nigerians in Rome to Dominicans in Amsterdam and Paris. Sex work as labor, reflecting limited opportunities in a globally unequal economic system, must figure centrally in our research, as must the overrepresentation of Black women in Europe's prisons. And if Black women come to Europe to do sex work, white men go to South Africa and Gambia, to Brazil and the Dominican Republic for sex workers.[17]

As Michelle Wright reminds us in this volume, we haven't even begun to do significant research on issues around sexuality (and, we might add, transgender issues) beyond masculinity and the feminine mystique, images in media, and performance; we have very little published work on these issues, on the experiences of Blacks of often deliberately ambiguous gender identity, of the responses to them and their responses to those responses. We know there are small but significant communities. The need for multidisciplinary work is also evident. And the media must focus centrally, given the globalized images of Black women in television, film, and advertising, especially for tourism. Much has been done on Josephine Baker in this respect. This an excellent point of departure, and work will continue. But many more women are present, writing, performing in theatre and film. We need to document.

Literature must figure prominently, too—we must work hard to identify and explore writing by Black women in fiction and nonfiction, in poems. Our specialists on individual nations will know this literature; Di Maio in this volume provides rich documentation. Let's have more of this.

Interracial marriage and the identities of people of mixed racial descent also figure largely in Europe, and far larger than in the United States, given the distinctive history of these phenomena in Europe and the far higher rates of dating and marriage. For example, rates of interracial marriages between Blacks and whites in Britain are 35 percent for Black women, 40 percent for Black men. The proportion of people of mixed origins among Germans is also high. Implications for racial identity are profound, and for changing notions of belonging and identification with the diaspora.

Last but not least, as someone born outside the capital of Britain, let me remind readers that there are Blacks outside the capitals of these nations. Starting with these capitals is of course understandable and an excellent point of departure, but let's move on. Let's not continue to reduce France to Paris, Britain to London, Germany to Berlin, or Italy to Rome. If we really want to understand the Black presence in Europe, and we really want to study space and place, then we can only do this successfully by traveling outside the capitals. Study of this kind will enrich our understanding of the variety and vitality of Blacks across Europe.[18]

(Dubious!) Comparisons with the United States

Many readers will have realized that up to this point I have not made reference to the United States. This has been deliberate. Let me say why. Research and writing on Blacks in the United States has been tremendously useful in the work on Europe, the Caribbean, and the United States. I'm hopeful of the contribution the extant literature on Black USA can contribute to the study of the Black diaspora in Europe but cautious, hesitant even, about the ways in which it might distort our focus—the questions asked, the concepts used, the methodologies deployed, and the empirical research conducted. These points connect with some of the observations made by Wright about the sheer volume and resources of the U.S. academy, with Stovall's idea of the "African Americanization of France," as well as with the deliberations of Wekker.

The Black diaspora in Europe is in large part, and always has been, dominated by the discussions of the Black diaspora in the United States. Josephine Baker is the most prominent example here, and Blacks in the American military are also known. So too, are African American cultural products in music (from jazz and soul to rap and hip-hop), in religion, in political thought, in film and literature, and in pan-Africanism. The lives of Black Americans reiterate themselves in the lives of Blacks in Europe. As a teenager in England, my first readings were of *Black Bourgeoisie* by E. Franklin Frazier, *The Autobiography of Malcolm X*, *Soledad Brother*, and *Angela Davis: An Autobiography.*

Comparisons with the Black United States offers lots of potential—concepts, theories, methods. It is almost impossible in Britain, perhaps even in Europe, for work on Black women, by Black women, to fail to mention key African American feminists from Angela Davis and June Jordan to Barbara T. Christian and Patricia Williams, from Alice Walker and Toni Morrison to bell hooks. This has been unavoidable and also necessary and useful. But my fear is that concepts from elsewhere will prevent the emergence of appropriate, location-specific concepts developing in Europe.

Let me just mention three: *ghetto*, *race riot*, and *who is Black*. In the United States, the concept of a ghetto refers to a predominantly Black, class-stratified neighborhood, with Harlem in New York, Watts or South Central in Los Angeles, and the south side of Chicago being well-known examples.[19] In contrast, in the UK it means any neighborhood with 20 percent or 30 percent people of color, including Black, Asians, and others—with Brixton in London, Handsworth in Birmingham, Moss Side in Manchester, St Paul's in Bristol, and Toxteth in Liverpool being well-known examples.[20] Black Liverpool, for example, had in the 1991 census less than 7,000 people—in a city of 452,000—that is, 1.5 percent. It is called a ghetto still. Historically in the United States, a race riot involved white people, often with the support of the police, in direct conflict with Blacks. In Great Britain, a race riot involves Blacks and whites against the police. In France, it involves white French and North Africans (not usually called Black) against the police.[21]

The definition of who is Black varies considerably. If you were to go to some Black organizations in Britain, you would be surprised that they have very few people of African descent. One example is Southall Black Sisters in London, which involves primarily Bangladeshi and Pakistani women. Other organizations have Blacks, Indians, and other ethnic groups in them.[22] As I have argued elsewhere, some books that compare Blacks in the United States and Britain, failing to draw the distinction between the definitions, end up with false numbers.[23] These three concepts reveal some of the pitfalls of uncritical borrowings from the United States.

Yes, we will continue to make reference, implicit and explicit, to the African diaspora in the United States, but we must also insist upon the need to analyze Blacks in Europe in terms of concepts and theories developed in that context. Readers of this anthology will be impressed by the ways in which the authors have resisted the strong pull to analyze the Black diaspora in Europe primarily through the lens of the African diaspora in the United States.

Establishing Our Priorities

One of the strengths of an anthology like this one is that it urges us to contemplate the many options before us and to consider our priorities. In this anthology, we urge readers to deliberate on the options. What projects must command our attention? What data must we collect—especially before we lose them? Consider, for example, the *Empire Windrush*—the ship that arrived in Southampton in 1948 and is usually seen as the start of West Indian migration to Britain. Right now, any of those several hundred West Indians who are still alive are in their eighties. Marika Sherwood runs an organization that documents Black life and history in Britain, and she urges us to spend more attention on history—people are dying, communities are being transformed, documents and data are being lost. She insists that there is too much preoccupation with the present, and we are going to lose forever the history of these communities. This fact insists upon an urgent need to interview *Empire Windrush* arrivants. What disciplines are most important? In this anthology, we hear from multiple disciplines including history, anthropology, cultural studies, sociology. The editors believe that this demonstrates the importance of multidisciplinary approaches to the Black diaspora. We hope that this volume will inspire people to produce far more literature, including novels, poems, political writings, memoirs. We also need to locate and disseminate far more photographs.

A primary concern is the need for what I call the excavation and archeology of the Black present. Concrete, empirical, detailed studies of individuals, families, neighborhoods, communities, and cities. We simply don't have the data—on lives and histories and experiences. Anthologies such as this one can have a direct influence on the next generation of scholars in these areas. I would urge us to consider the range of topics and to bring to the attention of younger scholars—graduate students—the possibilities and limitations that will confront them.

Establishing priorities are all the more urgent because of the dramatically changing situation in Europe. Blacks were always a minority in Europe, and as the European Union expands, they are becoming a smaller and smaller minority. Besides, the color and culture of immigrants to Europe has changed. Only in Britain were most immigrants Black, but that had changed by the 1980s. Now most immigrants to Britain are white, and most immigrants to Europe are Muslim. At the present time, Muslims are the largest minority in Europe and, in the aftermath of the war on terror, Islamophobia is a far more central focus of attention than Blacks. This means there are less and less resources for Blacks and less attention to them as they are rendered marginal.

The Structure of the Book

The book is structured to take up the many issues pertinent to the Black diaspora in Europe. What is Europe and who is European? Who is Black in Europe, who is a Black European? What is the Black diaspora in Europe, historically and at present, and who is included or excluded from that diaspora? Some chapters address their issues to Europe as a whole, and others subject the issues to greater empirical scrutiny in individual nations, or in comparisons across specific nations. And collectively, the authors deploy the tools of multiple disciplines to highlight the most salient issues.

Blakely's chapter provides an excellent history and the broad demographic context to the Black presence across Europe. Blakely demonstrates that in the face of specific national histories, divergent contemporary racial demographics, and political and social structures, generalizations about the Black presence across the continent can be made. He considers nations usually ignored, for example, Russia. He documents the early Black presence in particular nations and articulates how the experiences of Blacks in individual nations today complicate our understanding of the diaspora.

Brown takes up the issue of defining the diasporic, particularly in terms of collective and individual subjectivities. Using her family reunion as the focus of analysis and linking this analysis to her recent ethnographic work in the port city of Liverpool, England, she contends that diaspora is defined more by relationships, and less by displacement and dislocation. She concludes by reminding us how the work of one of the earlier analysts of the diaspora—St. Clair Drake—still has import in contemporary analysis.

Di Maio focuses her attention on immigration, diaspora, and belonging in Italy. In the study of the Black presence in Europe, Italy is usually neglected. In recent decades, this has changed, and an exploration of Italy, as Di Maio demonstrates, provides insights into a nation that offers divergent patterns for Europe. She focuses on literature produced by migrants that express their feelings of belonging and loss, and of aspirations towards the nations from which they, or their parents, come. Such stories provide more nuanced details about these issues than are usually provided in analyses by social scientists. The rich, textured descriptions that Di Maio recounts testify to the value of multidisciplinary contributions to understanding the black diaspora in Europe and to the data and evidence that such insights provide.

Hondius explores the history of the Black presence in the Netherlands as a context for understanding issues of memory and recollection, as well as the ambivalence towards skin color so manifestly demonstrated by the majority of the Dutch population today. She documents the arrival of Blacks in the Netherlands at the end of the sixteenth century, their initial experiences, and how they were, subsequently, erased from the historical record and, equally importantly, from Dutch collective memory. Her chapter also demonstrates the ways in which attitudes towards Blacks in Europe—including their presence and history—can vary fundamentally from nation to nation.

The sociohistorical significance of the Black American presence in France, its causes of migration, and present African-origin demographics have prompted Stovall to examine comparatively the Black histories of the United States and France. In so doing, he observes that since the mid-twentieth century there has been a convergence between the life worlds of Blacks of the two nations, thereby unsettling a trope cherished in French society and upon which African American expatriation has been predicated—color-blindness. Nowhere is this more apparent than in the forms of exclusions experienced by Blacks in both countries and the discourses of race that they have evoked. "Could it be," queries Stovall, "that African Americans who come to Paris today in search of the legendary color-blind paradise might only find a world very similar to the one they left behind?"

Wekker addresses the obstacles that confront us as we attempt to imagine Black Europe. Examining the various layers of these obstacles, she tells us, like just so many layers of an onion, allows us to interrogate the pitfalls and potential of the challenge. She begins with the wider geopolitical and power dynamics of such an imagining, explores some of the "powerful contradictions" of the Black presence in Europe, and then deploys the specifics of the Netherlands to explore "racial Europeanization" in the Dutch context. All Blacks are not created equal, her work draws to our attention, and this is evident in competing definitions of blackness, particularly as they are played out across the Atlantic theater.

France is fertile ground in this volume for explorations of racialized formations that invite us to theorize belonging and solidarity constructs among diaspora Blacks who inhabit French nation-space. To this end, Keaton explores what she calls "Black migration narratives of inclusion," that is, accounts of the positive reception of Black Americans in Parisian society that foster the fallacy of color-blindness. Juxtaposing contemporary Black American expatriate narrative to the 2005 "riots" in France, Keaton asks how we might interpret the differing reception of Blacks vis-à-vis the social realities of race suffered by France's racialized "others," namely African origin youth residing in the "Other France," the impoverished public housing projects in the French suburbs.

Recently, as Constant observes, there has been an explosion of racialized events in France that has led to the resurrection of what remains a taboo topic: race consciousness and the notion of race as an explanatory variable of social inequality in French society. While highlighting the necessary distinctions between U.S. and French conceptualizations of race in both theory and practice, Constant invites a debate on the question of race in France by interrogating widely held political assumptions of race neutrality. As he argues, "the French race-neutral model has been far more an ideal than an empirical model: color-blind in theory, [France] has always been race-coded in practice."

Julien provides an analysis of the most famous and symbolically important African American to have visited France in the mid-twentieth century: Josephine Baker. She focuses on the two most popular movies in which she played a leading role, *Zou Zou* and *Princesse Tam Tam*. Via a detailed assessment of the racial symbolism of the movies, she shows how they work historically to reify and affirm racial difference in the French context, and she contends that they help us identify patterns of continuity at the present time.

Francis examines Josephine Baker as a cinematic phenomenon that reveals key aspects of performance and transnationality. The "terrain and methodology" of her essay concerns "stardom and how it was made and what it expressed." Comparing Baker with other Black women in film, especially Black Americans, Francis argues that Baker's success "functioned as part of a vindicationist uplift narrative" for Black movie audiences. She asks, "Does transnationality require performativity? And is this relationship gendered—or rather how is it gendered and raced?" Her answer is that Baker, and Black dance, "present a complex relationship between performance and text around the question of technology."

Campt focuses on Germany and explores questions of national distinctions and transnational identities via the lens of visual culture and the "indexicality of race." How do we theorize diaspora as an explicitly transnational formation that parochializes the United States, she asks, and what do visual representations add to this initiative? Examining a range of photographic representations of "Afro-Germans" in early twentieth-century Germany—photographs where "race becomes visible in ways that are inextricable from gendered embodiments of national belonging"—provides an opportunity to advance such an enterprise.

Weheliye dissects ideas of the "we" that are affirmed or implied in notions of the community, the nation, the people, and the diaspora. Exploring diaspora's promise as "a virtual technology of collectivity," he examines recent articulations of Afro-German music to explore the specifics of German identity, as well as the broader problems of national and diasporic identity in Europe.

Sharpley-Whiting and Patterson use the case of France and its overseas territories to highlight the problems in defining the geographical and political contours of Europe and Black Europe. The existence of these territories, legally part of the European Union, historically part of the French nation, and geographically isolated from Europe, pose problems for defining Black Europe.

Taking the situation of Blacks in Britain as a point of departure, Nimako and Small question the ways in which blackness is defined both inclusively and exclusively and explore the implications of the arrival in Europe, in recent decades, of more and more Africans from the continent. They highlight the marginality of Blacks in the European Union—both demographically and in terms of economic and political power—and discuss relations between Europe and the various nations of Africa. They articulate the conundrum of positionality and strategy, as Blacks in Europe, and African nations outside Europe, negotiate with the stakeholders of the European project writ large in the competition for access to resources and power.

Wright is concerned with the competing ways in which blackness is currently defined, with the historical events invoked to define blackness, and with how other, arguably equally important, events, are left out of the reckoning. In describing frameworks of knowledge production, she asks why and how dominant definitions of blackness continue to so flagrantly exclude women and gays, and how might the analytical inclusion of gender and sexuality enrich our understanding of power and struggle? Interrogation of these practices is necessary so that we can further accommodate the irreducible diversity within the African diaspora.

Conclusion

On behalf of the editors I want to once again thank all the presenters at the 2005 conference at Northwestern University for urging us to examine the black diaspora in Europe. From that conference has come this anthology. What the anthology demonstrates, among other things, is that as we study the Black diaspora in Europe we are spoiled for choice, with a plethora of issues, wonderful opportunities for innovative substantive research, and a sense of urgency on a number of research topics. We have a lot of hard work ahead of us—the usual scenarios of limited resources, unlimited topics, and the practicalities of getting a job, securing tenure, not to mention those transatlantic flights to visit the archives and the communities whose lives we are attempting to document.

And yet I'm optimistic. The challenge promises to be fulfilling, the contributions that our research will make promise to be important, and it is so very necessary to continue to document how the Black diaspora in Europe enriches our understanding of the Black diaspora elsewhere, as well as social relations in Europe and of the world. To paraphrase the words of Sivanadan, we must do it because the study of the Black diaspora in Europe broadens our mind, expands our horizons, enlivens our passions, and enriches our lives.

Notes

1. A useful documentation of the obstacles confronted by blacks and other people of color in Europe—immigrants who are victims treated as suspects—can be found in Liz Fekete and Frances Webber, *Inside Racist Europe* (London: Institute of Race Relations, 1994).

2. Talking about Liverpool, noted historian David Richardson tells us, "Between 1780 and 1807 over three quarters of all English ships involved in the English slave trade were fitted out in the port. Thus Liverpool was not only the largest single English slaving port in the eighteenth century. After 1780, it was also the undisputed slaving capital of England and by far the largest slave port in the Atlantic world." David Richardson, "Liverpool and the English Slave Trade," in Anthony Tibbles, ed., *Transatlantic Slavery: Against Human Dignity* (London: HMSO, 1994), 73.

3. Centre for Contemporary Cultural Studies, *The Empire Strikes Back: Race and Racism in '70s Britain* (London: Allen and Unwin, 1982).

4. Problems with the concept of "race relations" have been well documented. See Michael Banton, *The Idea of Race* (London: Tavistock, 1977); Robert Miles, *Racism and Migrant Labour* (London: Routledge and Kegan Paul, 1982); Robert Miles, *Racism after "Race Relations"* (London: Routledge, 1993).

5. Ambalavaner Sivanandan, *A Different Hunger: Writings on Black Resistance* (London: Pluto Press, 1982).

6. Valerie Amos and Pratibha Parmar "Challenging Imperial Feminism," *Feminist Review* 17 (Autumn 1984): 3–19.

7. Amos was appointed a government whip in the House of Lords in 1998. She was created a life peer in August 1997. After holding various positions, Baroness Amos became leader of the House of Lords and president of the Council in October 2003.

8. Carby is professor and chair of the department of African American studies at Yale University; Solomos is professor and chair of the department of sociology at City University of the University of London; Gilroy is professor of sociology at the London School of Economics, University of London; and Parmar is an award-winning filmmaker who lives in London.

9. For a rich, nuanced analysis of these identities in Liverpool, see Mark Christian, *Multiracial Identity: An International Perspective* (London: Macmillan Press, 2003).

10. See Andrew Pilkington, *Racial Disadvantage and Ethnic Diversity in Britain* (Basingstoke and New York: Palgrave, Macmillan, 2003), 36. For a discussion of concepts of race and race mixture, see Charlie Own, "'Mixed Race' in Official Statistics," in David Parker and Miri Song, eds., *Rethinking "Mixed Race"* (London: Pluto Press, 2001).

11. For the 1981 data, see Lord Gifford, Wally Brown, and Ruth Bundey, *Loosen the Shackles: First Report of the Liverpool 8 Inquiry into Race Relations in Liverpool* (London: Karia Press, 1989), 37. For the 1992 data, see Jacqueline Nassy Brown, *Dropping Anchor, Setting Sail: Geographies of Race in Black Liverpool* (Princeton: Princeton University

Press, 2005), 32, where she cites Office of Population Census and Surveys, 1992 County Monitor. 1991 Census: Merseyside, Government Statistical Service.

12. Colin Brown, *Black and White Britain: The Third PSI Survey* (London: Heinemann Education Books, 1983).

13. A. Rattansi and Sallie Westwood, eds., *Racism, Modernity, and Identity: On the Western Front* (Cambridge: Polity Press, 1994). A 2006 edition of the *Economist*, that self-proclaimed bastion of global capitalism, noted that even powerful Europeans can't decide what the main values of Europe are.

14. Today's European Union began in 1951 as the European Coal and Steel Community with six members: Belgium, West Germany, Luxembourg, France, Italy, and the Netherlands. The European Economic Community was formed in 1957, and popularly called the "Common Market." Denmark, Ireland, and the United Kingdom joined in 1973, Greece in 1981, and Spain and Portugal in 1986. Austria, Sweden, and Finland joined in 1995, making a total of fifteen nations. A further ten nations joined in 2004: Cyprus, the Czech Republic, Estonia, Hungary, Latvia, Lithuania, Malta, Poland, Slovakia, and Slovenia, making a total of twenty-seven nations, with over 450 million people. Bulgaria and Romania joined in 2007.

15. Philomena Essed in the Netherlands, Jayne Ifekwunigwe and Gargi Bhattacharyya in Britain, Elisa Joy White in the Republic of Ireland. Philomena Essed, *Everyday Racism: Reports from Women of Two Cultures* (Alamedia, CA: Hunter House, 1990); Jayne O. Ifekwunigwe, *Scattered Belongings: Cultural Paradoxes of "Race," Nation, and Gender* (London: Routledge, 1999); Gargi Bhattacharyya, *Tales of Dark-Skinned Women: Race, Gender, and Global Culture* (London: UCI Press, 1998).

16. Trica Danielle Keaton, *Muslim Girls and the Other France: Race, Identity Politics, and Social Exclusion* (Bloomington: Indiana University Press, 2006).

17. Kamala Kempadoo and Joe Doezema, *Global Sex Workers: Rights, Resistance, and Redefinition* (New York: Routledge, 1998).

18. In Britain, Ramdin documents the experiences of blacks outside London. Ron Ramdin, *The Making of the Black Working Class in Britain* (London: Wildwood House, 1987). So, too, does Christian, *Multiracial Identity.* See also Chris Mullard, *Black Britain* (London: Allen and Unwin, 1973), and Stephen Small, "Racialized Relations in Liverpool: A Contemporary Anomaly," *New Community* 11, no. 4 (1991): 511–37. A number of interesting insights into variations for blacks around Europe can be found in Caryl Phillips, *The European Tribe* (Boston: Faber and Faber, 1987).

19. Wilson argues that there is far less class stratification in American ghettoes today and that "unlike in previous years, today's ghetto residents represent almost exclusively the most disadvantaged segments of the urban black community." William Julius Wilson, *The Truly Disadvantaged: The Inner City, the Underclass, and Public Policy* (Chicago: University of Chicago Press, 1987), 143.

20. Susan J. Smith, *The Politics of "Race" and Residence* (Oxford: Polity Press, 1989). Her analysis demonstrates that although people in England often talked of "ghettoes" and the need to avoid "ghettoization," the evidence demonstrated that "neither the size nor the concentration of the black population in Britain has allowed 'ghettoization' to develop on a scale or intensity comparable to that in the USA." Smith stresses, however,

that segregation is "marked and enduring" (18). For a detailed comparison of Britain and the United States, see also Ceri Peach, "Urban Concentration and Segregation in Europe since 1945," in Malcolm Cross, ed., *Ethnic Minorities and Industrial Change in Europe and North America* (Cambridge: Cambridge University Press, 1992). And for Bristol, see Ken Pryce, *Endless Pressure* (Harmondsworth: Penguin Books, 1979).

21. Report of the National Advisory Commission on Civil Disorders, New York, 1968 (the so-called Kerner Commission); Lord Scarman, *The Scarman Report: The Brixton Disorders; 10–12 April 1981* (Harmondsworth: Pelican, 1982).

22. Julia Sudbury, *"Other Kinds of Dreams": Black Women's Organisations and the Politics of Transformation* (London: Routledge, 1998). It is important to note that these ethnic groups do not see themselves as "black" in terms of sharing African descent but rather "black" as a political category for social organization. In this sense, to be "black" in Britain corresponds better to the concept of "people of color" in the United States than it does to "black" in the United States.

23. Stephen Small, *Racialised Barriers: The Black Experience in the United States and England in the 1980s* (London: Routledge, 1994). See also Stephen Small, "Unravelling Racialised Relations in the United States of America and the United States of Europe," in John Wrench and John Solomos, eds., *Racism and Migration in Western Europe* (Oxford: Berg, 1993), 233–49.

SECTION 1

Historical Dimensions of Blackness in Europe

1

The Emergence of Afro-Europe: A Preliminary Sketch

ALLISON BLAKELY

A virtual explosion of Black African immigration in Europe over the past few decades, whose magnitude and significance are not yet widely recognized by scholars nor the general public, is creating an unprecedented increase in Europe's black population and a predictable negative response. While even the participants themselves are only beginning to sense a degree of group identity—largely forced upon them by the shared experience of discrimination and racism expressed in unmistakable common patterns—the Black population in Europe has finally achieved a size and visibility that invites comparison with the involuntary definition of community that shaped the concept of *African American* among the descendants of enslaved Africans in North America. This analogy becomes all the more tempting when one considers the evolving idea and reality of the still-growing, twenty-seven-nation European Union with its porous borders and the fledgling European Parliament. Add to this Internet Web sites and other electronic media that taken altogether constitute a new, transnational dimension for cultural conceptualization and organization whose potential impact is yet to be measured.

The definition of *Black* employed here is inherently ambiguous, because the concepts related to this have always been somewhat ambiguous and arbitrary, and moreover this definition was originally imposed on people of African descent by others. I am, therefore, not here proposing a new definition, only offering observations on how the most prevalent convention may be becoming operative in Europe. With respect to France and other countries that discourage formal stipulation of racial or ethnic categories by law or tradition, I am simply counting those who within those societies routinely suffer personal indignities and adverse discrimination due to their skin color or known Black African ancestry, regardless of census categories. It is also important to note here that the precise number of Blacks is not essential to my central discourse, as long as it is admitted that the level and breadth of distribution is unprecedented and has become of social concern.

The largest countries in Western Europe, the United Kingdom, France, and Germany, have a long and well-known history of immigration of Blacks, with the United Kingdom having now around 1.5 million Blacks in its population of 60 million, and France probably over 2.5 million out of a comparable total population. Germany, with a larger total population of over 80 million has only around 168,000 from sub-Saharan Africa, which can be explained by obvious historical and geographical factors. Just a hint of the scope of what I am calling "Afro-Europe" can be seen in the fact that it now ranges from Ireland in the extreme northwest, where the Black population has quietly risen above 30,000; to the Netherlands, where it is half a million; to Scandinavia, where apart from Sweden the numbers are relatively small but the related problems are still surfacing; to Russia, with lingering remnants of the tens of thousands of African

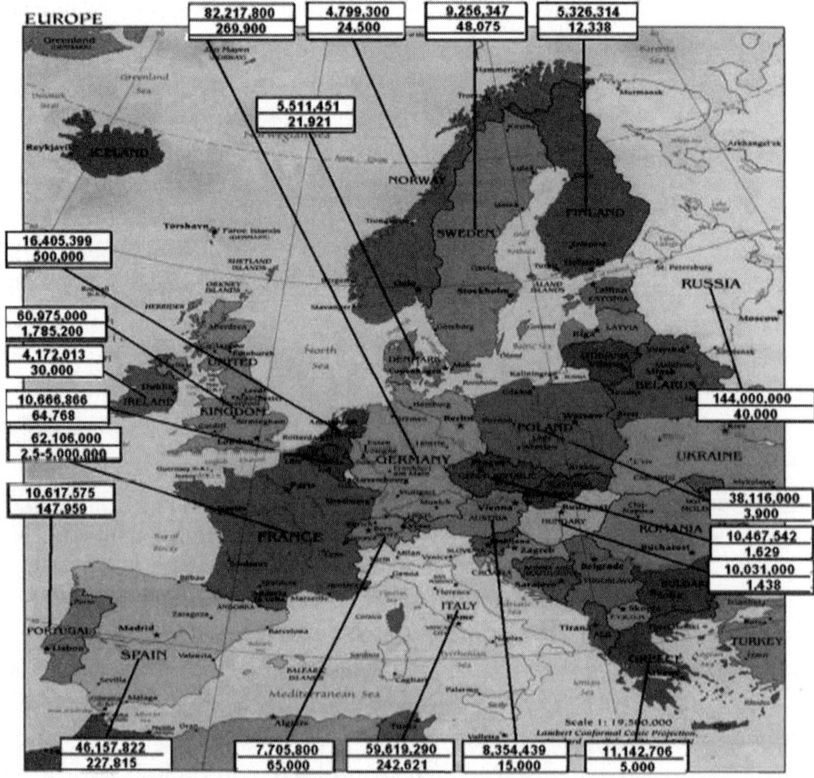

Figure 1.1. Approximate Black populations in Europe, composed and compiled by the author.

students who trained there under the Soviet regime; on around to Italy and Spain on the Mediterranean. The rapid rate at which this level of Black population has materialized and continues to be augmented by the hundreds of thousands of immigrants pouring into Europe annually—despite recent efforts to stem the tide—gives further support for the metaphor of explosion. While the percentage of Europeans of Black African descent is still under 2 percent, the social construct of "blackness" has throughout modern times carried a significance that cannot be measured simply in numbers.[1]

Transition from Africans in Europe to Afro-Europe

The value of generalizations and parallels drawn in the present effort at a comparative overview of Europe on this subject should be weighed against a constant awareness of the great regional, historical, and cultural diversity of the societies in question. The same is, of course, true of aspects of American history mentioned in places. This said, there is all-too-abundant graphic evidence of the negative backlash I have alluded to and the parallels with the African American experience that also relegated groups of diverse African origins to a collective category of inferiority. The ethnically charged protests that spread to 300 cities in France in late October and early November 2005, featuring deadly violence and thousands of burning automobiles, easily evoked scenes from the major urban riots in the United States in the 1960s, or the disturbances in 1981 in London's Brixton district, followed a few months later by a much larger one in Liverpool's Toxteth district. The underlying causes Lord Leslie Scarman identified in the government inquiry, reported in November 1981, were reminiscent of the 1968 Kerner Commission Report on conditions in the United States that had attributed the American riots to the failures of American society to integrate African American rural-to-urban migrants and their descendants, as reflected by high unemployment, abusive police practices, substandard housing, inadequate education, poor recreation facilities and programs, and inadequate response from established institutions. Now, a few decades later, a survey of reports emerging from all the countries to be discussed here read like excerpts from the Kerner and Scarman inquiries. Attorneys for the families of the two teenagers killed in the more recent violence in France filed a complaint with the courts charging what amounted to racial profiling and police negligence strikingly reminiscent of perennial complaints of police misconduct that is all too familiar in the United States' inner cities.[2] While much of the world was more surprised to learn of France's clusters of suburban (*banlieue*) poor than it was of those abandoned in New Orleans during Hurricane Katrina earlier in 2005, such ghetto-like settlements of ethnic and religious immigrants in Europe are not unique to France.

Consider, for example, the fact that now more than 70,000 Somalis live in and around London. Predictably, the new arrivals live in some of the poorest neighborhoods. Similarly, Cape Verdeans, owing to the Portuguese dimension of their colonial past, have a population in the shantytowns of Lisbon comparable to that of the Somalis in London; 50,000 to 70,000 migrated to Portugal since the 1950s to find work and better lives.[3] Poignant testimony of the persistence of immigration despite hardships is that over a thousand North Africans of various origins have perished in the waters between Gibraltar and Spain in recent years. Meanwhile, equally compelling evidence of the backlash that awaits new arrivals in some parts of Europe is that in Russia alone, authorities count some 50,000 youths organized into skinhead gangs, while the African diplomatic corps in Moscow lodges official complaints in vain about brazen, daylight assaults on their Black officials and other Africans resident in Russia, on the streets of Moscow, St. Petersburg, and other cities. A central assertion underlying the present essay is that a Black identity is being forced by circumstances upon even those individuals and groups that would prefer otherwise. It should also be noted that the current quest for identity among Blacks in Europe is not exactly the same as that earlier for the descendants of enslaved Africans in America. Most are directly from Africa, or from a former European colony with a Black majority. Although this transition to a Europe with a conspicuous Black population has seemed to come about suddenly, and largely unnoticed, it in fact has transpired along differing paths and at paces distinctive to each European society in question. What this population that I view as having an incipient overarching Black identity all share is a common background deeply rooted in the history of the European colonial empires and their engagement in the Atlantic slave trade.

The current European Black population represents three main categories of migration: (1) Blacks who were already connected to European countries through former colonial ties, thus primarily Great Britain, France, the Netherlands, Spain, Portugal, Belgium, and Germany; (2) refugees from turmoil in Africa seeking political asylum, especially in Switzerland, Finland, Sweden, Denmark, Norway, and the Netherlands; and (3) students attracted by educational opportunities in Russia, the Czech Republic, Slovakia, Poland, Hungary, Bulgaria, East Germany, and Latvia. Then there are others primarily seeking employment who for various reasons are drawn to Italy, Ireland, and Greece. Globalization of industrial capitalism and the growing reality of an economic world without borders is perhaps the most immediate influential development affecting the current migrations. Just as populations within Africa and the Caribbean first moved to local regions more industrially active, thereby affording more jobs, the two major regions they moved to abroad, Europe and the United States, are the world's leading industrial areas, and at the same time are experiencing declines in birthrate that threaten economic prosperity. Against the backdrop of the massive, still ongoing rural-to-urban migration within China, for example, of over 200 million during this same era, the dramatic upsurge of primarily labor migration into Europe from Africa and Asia is not so surprising. A comparative overview of the impact of these recent migrations on racial and cultural identities of peoples of Black African descent in various European societies and reflection on the extent to which this collectively resembles the African American experience may be of some value for understanding the process unfolding, both for the individuals and groups experiencing it and the respective governments involved. The Black populations in these host societies are aiming at integration or assimilation on the one hand and formulation of racial and cultural identity on the other. The predominance of the nation-state as the basic form of social organization in the course of the Industrial Revolution, which also inspired cultural nationalism, now finds its counterpart in the aspiration of migrants for either some degree of integration into the host societies or strong consciousness and organization along ethnic lines in order to survive and prosper.

In a world that seems to be constantly shrinking, in inverse correlation with the expansion of new technologies, it is no longer difficult to suspend in our minds the artificial geographical borders around the globe. However, the historical significance of human differences based on the artificial constructs of race and color are more difficult to remove even in our imagination. Thus the subject of Blacks in Europe is neither as nebulous nor artificial as it should be in a more perfect world. Regarding my implied comparison with North America, there are of course obvious parallels between the origins of the Black populations in Europe and the Americas. Some of the differences in the present perceptions and realities may be accounted for by the fact that the leading European countries did not favor the actual practice of slavery within their societies in the modern era. Of all the great Western powers, only the United States did.[4] This accounts for distinctive differences in racial definitions and social attitudes compared to European countries—that is, unabashed lingering premodern assumptions in the United States, as opposed to hidden ones. This explains in part a widely held, false impression, both at home and abroad, that Europe lacked the basis for the notoriously bad race relations characterizing the United States. Europe did play an ironically interesting earlier role as a sort of laboratory for Black freedom of expression, for example, nurturing major figures of the Harlem Renaissance in France. However, Black emigrants' initial sense of euphoria was in most cases later tempered by closer familiarity with how they were really regarded.[5] A good illustration of the operation of the circum-Atlantic cultural exchange within the African diaspora during the early twentieth century is that the Harlem Renaissance was in turn part of the inspiration for the Négritude movement founded by African and Afro-Caribbean intellectuals in France at the beginning of the 1930s. While the primary movers, Léopold Sédar Senghor and Aimé Césaire, drew most deeply from European and African cultural wells for this, Senghor directly acknowledged influence from W.E.B. Du Bois's writings from the start of the century and viewed the Harlem Renaissance as the prototype for their movement.[6] Likewise, Scandinavia, the Netherlands, Switzerland, and Soviet Russia enjoyed especially positive reputations in the early twentieth century as societies that were tolerant concerning concepts of race and social justice.

While this view has some validity in relative terms, it tends to obscure the centuries-old, shared tradition of color prejudice and racism in western civilization that is far more essential for an understanding of what is happening now in Europe. By the end of the eighteenth century, the claim that Blacks were naturally inferior became the prevalent justification for the Atlantic slave trade and slavery in European colonies in the Americas. At the same time, modern capitalism found profit in popularizing debasing stereotypes, for example, in brand names for products alluding to Blacks as exotic, erotic, or innately servile. All the way into the twenty-first century, lighthearted racism has supported the sale of such pastries as the *Negerkuss* or *Negerzoen* (Negro's kiss) and *Mohrenkopf* (Moor's head) in Germany, France, the Netherlands, Scandinavia, and Switzerland. A recent reminder in Sweden is controversy over an ice cream brand name, *Nogger Black*. In the Netherlands, the main cookie company producing *Negerzoen*, Van der Breggen, decided in March 2006 to change the name to *Buys Zoenen*. However, since 96 percent of the 5,000 respondents of a poll were of the opinion that the original name was not racist, it seems likely that the name will continue to be used by the general public.[7] Whether these popular treats seriously represent racism or not, the very existence of the controversy is commentary on the legacy of racism.

Over recent centuries, modern science has lent its prestige to further reinforce the kind of racism that already had produced blatantly flawed scientific findings concerning Africans. Further complicating study and discussion of this issue is the broad spectrum of definitions concerning Black African identity. Of all the world's societies, only the United States featured a definition of Black identity that meant anyone with known Black African ancestry. European societies, those in the remainder of the Americas, Africa, and the rest of the world placed more significance on varying shades of color. Hence one encounters such terms as *mulatto, Black, Ethiopian, African, moro, nero, negro, nègre, preto, indiani* in Europe, and the extreme case in Brazil where dozens of terms eventually came to be adopted to describe degrees of color and related social status. This results in great ambiguity concerning who might be considered Black, and admittedly renders generalization about Blacks in Europe problematic. The powerful appeal and ancient vintage of stereotypes is evident in the fact that the caricature

Figure 1.2. Black stereotypes in American and European children's stories: first page from *The Story of the Black Boys.*

of the black slave as happy-go-lucky, lazy, and irresponsible, which is usually associated with nineteenth-century North America, was already popular in sixteenth-century Europe. While there were instances of admiration for individual Africans who distinguished themselves in various pursuits, pervasive color prejudice tended to ensure that these would be viewed as exceptions to the merits of Africans in general. The denigrating images of Africans in western civilization overshadowed others present that might have allowed a more balanced picture of the roles of Africans.

While there were many black servants, slaves, and even some executioners in early modern Europe and the European empires, there were also many free

Figure 1.3. Black stereotypes in American and European children's stories: a picture of a game named after the story *Little Black Sambo,* along with other related stereotypes. Courtesy of photographer Roland Freeman.

among the ordinary populace, working in such occupations as musicians, soldiers, and sailors. Moreover, the European elites occasionally included Africans who were nobles, government officials, intellectuals, priests, and even saints. Invoking the mythic "Curse of Ham" as a basis for enslaving Blacks did not alter the veneration of Black Madonnas at hundreds of churches in Europe and

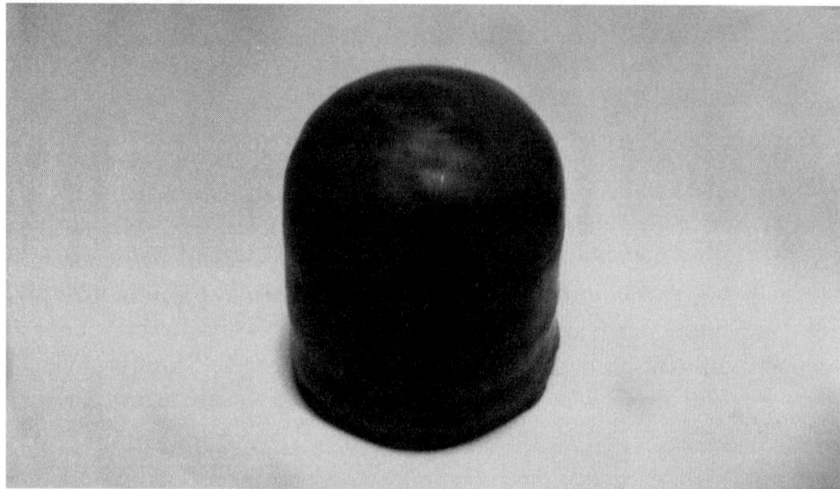

Figure 1.4. A *Negerzoen* (Negro's kiss) confection from the Netherlands. http://commons.wikimedia.org/wiki/Image:Schokokuss2.jpg?uselang=nl.

the Americas. While travel literature and the graphic arts, including marginal decoration on maps, at times reinforced misleading stereotypes about Africa and Africans, the arts in other instances featured beautiful representations of Africans, for instance, the Black king in countless renditions of the adoration of the Magi. And while folklore, music, poems, and plays carried some negative images, they also at times demonstrated admiration for qualities thought of as African. Actual history thus provided ample material for positive images to predominate; the chosen course of socioeconomic and intellectual developments determined otherwise.[8] A comparative look at the image of Blacks in Western popular culture on both sides of the Atlantic reveals deeply seated, shared prejudices that served as fertile soil for the rapid spread of the racialized social tensions now evident across Europe.

The Challenges and Responses

In the case of the former European colonial powers, it should not be surprising that they inherited significant populations of Black African descent. All that was needed was a greater demand for labor and a weakening of restrictions that for centuries had limited the influx of African populations. Present-day declining European birthrates create a stimulus like that which led to a Black population approaching a quarter of a million in Spain and Portugal in the fifteenth and early sixteenth century in the wake of the bubonic plague. In waging the two world wars of the first half of the twentieth century, costing tens of millions of lives, and on the crest of unprecedented industrialization, the European powers inflicted upon themselves a similar depletion of labor supply and greater dependence on their former colonial subjects. Nevertheless, in the European countries most affected by immigration issues, as also in the United States, the obvious demand for this labor supply continues to be met by strong nationalistic sentiment wishing to deny the need and its desirability. A good example of these internal contradictions is the case of France, where public officials still express pride in what are considered the civilizing benefits of the French colonial past but, similar to other countries, in 2006 passed a law restricting further immigration even from former colonies of those with certain skills. Added to the labor demand is the inescapable human legacy of empires that included Black Africans, many of whose descendants became citizens at the end of empire. This is especially the case with France and Great Britain. For present purposes, the United Kingdom may be viewed as the model of a former colonial power that directly inherited a Black population. Already by the late eighteenth century, there may have been a Black population in England approaching 30,000. Eventually Black subjects from the Caribbean and Africa have had to be accommodated for mutual benefit, just as the descendants of enslaved Africans in the United States have had to be.

It is perhaps England's role as the most extensive of all the maritime empires that accounts for the fact that the British now appear the most ready to embrace multiculturalism and accept the reality that being British need not mean being white. Tariq Modood, a sociologist at the University of Bristol, observes the following:

> In terms of positive reception of migrants . . . Britain, in particular cities such as London, has been remarkably receptive and self-transformative. I think this is related to the fact that ethnic minority political mobilization in Britain began with a set of factors that enabled it to reach a degree of ideological assertiveness, prominence, and civic impact in a limited period of time that seems without parallel in Western Europe . . . French history does have parallels with the British, though the comparison only highlights that in both imperial and contemporary settings the French are less tolerant of cultural plurality than the British.[9]

In recent years, there has been a noticeable increase in overarching organization of Blacks there, usually in combination with Indians, who in Britain have long been referred to as "Blacks." There have been signs of progress in social integration. For example, the 30,000–member London municipal police force is over 7 percent nonwhite, with an even higher percentage of minorities being trained. Furthermore, a small number of members of minorities serve in the 659–seat House of Commons; Paul Boateng in 2002 became the first Black cabinet member as Tony Blair's chief secretary of the treasury; and Baroness Valerie Ann Amos of the Labour Party, a life peer, served as leader of the House of Lords from October 2003 to June 2007, and as a consequence the first Black woman to sit in the cabinet of the United Kingdom. Nonwhites are also becoming prominent in the news media and in such professions as medicine and law.[10]

France, on the other hand, where over 2.5 million of her population of 60 million is Black, including her overseas territories in the West Indies, is a former colonial power that officially opposes what is considered "identity politics," and prefers to be "color-blind" and not list such categories as skin color or racial grouping. Nevertheless, in France too Blacks experience constant discrimination resulting from color bias, although not as much as non-Black North Africans, especially Algerians and Moroccans. The rioting in late 2005 that began after the controversial deaths of two teenagers who were pursued by the police in the Paris suburb of Clichy-sous-Bois was led by members of frustrated African ethnic and religious minorities, about 30 percent of whom were estimated to be Black. Before the violence subsided, 220 policemen were injured, more than 6,000 people had been arrested, about 10,000 automobiles had been burned, and 300 buildings damaged. The government's response to this crisis, which centered on frayed relations between native French on the one side and immigrants and their France-born children on the other, represented a dramatic and tragic illustration of the practical implications of color-blindness. It became clear that the authorities lacked even a vocabulary to discuss the crisis intelligently, let alone strategies to quell it, since in their minds there could be no ghettos in France, notwithstanding the housing of approximately 2 million immigrants in 300 high-rises, many of which are substandard. Nor could French leaders of any political stripe admit of a possibility of the periodic violent outbursts that are inherent in communities of systematically disadvantaged people that the dominant society chooses not to see.[11] Also disturbing is that the hard-line reaction of then Interior Minister Nicolas Sarkozy and Prime Minister Dominique de Villepin appeared to resonate better with the French public than did the more conciliatory stance of President Jacques Chirac.

The even more massive public protests in France in the spring of 2006 against a proposed law that sought to weaken the civil rights of young adults related to employment—employers gained arbitrary rights to terminate employment within the first two years—also contained a cultural component that may have been a carryover from the earlier social unrest. These strikes and protests, led by students and labor unions, included a subcurrent of more violent activity by some youths. While the government and most commentators viewed this as purely criminal activity, it also may reveal an element of class struggle, featuring some of those unemployed at a much higher rate than the students and venting their frustration that their plight was not addressed by the new legislation as the government claimed. Journalists making follow-up visits a year later to Clichy-sous-Bois and Épinay-sur-Seine, another suburb affected by the 2005 unrest, found tensions still high and more minor outbreaks of violence. The persistence of such tensions was further demonstrated in November 2007, after two teenagers in the suburban town of Villiers-le-Bel died when their motorbike collided with a police car. Rioting broke out for two nights, resulting in injuries to around 120 of the hundreds of police officers mobilized. At a town meeting called to calm the atmosphere, the perennial issues of housing, jobs, and ethnic profiling were once again raised by the public. Meanwhile at the government level, Nicolas Sarkozy, now enjoying his new role as president of the republic, blamed the rioting on a "thugocracy" and denied that it was related to social ills.[12] On the positive side in recent French history, in the 2002 presidential election Christiane Taubira, an economist from French Guiana, became the first Black candidate for president and drew 660,000 votes, 2.3 percent of the total. Blacks have also in rare instances served in the National Assembly or in regional parliaments, mostly representing French territories abroad—and as many as 100 have been elected to city councils around the country, albeit out of thousands in total.

Most of the patterns of the European Black experience traced here are paralleled in several European countries. The half-million population of Black African descent in the densely packed Dutch population of 16 million also came about as a result of a once-vast empire. Unusually detailed study of related problems by the National Bureau of Statistics provides a picture of issues and patterns there that may also be instructive concerning Black communities in other European countries that provide little such documentation. I will forego presenting this in depth here due to space limitations and publication elsewhere.[13] A closer look at the experiences of the Somalis and Cape Verdeans mentioned earlier may serve as an example of the common patterns. In the United Kingdom, Somalis first came in significant numbers as military recruits in WWI. After the war, many remained in such port cities as Cardiff, London, and Liverpool. Intending to work and send money home, they were called "the fortune men" by fellow countrymen. Some point to this attitude of temporary residency to explain the reticence to acquire English language and culture more fully. Some of those residing in housing projects in and around London experienced cultural conflict with Jamaicans, who taunted them for being new arrivals, sometimes referring to them as "scum," "asylum boys," and "parasites." While immigration has occurred on a much smaller scale, the Somalis have fared little better in the smaller European countries such as Sweden, where they number 12,000; Denmark, with 13,000; and Finland with 6,000. The latter two governments unsuccessfully attempted to negotiate formal plans of resettlement with the Somali government. Among the Cape Verdeans in Lisbon, the majority, especially the most visibly black and of mixed parentage, find themselves in shantytowns alongside the Gypsies (Roma) and other poor and encounter much difficulty due to language differences.[14]

Spain, whose empire once included the Netherlands and Belgium, is one of the prime entry points for immigrants from Africa, and counts over a quarter of a million immigrants in her population of some 42 million. Only about 45,000 of these are Black Africans. This is in part because Spain was no longer a great maritime power when the scramble for Africa began, and had lost even her American slave colonies a century earlier than the British and French. Although the official Spanish attitude concerning color prejudice is reminiscent of the French, conspicuous signs of racist thought have surfaced in recent years. During the 1992 Olympic Games held in Barcelona, a museum exhibit of the stuffed corpse of an African man that had been on display in the town of Banyoles in the north of Spain since 1916 came to light. Its origins have been traced to South Africa, where, immediately after his burial, his body was stolen from the grave by two famous French taxidermists, the Verraux brothers, who took it to Paris with thousands of artifacts and wildlife for display. It eventually came to rest in Banyoles after a Spanish naturalist purchased it and displayed it at the 1888 Barcelona World Exhibition. Despite public outcry from Africans about the exhibit in the 1990s, the local officials and public were apparently so attached to it as a tourist attraction that they launched a campaign to keep it, including T-shirts with supportive slogans and Easter chocolates in the image of *El Negro.* It was finally surrendered in 2000 to Botswana, where it was buried.[15]

Additional, more recent notoriety resulted from blatant racist taunting by the crowd of 55,000 at a soccer match in Madrid's Bernabeu stadium in November 2004. Racist treatment of Black soccer players has been a Europe-wide phenomenon but had subsided considerably since the 1970s and 1980s, when organized public efforts in the United Kingdom, the Netherlands, Ireland, and other countries where it was rampant toned it down. During that era, it was also dangerous for Black fans to attend soccer matches in those countries, even though increasingly some of the leading players were Black. A recent reminder that such ugly attitudes are still latent occurred at a match in Halle on March 25, 2006. When disgruntled fans shouted racial epithets and spat at Adebowale Ogungbure, a Nigerian midfielder on one of the teams, he responded angrily with a Hitler salute. Adding further insult, he was charged with violating the German constitution, which prohibits this gesture. While those charges were dropped, tension surrounding Black soccer stars in Europe continues, in spite of the continued increase in their numbers. For instance, the runner-up French team in the 2006 World Cup championship was predominantly Black, and its captain was the superstar Zinedine Zidane, a French Algerian.[16]

Portugal, which shared Spain's history as one of the very first of the modern European colonial powers, now only counts around 110,000 immigrants in her population of around 10 million. The majority are Black and come from former African colonies relinquished only in the mid-1970s, after years of liberation struggles in Angola, Mozambique, and Guinea-Bissau. Cape Verde was the home of the second-largest contingent that moved to Portugal. There, too, initiatives have had to be taken against racism, especially after a riot in 1995 in Lisbon where dozens of skinheads rampaged in a neighborhood of Lisbon and murdered a young citizen from Angola.[17] Belgium, although once exploiting sizeable holdings in central Africa, has a relatively small African population of around 22,000, apparently because the more recent French influence in the former Congo has made France a more attractive destination for Africans departing for Europe. Yet Belgium experienced one of the most heinous racial incidents of all, when a black-clad teenager went on a rampage with a hunting rifle in May 2006 during which he wounded a woman of Turkish descent and killed a black woman from Mali and the two-year-old white girl in her care.[18]

While Germany arrived very late to the competition for colonies, a Black population numbering in the hundreds was present for centuries. This included even some former slaves from America who during the American Revolutionary War were among those recruited by the British to serve under their Hessian mercenaries. Some accompanied their defeated commanders back to Germany after the war. The current Black population, which has arrived largely over the past century, received its main growth spurts from the military occupations in the wake of both world wars. It is estimated to be around 167,000, although German census categories do not use racial designations. It consists of Afro-Germans, Africans, African Americans, and Black Caribbeans. Since unification in 1990, the number directly from Africa has doubled to around 14,000. Even German-born Blacks experience discrimination in housing and employment that is largely not punishable by law. There are some positive signs since the 1990s, for example, Nigerian Adewale Adekoyeni became the first Black judge in Hamburg; and there is a high-profile presence in the media and music. However, even those whose families have resided in Germany for generations are confronted with a pervasive German attitude that does not allow colored citizens to be considered German.[19] A January 2009 three-part series on National Public Radio in the United States probing European reactions to the election of President Barack Obama included the observation from a member of the German Council on Foreign Relations that the German concept of identity is predicated on exclusion of those from elsewhere.[20] Perhaps more surprising is that although in Germany Hitler's *Mein Kampf* is banned by law, neo-Nazi groups are tolerated and Afro-Germans dare not go out on the street on Hitler's birthday for fear of physical assaults by skinhead bands. The savage beating of an Ethiopian irrigation engineer in Potsdam in April 2006 and a less serious racist attack in Berlin prompted the German government to take special measures in anticipation of the soccer World Cup there in June, featuring many teams with Black players.[21]

The new Russian state, even after its reduction from the immense expanse of the former Soviet Union, still has a population of 150 million, dwarfing all of her European neighbors to the west. While a small African presence in Russia extends back centuries, a population of sufficient size to be noticed in such a large country materialized only in the second half of the twentieth century. Oriented toward the West, Russia encompasses both European and Asiatic territories and culture. However, attitudes in Russia prior to the twentieth century concerning Blacks were shaped by biases common to all Western societies. During the Soviet regime, official doctrine magnified Russian consciousness of Africa and Blacks far out of proportion to any actual Black presence and enforced at least public respect for Blacks, although there is clear evidence that racist attitudes, and even treatment, persisted even then. The story of the recent African diaspora in Russia centers on the legacy of Cold War policies that brought more than 50,000 African students to Russia for extended study. It is within this historical context that Russia serves as the prime example of African migration to Europe for education in countries that were not former colonial powers. This is especially true of countries that during the Cold War were part of the Soviet Communist orbit, including Czechoslovakia, Poland, Hungary, Bulgaria, East Germany, and Latvia.

Some of the tens of thousands of Africans stayed in Russia, just as smaller numbers remained in the smaller countries and still continue to come on a much-reduced scale despite racial tensions. Around 17,000 mixed-race children have recently been identified in Russia by the Russian Interracial Children's Charity Fund, "METIS," based in Moscow. Many now live in dire straits in an impoverished post-Soviet society that has little regard for this population now that the ideological motivation for their advancement is past. Incidents of racially motivated physical assaults and other xenophobic behavior have become the norm. There is not even a question of real assimilation into Russian society, which has thus far shown little response to a growing litany of eloquent, passionate appeals for relief from unconscionable violence. In March 2006, a knife attack on a nine-year-old girl of mixed parentage at the entrance of her apartment building by two young assailants occurred in the same week as a verdict exonerating those accused of murdering another nine-year-old two years earlier. Just months before, a student from the Congo was beaten to death by attackers who were charged only with attempted murder.

Only in early 2006 did the Russian government reluctantly begin moving toward criminalizing racial hate crimes, amid persisting public apathy reminiscent of that in the United States, where there was no national law against lynching until the 1950s. The incident that finally brought action was the gruesome murder of twenty-eight-year-old Samba Lamsar, a Senegalese student, on the street in St. Petersburg on April 7. A shotgun with a swastika carved in its stock was left at the scene. Even then the government began to take legislative action only after a public outcry that climaxed in an unauthorized street protest of some 3,500, organized mainly through the Internet.[22] Africans in the Czech Republic estimate that the roughly 3,000 there at present are experiencing a sufficient level of violence to warrant organized efforts to mobilize the public against racism. Conditions in Slovakia are particularly distressful, with the roughly 500 Africans settled there, mainly former students, repeatedly harassed by skinheads (estimated by the police to number around 300 in the country). In Hungary too, the skinheads are very active. Reports from Bulgaria in 2005 reflected woeful experiences among the several hundred Blacks counted there.[23]

Switzerland, a country long famous for a high living standard, neutrality in international conflicts, and for highly civil behavior, is an example of a country refugees have considered ideal for asylum. There are now around 50,000 Black Africans living there, and although Switzerland once prided itself on being above racial problems, there now is a federal commission against racism, which in March 2000 cosponsored with the University of Bern a national conference against racism. There were numerous presentations by scholars and other professionals, most of whom were of color and originally from Africa, Asia, and the United States. They treated a broad spectrum of issues related to race and identity. The Netherlands, Finland, Sweden, Denmark, and Norway have been other popular destinations for asylum seekers. Exceptionally supportive state welfare systems are another attraction in those countries favoring socialist governments, although benefits even for citizens have been significantly curtailed in recent years.

In Finland and Sweden, racism is being discussed more than ever before. In the case of Sweden, this is particularly striking in light of the fact that Swedish economist Gunnar Myrdal headed the Carnegie Corporation's collaborative project that produced his famous study *The American Dilemma* in 1944, which was part of what enhanced Sweden's positive image in African-American intellectual circles. Current developments in Europe are making it clear that the tension between humanitarian ideals and practice highlighted in that work are just as pronounced in Western societies in general as they were and are in the United States. While the number of Blacks in Sweden is still relatively small at 55,000, its immigrant population is now about 10 percent of the population of 9 million. A White Power movement has increased its activity, and antidiscrimination legislation has been needed. Meanwhile, Norway was rocked in 2001 by the unusual occurrence of a racially motivated murder of a mixed-parentage teenager by members of Norway's small neo-Nazi community.[24]

The experiences of Italy, Ireland, and Greece are good examples of European countries not deeply involved in the African slave trade and colonialism, nor in ideological recruitment, but that nevertheless have attracted a recent surge in African migration mainly seeking employment. Italy, which like Germany only became unified in the nineteenth century, was also a late arrival to colonization in Africa, and even less successful. However, today Italy is receiving more than 100,000 immigrants a year, as one of the most attractive gateways into Europe and a popular labor market itself. Concerning the Black population, now approaching 200,000, there are around 53,000 Senegalese and upwards of 20,000 Nigerians. While life is not easy in material terms for these newcomers, Italy has stood out as a country where public attitudes appear more tolerant of cultural differences; public leaders have expressed determination to learn from the lessons of the British, French, and Germans to avoid predictable racial problems that are beginning to manifest themselves. However, one discouraging sign is that Italy maintains one of the most restrictive citizenship laws for immigrants.[25]

What is particularly striking about the new immigration to Ireland and Greece is the pace. The immigrant population in Greece increased from 2 percent to 7 percent of the total population of 11 million during the past decade. Although the black population of Greece numbers only in the hundreds, Athens can boast of the election of an African American woman to her city council. Yvette Jarvis, a former basketball star from Boston University, played professionally in Athens, where she was dubbed "the Black Venus," married a Greek, and settled in Athens. The main complaints of immigrants to Greece revolve around restrictions on gaining permanent legal residence. The total immigrant population of Ireland from all origins grew from around 4,000 in 1997 to 40,000 in 2001. According to United Nations High Commissioner for Refugees reports, most immigrants to Ireland come from Nigeria, Romania, Congo, Libya, and Algeria. While officially a very large proportion of these register as asylum seekers, the demand for labor there and the rate of the immigrant influx suggest that jobs are the real magnet, especially with such recently arrived high-tech firms as Microsoft, Intel, and Dell Computers. Unfortunately racial incidents in Belfast alone have begun to be counted in the hundreds, although there are positive signs of cultural adjustment as well.[26]

The Question of Identity and Future Prospects

One of the most tangible changes among the black population now taking shape in Europe from that present earlier is an expressed black consciousness and striving toward respectable identity, at times emphasizing group identity and at times on the individual level. One reason it makes sense to speak in terms of an "Afro-Europe" is that increasing signs of some form of black community are appearing. Here I should note that, just as the postcolonial period of migration has accounted for most of the African population in Europe, a related wave also has transformed the demographics of the United States, so that the descendants of slaves there are losing their majority status among those not of European descent. Nevertheless, some leaders in the burgeoning black communities in Europe are still looking to the North American Black experience for organizational models. For instance, Blacks in England have celebrated a Black History Month in October since 1987. In Berlin for over a decade now, a Black History Month has been celebrated in February like in the United States, with thousands attending related cultural events, although many Germans remain unaware of the still small black population. Czech Africans have designated November as Black History Month since 2002, and there is a similar proclamation of Black History Month at the end of the year by a Surinamer bookseller in the Netherlands, Sarafina Books.

In 2002, an organization called *Conscience noire* sponsored a conference in Paris featuring films and speeches on Black pride, hair braiding in African styles, heated discussion about the difficulties of maintaining African families and traditions in France, and about declining respect between Black men and Black women. Black communities in several countries have staged beauty contests and fashion shows. African shops, hair salons, restaurants, and nightclubs abound not only in London and Paris, but also Ireland, the Netherlands, Russia, and Denmark. A small section of Parnell Street in central Dublin has been dubbed "Little Africa," an appellation shared with a town of some seven to eight thousand Africans near Naples. Published guides (aka yellow pages) to all sorts of Black establishments can be found in Paris and Amsterdam. Majority Black churches are springing up within all of the sizeable Black communities. In several European countries as well as the United States, the past decade has witnessed a flurry of legislation, monuments, museums, and other activity aimed at expressions of acknowledgment and atonement or reparations for European involvement in the African slave trade.[27]

Conscious formulation of concepts of Black identity is in progress both in academic circles and among Black professionals in the community. Examples of the latter are ISD (*Initiative Schwarze Deutsche*), an alliance of Afro- and Asian Germans founded in 1986, and MAT (*La Maison de L'Afrique à Toulouse*), an African pride organization in Toulouse. After the riots in the suburbs, some sixty French organizations for Black people formed a federation to fight racial

Figure 1.5. A flier from a 2002 black consciousness conference in Paris. Photo by the author.

discrimination, with Patrick Lozes, a Black pharmacist from Benin who has also run for national office, as its first president. Named the CRAN (Le Conseil Représentatif des Associations Noires), it seeks to involve political parties, unions, and other bodies in fighting discrimination. The CRAN's activities illustrate a transition from organized efforts that are primarily antiracist into those that are assertively pro-Black. This appears to be a trend in the European countries with large Black populations.[28] While the number of black scholars in European higher education remains very small, organized study of related issues is well underway in the major countries. There are as well various policy institutes and think tanks that devote special attention to relevant issues. The Institute of Race Relations, based in London and established in the 1950s as an independent educational charity organization to conduct and publish research on race relations throughout the world, has since 1972 focused especially on racism in Britain and the rest of Europe. Most university programs related to Black subjects focus on African and African American studies, such as the *Cercle d'Etudes Afro-Américaines,* Paris; and the Collegium for African American Studies (CAAR). The latter is based in Europe, but claims a membership of over 250 scholars in twenty countries.

Special interest is now beginning to be shown to the history of Blacks in Europe. Over the past few years, both in Europe and the United States the subject of Blacks in Europe has moved beyond the appearance of related panels at conventions of the major disciplines to full-blown conferences. Another example within academic circles is the existence of the Black European Studies Center at the University of Mainz, which was established with funding for three years and hosted a conference in November 2005 and another in Berlin in July 2006. Both conferences featured impassioned discussions on questions of European black identity, who should define it, and who can best pursue Black European studies. Paradoxically, the occurrence of such discussion belies the denial of some Afro-Europeans who questioned the relevance of African American history for their situation, since precisely such discussion has continued for centuries in the United States. Further evidence of a growing visibility of these issues is a course offered at Middlesex University's summer school called "Black London." Initiated in 2004 in a program cosponsored by the Black and Asian Studies Association and Institute of Commonwealth Studies, it focuses on London's African, Caribbean, and South Asian populations in exploring issues of cultural diversity in modern Britain. In France, a law passed in 2001 recognizing slavery as a crime against humanity also included a requirement that lessons on slavery be part of the school curriculum. In 2006, political conservatives and centrists unsuccessfully tried to remove the latter provision in retaliation for the abandonment of another recent law that would have required highlighting the "positive role" of French colonialism.[29]

Figure 1.6. An announcement for a course on Black London offered at Middlesex University Summer School. Photograph courtesy of Hakim Adi.

It is not clear at this point whether formulation of Black identity in Europe is going to hearken back to the sort of cultural emphasis expressed in the Négritude movement of the early twentieth century or some more pragmatic political variant that might exploit the fact that European political systems, in contrast to the United States, are truly multiparty in a way that can afford significant leverage to minority constituencies. Most of the organizational efforts in Europe surrounding the identity question reject a narrow focus on blackness and emphasize alliance with others suffering from ethnic or racial discrimination, and educating the general public about the plight of immigrants. This can be seen in the principles espoused by the African Network in Austria; the Africa Solidarity Centre in Dublin; the African Union social organization in St. Petersburg; the Afro-Latvian Association launched in Riga in 2004; Humanitas Afrika in Prague; Solid Africa, an African student organization based in Bratislava, Slovakia; and the African Civil Society, also called the Africa Centre, in Finland (ACSF). The *Collectif des Antillais, Guyanais, Réunionnais* (Collective of Antillians, Guyanese, and the Reunion), the largest activist organization of French citizens from French territories abroad, was founded in 2004 in Paris, boasts of a membership and sympathizer base of over 40,000, including some members of Parliament, and has mounted numerous demonstrations and a media campaign against racism. This shows that racial problems in France are not limited to immigrants. A study of twenty-seven Cape Verdean neighborhood associations in the Lisbon metropolitan area revealed that while most are comprised of Cape Verdeans, some represent Cape Verdean-majority neighborhoods where others also reside. These associations, most of which are subsidized in part by the local government, pursue interests ranging from basic socioeconomic welfare to political and cultural activities. The question of identity is also an ongoing issue, as indicated in the following response from one interviewee: "Portuguese society doesn't see them (youth) as Portuguese because of skin colour. The mentality that exists is: 'they are black therefore they are African.' On the other hand, the young generation doesn't know Cape Verde, and they don't identify with their parents' version of being Cape Verdean. As a result of that they end up not knowing who they are and how to define themselves, and because of that, they start searching for an identity and end up finding it in other forms of being African, primarily in Afro-Americanism."[30]

Regarding the reactions of the European majorities to this quest for identity, it is important to keep in mind that a corollary to the search for Black identity is self-conscious reflection by Europeans about their own identity, which was also the case when they first imposed a Black identity on Africans centuries ago. Indeed, the current European confrontation with the sudden swell in non-Western immigrant populations has in some countries brought about the most thorough of such introspection since the Europeans encountered the non-West in the age of exploration. A recent shift to the political right, at least temporarily, in Western countries in general, coupled with occurrences of unfamiliar forms of violent conflict serve to shake confidence about consensus and complicate the question of options for the immigrant populations. Current events in Europe offer many more vital questions than answers concerning the probable course of the future. In light of the recent upsurge of violent confrontations and organized protests, it seems especially prudent to gain a better understanding of the immediate causes of such outbursts. For example, is there a critical mass of Black or immigrant population at which trouble may be anticipated? Research now underway by some economists on the impact of the riots of the 1960s in the United States suggests that the crucial factor predictive of violence was the density of Black population in a given city, irrespective of high unemployment, low wages, and other such conditions.[31] If valid, this discovery might have valuable policy implications for European societies looking to ward off problems. The onset of the ongoing, global economic crisis of historic dimensions that startled the world in 2008 reinforces the urgency of these questions.

Another interesting question is why racial incidents have been more prevalent and more brutal the farther east one looks in Europe. Is this a result of less exposure to the outside world historically, a less deeply grounded tradition of democracy and more lingering respect for class hierarchies, or simple correlation with economic conditions? All of these demand further study. One major difference in the situation of Blacks in Europe compared to that of African Americans in terms of integration into their local societies, in addition to the differences in definition of "blackness," is that they are generally not the main targets for discrimination. That role most often falls to small native minorities who are despised for historical reasons, and especially to Muslim populations because of the distinctive religious and cultural differences. Blacks' assimilation or integration into European societies is therefore not as intractable as that in the more rigidly color-conscious United States. Nevertheless, it remains to be seen whether the age-old color stigma might leave Blacks in Europe in a special new category for exclusion.[32]

Notes

1. Estimates of the Black population in Europe are inherently imprecise, not only due to variant categorization of Blacks and deliberate rejection of any such category in many countries, but also because of the presence of uncounted undocumented immigrants. The estimates presented here reflect my own assessment, based primarily on official statistics but taking into account estimates by nongovernmental organizations as well. In the case of France, the clearest sort of documentation can only be found regarding the country of origin of immigrants, for example, from the National Institute of Demographic Studies, which for 1999 showed around a third of a million such immigrants, apart from French citizens from the same place and other Black residents of France. I am, however, persuaded by the findings of reputable scholars and journalists who consistently advance estimates ranging from 2.5 million to 5 million. By this standard, I am using a conservative estimate. See Michéle Lamont and Éloi Laurent, "Identity: France Shows its True Colors," *International Herald Tribune,* June 6, 2006; John Tagliabue, "Taunts on Race Can Boomerang," *New York Times,* Sept. 21, 2005; and the *Institute national d'études démographiques* at http://www.ined.fr/fr/pop_chiffres/france/immigres_etrangers/pays_naissance_1999/ (accessed May 12, 2008). That such uncertainty of Black population estimates for Europe has always been the case can be seen from historical accounts of the Black population in the United Kingdom. For example, see Norma Myers, *Reconstructing the Black Past: Blacks in Britain 1780–1830* (London: Frank Cass, 1996); O. Shyllon Folarin, *Black Slaves in Britain* (London: Institute for Race Relations and Oxford University Press, 1974); and James Walvin, ed., *Black and White: The Blacks and English Society 1555–1945* (London: Alan Lane and Penguin Press, 1973). I have based my estimate of the Black population in Germany, the European country with the third-largest Black population, on the figures provided in the *Statistisches Bundesamt Deutschland* by subtracting from the total of 276,973 for all of Africa the numbers indicated there for

specific African countries above the Sahara. See http://www.destatis.de/basis/e/bevoe/bevoetab10.htm (accessed May 12, 2008). Examples of other readily accessible sources on the current black population across Europe are the United Kingdom Statistics Authority: http://www.statistics.gov.uk; Organization for Economic Development and Cooperation, http://www.oecd.org/home/0,2987,en_2649_201185_1_1_1_1_1,00.html; http://www.migrationinformation.org/resources; *Institute Nationale d'Etudes Demographiques*, http://www.ined.fr/fr/pop_chiffres/france/structure_population/pyramide_ages/; *Central Bureau voor de Statistiek* of the Netherlands; *Instituto Nazionale di Statistica*, http://www.istat.it/salastampa/comunicati/non_calendario/20051027_00/testointegrale.pdf; Federal Statistical Office of Germany, http://www.destatis.de/basis/e/bevoe/bevoetab10.htm; and N. L. Krylova and S.V. Prozhogina, *Metisy: kto oni? Problemy sotsializatsii I samoidentifikatsii* (Moscow: Russian Academy of Sciences, 2004), 46–50. All URLs accessed May 12, 2008. My survey of statistics was aided greatly by Abel Djassi Amado, a research assistant.

2. Leslie George Scarman, *The Brixton Disorders 10–12 April 1981: Report of an Inquiry* (Cmnd.; 7648) (London: Hmso, 1968); *United States Report of the National Advisory Commission on Civil Disorders* (New York: Bantam Books, 1968); Jean-Pierre Mignard and Emmanuel Tordjman, *L'Affaire Clichy: Morts pour rien* (Paris: Éditions Stock, 2006). For further background on the living conditions of French Arabs and Africans in the Paris suburbs, see Trica Danielle Keaton, *Muslim Girls and the Other France: Race, Identity Politics, and Social Exclusion* (Bloomington: Indiana University Press, 2006).

3. One article quotes Mohamoud Nur, a Somali social worker, who estimates the Somali population in London at 150,000. Most accounts admit that the precise number is unknown but is considerably higher than official government figures. See Alan Cowell and Raymond Bonner, "New Questions Asked in London Bombings," *New York Times*, Aug. 16, 2005; "Thousands of Somalis and Eritreans Claim Asylum Each Year; London Bombings," *Evening Standard*, July 27, 2005; and Ambrose Evans-Prichard, "Somalis Exiting Netherlands for Britain," *London Daily Telegraph*, Jan. 6, 2005. I am indebted to Natoschia Scruggs for first bringing to my attention the breadth of the Somali diaspora. Their communities in the United States have also gained attention. For example, see William Finnegan, "Letter from Maine: New in Town; the Somalis of Lewiston," *New Yorker* (Dec. 8, 2006): 46–58. On the Cape Verdean population in Portugal, see *Instituto Nacional de Estatistica Portugal*, http://www.ine.pt/xportal/xmain?xpid=INE&xpgid=ine_main (accessed May 12, 2008).

4. For example, Sue Peabody's insightful investigation of the presence of slavery within France shows that, although there were scattered instances of black slaves residing in France for centuries, official efforts at prohibiting the practice were persistent, and their presence was never sufficient to be a defining economic or social feature of modern European societies, as it was in the South in the United States—there exercising great influence on the politics, economy, law, and value system of the entire country. Sue Peabody, *"There Are No Slaves in France": The Political Culture of Race and Slavery in the Ancien Régime* (New York: Oxford University Press, 1996).

5. For more on this, see Tyler Stovall, *Paris Noir: African Americans in the City of Light* (New York: Houghton Mifflin, 1996); Brent Hayes Edwards, *The Practice of Diaspora:*

Literature, Translation, and the Rise of Black Internationalism (Cambridge: Harvard University Press, 2003); Theresa Leininger-Miller, *New Negro Artists in Paris: African American Painters and Sculptors in the City of Light, 1922–1934* (New Brunswick, N.J.: Rutgers University Press, 2000); Elizabeth Ezra, *The Colonial Unconscious: Race and Culture in Interwar France* (Ithaca, N.Y.: Cornell University Press, 2000); and Carole Marks and Diana Edkins, *The Power of Pride: Stylemakers and Rulebreakers of the Harlem Renaissance* (New York: Crown Publishers, 1999).

6. Léopold Senghor, *Liberté V: Le dialogue des cultures* (Paris: Seuil, 1993); Aimé Césaire, *Discours sur le colonialisme* (Paris: Presence Africaine, 1955); Janet G. Vaillant, *Black, French, and African: A Life of Léopold Sédar Senghor* (Cambridge, Mass.: Harvard University Press, 1990).

7. "Ice Cream Giant Slammed for 'Racist' Ads," *The Local* (Sweden's News in English), based on an article in the *Svenska Dagbladet,* Apr. 13, 2005. "*Negerzoen wordt zoen,*" *De Telegraaf,* http://www.telegraaf.nl, Mar. 23, 2006.

8. For further background on the image of blacks, see, for example, Jean Devisse and Michel Mollat, *The Image of the Black in Western Art, II, From the Early Christian Era to the "Age of Discovery,"* vol. 2, *Africans in the Christian Ordinance of the World (Fourteenth to the Sixteenth Century)* (Cambridge: Harvard University Press, 1979); Allison Blakely, *Blacks in the Dutch World: The Evolution of Racial Imagery in a Modern Society* (Bloomington: Indiana University Press, 1994); Jan Nederveen Pieterse, *White on Black: Images of Africa and Blacks in Western Popular Culture* (New Haven: Yale University Press, 1995); Leora Auslander and Thomas Holt, "Sambo in Paris: Race and Racism in the Iconography of the Everyday," in Sue Peabody and Tyler Stovall, eds., *The Color of Liberty: Histories of Race in France* (Durham: Duke University Press, 2003), 147–84; T. F. Earle and K.J.P. Lowe, eds., *Black Africans in Renaissance Europe* (New York: Cambridge University Press, 2005); Emmanuel Chukwudi Eze, ed., *Race and the Enlightenment* (Oxford: Blackwell, 1997); and Stephen Jay Gould, *The Mismeasure of Man* (New York: W. W. Norton, 1996).

9. Tariq Modood, *Multicultural Politics: Racism, Ethnicity, and Muslims in Britain* (Minneapolis: University of Minnesota Press, 2005), 191–93.

10. An insightful, comprehensive overview on these developments in Europe is an online article by Johanna Maula, director of the International Cultural Centre of Helsinki, "Posses of Rabble or Calling for Minority Rights?" *Helsinki Times,* Nov. 30, 2005, 1. I am especially indebted to Leroy P. Hardy Jr. for voluntarily aiding my tracking of related current developments all across Europe.

11. John Tagliabue, "French Lesson: Taunts on Race Can Boomerang," *New York Times,* Sept. 21, 2005. On the deeper historical dimensions of these issues, see Tyler Stovall, "From Red Belt to Black Belt: Race, Class, and Urban Marginality in Twentieth-Century Paris," in Peabody and Stovall, *The Color of Liberty,* 351–69.

12. Molly Moore, "Huge Protest Puts France to the Test," *Washington Post,* Mar. 29, 2006; Jeffrey Stinson, "Fear of Replay of '05 Riots Has French on Edge," *USA Today,* Oct. 27, 2006; Elaine Sciolino and Ariane Bernard, "Anger Festering in French Areas Scarred in Riots," *New York Times,* Oct. 20, 2006; John Ward Anderson, "Paris Suburb Hit by Rioting Tries Healing Power of Talk," *Washington Post,* Dec. 3, 2007.

13. See my "African Diaspora in the Netherlands," in *Encyclopedia of Diasporas: Immigrant and Refugee Cultures Around the World,* vol. 2 (New York: Kluwer Academic/Plenum Publishers, 2004), 593–602. See also Ineke van Kessel and Nina Tellegen, eds., *Afrikanen in Nederland* (Amsterdam: Koninklijk Instituut de Tropen, 2000); Gert Oostindie, *Paradise Overseas; The Dutch Caribbean: Colonialism and its Transatlantic Legacies* (Oxford: Macmillan, 2005); and my *Blacks in the Dutch World.*

14. For a brief overview of Somali history in England, see http://www.portcities.org.uk/london/server/show/ConNarrative.109/chapterId/2320/The-Somali-Community-in- (accessed May 12, 2008). On Cape Verdeans in Portugal, see Joao Sardinha, "Cape Verdean Associations in the Metropolitan Area of Lisbon and Their Role in the Integration of the Cape Verdean Community into Portuguese Society," The Faculty of Social Sciences and Humanities of the New University of Lisbon, http://e-geo.fcsh.unl.pt/pdf/linhaad_joao_sardinha.

15. Neil Parsons, "El Negro of Banyoles," paper presented at a conference sponsored by the University of Botswana history department, May 24, 2001.

16. Eva Lodde, Mike Glindmeier, and Jens Todt, "Racism in Soccer: Player Silences German Racists with Hitler Salute," *Spiegel Online,* Apr. 3, 2006, http://www.Spiegel.de/international/0,1518,409517,00.html (accessed May 12, 2008); John Ward Anderson, "A Multi-Hued National Team Thrills Racially Uneasy France," *The Washington Post,* July 7, 2006.

17. Libero Della Piana, "Choose Your World: Race in Portugal and the New Europe," *Color Lines Magazine* 2, no. 4 (Winter 1999–2000): 1.

18. Raf Casert, "Rise of Racist Violence Concerns Belgium," San Francisco Chronicle, May 12, 2006, http://www.sfgate.com/cgi-bin/article.cgi?f=/n/a/2006/05/12/international/i111913D17.DTL.

19. Lucian Kim, "Grappling with Being Black . . . and German," *Christian Science Monitor,* Feb. 4, 1999, 7. See also David McBride, Leroy Hopkins, and Aisha Blackshire-Belay, eds., *Crosscurrents: African Americans, Africa, and Germany in the Modern World* (Columbia, S.C.: Camden House, 1998).

20. Sylvia Poggioli, "Race and Politics in Europe Today: German Minorities Still Fight To Be Seen, Heard," National Public Radio, Jan. 9, 2009, http://www.npr.org/templates/story/story.php?storyId=99189120, 3.

21. Colin Nickerson, "Racial Attacks in Germany Stir World Cup Fear," *Boston Globe,* Apr. 24, 2006.

22. "V Sankt-Peterburge soversheno prestuplenie, zhertvoi kotorogo stala temnokozhaia devochka," *Pervyi Kanal Novosti,* Mar. 26, 2006; "Antifashistskii miting v Sankt-Peterburge byl cobran po elektronnoi pochte," *Pervyi Kanal* (Channel 1), Apr. 11, 2006. On the move toward legislation, see related *Pervyi Kanal* articles on Apr. 13 and 16. A 2006 report from Amnesty International highlighted racist killings in Russia: "Russian Racism 'Out of Control,'" May 4, 2006, http://thereport.amnesty.org/eng/regions/europe-and-central-asia/russian-federation.

23. Jarka Halkova, "Fighting Borrowed Prejudices about Africa," Nov. 12, 2004, Radio Prague Archives. Matthew J. Reynolds, "African Expats Long for Safe Streets," *Slovak Spectator,* June 26, 2000; *The Skinhead International: A Worldwide Survey of Neo-Nazi*

Skinheads (New York: Anti-Defamation League, 1995); "Higher Deficit Feared . . . Libya Quagmire . . . The Art of Hospitality," *Sofia Echo,* Sept. 2–8, 2005.

24. Lars Bevanger, "Norway Coming to Terms with Racism," BBC, http://news.bbc.co.uk/1/hi/world/europe/1161853.stm.

25. William Horsley, "The New Italians," BBC, http://news.bbc.co.uk/2/hi/europe/1480168.stm.

26. Jenna Milly, "Ireland Tackles Refugee Influx," CNN.com, 2003.

27. Poggioli, "Race and Politics in Europe Today: Immigrants Forced to Margins of Italian Society," Jan. 14, 2009, 1; Gert Oostindie, *Het verleden onder ogen: Herdenking van de slavernij* (The Hague: Arena/Prins Claus Fonds, 1999).

28. *Farbe bekennen: Afro-deutsche Frauen auf den Spuren ihrer Geschichte* (Frankfurt am Main: Fischer Taschenbuch Verlag, 1992). France is the country in which the liveliest discourse from a wide variety of commentators is transpiring over the question of black identity, especially in the wake of the riots in late 2005. See, for example, Pap Ndiaye, *La condition noire: essai sur une minorité française* (Paris: Calmann-Lévy, 2008); history professor Myriam Cottias, *La question noire: Histoire d'une construction coloniale* (Paris: Bayard, 2007); Senegal-born State Secretary for Human Rights under the Ministry of Foreign Affairs, and a member of Sarkozy's UMP, Rama Yade-Zimet, *Noirs de France* (Paris: Calmann-lévy, 2007); Bénin-born pharmacist and first president of CRAN Patrick Lozes, *Nous, les Noirs de France* (Paris: Éditions Danger Public, 2007); urban planning instructor Jean-Baptiste Onana, *Sois nègre et tais-toi!* (Nantes: Éditions du temps, 2007); member of the National Assembly representing Guyana, her birthplace, member of the PRG, presidential candidate in 2002, and author of the law declaring French participation in slavery a crime against humanity, Christiane Taubira, *Rendez-vous avec La Républic* (Paris: Éditions La Découverte, 2007); North American history professor François Durpaire, *France blanche, colère noire* (Paris: Odile Jacob, 2006); Cameroon-born sociocultural consultant Gaston Kelman, *Je suis noir et je n'aime pas le manioc* (Paris: Éditions Max Milo, 2004); historical writer, Commission on the Rights of Man member, and child of Caribbean parents Claude Ribbe, *Les Nègres de la République* (Monaco: Éditions Alphée, 2001); journalists and historical writers Geraldine Faes and Stephen Smith, *Noir et Français* (Paris: Éditions du Panama, 2006).

29. Angela Doland, "France Examines Scars Left by Slavery: Commemoration Falls Shy, Some Say," *Boston Globe,* May 11, 2006.

30. Sardinha, "Cape Verdean Associations," 21.

31. Two economists engaged in such studies are William J. Collins and Robert A. Margo, "The Labor Market Effects of the 1960s Riots," Working Paper 10243, Working Paper Series, 2004, National Bureau of Economic Research, Inc. (this and related papers available at http://www.nber.org).

32. For thoughtful reflections on the broader parameters of this question, see Thomas Holt, *The Problem of Race in the Twenty-first Century* (Cambridge: Harvard University Press, 2000).

2

Blacks in Early Modern Europe: New Research from the Netherlands

DIENKE HONDIUS

> The tardy recognition of a color-consciousness long present but earlier denied has produced the paradox in which a society not free of racism must remain race-conscious for a while in order to end race consciousness.
>
> Allison Blakely, *Blacks in the Dutch World: The Evolution of Racial Imagery in a Modern Society*

During four centuries of European ideas and action with regard to race and racism, the impact of visible difference, in particular skin tone, has remained significant. Yet in Europe, color can appear to be ignored. In a study about the acceptance of intermarriage as a test for tolerance, I interviewed dozens of mixed couples living in the Netherlands about the reactions they had received from family and friends. What turned out to be most ambiguous was how the couples themselves spoke about the impact of skin color difference. In one and the same sentence, they would tell me that color, skin tone, is completely unimportant yet crucial, that color to them was something they did not see yet was always there; they would deny and stress color simultaneously. This ambivalence, the individual struggles with racial difference, sparked my interest for the long-term nature of race relations in Europe.[1]

In Western Europe, one of the legacies of the history of the Holocaust is what I call the *antiracist norm:* the norm that says that racial difference does not matter. Racial difference, the concept of race, the word race (*ras,* in Dutch, like *rasse,* in German), are consciously ignored: race may not have any space in public discourse. In public policy, *race* is not a word we ever hear in Dutch. That is very different from how race is used in English. Yet visible difference is a fact of life, and hard to deny or ignore. The combination of the antiracist norm and the fact of visible blackness and whiteness creates a source of tension in present-day life, and this is what mixed couples voiced in the interviews I had with them. Underlying this ambivalence are four centuries of race relations.

Variety in skin tones in Europe is common but also still new—in some places more than others. In the Netherlands, a significant Black presence is only thirty years old. Only now are the Dutch beginning to acknowledge the history and the legacy of our four centuries of empire, the involvement in and the profits of the slave trade and slavery in the colonies—only now, as a result of the Black presence in the country today. Among the first results of this late, new, still hesitant and always controversial move to accept the legacy of colonialism and racism are monuments to recognize the involvement in the slave trade and slavery, in Amsterdam (2002) and Middelburg (2005). Research projects are under way. Education packs are being made. Transnational family histories and genealogies are studied. These are indications that we are at a juncture. However, there remain areas that are still too sensitive for most white Dutch to change. Black Pete (*Zwarte Piet*), the Black and supposedly funny stereotypical servant and helper of Saint Nicholas, always portrayed as "pitch black," with thick red lips, wide-open eyes, gold earrings, and dressed like a doll, is the most well-known example. His presence in the yearly festival in December is defended as Dutch heritage that should not be taken away. But Black Pete has slowly become more controversial.

Two small but significant victories, as I see it, were won very recently: first, a change in the Dutch dictionary, and second, a change in the name of a well-known sweet, the so-called Negro's kiss: *Negerzoen*. It is a cookie topped with sugared egg white cream covered in dark chocolate. Four years ago, a grassroots committee of Black Dutch activists with Surinamese roots began a campaign against the word *neger*, negro. The first target was the Dutch dictionary Van Dale, in which the definition of *neger* was "person belonging to one of the black races from Africa; *nikker* [nigger], *roetmop* [literally, "lump of soot"]." Only in the latest, 2005 edition was this added to the definition: "descendant from the negro slaves who were in former times imported in America (perceived by some as a term of abuse)."[7] *Neger* is no longer a neutral term to use for nonwhite, dark-skinned people, but is acknowledged to be a pejorative, a negative term as well. I am convinced that without the activism of the small committee, this would not have been changed. Interestingly, there is as yet no public alternative for *neger*.

The sweet Negro's kiss was the second target, and in March 2006 the company that has produced these sweets since the 1920s announced that, following new marketing research, they had come to the conclusion that the name *Negerzoen* was no longer "of this time": they decided to change the name to Kisses, preceded by the company name, "Buys," so *Buys Negerzoenen* has changed to *Buys Zoenen*. This decision has provoked thousands of reactions, most of which were negatively loaded: varying from outright racism to resignation, shrugging, well-alright-then lack of understanding. Very, very few if any white Dutch welcomed this decision: the positive reactions that I personally have heard were from Caribbean and Surinamese Dutch—yet the decision to change the name is a fact; it has to be tolerated.

One might say, what's all the fuss about one word, about one little sweet? However, it is in these small incidents that one can feel the significant Dutch defense mode: changing the "Negro's kiss," avoiding the word *neger,* is seen as unnecessary, as politically correct, or simply as strange and unimportant. Yet it is done, it has been noted, and I suppose many people have heard about it and now finally know that there are people who really do not like the word *neger.* Therefore, I regard both the dictionary and the sweet company's decision to change as significant steps forward. It will perhaps open the way to more interest for the history of Dutch and European race relations. Against this context, then, now I will go back four centuries to the first beginnings of this long narrative in order to better contextualize it historically.

African-European Encounters: The Repetition of Surprise

In the early modern meetings between white Europeans and Africans, as recorded in sixteenth- and seventeenth-century records of travels to Africa, the European surprise about blackness is a major aspect. Dark skin color made a deep impression and is always noted. Not heavy-handed, there is no moral weight attached to the early observations—but blackness is always mentioned, put into words: *Swart, Negro, Swartig, Neger*—and the opposite, *Blank,* comes up quickly too. No immediate racial classification is made: more the expression of surprise and also a positive appreciation and admiration of the wonders of God's creation can be found.

The history of these meetings is not recorded by both sides. We are depending on written records by white Europeans. What we can find are their perceptions, and through their perceptions, we can trace glimpses, remnants, of the reactions of the Africans. The asymmetry was there then—in terms of power, of mobility: who had the ship, who could travel, who wrote down his impressions—and it has remained with us until today. The travelogues express the idea that the writer is a pioneer: the first to see, to meet, and to experience difference in these meetings with Africans. It seems that every white person experienced this as new, surprising, and significant: the first meeting with Black people. So there is now a four-centuries-old European history of the repetition of surprise. Well into the late twentieth century, every white boy, girl, man, or woman seems able to remember his or her first meeting with a nonwhite person.

One of the explanations I see for this repetition of surprise is the general and long-term absence in Europe of Blacks even though most European nations had significant empires with Black populations who were exploited, enslaved, put to work for the mother country, and treated as inferior. The fact that the "colonial subjects" remained far away from Europe, over the ocean, has long been regarded as a coincidence. However, as I will explain with some examples, the absence of Blacks in Europe was the result of a series of conscious decisions and specific laws, intended to keep slavery invisible and Europe white. Given these centuries of restriction, Blacks and Africans in Europe remained exceptional and different, generally being "the only one" in their immediate surroundings. This kept the surprise factor intact. The very few Africans and Asians who did manage to make it to Europe, usually for a short period in their lives, were generally received with curiosity and surprise, and much less frequently with hatred or outright rejection. A strong tendency of white paternalism, the law, and the small numbers of nonwhites helped to sustain deeply ingrained racial inequalities and Black minority status for centuries—for so long, in fact, that currently Europe is experiencing a new phenomenon: the permanent, ordinary, daily interaction between whites and nonwhites. Three examples of early Black presence in the Netherlands show the beginnings of a long-term pattern of European race relations.

African Men, Women, and Children in Middelburg in 1596

In November 1596, 130 "Moors" arrived in Middelburg, in the southwest Netherlands. It is the oldest story about a group of Africans entering the Netherlands, and it has left a somewhat positive image: the "Moors"—a term that in Dutch at the time was generally used for dark-skinned people of African origin, without the association of Muslim descent that is known from Spain and southern Europe—were liberated in Zeeland when a Portuguese merchant ship was captured; and their liberation is regarded as something to be proud of. My conclusion is quite different: they left soon and were sold as slaves in the West Indies after all.

From the second half of sixteenth century onwards, individual merchants tried their luck and set off, first to southern Europe, later to the Mediterranean, the North African coast, and soon also to more southern West African and down to South African coasts in the seventeenth century. At the end of the sixteenth century, these pioneers, private entrepreneurs, and adventurous individuals, pirates, and looters, were seen by the local and national authorities as both a threat and a challenge, a chance for profit. This marks the beginning of state involvement, with the Dutch East and West India Companies established at the beginning of the seventeenth century, and trade monopolies being handed out. The critical objective was to control private trade and to bring in profit for the state, as well as for the private traders complicit with these activities.

Shipbuilding developed fast, and the Dutch were able to build lots of ships that were fast and strong in comparison with ships of other European nations. They competed and followed the example of the Portuguese, and the Dutch were able to take over colonies and settlements from the Portuguese both on the African coast and in the Americas. The Portuguese and the Spanish were already beginning to trade in slaves at the time, and African people as servants and other workers were beginning to be a more common sight in Portuguese and Spanish cities. The Dutch did not immediately involve themselves with the slave trade, but after several decades they saw a clear commercial opportunity and in the first half of the seventeenth century, the Dutch were world leaders in the slave trade. After that, the English and French became much more important, and the Dutch involvement was by comparison smaller. However, the slave trade by Dutch merchants continued until the end of the nineteenth century. After the formal abolition of the slave trade and of slavery, Dutch private merchants continued to seek a profit. The privateers—or pirates—were primarily interested in sugar, gold, ivory (elephant's teeth), and salt. They traded also in pearls, fur, and tobacco, both as regular traders and as looters.[3]

"All Baptized Christians"

The ship that was captured from a Portuguese merchant was brought to Middelburg. It did not contain sugar or tobacco, but more than a hundred Moors: men, women, and children. Why the captain returned to Middelburg is not clear. The ship came *"uyt Guynéa"* and was probably going to Brazil or the Caribbean, the West Indies. Possibly the ship had to be repaired. It is very likely that the captain intended to sell his human cargo. This can be seen from the phrasing of the minutes of the States of Zeeland, the local authorities dealing with this incident, and the burgermaster of Middelburg, Adriaen Heindricxssen ten Haeff, on November 15, 1596. They explicitly prohibit the sale of the Moors: they are not to be held or sold as slaves but to be set free. Why could they not be sold according to the Zeeland authorities? The minutes are clear: "here were brought with ships from Guynéa, in which many Moors, as much as hundred, Men as well as Women and Children, being all baptized (christened) Christians, and that they for that reason do not deserve to be held by anyone or to be sold as Slaves, but are to be set in their free liberty, without anyone pretending them to be his property."[4]

The mentioning of the group being "all baptized (christened) Christians" is an important point since that was the reason they had to be liberated. For Dutch (Zeeuws) Calvinist protestant authorities, baptism was a holy sacrament that had to be taken seriously. These Africans, however, were not baptized by Dutch Protestants, but by Portuguese Roman Catholics. The Portuguese Catholic practice of christening differed markedly from that of Dutch Protestants, and in general the Dutch regarded Roman Catholics as enemies and dangerous heathens. In the Portuguese-controlled coastal areas in Africa and Asia, baptism had become a common practice. Everyone who was to go on a ship was baptized, as a kind of insurance, "to be on the safe side." There were no conditions attached in terms of promising to live as Christians. In contrast, the baptism practice of Dutch reformed Christians is the last step in an exclusive process. The person to be baptized—or, in the case of a child, his or her parents—had to ask permission from the local church authorities and answer a number of specific questions. Parents had to promise to raise the child as a Christian and to give it their best example. Refusal of the request to be baptized was not uncommon. This significant difference in the "weight" attached to baptism appears not to have been important in the case of the Moors of Middelburg: their status as baptized Christians was not a matter of debate or doubt.

The American historian John Thornton discovered in the archives of Evora in Portugal how the Portuguese went about their baptism of slaves in Africa. They made baptism obligatory, mandatory: Thornton found reference to a law from the end of the sixteenth, perhaps the early beginning of the seventeenth century in Angola, stating that "Portuguese law required all African slaves to be baptized and made Christians before their arrival in America." Thornton shows that this was not just a formality. From 1575 onwards, Portuguese Jesuit priests had started a Christian community that had grown into what he calls a mixed Christian-Angolan, "Afro-Christian syncretic church," in which the local language Kimbundu was spoken. In that language, the enslaved were also baptized, according to Thornton: "The basic catechism, for those captives awaiting embarkation or on board ship probably followed the outlines set down in a late sixteenth century text, though undoubtedly delivered in Kimbundu."[5]

The group of Africans in Middelburg had likely experienced an Angolese-Portuguese Christian baptism. However, just how important their being baptized really was to the Portuguese is an open question. Perhaps baptism is not the point. Perhaps it is more important that African slaves, the most direct proof of the newly developing involvement of Dutch merchants in the slave trade, did not become visible in the Netherlands.

Exhibition Day in Middelburg

The Middelburgers were invited to come and see the Moors, by an announcement made in the churches: "Next Sunday will be announced in the Churches, that the Moors in question, the women, as well as men and children, will be set in their natural liberty, by the Council here, and by the Magistrate of Middelburg, on behalf of the States of Zeeland, with the appropriate solemnity [ceremony], to be able to proceed with their free will in such work, trade, craft or service as they wish. That therefore anyone that same day will be able to find them in the Hoff van Zeelandt in Middelburg, called the Abdye [seat of the local government], in order to appoint some of the Moors, to accept them, to raise them in God's fear."[6] We assume that the announcement and the exhibition day indeed took place in Middelburg's city center. However, no trace or report of this remarkable event can be found. It is possible that some of the Africans found work as farm workers, domestics, or soldiers.

Most Likely from Angola

It was a substantial group of men, women, and children, but we know none of their names. The only indication of the place they came from is "Guynéa," but that was a general name for most West Africa. According to the American historians John Thornton and Linda Heywood, Angola and the neighboring area of the south of Congo would be the most likely region of origin, since it was a ship captured from the Portuguese, and since there were already frequent slave transports from Portuguese Angola during this period.[7] Thornton wrote, "By the end of the [sixteenth] century, Luanda-based merchants had developed a series of trading networks east across Kongo to the Maleba Pool area."[8]

People at risk of being enslaved in these years were those who were left behind during heavy fights in the Angola interior area of Ndongo. They were captured by local groups of warriors called Imbangala, who sold them to the Portuguese as slaves, writes Thornton: "Old people, some women, and most children were ordered to retire to hills or other inaccessible places until the fighting was over, while the men prepared for battle. . . . Some women accompanied the armies to cook for and comfort the soldiers. . . . The remaining civilians who had not taken adequate shelter in hills or forests were vulnerable to enslavement."[9]

A British sailor, Andrew Battell, captured by the Portuguese and working for them as forced laborer, wrote an eyewitness report of these events:[10] "In the late 1590s, a group of Portuguese merchants had organized four voyages that included Battell to the area for the express purpose of buying captives for export."[11]

I think it is likely that one of these transports was intercepted by Dutch privateers; it happened often and also over a longer period of time. A second indication for Angola as a region of origin is the fact that they were Christians, writes Heywood: "Angolans (either from Kongo or some parts of the Portuguese territory and its neighbors) were the most likely source of a large number of Christians."[12]

What Became of Them?

Of such a large group entering the small town of Middelburg, one expects to find some historical traces of them. The Leiden historian Pieter Emmer suggests that "a large part of the slaves will no doubt have been transported directly to the market in Antwerp, where slaves were regularly traded." However, there is no indication of this at all.[13] It is certain that there were more Africans in Antwerp, but an organized trip of a group of Africans, or an agreement between traders from Zeeland and Antwerp are both highly unlikely. The city of Antwerp could not be reached at the time because the Schelde River was already closed off and the Antwerpen Exchange was no longer active. Some of the Africans may have reached Antwerp but not the whole group.

There were some other Africans in Zeeland at the time. Every now and then, an individual was taken into the Middelburg hospital "Gasthuis" for the poor. On May 28, 1591, there was "a Moor who we can not understand" ("*eenen moor die men niet can verstaen*"). He died on April 3, 1593, having spent almost two years in the poor house. That same year we know of the arrival of "a Moor called Ioors" ("*een mooriaen genaempt ioors*") on May 22, 1593, and later also a "Moorinne with child" ("*moorinne met kind*").[14] The large group of Africans who came into the city in 1596 would definitely qualify for entrance in the Gasthuis, which generally welcomed strangers who were ill, soldiers, sailors, those who had not lived in the city more than a year and six weeks, and people who could not be supported by the church. There is, however, no mention of any group of Moors after 1596.[15]

No Traces in the Archives

The substantial and detailed minutes of the churches in Zeeland do not mention the Moors either. I found this surprising, since the local authorities announced their liberation because they were baptized. There are also substantial military archives, including lists of names of soldiers. No names that would indicate African origins can be found here, either. I have not found any archives of schools. One would expect that the children among the group would have to go to school at some point. Unfortunately the baptismal, marriage, and burial records of 1596 were destroyed by fire during World War II, when Middelburg was bombed. In 1901, the archivist J. H. de Stoppelaar saw these archives; he writes, "Many of the blacks who were accepted, enjoyed the freedom they were given only for a short time; according to the 'register of dead bodies of those who are buried in the cemeteries,' no less than nine 'moors from Indie' were buried in the period from 4 January until 3 March 1597."[16] The number and the time make it likely that these nine people belonged to the group. Further research is unfortunately impossible due to the loss of the burned archives. The fact that nothing about this group can be found strongly suggests their chances of having remained in Zeeland as a group were slim. Individual life histories remain plausible, of course. Yet, I think that the lack of traces of this group, considering the substantial archives and variation of sources in Zeeland, is an important given. Did the Africans leave?

Shipowner Pieter van der Haegen and Captain Melchior van den Kerckhoven

The Dutch shipowner and the captain involved left more traces. Their economic interests were at stake when they were prohibited to sell "their" Moors in Zeeland. Their reaction was significant. Merchant Pieter van der Haegen from Rotterdam was the shipowner, and therefore also the owner of the human cargo. Van der Haegen had lived in Hamburg earlier, as well as in Amsterdam in 1591.[17] In Amsterdam he was a merchant in textiles.[18] From Amsterdam he settled in Rotterdam and entered the shipping business in 1596. He was known as an enterprising but not a cautious man: "More a speculator than a decent merchant" (*Eerder een speculant dan een degelijk koopman).*[19] He was among the pioneers in international trade, but the trips he organized in 1599 all ended in loss. He lost his capital and moved to Middelburg in 1603.[20] He had a bad reputation; for example, a Leyden professor Baudius wrote a letter to Hugo de Groot in 1607 about all sorts of scandals in merchant families: "Vanderhagio," he says, was "a famous mauvais sujet, who was not much better than a Roman slave brute."[21] Melchior van den Kerckhoven was a pirate, and captain on Van der Haegen's ships. He had a bad reputation as a looter of everything he could get his hands on "by plundering friend and foe along the African coast" ("*door langs de Afrikaansche kust vriend en vijand te plunderen*").[22] Since he worked for Van der Haegen before as well as after 1596, it is most likely that this Van Kerckhoven captured the Portuguese ship with slaves and brought it to Middelburg.

The crew on the ships were Portuguese or Spanish, because only these nations were allowed to trade in the West Indies.[23] In 1597 and also in 1601, Van der Haegen, together with the Rotterdam banker Hans van der Veken, sent a number of ships to the East Indies. They lost a lot of money, but they kept trying.[24] Van der Veken's motto was "Happiness is persistent for those who deserve it" ("*Het geluk is standvastig voor wie het verdient*").[25] Kerckhoven did not stop either, moving on to Nova Zembla, the North Cape, as well as North America, reaching the Hudson river area in 1609.[26]

Carte Blanche: Obtaining Permission from the National Government

The States of Zeeland decided that the Moors could not be sold. That, however, did not make them the possession of the local authorities. Shipowner Van der Haegen still considered them his property, and he refused to accept the decision. He went to the national government, the States General ("Staten Generaal") in The Hague, and filed a request, first on November 23, and also on November 28, 1596, to obtain permission to bring the Moors and the Portuguese crew of the ships to Portugal and the West Indies after all. The exact texts of these requests have not yet been found, but the States General minutes quote from them. On November 23, Van der Haegen requests of the government, "that they would allow him to bring one of the four Portuguese pilots who arrived recently in Zeeland with approximately hundred and thirty Moors, to Portugal to bring them on land, and that he also, next to some of the same pilots in his service, would be allowed to bring from there onwards ten or twelve Portuguese sailors in order to finish his planned trip to the West Indies. After considerable deliberation the request of the transport of the Moors was turned down."[27]

This decision implies that the Moors could not be taken away but that the Portuguese crew as well as the ship could be moved. Within a week, Van der Haegen filed a second request; the following quotes come from the States General minutes: "After a second request of Van der Hagen it was decided on 28 November, that he could do with the Moors 'as he sees fit'" ("*Op een tweede request van Van der Hagen werd 28 november beschikt, dat hij met de Mooren kon doen, 'soe hy 't verstaet*'"), with the addition that the States General were not prepared to take any further decision about this request (*doch dat de Staten niet van plan waren verder een besluit omtrent dit verzoek te nemen'*).[28] The national authorities gave Van der Haegen permission to do with them as he pleases; they do not want to be involved in it any further.

These findings lead me to conclude that it is most likely that Van der Haegen subsequently had the Moors in Middelburg taken away on his ship, that they left the Netherlands after all. This is the most likely course of action. The Africans perhaps remained on the ship before and after the exhibition day in Middelburg, and possibly also in the Hoff van Zeeland, the seat of the local government; but these were offices. A group of 130 men, women, and children could not stay there for a longer period of time. Something had to be done.

Melchior van Kerckhoven indeed left very soon with ships owned by Van der Haegen. There are no indications that the ship in Middelburg was no longer at their disposal.[29] My conclusion is that Pieter van der Haegen had the group of Moors from Middelburg picked up by Melchior van Kerckhoven, who brought them via Portugal to the West Indies, where they were sold as slaves after all. Possibly not the whole group; perhaps some Africans were left behind in Middelburg who had found work in the meantime. Nine of them died within a few months, but the rest of the group did not stay in Zeeland. My conclusion is that the stay of most of them in Middelburg did not last longer than a few weeks.

Perhaps more research is possible. Chances to find more information about the group as a whole I regard as slim. Traces of individual Africans may still be found, for example, in private archives of families in Zeeland, indicating names of African domestics or other personnel. International archives possibly contain more information, about the African origins of the group, about the Portuguese crew, and the further travels of Van der Haghen and Van Kerckhoven to the West Indies.

Another discovery was that not only the captain of the ship but also several of the local dignitaries involved in the decision to free the Moors in Middelburg, in particular Mayor ten Haeff, became active in the African trade immediately afterwards. Rather than benevolently freeing the enslaved, the episode encouraged them to join this new form of trade that showed great commercial promise, as soon as possible. These discoveries give an entirely new twist to the story. I am now inclined to question the importance of the fact that the Africans were baptized Christians. If their status as Christians was really important for the authorities in Zeeland, local churches could have done something to welcome their new brothers and sisters; there is no sign of that at all. After the national government overruled the local authorities of Zeeland, no further reaction can be found from them, either. The fact that the same people who decided that the Africans had to be set free became involved in the trade as soon as they could is significant. I think that these facts strongly contradict an interpretation of the local authorities' decision to liberate the Africans as a humanitarian act.

Slavery: Not Here in Europe

The message that the Zeeland authorities were sending out was multilayered.

- To the individual shipowner and captain, the message was you made a mistake; don't try this here.
- To the wider community of merchants and captains, the message was you cannot sell slaves here in Zeeland; this is not the way to make money with this trade.
- To the general population, the message was presented as something more positive: there is no slavery in Zeeland, and baptized slaves will have to be treated as employees and raised as Christians.

In retrospect, we can see that all three layers of this message were effective. It served first of all as a geographic boundary: it kept the visible realities of the slave trade away from the Netherlands. The story lived on in local tradition as an example of the freedom-loving nature of the people of Zeeland, a tradition established in 1581. As the Leiden historian Johanna Kardux reminds us, in the 1581 *"Akte van Verlatinge,"* the Dutch declared their independence from Spain, conceiving the foundation of their nation as a rejection of slavery and thus justifying the right to revolt.[30]

This separation of what could be done "here" in Europe and "there," elsewhere, was helpful in ignoring the role that the port cities of Zeeland played in the triangular transatlantic trade of slaves from Africa to the West Indies and

North America. After the Dutch West Indies Trade Company lost its monopoly in 1730, Middelburg became the center of the Dutch slave trade. Ships fitted out in Zeeland carried about 30 percent of the trade between 1601 and 1803, transporting a total of 180,000 slaves, a fact omitted from the self-congratulatory folklore about the Africans in Middelburg.

Keeping Slavery an Ocean Away

Responding to my findings with regard to this history, Johanna Kardux and the American historian James Horton conclude that "the public memory of the events was in fact an act of collective forgetting."[31] Although the story was indeed mostly forgotten, another, more active interpretation is possible. Because this is not just a Dutch story. Not only in the Netherlands or Zeeland, but also in Britain and France there are histories of enslaved and freed Africans who found their way to Europe in small numbers from the sixteenth century onwards. And we know that in Portugal and Spain, larger numbers of Africans lived in the southern cities from the fifteenth century onwards.

The legal history of these "incidents" and "exceptions" is interesting, as the American historian Daniel Hulsebosch writes in a recent article.[32] One significant moment is the Somerset case and the decision Judge Mansfield made in 1770 in London. James Somerset was a slave brought to Britain by his West Indian owner and subsequently freed. However, this former owner decided to return to Jamaica and wanted Somerset to come with him. Somerset refused and fled; a trial followed. It was a test case: which law was valid for whom? Judge Mansfield decided that Somerset could remain free in Britain. This case has been generally interpreted as the origins of the abolitionist movement and an early indication that slavery would come to an end; it has entered the history books as the proof of liberty in Britain—similar to the Middelburg Moors liberation story. However, Hulsebosch reconstructs the case within a much wider, Atlantic context. This decision, he says, had both European, local, and national functions as well. "The participants in Somerset's Case were most concerned to reconcile this tension: to keep slavery in the empire while keeping it out of England."[33] The decision to liberate one slave in England implied that slavery elsewhere could continue: "The decision left the institution of colonial slavery almost untouched while at the same time insulating England from slavery, the power of returning West Indian planters, and despotism. . . . Indeed, the participants in Somerset's Case assumed the legality of colonial slavery."

Similarly, the 1596 ruling to liberate the Moors in Middelburg was an active effort to keep the immediate, visible consequences of the Atlantic slave trade out of Zeeland; but the national government overruled the decision by allowing the captain to do with the Africans as he saw fit—that is, someplace other than Zeeland. The line that was drawn here was a local, geographical one: there could be no visible slavery in Europe. As Hulsebosch wrote, "The primary argument here was to keep slavery an ocean away. The judges agreed with that argument."

Temporary Stay

Although slave owners traveled freely to and from the Netherlands during the centuries of slave trade and slavery, there was no significant black presence during all those years—or at least, as far as we knew. There is now evidence that there may have been more. Servants were among the few Africans who managed to settle in Europe during the colonial era. They usually remained only a few years. This temporary stay in Europe is not only the case for the very early story of the Moors in Middelburg, but also for other Africans who came to the Netherlands such as Jacobus Capitein, Tannetje Vrijheid, Jan Kompany, Aquasi Boachi, and Kwamin Pokoo.[34] Did they stay or leave voluntarily or was there coercion? I am convinced that we can find out much more about this, both through local archive research and through international comparative research.

Blackness is not always mentioned in European records, as Allison Blakely notes in his pathbreaking and inspiring study "Blacks in the Dutch World":

> In these early centuries within the Netherlands it was rather easy for blacks to melt into Dutch society once they entered. Unlike the situation in the colonies, a tinge of color did not define a person as black. This reticence to accentuate differences may stem in part from the general spirit of accommodation which became traditional in the Netherlands, but may also be due to a lingering uneasiness with the participation in the African slave trade and slavery, which remained outlawed at home. A different definition of the descendants of the early black immigrants to the Netherlands would probably show a significantly higher "black" population than is now counted.[35]

The intriguing presence and absence of Africans in European history can be explained to some extent by the official absence of slavery on European soil: since slavery did not officially exist, no official emancipation or liberation was possible, and everything remained informal, as the Amsterdam archivist Lydia Hagoort notes in her study of the Portuguese Jewish cemetery of Amsterdam in which she found records of dozens of Blacks, both enslaved and free, in the seventeenth century.[36]

In the absence of a racial classification in European national records, and in the knowledge that there is more to find, we need other tools to explore the lives of Blacks in early modern Europe. A combination of detailed archive research and art history is currently proving to be successful.

Africans in Amsterdam: Rembrandt's View

From new research in community and notary records, it is now certain that by the early seventeenth century, quite a few black people had found their way into Amsterdam. Until now, only in Antwerpen was there proof of an early black presence. Evidence of this Black presence in Amsterdam has been found in the archives of the Portuguese Jewish community, especially the cemetery records, which were thoroughly researched by Amsterdam city archivist Lydia Hagoort, as well as in the archives of notaries working in the city at the time.[37] It is certain that there are also more histories of piracy involving enslaved Blacks, similar to the 1596 story. One example comes from the Amsterdam notary's office archives. Four Portuguese merchants, Izak Brazilai, Antonio Mendes, Rodrigo Alvares Drago, and Antonio Henriques Alvin, left statements with Amsterdam notaries in February 1626 after having survived takeover of their ship by Dutch privateers. The Portuguese merchants were allowed to come to Amsterdam following their request, and they come to the city with their "negroes and negresses."[38]

> Drago declares that in October 1625 when together with Alvin, he made his way from Pernambuco [Brazil] to Viana [do Castelo, North Portugal] with the ship De Engel Rafael of skipper Gaspar Maciel Entaon, this ship was seized by a certain Captain Jacob who took them to Vlissingen. There, they and the rest of the crew were released, each with one Spanish pistole and money. The others of the crew went to Rouen; he and Alvin went to Amsterdam with three negroes and five negresses that belonged to Alvin. All declare that Alvin remained in Amsterdam with the eight negroes for about three months and that he was free to go where he pleased and that he could leave with them whenever he wanted.

This group must have been seen in Vlissingen first, and then have lived in Amsterdam from October/November 1625 until February 1626 at least.[39] There are many more individual stories of Africans in the Netherlands, not only enslaved, but also free, hidden in these and other archives. The same is true for individual histories of Asians entering Europe, as new research reveals.[40] This evidence of an early modern African and Asian presence has consequences for the way we look at seventeenth-century Europe. Exciting connections of simultaneity appear when archival research is merged with history of art.

The world famous painter Rembrandt van Rijn worked from Leiden, but he began to spend more and more time in Amsterdam after 1625, settling there permanently in 1631. When we look at the addresses of Rembrandt, the very same street names are found that were mentioned in the notary records mentioning Black women and men. From 1631 to 1634, Rembrandt lived in the house of art dealer Hendrik van Uyleburgh on Jodenbreestraat 2. He remained in the neighbourhood, and from 1639 onwards he owned a house on St. Anthoniesbreestraat, which is now called Jodenbreestraat 4–6, still known as the Rembrandt house today. This "Breestraat," and particularly the "cellars," are mentioned by several notaries—because of the people who live there or who are seen there. It was the heart of the Jewish neighborhood, where some houses were owned by Portuguese Jewish merchants, others kept as warehouses, and the cellars and attics used for the poor.[41] In these same years, Rembrandt made several drawings, sketches, and later paintings with black men and women, as art historian Elmer Kolfin has recently presented.[42] Until recently, it was thought that Rembrandt had traveled to Antwerpen where he might have seen some black people and that he had later drawn and painted from memory—for example, his famous painting of two Black men, which can be seen at the Mauritshuis museum in The Hague. Our research shows that Rembrandt only had to look out of his window, and only had to set one foot out of his door on Jodenbreestraat, perhaps even in the cellar of his own house, to be able to meet black men and women in Amsterdam.

Notes

1. Dienke Hondius, "Gemengde huwelijken, gemengde gevoelens: Aanvaarding en ontwijking van etnisch en religieus verschil," PhD diss., University of Amsterdam/SDU Publishers, The Hague, 1999 and 2001.

2. October 2005, new full-print edition of the Dutch dictionary Grote Van Dale (XIV), 14th edition (Utrecht: Van Dale Publishers, 2005). However, the Van Dale Company, www.vandale.nl, has an online dictionary that still only mentions the first sentence: "Neger: persoon behorend tot één van de zwarte rassen uit Afrika" (person belonging to one of the black races of Africa).

3. See also Dienke Hondius, "Afrikanen in Zeeland, Moren in Middelburg," *Zeeland: Tijdschrift van het Koninklijk Zeeuwsch Genootschap der Wetenschappen* 14, no. 1 (March 2005), *Zeeland en het slavernijverleden,* 13–24; Dienke Hondius, "Black Africans in Early Seventeenth Century Amsterdam," in Kate Lowe, ed., *Renaissance and Reformation (Renaissance et Réforme)* 31 no. 2 (Spring 2008): 89–105. Special issue: "Sub-Saharan Africa and Renaissance and Reformation Europe: New Findings and New Perspectives," http://www.crrs.ca/renref. The archives of the Middelburgsche Commercie Compagnie, a private company active in the slave trade, have been kept in excellent condition in the Zeeuws Archief in Middelburg, Netherlands, http://www.zeeuwsarchief.nl.

4. Translations are mine unless otherwise noted. Dutch original text: "Dat hier waeren ingebracht mette Schepen uyt Guynéa, hier in gecommen veele Mooren, wel by de hondert, zoo Mans ald Vrouwen ende Kinderen, wesende alle gedoopte Christenen, ende dat die daeromme nyet en behooren by yemanden gehouden oft vercocht te worden als Slaeven, maer gestelt in heure vrye liberteyt, zonder dat yemandt van derselver eydgendom behoort te pretenderen." The text of the decision on Nov. 15, 1596, says, "Op 't vertooch van den Burgemeestere Adriaen Heindricxssen ten Haefft, dat hier waeren ingebracht mette Schepen uyt Guynéa, hier in gecommen veele Mooren, wel

by de hondert, zoo Mans ald Vrouwen ende Kinderen, wesende alle gedoopte Christenen, ende dat die daeromme nyet en behooren by yemanden gehouden oft vercocht te worden als Slaeven, maer gestelt in heure vrye liberteyt, zonder dat yemandt van derselver eydgendom behoort te pretenderen; is geresolveert, dat men Sondaege naestcommende, zal in de Kercken doen vercondigen, dat de voorschr. Mooren, zoo Vrouwen, als Manspersoonen ende Kinderen, Maendaege naestcommende by den Raede alhier, ende den Magistraet van Middelburch, gestelt zullen werden, vanwegen den Staten van Zeelandt, in heure natuerlicke lyberteyt, mette solempniteyt daer toe behoorende, om met hunnen vryen wille hun te mogen begeven tot zulcken styl, ambacht oft dienst, als hun zal gelieven, dat daer omme een yeder ten zelven daege, hem zal mogen vinden in 't Hoff van Zeelandt, tot Middelburch, geseyt d'Abdye, om zoo eenige van de voorschr. Mooren, hun begeeren te appoincteren met yemanden, deselve te aenveerden, om op te bringen in Godts vreese." Zeeuws Archief, Middelburg, Archief Staten van Zeeland, Notulenboeken, Nov. 15, 1596.

5. John Thornton, "The African Experience of the '20. and Odd Negroes' Arriving in Virginia in 1619," *William and Mary Quarterly* 55, no. 3 (1998): 421–34, quotation on 434.

6. Dutch original text: "Sondaege naestcommende, zal in de Kercken doen vercondigen, dat de voorschr. Mooren, zoo Vrouwen, als Manspersoonen ende Kinderen, Maendaege naestcommende by den Raede alhier, ende den Magistraet van Middelburch, gestelt zullen werden, vanwegen den Staten van Zeelandt, in heure natuerlicke lyberteyt, mette solempniteyt [plechtigheid] daer toe behoorende, om met hunnen vryen wille hun te mogen begeven tot zulcken styl, ambacht oft dienst, als hun zal gelieven, dat daer omme een yeder ten zelven daege, hem zal mogen vinden in 't Hoff van Zeelandt, tot Middelburch, geseyt d'Abdye, om zoo eenige van de voorschr. Mooren, hun begeeren te appoincteren met yemanden, deselve te aenveerden, om op te bringen in Godts vreese." Zeeuws Archief, Archief Staten van Zeeland, Notulenboeken, Nov. 15, 1596.

7. Linda Heywood and John Thornton, conversation with author, Boston University, November 2003.

8. Thornton, "The African Experience," 421–34.

9. Ibid., 429.

10. Andrew Battell, "The Strange Adventures of Andrew Battel of Leigh in Essex," in Samuel Purchas, *Purchas His Pilgrimes* (London: Fetherstone, 1625; reprints 1901, 1967).

11. Thornton, "The African Experience," 427.

12. I thank Linda Heywood for her suggestions for my research. Linda Heywood, e-mail message to author, June 24, 2004.

13. Emmer said, "Een groot deel van de slaven zal ongetwijfeld linea recta naar de markt te Antwerpen zijn gebracht, waar regelmatig slaven werden verhandeld" ("A major part of the slaves will undoubtedly have been brought directly to the market in Antwerp, where slaves were sold regularly"). Pieter Emmer, *De Nederlandse slavenhandel* (Amsterdam: Arbeiderspers, 2000), 34.

14. Johanna Louise Kool-Blokland, "De zorg gewogen: Zeven eeuwen godshuizen in Middelburg," dissertatie, Universiteit Tilburg, 1990. Uitgave Kon. Zeeuwsch Genootschap der Wetenschappen, Middelburg 1990, 86–87. I thank Roelof Koops, director of the Zeeuws Archief, who pointed this source out to me.

15. Ibid., 127.

16. Dutch text: "Velen van de zwarten, die aanvaard werden, hadden slechts een kortstondig genot van de hun geschonken vrijheid; volgens het 'register van de doode lichamen derghenen die op de kerckhoven begraven syn' werden er van 4 januari tot 3 maart 1597 niet minder dan negen 'mooren wt Indie' ter aarde besteld." J. H. de Stoppelaar, *Balthasar de Moucheron. Een bladzijde uit de Nederlandsche Handelgeschiedenis tijdens den Tachtigjarigen Oorlog* (Den Haag: Martinus Nijhoff, 1901), 61–62.

17. In 1591, his wife's name is Suzanna Cobbouts; they registered their will on December 30 of the same year (source: Amsterdamsche Notarisprotocollen, notaris Jacob Gijsberts, O. 209). At the time they had four children: Susanna, Jan, Maria and Sara, as well as a daughter from an earlier marriage of the wife, Grietgen van der Velde, daughter of Peter van der Velde.

18. Aanteekeningen Bijlsma, Gemeentearchief Rotterdam.

19. F. C. Wieder, "De reis van Mahu en de Cordes" (Den Haag: Martinus Nijhoff, 1923), 7.

20. Amsterdamsche Notarisprotocollen. J. F. Bruyningh Z., 61, 93, twee akten van 20 Augustus 1603, p. 116.

21. Dutch text: "een fameus mauvais sujet (inclytus nepos), die niet veel beter was dan een Romeinsche slavenbeul (tribunus vapularis)." J. H. de Stoppelaar, Balthasar de Moucheron, *Den Haag,* Nijhoff 1901, p. 101, noot 12. Letter by Professor Domnicus Baudius, Leiden, to Hugo de Groot (Grotius) in The Hague, Oct. 7, 1607: "inclyto nepote Vanderhagio, quo nemo tempestate nostra doctius corvos hiantes ludit et ductat dolis, ni Moucheronem forte compares planum isti tribuno vapulari." See also *Rotterdams Welvaren 1550–1650* (The Hague: Martinus Nijhoff, 1919), 59/81.

22. In 1599, therefore he falls into disrepute; later he is taken prisoner in Venice as a pirate. Pieter van der Haegen equipped immediately afterwards in November 1596 four ships: *St. Jacob, St. Pieter, De Zwarte Leeuw,* and *De Drie Koningen.* His financer is Hendrick Anthonisz Wissel, known as a "financial genius, who also was involved in establishing new banks." Melchior van den Kerckhoven directed these ships.

23. On the ship *Drie Koningen,* two Portuguese, Laurens André and Willem Palmar, were in charge together with a Portuguese crew. Van der Haegen worked with Portuguese partners: for example, on the Canary Islands and the Cape Verdian islands he worked with Jan de Cabrajos, who had permanent representatives in San Thomé, Spiritu Santo, and Rio de Janeiro. In the archives of the Antwerp and Leyden merchant Daniël van der Meulen, a letter of Van der Haegen was found: GA Leiden, FA vd Meulen, inv.nr. 365. The Rotterdam historian Jeroen Blaak found another trace of a young trader in slaves named Steven van der Haghen, 1563–1624. This adventurous young man traveled throughout Europe from the age of ten years onwards and lived a few years in Spain and Italy. In 1585 he worked with a shipper from Hoorn and they became involved in trade, first to Italy and later to Carthagena. "Ende in Carthagena vonden een Neerlands coopman genaempt Lenaert Castro, den welcken handelde op Barberien, ende hadde veel slaven ende slavinnen, die hij oock vercocht."

Van der Haghen mentions another trip in 1597 to "Guinea," without mentioning what was traded there. P. A. Tiele, ed., "Steven van der Haghen's avonturen van 1575 tota 1597 door hem zelven verhaald," *Bijdragen en mededeelingen van het Historisch Genootschap* 6 (1883): 377–421; 402–3.

24. J.H. de Stoppelaar, "Balthasar de Moucheron," *Den Haag,* Nijhoff 1901, p. 73, noot 13. In 1601 Van der Haegen worked with De Moucheron as well.

25. The Latin phrase is *Stabilis Fortuna Merenti.* Noortje de Roy van Zuydewijn, "Van koopman tot icoon. Johan van der Veken en de Zuidnederlandse immigranten in Rotterdam rond 1600" (From Merchant to Icon: Johan van der Veken and the Southnetherlands' Immigrants in Rotterdam around 1600) (Amsterdam: Prometheus en Bert Bakker Publishers, 2002), 9. See also R. Bijlsma, "Het bedrijf van de Magellaensche Compagnie," in *Rotterdams Jaarboekje 1917,* Series 2 (1913–1922), Rotterdam City Archives, Rotterdam, p. 26–44.

26. Kerckhoven is also mentioned by the Swedish historian Nystroem, in his "History of Georgaphy and the Geographic Discoveries until the Beginning of the Nineteenth Century." Johan Fredrik Nystroem, "Geografiens och de geografiska uppaeckternas historia (1899)," 250. http://runeberg.org/geohist/0418.html.

27. "Dat men hem soude toelaten een van de vier Portugiesche piloten, die onlancx in Zeelant gearriveert zijn met omtrent hondert derttich Mooren, na Portugael te moegen brengen ende an 't lant te setten, ende dat hy, suppliant, neffens eenige derselver piloten, in zynen dienst wesende, van dairaff thin ofte twelff Portugiessche bootsgesellen tot volvueren van zyne voirgenomen reyse op West Indin soude moegen nemen. Na behoirlycke diliberatie is 't voirsz. Versuick van het transport der Mooren affgeslagen." N. Japikse, Resolutiën der Staten Generaal, deel 9, 1596/97. Nijhoff, *Den Haag* 1926, p. 333/334, no. 406.

28. N. Japikse, ibid., p. 334, noot 1, R.i.d.p.p. In the following years, Van der Haegen was in regular contact with the national Staten Generaal about other requests. We can see that he acquired a certain name for himself, from the minutes, the Resoluties, at several occasions. Nationaal Archief, Resoluties Staten Generaal 1596, archief 1.01.03, inv. Nr. 22, Nov. 29, 1596.

29. No further traces of this ship were found in the archives of the admiralty; the ship was not sold. I thank Ivo van Loo, Zeeuws Archief, for checking this in his files on these archives regarding the private trade in Zeeland in the sixteenth and seventeenth century. E-mail to author, Feb. 24, 2004.

30. "The *Akte van Verlatinge,* the 1581 Dutch declaration of independence from Spain, which may have been a model for the American Declaration of Independence, justifies the revolt against the King of Spain by arguing that 'God did not create the People Slaves to their Prince.' Like the Americans, the Dutch conceived of the foundation of their nation as a rejection of slavery. The right of revolution was further justified thus: '[when the Prince, i.e., the King of Spain] oppresses [the People] . . . exacting from them slavish Compliance, then he is no longer a Prince but a Tyrant.'" Johanna Kardux, quoting Stephen E. Lucas, "The Plakkaat Van Verlatinge: A Neglected Model for the American Declaration of Independence," in Rosemarijn Hoefte and Johanna C. Kardux, eds., *Connecting Cultures: The Netherlands in Five Centuries of Translatlantic Exchange* (Amsterdam: VU University Press, 1992), 192.

31. J. C. Kardux and James O. Horton, "Slavery and Public Memory in the United

States and the Netherlands," *New York Journal of American History* 66, no. 2 (2005): 35–52. See also J. C. Kardux, "Monuments of the Black Atlantic: Slavery Memorials in the United States and the Netherlands," in Heike Raphael-Hernandez, ed., *Blackening Europe: The African American Presence* (New York: Routledge, 2003), 87–105.

32. Daniel Hulsebosch, "Nothing but Liberty: Somerset's Case and the British Empire," *Law and History Review* 24, no. 3 (2006): 647–58.

33. Ibid. Hulsebosch concludes that Somerset's lawyers' primary goal was "to keep slavery an ocean away." "The empire's legal pluralism allowed Mansfield to rationalize the brutality of slavery while locating it offshore, thus facilitating the coexistence of slavery and freedom" (15–16 in online version). See also Daniel J. Hulsebosch, *Constituting Empire: New York and the Transformation of Constitutionalism in the Atlantic World, 1664—1830* (Chapel Hill: University of North Carolina Press, 2005).

34. The author is preparing a book with more of these individual histories. See also Raphael-Hernandez, ed., *Blackening Europe.*

35. Allison Blakely, *Blacks in the Dutch World: The Evolution of Racial Imagery in a Modern Society* (Bloomington: Indiana University Press, 1993), 230.

36. Lydia Hagoort, *Het Beth Haim in Ouderkerk aan de Amstel: De begraafplaats van de Portugese Joden in Amsterdam, 1614–1945* (Hilversum: Verloren, 2005), 39.

37. For their help with this research, I am indebted to Lydia Hagoort and Eric Schmitz of the Gemeentearchief Amsterdam, who helped me read the records. City Archives Amsterdam: Gemeentearchief Amsterdam, Archieven Notariaat, Archiefnr. 5075, inventaris nr. 941, notaris Daniel Bredan, Minuutacten 1632. Additional information may be found in Archiefnr. 5372, Amsterdamse Notarissen 16e-18e eeuw, ongeinventariseerde archieven.

38. Nr. 3403, Feb. 19, 1626.

39. Studia Rosenthaliana, vol. 32–33, 1998–99. Notariaats Archieven, Gemeentelijk Archief Amsterdam, 392A, fol. 84–84V, Notarissen Jacob and Nicolaes Jacobs.

40. Ongoing research by the author. Conference paper presented at Black European Studies Conference, Berlin, Freie Universität, July 29–31, 2006.

41. For more details, see Dienke Hondius, "Black Africans in Early Seventeenth Century Amsterdam," in Kate Lowe, ed., *Renaissance and Reformation (Renaissance et Réforme)* 31 no. 2 (Spring 2008): 89–105; http://www.crrs.ca/renref.

42. Elmer Kolfin, art historian at University of Amsterdam, conference paper, Black European Studies Conference, Berlin, Freie Universität, July 29–31, 2006.

3

Now You See It, Now You Don't: Josephine Baker's Films of the 1930s and the Problem of Color

EILEEN JULIEN

After Josephine Baker's meteoric rise as a dancer in Parisian music halls in the 1920s, her manager, Pepito Abatino, sought another stage for Baker: the popular and far-reaching medium of cinema that would help propel this African American woman of humble origins to unimaginable fame around the world. There is a consensus among Baker's biographers that the major feature films she made in the 1930s, *Zou Zou* (1934) and *Princesse Tam Tam* (1935), were vehicles to display her personality and extraordinary talent as a dancer and singer.[1] Musical interludes in which Baker dances and sings and grandiose stage show spectacles are thus at the heart of both films, but as collaborative productions[2] in which plots and character development were clearly negotiated, the films also embody French attitudes and dilemmas of the 1930s. Elizabeth Ezra has written that in 1934, the year *Zou Zou* was released, "traditional structures of community were being threatened by both the right and left" and that "film was rapidly creating new representations of community as well as new communities of spectators" (102). Here I will focus on Baker's films as vehicles for *French* exploration of racial identity and national belonging.

The historical context of these films and their inquiries into racial dynamics was French colonialism, based on the notion of racial hierarchy and imbued with a sense of a grand civilizing mission. In the 1930s, colonialism and its racial mind-set were in their heyday. In broad terms, French colonial policy was premised on the idea that colonial citizens and subjects could "overcome" their origins and concomitant racial identity and—through education and the acquisition of French language—be *assimilated*.[3] Despite this assimilationist rhetoric, however, Baker's films project an anxiety about the possibility of embracing people of color in the French nation. Did the French people buy the elite, imperializing rhetoric? Could people of color be assimilated? And by association, could lower-class French men and women themselves be assimilated?

Josephine Baker arrived in France in September 1925. She was part of a continuous wave of African Americans washing up on French shores. As early as the nineteenth century, the French had welcomed free New Orleanians of color such as the playwright Victor Séjour or the famed black American painter Henry Ossawa Tanner. They were followed in the twentieth century by black soldiers who fought in World War I and innumerable jazzmen including, most famously, Sidney Bechet. The legend of French openness that spread with veterans returning to the United States brought to French shores an ever-increasing trickle of American blacks fleeing myriad guises of racism and lack of opportunity in the United States. By mid-century, this movement would encompass many talented and charismatic figures, including writers Langston Hughes, Claude McKay, Jessie Fauset, Richard Wright, Chester Himes, James Baldwin, musicians Duke Ellington and Dizzy Gillepsie, and visual artists Augusta Savage, Aaron Douglas, William Johnson, Hale Woodruff, Lois Mailou Jones, and Richmond Barthé.[4] France's embrace of these dark Americans was altogether different from its relationship to its colonial citizens and subjects.[5]

When Josephine Baker and the dance troupe organized by Caroline Dudley began rehearsals in September 1925 for the opening of the *Revue Nègre,* which would take place just a few days later, France was in fact in the throes of *negrophilia,* an esthetic manifested prominently in the visual arts, music, and performance. Negrophilia was a complex, ambiguous phenomenon, conflating European notions of Africa and African American life and performance. Gérard Le Coat argues, for example, that the directors were disappointed when they saw the group of African American performers rehearse: their show, "done with great precision and nuance, had nothing 'truly *nègre*' about it. . . . On one side were professionals seeking respectability that the American context refused them. . . . [Blacks who wanted to] show Whites that they [were] just as refined. On the other side, Parisian *Gentlemen* who [wanted] *the savage,* who [imagined] natives who have just stepped out of virgin forests. Baker and the troupe were directed by the French directors and their consultant Jacques-Charles to enact the "primitive" in the performance they would do (27).

There was not, of course, an unambiguous embrace of this primitivism that Baker would come to symbolize. Baker's astonishing dancing her unimaginably agile body and "primitive" energy—in the *Revue Nègre* (1925), the *Folies Bergères* (1926), and the *Bal Nègre* (1927), was greeted in the French press with both hysterical acclaim and indignation. During tours in Germany and Austria, she set off a wave of scandal. For many, Baker's physique and extraordinary dancing represented a cultural antidote to a civilization that had produced an effete aristocracy, flaccid bourgeoisie, and the catastrophic "Great War." For others, Baker symbolized the menace of degeneration.

While *Zou Zou* and *Princesse Tam Tam* focus especially on dance and stage show spectacle, their narrative form is significant. Both films locate themselves within two traditions: first, the gendered "rags to riches" transformation, enacted also in the journey from "periphery" to metropolis; and second, the romance or love story, a narrative genre that can be read meaningfully with respect to social and national issues (Julien). In both *Zou Zou* and *Princesse Tam Tam,* the form of romance is unrequited love, as it was in Baker's silent film of 1927, *La Sirène des Tropiques:* The island girl Papitou falls in love with a Frenchman who is on a mission in the tropics and who chooses to remain faithful to his French girlfriend back home. The triple iteration of the story of unrequited love can hardly be accidental.

Just as the use of symbolism, allegory, or temporal and spatial distancing allows for a less threatening investigation of thorny issues, it seems clear that Josephine Baker provided a comfortable purchase for French spectators on the question of race and belonging in the 1930s. Elizabeth Ezra has written that Baker was "popular . . . precisely because she was so hard to place; a floating signifier of cultural difference [representing] many different things to different people" (99). Not only was Baker *not* a French colonial subject or citizen but, as a victim of American racism, she bolstered French claims to have created the premier republic of "liberté, égalité, fraternité."[6]

By casting Baker as a Martinican woman in the one instance and a Tunisian shepherdess in the other, these films also treat the acute question of racial identity and national belonging more plausibly, perhaps less scandalously by focusing on persons of color from societies considered closer to the civilized West than was "black" Africa, the most egregious site of the primitive. Martinique, still a colony in the 1930s, would become officially a full-fledged French *département* in 1946. By virtue of interracial mixing, Antilleans were considered higher up on the civilizational scale than were the Senegalese, for example, who had been conscripted by the French for World War I and World War II (Fanon, 20). Tunisia, a French protectorate since 1881, boasted not only of Roman history with ruins to prove it but was, from an Orientalist point of view, part of the Arab world that had once been a great civilization even if it was now decadent and lapsed. Moreover, while the women Baker plays are beautiful and sexy, the films, made for mass audiences, work to undermine their seductiveness: They are cute, comic, childlike, and therefore more easily dismissed. They are surely less threatening to the social order than a dark male protagonist would be.

Together, *Zou Zou* and *Princesse Tam Tam* suggest two opposing approaches to the question of difference, specifically the place of racial difference in the French nation. The first pledges allegiance to Enlightenment ideals in which race as a marker of difference does not matter. Zou Zou's racial identity is skin deep, having virtually no acknowledged relationship to identity, culture, and power. In an ambiguous twist—that one would like to think refreshingly progressive—race seems to have no bearing on Zou Zou's remarkable gifts as a dancer. If we do not admit of difference, the film suggests on its surface, there is none. *Princesse Tam Tam,* on the other hand, admits of difference with a wallop, imagining it as profoundly incompatible. Thus while class and gender identities are a critical dimension of plot and representation in *Zou Zou,* racial identity is invisible or deemed meaningless: Presumably the spectator, like Zou Zou's entourage, does not notice it or simply ignores it. But if racial identity is never acknowledged by the film, it is a silent specter, the only conceivable explanation for Zou Zou's woes, and thus always visible to the contemporary spectator. In *Princesse Tam Tam,* race (intersecting with class and gender) is tied to culture and is continuously performed. Despite these radically different articulations, both films lead to precisely the same conclusions: racial or cultural incompatibility and the impossibility of bridging racial and cultural differences.

Although some biographers of Baker seem to have missed this nuance, *Tam Tam* presents a story within a story.[7] Max de Mirecourt ("short-sighted"?), an aristocrat and second-rate author, blames his current writer's block on his wife's rich lifestyle and pretentious, boring, upper-class friends. He goes off to Africa, a pure, natural haven, for inspiration. He discovers a shepherdess, Alwina (Baker), whose spontaneity, playfulness, and childlikeness are refreshing in contrast to the snobbish, "civilized" French tourists whom he encounters. But Max is still incapable of meeting his publisher's deadline until he learns that Lucie, his wife back in Paris, is seeing the famous and wealthy maharajah of Datane.[8] Max sits down one evening and by morning has cranked out a bestseller, a Pygmalion story.

The novel takes place diegetically, as in a dream, before the film's spectator: In order to spite his wife and make her jealous, Max, promising Alwina clothes and, above all, food, lures the naïve young woman, who is also supposedly in love with him, to Paris. She has been made over, with piano and math lessons and stylish clothes. Once in the "City of Light," the "Princess of Palindor" is all the rage, and Max parades her before "tout Paris." Alwina grows tired of the charade and one evening goes out on her own. In a reverse Cinderella motif, she throws off her fake identity and gets down, black American style, in a nightclub, where she is seen by one of Lucie's friends. Lucie, confident with the knowledge of the princess's fake identity, persuades the maharajah (as Baker apparently had done) to throw an elaborate party in her honor. Roused by the music and drums and plied with alcohol by Lucie's friend, the princess jumps to the floor, sheds her sophisticated clothing, and does a "savage" dance. It would seem that Lucie is set to triumph and Max to be defeated when the men at the party rush to carry Alwina out on their shoulders in elation, signaling that she is a sensation. Lucie and Max make up. The maharajah consoles Alwina and encourages her to return to her native land.

The camera signals the end of the diegetic plot by focusing at that moment on the maharajah's exotic Oriental urn with smoke billowing above it. It is morning in Tunisia. Max is passionately describing the novel's ending to his assistant Coton, when Alwina, eating messily, enters and begs Max to take her with him to Paris. Max replies that she is better off where she is. A French newspaper headline, signaling the return to Paris, announces the success of Max's new novel, which he is signing at a bookstore. Back in Tunisia, the spectator rediscovers Alwina, now a happy spouse and mother. Ducks and chickens have overrun Max's former abode and the camera closes with a shot of a donkey chewing up the cover of his novel, *Civilization.*

There are moments of comic critique in the film, such as this closing sequence, and other blows to the concept of civilization. In a tradition going back to Montesquieu's *Lettres persanes* (Persian Letters, 1721) and Montaigne's essay "Des Cannibales" (On Cannibals," 1580), *Tam Tam* makes use of the "primitive" precisely to offer a critique of the "civilized." The film effects this critique cinematically through its continual juxtaposition, often through a dissolve with graphic matches. Alwina's native Tunisia and Parisian society are co-temporal but spatially and visually contrasted: exteriors, expansive space, sunlight, and sea, on the one hand, versus interiors, enclosure, telephone and radio, glass flowers, birds, fish, and palm trees, on the other. Not surprisingly, Paris/civilization is shown to be artificial, shallow, self-absorbed, and uninformed. News about the princess spreads like wildfire among gossiping Parisian women on the telephone, just as Lucie's flirtation with the maharajah is depicted cinematically as the subject of all eyes. These humorous scenes suggest the boredom and nosiness of high society. Lucie, conflating sites of the "primitive," asks the maharajah if he knows the princess, since Palindor "must be close to where you live." (Ironically, she is right, of course, because Palindor and the East are here only Orientalist inventions, whatever Parisians imagine them to be.) Coton argues that once Alwina knows how to lie she will have become "civilized," and Alwina herself concludes early on that bare feet are better than shoes and that hunger and mealtime are not necessarily the same thing. There is also a satiric visual comment on sexual conquest when the maharajah is speaking to Lucie on the phone: The final butterfly he needs for his collection, as if by magic, lands in place. But these barbs thrown at civilization's excesses and failings, including gender games, leave "civilization" and "the savage" in place. While there is theatricality, satire, and self-reflexivity because of the film's juxtapositions, it is impossible to tell to what extent the public or even the filmmakers understood the film's fundamental vocabulary as modernist cliché. The oxymoronic title of the film, for example, does not undermine the authority of its terms so much as suggest that the princess is of ridiculous, if not barbarous, royalty and lineage.

When in the final scene the donkey chews up the cover of Max's novel, several interpretations are possible. Max's woes as a writer, the hot air of his novels, *The Troubled Soul, Hearts and Flames, Civilization,* and so on can be read as a commentary on the crisis of upper-class literature and culture between the wars. Indeed the novelistic plot itself and its motivation in petty jealousies suggest the very vacuity and decadence that Max is trying to escape by embracing a supposed African innocence. This is clearly a culture worthy of the assaults of Surrealists and Marxists. But the final scene also would seem to assert the vanity of civilization in general. It restates the film's basic dichotomies: first, nature/Africa is beyond the reach of civilizing; second, one only need turn one's eyes, and the native/nature will reassert its primacy over civilization.

The film challenges therefore the premise of the colonial policy of *assimilation,* that colonial citizens and subjects would become Frenchmen through education and training. Here, the veneer of civilization that Max foists on Alwina is thin, indeed. When she breaks out in dance, the "restless native" underneath rises once again to the surface. The film thus affirms what was, according to Brett Berliner, an entrenched popular belief regardless of assimilationist discourse. Berliner supports this argument with a sobering account of Paul Morand's collection of stories in *Magie noire* (1928) and in particular the short story "Congo," which narrates the "immense vitality" of a Josephine Baker-like performer and the menacing, transformative power of drums, not only over Africans but over Europeans as well (Berliner, 226–29).

The camera in the final scenes of *Princesse Tam Tam* effects this transformation for Alwina and the spectator. At the maharajah's party, Alwina, who is alone at her table, is taunted by Lucie's friend who is close to her face when the music intensifies. The camera focuses on Alwina's face and captures her barely containable excitement. When the drum—clearly originating in sub-Saharan (as opposed to North) Africa in a further conflation of sites of the "primitive" world—begins to dominate the other instruments in a Cuban-style rumba and Alwina's senses are overwhelmed, she slips off her gold lamé dress and jumps to center stage. The tight close-ups between the drum/drummer and Alwina's ecstatic, delirious face thereby drown the spectator as well in the same powerful call of the music and, ultimately, of the savage.[9]

Because the stories of transformation and unrequited love that are at the heart of the film take place in Max's fantasy, *the novel,* it is nicely contained for the film's public, who can indulge in the primitive and exotic and then step out of this experimental world and back into the presumed order, stability, and safe familiarity of the real one. The maharajah does double duty, not only as Lucie's would-be lover but as a colored advocate for the importance of racial purity and separation. He pushes Alwina to abandon hope of a real relationship with Max or any white man when he tells her in the final scene in Paris, "Build nothing with them."

Of course, given its contrived plot and premises, the film almost makes one long for ethnographic authenticity. Apart from the historic ruins at Dougga and the initial market and street sequences with local adults and children who are the backdrop for Baker's antics and dancing, there is no Tunisian culture in the film. Tunisia (soon to be Palindor) is one of a million interchangeable sites on the primitive end of the civilizational spectrum. Similarly, apart from the Tunisians mentioned above and the drummer and musicians, every dark-skinned character worthy of a close-up—from Max's servant Tahar ("Dar," in one set of subtitles) to the maharajah and the colored patrons in the Parisian bar—are in blackface.[10] Baker herself as a Tunisian shepherdess has none of the body language of a North African. There seems to have been a conspiracy between producers and public that sheer invention would do. For her French public at least, this fantasy is not only unproblematic, it is crucial. In an important article on Baker's dancing and body, Terri Francis notes that "African-American performers like Baker uniquely permitted the combination of (fantastical) references to ancient Africa and to modern black America—bypassing actual, contemporary Africa" (830). Given the colonial context, then, Baker as a performer and star served an essential ideological function. Her dancing, which drew on African in addition to African American traditions, allowed for a guiltless embrace of Africa without Africans, an esthetics without politics.

While *Tam Tam* is a Pygmalion fantasy in which issues of national, class, and racial identities are literally and figuratively at center stage along with Baker's dancing, *Zou Zou* has a thicker plot in the realist mode, with crime, suspense, punishment, friendship and attendant joys and pains, and several subjectivities in the making. While spectators of *Tam Tam* are conscious of the film's satire and contrivance and therefore watch its story unfold with a certain detachment, *Zou Zou* works through the spectator's identification with the heroine. *Zou Zou* takes the issue of racial identity to a different class—workers and a lesser bourgeoisie.

Zou Zou opens with an outdoor, nighttime circus scene.[11] Throngs of working-class adults and their kids mill about before tents and rides. A carnival barker calls them to come see what he describes alternately as a miracle and a *phénomène* (according to the film subtitles, "a freak of nature"): twins, the children of a redskin ("*Peau rouge*") father and Chinese mother, who rejected them, he explains, because the children were of a different color than their parents. The young colored girl Zou Zou and young white boy Jean appear. They are being raised as sister and brother by the barker, their adoptive father, Papa Melé, whose name—could it be coincidence?—suggests "mixing." Ezra reads Papa

Melé's embrace of these two children as an allegory of French assimilation, in which the circus itself represents childhood innocence and intimate community (101). In private, Papa Melé assuages the children's doubts and fears about their origins and suggests that Jean will always take care of Zou Zou. Jean, on the other hand, dreams of taking to the seas and is not sure that Zou Zou will be able to accompany him.

Years later, Jean (now played by Jean Gabin) returns from seafaring to his family. Zou Zou (Baker) is clearly enamored of him, as they walk the waterfront of Toulon. The family moves to Paris, where Papa Melé finds work, Jean becomes a stagehand at a music hall, and Zou Zou joins the Vallée laundry where she works with a half-dozen affable young (white) women. An important client of the laundry is Miss Barbara, the star at the music hall to whom Zou Zou and her girlfriend Claire Vallée deliver linens. Unbeknownst to Zou Zou, Jean falls in love with Claire.

One evening, he is arrested for murder, and Zou Zou agrees at last to perform at the music hall in order to earn money to help him. She identifies the real murderer, and Jean is released. But Zou Zou discovers the love between Jean and Claire, and the film closes on Zou Zou, transformed from naïve and ordinary laundress to famous star, beautiful but lonely, singing plaintively in a birdcage while two lovers embrace on a nearby bridge.

Elizabeth Ezra argues for a relationship between the title of the film and the name given to African soldiers, *les zouaves,* finding evidence for it in Zou Zou's playful dance routine in which she imitates the stance of soldiers firing their guns. The title also provides critical insight of another sort into the film's agenda. Zou Zou is a diminutive, arguably cute, name. It seems that when the film was being shot, Baker had a small dog that she had named Zou Zou (Sauvage, 124). The eponymous character is appropriately childlike, making noises and faces of all sorts, adoring of children, caged birds, and a found puppy. These traits can be read in light of Frantz Fanon's remark: "They say the black man likes palaver, and as for me, when I pronounce 'palaver,' I see a group of jubilant children, launching unexpressive shouts to the world, crude sounds, children at play. . . . The black man likes palaver, and the road is not long to this new proposition: the black man is a child" (21, my translation). Zou Zou's inarticulateness and her infantilization are symptoms of racial identity that the film otherwise mostly chooses to ignore.

In *Zou Zou,* color and Creole identity are alluded to early on but then fade away. When the young Zou Zou of the circus asks why she is dark and Jean is not, Papa Melé replies that the stork dropped her in the chimney, which is to say color is just skin deep. In a strange scene, the camera also shows little Zou Zou looking at herself in a mirror and playing with the makeup of a chorus girl who discovers her and chases her out of the tent. Could the director have intended a racial commentary in this borrowing of powder? For there is an implicit yearning for racial normalcy in Zou Zou's gesture. Years later, Jean's white girlfriend in Manila—in a scene of buying and selling that recalls colonial economies and trade imbalances—remarks while watching a young, bare-breasted, dark-skinned girl dance that "they are all born with rhythm." Back in Toulon, Jean's sailor buddies see him walking with Zou Zou on the waterfront and tease him about his "petite Créole," to which he replies that Zou Zou is his sister and from Martinique. These episodes occur long before the main story, situated in Paris, is set in motion. Thereafter the issues they raise never resurface in any explicit way.

When Zou Zou finds herself among her coworkers at the laundry (*blanchisserie,* literally, the white-washing place), she is distinguishable only by her buoyancy, charm, and talent. No notice is given to her color. *Zou Zou,* I submit, works to make color if not invisible, then insignificant. The film seeks to affirm a humanist ideal of equality. It works superficially to disentangle Zou Zou and her world from the power of race, just as Papa Melé seeks to reassure the children early on that they are both equally loved by him because they are one and the same. Yet many aporia and tensions give the lie to the insignificance of race.

First, Zou Zou works at the laundry, delivers clothes to the music hall, and becomes the center of attraction in these spaces, but for this very reason, she is unique, not fully one of the girls. She performs *for* them but does not sing or dance *with* them (Ezra, 110). The famous sequence of Baker's dancing solo in silhouette is emblematic of this status. Zou Zou is dancing backstage for her own pleasure. Jean, urged on by his buddy, captures this private, intimate moment for public consumption by projecting her shadow against the stage curtain. (We film spectators are already consuming that image even before it is projected into the diegetic theater.) Just as Francis notes, the light and visual language in this performance venue is used to "transport an image of the live figure from the 'real' to the realm of myth" (840). Here Zou Zou becomes an icon of Baker as a spectacular, myth-sized exotic black body.

The decisive exclusion, then, arises from Zou Zou's impossible, unrequited love. Zou Zou has adult feelings but never manages to articulate them. They are captured only by camera shots of her face. Specifically, she is in love with her "brother," Jean Marchand (who, unlike her, has both a name and surname). But Zou Zou never communicates this love to him. She clearly notices, jealously and disapprovingly, the tattoo of a nude woman on Jean's arm. She catches him flirting with another woman and again is disapproving. Jean's sailor buddies on the Toulon waterfront notice Zou Zou's romantic attachment to him, but Jean does not. Like an adolescent, the now adult Zou Zou scribbles Jean's name on the tablecloth with water, an invisible ink, to be sure. She feels betrayed when she sees Miss Barbara and Jean kissing. While she misreads Jean's relationship to Miss Barbara in this scene, she correctly perceives his receptivity to other women. Zou Zou is not only inarticulate. She is oblivious to the budding romance between Jean and Claire and, through her invitations and sisterly love of Claire, pushes them together.

This is all the more striking when one considers the love triangle in which Miss Barbara figures. It surely is not incidental that the blond, sexy, volatile Miss Barbara has a strong Eastern European accent. A more dangerous lifestyle, an explicitly hot sexuality can be attributed to this marginal European. While it might be shocking to a certain morality to cast a dark-skinned Zou Zou as sexually alive, Miss Barbara, the mistress of Mr. Saint Lévy, a partner in the music hall, is in love with her Brazilian lover. She dubs Mr. Saint Lévy her "penguin," while her Brazilian man is her "jaguar." (Animal imagery—visual and verbal—is rife in these films.) Barbara is fed up with the Penguin, his money, and singing in the music hall. She is ready to sacrifice her professional life to run off to Brazil with the Jaguar, who even if he is not black in the strict sense of the term is nonetheless black by association—Brazil representing a land of racial mixing. The film offers up to its spectators not only the sight of Miss Barbara kissing Jean to thank him for helping her work up the nerve to split, but it also shows her in bed with the Jaguar. Zou Zou does not manage so much as an unchaste kiss and there are no compromising situations in which she can be filmed.

Brett Berliner has written that exoticism and ethno-eroticism were conflated with violence in the French imaginary of this period (205–33). There is a scene in the film that enters into these muddy waters. While Claire and Jean dance, Zou Zou sits quietly at her table, mooning over Jean whom she has urged yet again to dance with Claire. Julot, a hard-drinking patron, pulls Zou Zou out of her chair and onto the dance floor. She resists and Jean instantly comes over to protect his sister and her honor and knocks Julot out. Julot will be the victim of the murder for which Jean will be arrested. Zou Zou is quite obviously innocent, but this scene can be seen to confirm the popular perception of the working-class dance hall as risqué because of the cheek-to-cheek, groin-to-groin activity that seemed to have spilled over from clubs such as the *Bal nègre,* which were all the rage (Berliner 205–12). Zou Zou is surely read by Julot as tempting and easy by virtue of her skin.

Jean meanwhile is protected by the incest taboo and his firm commitment to Zou Zou's status as his sister. He never notices what a spectacular body she has. He is completely nonplussed, while his coworker ogles Zou Zou.

In the final scenes when Zou Zou goes to meet Jean whose release from prison she has made possible, she sees Claire and Jean embrace and her world crumbles. Perhaps appropriately, given Zou Zou's inarticulateness, these scenes are reminiscent of silent movies. There are no words.[12] Cinematically, the camera focuses tightly on Zou Zou's face; she is visibly distraught and nearly stumbles, walking in a pained daze. The drum—not the conga (or *djembe*) of *Princesse*

Tam Tam with primitive connotations, but rather a large orchestral drum, the timpani perhaps—grows in volume, pounding out a loud, increasingly fast rhythm, overwhelming the horns and strings (which themselves shift from the film's sweet, sentimental motif to a minor key), communicating extreme inner turmoil (much like an ad for a migraine remedy of a few decades back). The spectator is drawn into Zou Zou's pain and alienation that seem to have no metaphysical justification: To what might they be due, if not her difference? Like a drunkard, she wends her way back to the music hall, where a Paul Colin poster attests to Baker's/Zou Zou's fame. A workman slaps a banner across the poster, indicating Zou Zou has now given one hundred performances. In the final frames, this tragic mulatto is once again perched in the birdcage of her first performance. She may be from Martinique but sings nostalgically, perhaps symbolically, of France's lost colony, Haiti, "the home for which she longs."[13]

Josephine Baker accepted the role of the dark lover of uninterested white men—a fiction at terrible odds with historical reality—but she apparently was not always in agreement with these plot lines and character development. Phyllis Rose writes, for example, that Josephine Baker was not pleased with the ending of *Zou Zou:* "Why can't she have the man? It had been the same in *La Sirène des Tropiques:* she had to give up Pierre Batcheff. Josephine herself really wanted to get Gabin and asked Pepito why she could not. Would the public object because of her color? Pepito insisted that wasn't it. 'Zou-Zou is a star. She lives for her work. Like you,' he said. Pepito liked the story of the female star who has to give up the emotional side of her life as the price of stardom. Josephine did not" (162).

To the extent that Rose's description of this episode is accurate, it is clear that the narrative line in Baker's films was negotiated by the production team with their differing and sometimes conflictual worldviews, values, and experiences. Pepito might dismiss Zou Zou's racial identity as a factor in her failure to get her man, but the possibilities and limits of her roles were clearly on Baker's mind. Pepito's insistence on the unhappy conjugal ending as the cost of women's stardom also reveals a certain jealousy and attempt to control Baker. Paris, then, was not an uncomplicated space of freedom for Baker as an African American woman.

In an endless circle of life chasing art and art chasing life, Baker effectively became a French princess, symbol of France. And like Papa Melé, she created a "rainbow tribe" of adopted children in a daring bid to affirm, it would seem, that the performance of identity and community is more important than origins and is indeed the measure of who we are. Yet there is ambivalence in Baker's remarkable success, rooted as it was in African American and French mythologies. Object of adulation, recipient of the highest French honors, Baker's freedom was nonetheless not absolutely free but circumscribed by the persona she projected.

And what, finally, of the place of African Americans, via Baker, in crystallizing and theorizing the concept of African diaspora, especially given Didier

Gondola's argument that the African American myth of a nonracist France helped sustain French colonialism in Africa? The extraordinary trajectory of Josephine Baker in France seems to be a testament to the flexibility of the concept of blackness and of race more generally—of its shifting meanings, tied to historical moments, and social, national contexts. In this sense, it is also a reminder that while Africans and people of African descent share common roots, they nonetheless are products of different histories, languages, differential wealth and power, and so on. We are emphatically bound by racial identities or our presumed identities, but there is a cost to be paid in assuming that one stands for all.

Whether *Princesse Tam Tam* ever had appeal for North Africans or other colonized people is uncertain.[14] But today it is, of course, dated even for the French who now have concrete knowledge of former colonials and their children, some of whom live and work in a context of inequality and repression in France. The kind of blank slate that is Tunisia, the shepherdess made of whole (African American) cloth, her sensational Parisian transformation, and the confident (if superficially disavowed) modernity of *Tam Tam* are in jarring contrast to the realities that are now only too well known. *Tam Tam,* for all its humor, is passé, except perhaps in a Baker film festival.

Zou Zou, on the other hand, is apparently a film that still has appeal. In some sense, it continues to gratify and enforce social expectations, which suggests that the public, too, accepts the idea of higher costs to be paid by professional women. But there is a measure of self-delusion in Pepito's claim that color was not an issue. Baker became who she was precisely because she was a black American. And, as we have seen, what the film gives with one hand—a story in which color does not matter—it takes back with the other, Zou Zou's inexplicable exclusion. In that sense, the film strives to affirm French ideals but works nonetheless to shore up a sense of French belonging and community on the basis of tacit homogeneity. The working class, too, belongs to the nation—at the cost of maintaining the others, represented by Baker, at a distance.

Zou Zou and *Princesse Tam Tam* take opposing approaches to the question of racial difference in France—the first ignoring and suppressing difference, the second simultaneously fearing and embracing it as exoticism. But both films ultimately reify race and difference and affirm the importance of maintaining separate worlds. These varied approaches, with their nonetheless one and the same outcome, seem still very much alive today in the crisis of representation France is experiencing as the face of the French nation is gradually being transformed.

Notes

1. This would seem to be the case from conception to production: Pepito Abatino had devised the scenario and acted as "artistic" director for *Tam Tam*. The idea for *Zou Zou* came from Pepito's brother, G. Abatino, whose short story, according to the film credits,

became the basis of the screenplay. It seems that Pepito and Baker both invested their own funds in these films, and both films were produced by Arys Nissotti, a Tunisian casino owner whom the couple had met in 1928 (Rose 161; Wood 181). This surely helps explain why *Tam Tam* was set and filmed in Tunisia.

2. The screenplay for *Tam Tam* was written by Yves Mirande; Edmond Greville was its director. Carlo Rim wrote the script for *Zou Zou,* which was directed by Marc Allegret, apparently a nephew by adoption of the prominent writer André Gide.

3. Only Senegalese born in the four communes, St. Louis, Gorée, Rufisque, and Dakar, were recognized as citizens of France with full rights. Those born elsewhere in Senegal and in other French colonies were subjects, for whom a different legal status applied. Sheldon Gellar notes that colonial officials "embraced assimilationist colonial doctrines that declared the objective of French colonial policy to transfer French institutions and culture to the colonies to replace the allegedly more backward cultures they had encountered. However, assimilation was expensive and implied large investments in French education for African children and a dense French presence to directly oversee the colonized population. In the end, assimilation was simply not practical" (36).

4. See Michel Fabre's *From Harlem to Paris: Black American Writers in France, 1840–1980.* Stovall's *Paris Noir* presents a detailed account of the larger black American presence in twentieth-century Paris.

5. See, for example, James Baldwin's short story, "This Morning, This Evening, So Soon."

6. Didier Gondola denounces the myth, so popular among African Americans, of France as a land free of racial discrimination. He argues moreover that through their embrace of France as the land of racial freedom, "black American *émigrés* served as liminal figures," enabling French hegemony over colonized Africans (202).

7. Elizabeth Ezra reads, erroneously in my view, Mirecourt's book as "both the pretext and the narrative frame for the film's plot" (124). See also 114.

8. This is perhaps a less baroque twist of plot than it would seem, if Ean Wood is correct in his claim that Baker had a brief liaison with the maharajah of Kapurthala. As Terri Francis signals, it is difficult to separate "Baker's persona from her personhood, especially since she and her representatives often used elements of her private life in creating her public image" (828).

9. In subsequent decades, these motifs would be reworked to very different effects in the poetry of negritude, Senghor's "Femme noire" (Black Woman), published in 1948, for example, and in a diasporic novel, Paule Marshall's *Praisesong for the Widow* (1984).

10. It is difficult to interpret the meaning of blackface in this context as an esthetic shorn of U.S. connotations. Stovall writes, "Whereas in America blackface enabled theaters to present the black aesthetic without blacks, thus freezing them out of the white entertainment world, in Paris a white musician's use of blackface reflected the dominant position of blacks as jazz performers" (39). For an example beyond Europe, see Cole on the Ghanaian concert party (17–52).

11. Ezra signals the centrality of forms of popular dance and entertainment in *Zou Zou:* the circus, associated with community and innocence; the *bal populaire* in which participatory, ritualized dance also affirms community; and finally the music hall, where staged performance replaces intimacy (102–04).

12. This may also be related to Phyllis Rose's claim that because "of a lack of capital, filmmakers in France could not afford—as those in Germany and America could—to experiment with new techniques, so they were stuck with the old ones and improvised films . . . with joyous mediocrity" (160).

13. Ezra interprets this substitution of Haiti for Martinique as an expression of France's nostalgia for the diminishing returns and glory of empire (112–13).

14. Consider by contrast Sembène Ousmane's film narrative of the servant's journey from the colony to the metropole, *La noire de . . .* (Black Girl . . .).

References

Baldwin, James. "This Morning, This Evening, So Soon." *Going to Meet the Man.* New York: Dial Press, 1965, 123–69.

Berliner, Brett. *Ambivalent Desire.* Amherst: University of Massachusetts Press, 2002.

Cole, Catherine. *Ghana's Concert Party Theatre.* Bloomington: Indiana University Press, 2001.

Ezra, Elizabeth. *The Colonial Unconscious.* Ithaca: Cornell University Press, 2000.

Fabre, Michel. *From Harlem to Paris: Black American Writers in France, 1840–1980.* Urbana: University of Illinois Press, 1991.

Fanon, Frantz. *Peau noire, masques blancs.* Paris: Seuil, 1952.

Francis, Terri. "Embodied Fictions, Melancholy Migrations: Josephine Baker's Cinematic Celebrity." *Modern Fiction Studies* 51 (2005): 825–45.

Gellar, Sheldon. *Democracy in Senegal: Tocquevillian Analytics in Africa.* New York: Palgrave Macmillan, 2005.

Gondola, Ch. Didier. "'But I Ain't African, I'm American!': Black American Exiles and the Construction of Racial Identities in Twentieth-Century France." *Blackening Europe: The African American Presence.* Ed. Heike Raphael-Hernandez. New York: Routledge, 2004, 201–15.

Julien, Eileen. "The Romance of Africa: Three Narratives by African-American Women." *Beyond Dichotomies: Histories, Identities, Cultures, and the Challenge of Globalization.* Ed. Elisabeth Mudimbe-Boyi. Albany: State University of New York Press, 2002. 129–51.

Le Coat, Gérard. "Art nègre, jazz nègre, revue nègre: Esthétique primitiviste et syndrome raciste en France (1905–1935)." In *Carrefour de cultures: Mélanges offerts à Jacqueline Leiner.* Ed. Régis Antoine. Tübingen: Gunter Narr Verlag, 1993. 23–34.

Marshall, Paule. *Praisesong for the Widow.* New York: E. P. Dutton, 1984.

Morand, Paul. *Magie noire.* Paris: Bernard Grasset, 1928.

La noire de . . . Dir. Sembène Ousmane. With Thérèse M'bissine Diop, Anne-Marie Jelinek, Robert Fontaine. 1966.

Princesse Tam Tam. Dir. Edmond Greville. With Josephine Baker, Albert Préjean, Germaine Aussey. Arys Production, 1935.

Rose, Phyllis. *Jazz Cleopatra: Josephine Baker in Her Time.* 1989. New York: Random House, 1991.

Sauvage, Marcel. *Les Mémoires de Josephine Baker.* Paris: Editions Buchet/Chastel, n.d.

Senghor, Léopold Sédar, ed. "Femme noire." In *Anthologie de la nouvelle poésie nègre et malgache.* Paris: Presses Universitaires de France, 1948, 151.
La Sirène des Tropiques. Dir. Maria Nalpas and Henri Etiévant. With Josephine Baker, Pierre Batcheff, Regina Dalthy. 1927.
Stovall, Tyler. *Paris Noir: African Americans in the City of Light.* Boston: Houghton Mifflin, 1996.
Wood, Ean. *The Josephine Baker Story.* London: Sanctuary, 2000.
Zou Zou. Dir. Marc Allegret. With Josephine Baker, Jean Gabin, Yvette Lebon. Arys Production, 1934.

4

Pictures of "US"? Blackness, Diaspora, and the Afro-German Subject

TINA M. CAMPT

Diasporic Vision: Visualizing Black Europe and the Indexicality of Race

What is the *timeliness* of "Black Europe" in the current moment of African diaspora studies? Put another way, why think about "Black Europe" and why think about it just now? What kind of traction does the invocation of this term have (or perhaps lack) for the different European diasporic communities that might be seen to shelter under the expansive umbrella it seeks to extend? Finally, whose interests are served by such a composite term and to what extent does it paper over local, national, and hemispheric distinctions and definitions—distinctions and definitions of what constitutes "blackness" and what mediates our respective relationships to diaspora?

Such questions are pertinent, provocative, and sincere questions faced by scholars working on the African diaspora in Europe. We are scholars positioned by our knowledge of and abiding investment in the political, intellectual, and cultural formations induced by the violent displacements of the transatlantic slave trade. Yet like other scholars of the diaspora, our work on Europe's Black constituencies reminds us of the extent to which such formations will always necessarily exceed simple reduction to this or any other single point of historical origin. Our scholarship mirrors the diaspora itself through its location in equally dispersed but complexly linked geographic sites—sites that shape and situate our views of both the African diaspora and Europe. Yet we are also individuals positioned *as scholars* working within and outside of institutions that are "placed" in divergent (inter)disciplinary histories of field formation and with differential access to the resources of academic institutions. Hence, the questions posed above can be answered neither singularly nor definitively, but only indirectly, through particularly interested vantage points, forms of engagement, and practices of *viewing*. In other words, these are questions that I, in turn, will and can only attempt to address *obliquely* through the objects of my own very interested scholarship and scholarly location and literally, with an eye toward visualizing and transcribing certain critical elements of a "point of view."

As an African American feminist concerned with the transnational implications of the often inequitable relations among different communities within the African diaspora—relations characterized by the same uneven circulations of labor, culture, ideas, and capital through which the diaspora was and continues to be forged—I find it important to understand the emerging interest in Black Europe as part of a larger project of decentering the United States in the field of African diaspora studies in the twenty-first century. Parochializing U.S. models of race in relation to the equally complex forms of racial as well as gendered subject formation experienced by Black populations beyond the Americas and in Europe in particular is in no way a new project; it is the continuation of an older and ongoing tradition of the study of the African diaspora as an explicitly transnational formation that refuses to privilege any particular location over another.

This collection of essays and the public forum that was their initial arena of presentation provide a unique opportunity to consider the unsettled and potentially contentious questions posed above as issues that are critical to the present and future direction of African diaspora studies more broadly. The "unsettled" status of Black Europe and the African diaspora provides an occasion to see diaspora through a different lens, to take note of differences and similarities, and to appreciate the specificities of the particular national lenses and frames through which diaspora itself becomes visible. One of the major challenges posed by such a transnational approach to the African diaspora is how to think beyond our own established horizons of "blackness" toward less comfortable and requisitely complex conceptions of race. But to think our way toward new and more capacious horizons of race, Black politics, and culture, we must first apprehend who "we" are. Seeing ourselves or "picturing us" (to borrow Deborah Willis's elegant phrasing) is a necessarily defamiliarizing and decentering practice that reflects the fundamental and constituitive dynamic of diaspora itself. The pages that follow aim at just such a relational and defamiliarizing diasporic practice of viewing—one that expands both *who* and *how* we see diaspora, as well as who we picture *within* or *outside* a diasporic frame.

This essay takes up the challenge of visualizing Black Europe's relation to the African diaspora through what is arguably one of the crucial faculties we use to calibrate our definitions of race and blackness: vision or sight. When and where do we "see" the emergence of a Black German subject? Where do we encounter a visual instantiation of a Black subject who is internal to German society and partakes of a diasporic relation to this society that is neither transplanted, transitional, or transitory, but firmly grounded from within? I would argue that in early twentieth-century Germany, one important site where that subject materializes visually is in and through the medium of photography, specifically, Black German family photography. Often considered one of the most mundane forms of photography, I contend that it is precisely through their ordinariness and familiarity that family snapshots and portraits function as a complex site that refracts and reflects the politics of Black European diasporic formation.

African American artist and theorist of visual culture Coco Fusco has argued that photography is a particularly compelling cultural medium that individuals create and use to see themselves. As she writes, "Photography offers the promise of apprehending who we are, not only as private individuals but as members of social and cultural groups" (Fusco, 13). But what does it mean to make such a claim for a population like Black Germans—a community frequently lacking access to important visual cultural resources? What role can photography play in apprehending who Black Germans are, both as individuals and as part of the diaspora more broadly? This essay explores these questions through the lens of what theorists of visual culture have called "the indexicality of race," using racial indexicality to theorize some of the scripts of race, diaspora, and belonging these images compose and contest. As I will argue, these photographs offer one of the earliest articulations of Afro-German belonging and as objects that stage creative modes of belonging for Blacks as *Germans*—modes of belonging that urge us to consider *nation* as an essential framework through which diasporic membership is negotiated and the transnational politics of difference and solidarity are often necessarily forged.

Indexicality is most frequently associated with the work of Charles Sanders Pierce, who defined the index as a sign that refers us to a truly existing thing. His example was the bullet hole as an indexical sign for the shot, "for without the shot there would have been no hole; but there is a hole there, whether anybody has the sense to attribute it to a shot or not." Building on the theories of Pierce, Nicholas Mirzoeff writes that on the one hand, the photograph is held to be a directly indexical medium to the extent that it is marked by that which stands before the lens at the moment of exposure. Citing John Tagg's contention that on the other hand, photography is a medium with no inherent identity, rather a technology constituted through the relations of power with which it is invested, Mirzoeff insists that the photograph functions as a kind of screen upon which wider social forces become visible (Mirzoeff, 111). In other words, the photograph functions dialectically, as an index of that which it attempts to "capture" visually while simultaneously producing and becoming entangled and invested in the very meanings it produces. Photographic indexicality thus names a process of signification that involves forms of referencing that render race a meaningful category for understanding the images and individuals captured within the photographic frame. It is in this way that photography comes to serve as an important site for making race and racial difference visible, while at the same time propagating it as a meaningful category of humanity.

How is race indexed in Afro-German family photos? What scripts do they reference that make their representations of race register so profoundly against the grain? How are those scripts gendered at the same time that they are raced? And to what extent do these indexical frames translate transnationally within the diaspora? Black German family photography in the early twentieth century offers a dramatically different counterpoint to the dominant photography of Blacks circulating in Germany at the time. For the dominant photographic tradition of picturing Blacks *in Germany* has almost exclusively taken non-German Blacks as its object. Two primary visual referents dominate the photographic imaging of blackness in early twentieth-century Germany and persistently overshadow attempts to read submerged images of its own Black German subjects. The first is the stereotype of marauding Black masculinity—an image produced as a hyperbolic response to the historical presence of African colonial troops used by the French in the occupation of the Rhineland following World War I. The photographic images of Black occupation soldiers were propagated through their reproduction in numerous newspapers and in political cartoons and caricatures of both these soldiers and their Black German children throughout the 1920s.

In addition to this domestically produced photographic imagery, a second, more itinerate set of photographic images exercises an equally significant influence on the emergence of a Black German visual subject. It consists of the widely circulated photographic representations of early twentieth-century Black America: images that portrayed African American middle-class urbanity (for example, James Vanderzee's iconic photography of the Harlem Renaissance), rural depictions of the Black South and the poverty and oppression of Jim Crow segregation, and African American celebrities represented most significantly by the extensive iconography of Josephine Baker that proliferated throughout Europe. Together these two sets of iconic photography created a powerful dominant visual archive that structured the image of Blacks in Germany in significant ways. Each registers blackness in the German context as a foreignness that is both *gendered* (as hypermasculine or ultrafeminized) and *classed* (most often as a mobile, urban and cosmopolitan middle class, or an impoverished or "primitive" underclass), in ways that were ultimately deployed as a composite threat to German culture.

In the family photography of Black Germans in the early twentieth century, "blackness" becomes visible as racial difference in ways that were thoroughly gendered, yet the gendered embodiments figured in these images were also inextricable enactments of national belonging. As we will see, the domestic framing of this visual archive is particularly important, for these images of German domesticity also figure an explicitly gendered familial structure where racial difference is deeply embedded in both the family and the German nation. The families presented in these photographs are domestic constellations formed through diasporic dispersals and disavowed by the nation—yet they are family scenes that witness these individuals laying vigorous and visual claims to insistent modes of national belonging nevertheless. The domestic frame of these family archives thus gives us access to both a profoundly *German* diasporic subject who is racialized in ambivalent and contradictory ways, and a subject whose status in relation to the nation is affectively achieved through highly gendered forms of national belonging.

Family Matters: Race, Gender, and Belonging in Black German Photography

At first glance, the photo in figure 4.1 seems a relatively straightforward image: a baby photo, typical of so many others taken by countless families present and past. There seems little that is remarkable about such a photo. It could have been shot by any proud parent or family member attempting to capture an early moment in the life of a recent addition to the family. Looking more closely, the photo frames the infant as the undeniable center of attention. The child sits barefoot in a nonspecific, everyday garment and his clothing is anything but meticulous. One side of the garment is not quite properly placed, exposing his shoulder as if he had just wriggled out of a sleeve. It is at once casual and haphazard and at the same time effortful and intentional.

But perhaps we should step back, rather than forward, to appreciate more of the script this image writes for us. This photo was taken between 1921 and 1922. It is a photograph of Hans (Johann) Hauck, an Afro-German man born in 1920 and an individual about whom I have written extensively elsewhere (Campt 2004). Hauck was born in Frankfurt, Germany, and grew up in Dudweiler-Saarbrücken. He spent most of his life there until late in the war, but eventually returned several years after the war ended. He lived out the rest of his life in Dudweiler until his death in 2002. Stepping back even further, what is not at all apparent from the poses and expressions of this seemingly unremarkable German boy is the fact that he was the child of a German mother and an Algerian soldier stationed in Germany as part of the French colonial forces deployed in the occupation of the Rhineland following World War I. It tells us nothing of the public and diplomatic controversy surrounding this cohort of children and the ensuing propaganda campaign waged in German, French, and British newspapers that denounced the presence of these African troops and their biracial offspring as "the black scourge of European culture and civilization" (Lebzelter

Figure 4.1. Hans Hauck, circa 1921–22. All photos reproduced with permission of the United States Holocaust Memorial Museum, Washington, D.C. (hereafter, USHMM).

1985, Marks 1983, Nelson 1970, Reinders 1968). It gives no indication of the fact that eleven years later, the child pictured in this photograph was sterilized as one of the so-called Rhineland bastards vilified both in the interwar years and later in the National Socialist regime (Burleigh and Wippermann 1991; Campt 2004; El-Tayeb 2001; Friedländer 1995; Kesting 1992; Lusane 2003; Pommerin 1979; Proctor 1988).

But if we're honest, I would say that most of us would have to confess that the historical framing of this photo initiates a subtle shift in our view of the image.

We refocus our gaze on skin color, phenotype, hair texture, and the question of "blackness." We begin to invoke and attempt to apply our own regional and cultural definitions and criteria for assessing race as "blackness." Interrogating the optics of the photograph's rendering of race, we now ask how "Black," "brown," or "colored" is or was he? In what ways does the photo register the traces of race or the historical moment at which it was taken? Does it give us any indication or foreshadowing of his ultimate "fate" under the impending regime of National Socialist Germany? Do we see the imprint of the "Black Horror" or *"Schwarze Schmach"* in/on this image? Does it "color" or inscribe him as a "Rhineland bastard"—the discourse we assume indelibly shaped and circumscribed his life?

In many ways, such a response echoes one of the most persistent questions I encountered when presenting the oral accounts of Afro-Germans in the absence of these images. At the time, I was frequently confronted by the perplexing query, "So what did they actually look like?" Surprisingly to me, even in the face of these images—ostensibly, the visual documentation that would answer these questions—such questions persist and ironically have in fact multiplied. These images seem to invite and embolden a desire to explain or more often challenge or dismiss the racialized experiences of these individuals on the basis of their appearance, a phenomenon often expressed with the remark, "But he doesn't really look that 'Black' anyway." In these cases, the photographic image seems to work together with the details of Hauck's biography and our own understandings of what constitutes a Black subject to shift our focus to the issue of racial subjection and persecution. The simple fact of the date and circumstances of Hauck's birth in Germany as a child of the infamous Rhineland occupation acts as a kind of caption—an almost unavoidable historical captioning that attempts to fix a particular meaning to this image. Somehow looking at these photos seems to authorize us to question their subject's racial authenticity and search for a way of contradicting or disputing Hans's account based on our own ability or *in*ability to "see" Hans as Black, and to evaluate the legitimacy of his claims to racial vicitimization.

But what about the portrait in figure 4.2—how does it signify? Equipped with the background history of this individual I have provided, how should we read this image-text? Once again, the most obvious frames of reference seem to be oppositional ones: attempting to read race and/or blackness into the image according to our own culturally specific criteria, or reading it as archetypically German in ways that might seem to "whitewash" or erase the question of race. Like the previous image, this too is a portrait, but a family portrait of a different kind. It is a group photo that once again situates this family and the child in particular in a middle-class milieu. The individuals in the frame are posed, arranged almost symmetrically, balancing height, gender, and generation—two sisters flanking a brother or spouse, demonstrating the family bond with

Figure 4.2. Hauck, family portrait, circa 1926 (USHMM).

outstretched arms that link the generations and complete the kinship circle. A matriarch is seated centrally with grandchild to her left, his hand clasped inside of hers. The entire group is dressed in their Sunday best.

The more formal posing of this image reproduces traditional portraiture conventions and in the process actively constructs a particular image of this family. This portrait aspires to the image of a representative and respectable middle-class family of the era, thus placing the individuals captured within the frame in particular class positions. In this way, the image signifies the family's aspiration to middle-class conformity and typicality through its content, composition, and framing. As Marianne Hirsch has argued, family photography is a site through which the family itself expresses and projects its desires and aspirations for social status and self-creation (Hirsch 1997, 7–9). Family photographs are thus an active medium through which the family constructs and reproduces itself not necessarily as it is or was, but rather as it would like to be seen. In this context, the positioning of Hans Hauck as a biracial child of African descent in the photos of his white German family takes on special significance. As we shall see, his consistent figuration as an integral part of this family constitutes him as an *Afro-German subject* well in advance of the social and political discourses most often cited as enunciating this subject position several decades later.

Figure 4.3. Hauck, circa 1928 (USHMM).

The two photos of Hauck presented in figures 4.3 and 4.4 echo the previous portraits in telling ways. Here again, the backdrop is the family garden. As in the previous image, his haircut, the iconic *Prinz-Eisenherz-Schnitt,* remains, although in these images his hair seems fuller—perhaps revealing the return of its telltale wave. As with the first photo, we must also give voice to the silent traces and absent presences that lurk in its interstices. For a resurgent historical caption persistently haunts how we see and read each of these images. That caption is the ambivalence of race as blackness. As the child of an African colonial soldier, his heritage is a fact that, as Hauck recounted, signified loudly and with harrowing consequences throughout his life (see Campt, 94–99). Between 1935 and 1936, Hauck was sterilized in a secret campaign carried out by the Gestapo against the Afro-German children of the Rhineland occupation on the basis of

Figure 4.4. Hauck and mother, circa 1928 (USHMM).

his racial heritage and the dire threat these children were seen to pose to the purity of the Aryan race. Thus, regardless of how he was read or registered socially or optically, in the Third Reich Hauck's Algerian heritage was racialized as "Black" (*Negermischlinge*) according to the classifications of Nazi racial law, and his status became the justification for his sterilization.

Yet the ambiguity of race in these images prompts us nevertheless to probe these images for evidence of race as phenotypical blackness. But the photographs stubbornly resist our attempts to reduce them to such a simple reading. Looking at their composition and the portraiture techniques they reflect, these images project class status and milieu. This prototypical Weimar outfit and the *Prinz-Eisenherz-Schnitt* function as a kind of uniform that situates Hauck historically in a particular era, as well as socially, by integrating him into his generational cohort. Like a uniform, they also conspire to place him in a relation of conformity rather than exception to the dominant group. As I have argued elsewhere and will see even more vividly here, uniforms came to play a particularly central role in Hauck's life history.

Posed here with his mother—side-by-side, head almost touching head, his hand in hers, and in the garden yet again—the image maps the continuity of family spatially, physically, and affectively throughout this series of portraits. Each of the images we have seen was intended to capture their respective moments for posterity. They were retained long after the passage of that moment, and thus serve precisely this function. They are images that document inclusion, rather than exclusion, exception, or marginality. These photographs of a family embracing its biracial child reference familiar performances of German family life yet in ways that contest dominant scripts of national belonging that assume a fiction of German racial purity, and thus providing an important alternate account of both of German and diasporic subject formation.

Taken over time, these photos articulate not a momentary occurrence but the longevity of relation, connection, and indeed a kind of indigeneity that I would argue diasporic dwelling ultimately breeds. For although it begins with migration or displacement from a home *elsewhere,* diaspora (and the African diaspora in particular) is not necessarily an endless trajectory that perpetually suspends an eventual arrival *somewhere.* Put another way, I would argue that it is important to attend not only to questions of diasporic movement and forced and voluntary migration, but also to the ways that Black disaporic communities are also thoroughly *emplaced* and practice complex forms of homing and dwelling.

Rather than privileging questions of mobility, rupture, connection, and continuity with originary cultures and heritages, what is equally crucial to understanding the significance of the African diaspora is engaging the very local forms of identification and subjectivity that diasporics like Afro-Germans stake claims to. Departing from other influential formulations, I would contend that diaspora is not always intrinsically counternational. In fact, the (inter)generational dynamics of diasporic formation always make at least the provisional aspiration to *national* subjecthood a necessary part of any form of diasporic identity. In other words, diasporic subjects are never merely citizens of the world, nor are they ever wholly "transnational." Although many Blacks in the diaspora practice forms of belonging to multiple sites and communities due to the complex circumstances of migration, for others, belonging is an epistemological (rather than ontological) process of *emplacement* that involves active processes of articulation and identification. Here local rootedness and national belonging are the ground from which transnational and diasporic affinities, differences, allegiances, and solidarity must necessarily be forged.

The next two images (figures 4.5 and 4.6) are perhaps the most formal portraits in this collection: first communion and a wedding portrait. Props and ornaments are carefully positioned in relation to the photographic subject. The individuals themselves are posed with precision and centered, frozen in time for the camera. These are commemorative photos marking significant familial events. They are occasions around which families converge and that serve as rituals of kinship, connection, and belonging. As such, these photos signify as articulations of community, familial as well as cultural. As before, Hauck is central to each frame. He is in no way marginal or peripheral. His presence is consistent, even in these later photos taken following the death of his mother.

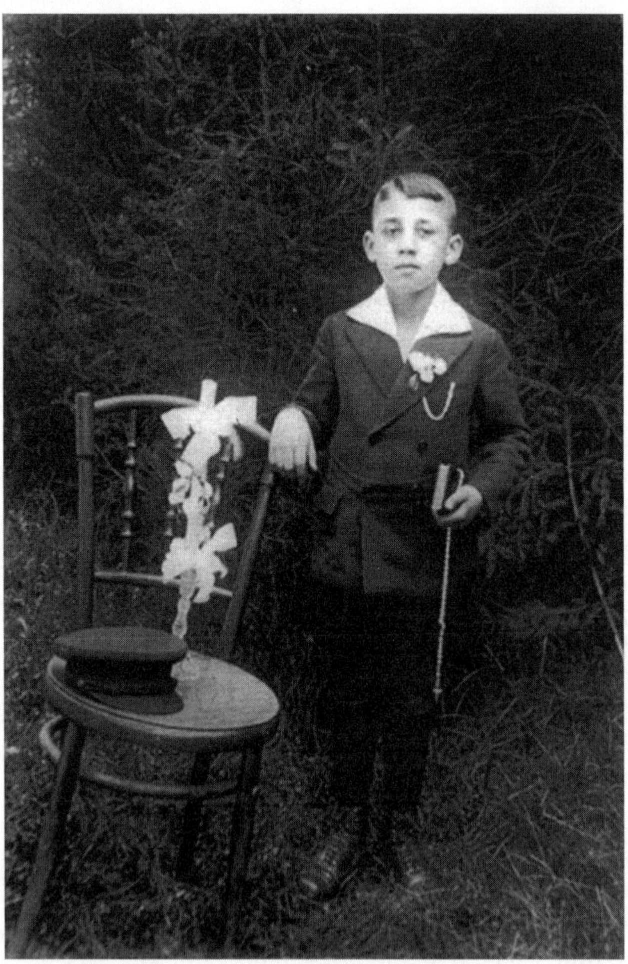

Figure 4.5. Communion, circa 1931 (USHMM).

Figure 4.6. Family wedding, circa 1932 (USHMM).

Each of these images mimics the professional photographic gaze of middle-class portraiture, indexing this genre of photography in ways that allow this family to project and claim respectable status as Germans by imaging family ties of intimacy, stability, and continuity. In the process, they reference forms of belonging that signify, stage, and perform family as "home"/homelife. This archive of domestic photography highlights practices of what I will term *diasporic home-making*—practices that are crucial to diasporic formation yet frequently papered-over by an emphasis on diasporic mobility. In an almost literal sense, these scenes of domesticity render white mothers and German families making homes for their biracial children and in the process producing domestic subjects in the places where diaspora eventually arrives and takes root. For both diasporic and transnational circulations produce not only temporary settlements but complex and creative practices of *home-making.*

These domestic photos portray Black Germans and their families *making home* in ways that offer an important "counter/part" (Brown, 99–100) to transnational studies of diasporic formation by emphasizing the significance of modes of local and national belonging in these processes. For in spite of his production as a racialized outsider, these images portray Hauck as in no way an "object" of curiosity or scorn, but rather a *subject*—indeed a "native" Black and German subject instantiated through his embedding in the existing structures of family. These photographs thus offer a powerful alternative representation of forms of belonging described much later by contemporary Black German authors as formative to their articulations of their African diasporic identities, yet well in advance of current discourses of multiculturalism. As such they witness modes of diasporic dwelling at a much earlier moment in German history, when articulations of national belonging in Germany were even more strenuously defined and policed along lines of racial and ethnic purity.

And now a very different set of photographs. Figures 4.7 and 4.8 are images that speak volumes to these same issues, yet through a very different set of structural optics. Unlike the previous series of photos, these images are institutional portraits. They are group photos that present individuals in the context of specific organizations. Both are organizations that typify the life of a youth in this period in Germany and both are institutional settings in which Hans Hauck was accepted as a member: in his primary school and as part of a group of trainee apprentices for the railroad. As classic examples of institutional photography, their composition seems less interesting than the preceding images, perhaps due to the fact that their staging is so straightforward and predictable. The arrangement of the members of the group has little to do with the individuals themselves—they are organized generically, with placement achieved by height alone and authority figures taking up positions on the sides. Here

Figure 4.7. School portrait (Hauck pictured top row, far left), circa 1928 (USHMM).

Figure 4.8. Railroad apprentice group (Hauck pictured second row, fourth from left), circa 1935–36 (USHMM).

the individual dissolves within the group, for it is only the group that matters. However, although their structuring may be unoriginal, they offer some of the most provocative images in this archive. For what sets these photos apart from the previous series of photos is the explicit emergence of gender to shape and define race and subjectivity in crucially constituent ways.

Both photos place Hauck in the context of specifically male groups. In the photo of his apprentice group, he resurfaces again at the center of the frame. This later photo was taken sometime around 1935–36. Lingering again on this image's silences, what it does not show is that Hauck's apprenticeship with the railroad was in fact a privileged position he acquired based on his membership in another more influential organization that literally enabled his acceptance at the railroad: the Hitler Youth. Hauck's membership in the intended bastion of Aryan youth indoctrination is noteworthy not only because of his African heritage but also because it occurred at a particular moment in the regional history of this institution. Hauck joined the Hilter Youth in a suburb of Saarbrücken in 1933 (the year of Hitler's seizure of power), during its period of voluntary membership and well before compulsory membership (*Jugenddienstpflicht*) was instituted in 1936. As he recounted, he joined the Hitler Youth "like all the other boys of his age." It was a group into which he was admitted in spite of his "non-Aryan" heritage—a fact facilitated by the locality of the group's structure, for the father of Hauck's childhood friend was the leader of the local chapter.

But to pose the question once again, how does this contextualization shape our view of Hauck's status in this image and this institution? Returning to the relation between the two portraits' compositions, in the transition between them, maleness morphs into masculinity through the uniforms and stoic posturing of its members as the image captures young boys in training. Hans, center stage yet again, is the only boy beyond the front row who adopts the defiant crossed-arm pose. The background of the photo threatens constantly to overpower the photograph, for the massive Nazi banner and swastikas dwarf both the individuals and the group and magnify the status of nation, nationalism, and fatherland. The photo thus fuses nation and masculinity and in the process produces an explicitly masculine and nationalist German subject.

Regardless of the interpretation we give them, each of these photographs provides only a partial account that surpasses any contextualizing caption we might give them. For example, they give no indication of the fact that in the very same period, just prior to his training as a railroad apprentice and during his membership in the Hitler Youth, he was sterilized by the Gestapo because of his African heritage. Does this fact influence or change our view of it?

Similar to the previous images, in figures 4.9 and 4.10 we see Hauck in uniform, though this time as a soldier after his induction into the German *Wehrmacht* in 1945. But we see no trace of what his experience was like as a part of the Nazi army. What these images do not tell us is that he saw the army as a "chance" to survive the Third Reich and that his decision to join up was made following a desperate attempt to flee this problem through a failed attempt at suicide in 1944. The photos gives us no hint of the fact that shortly after his induction into the army, Hauck was captured later on the Eastern front and held as a prisoner of war by the Russians from 1945 to 1949. Nor do we get any insight into the fact that, as Hauck explained it, being in the army was important to him because it was the first time he remembers "being treated as an equal" by his fellow Germans, and that his experience as a POW was noteworthy for him because, as he described it, "I was treated just like the other Germans. They [the Russians] didn't make any distinctions" (Hauck as cited in Campt, 121).

Like countless others in this regime, Hauck's racial persecution was not based on his skin color, but on his racialization as a non-Aryan and the threat he was seen to pose to the purity of the Aryan race based on blood. During this regime, membership in the national body was defined not only by race, but also through appropriate and sanctioned enactments of gender and gender roles. In Hauck's case, he was able to lay claim to visible/visual forms of masculinity through military organizations that legitimated him as a German as he transitioned from boyhood to manhood. Thus the military in some ways came to

Figure 4.9. Hauck and other soldiers, circa 1945 (USHMM).

replace the family later in his life as that which authorized his acceptance as a German during the war. But again, his status as a German subject was always already gendered and indeed contingent upon the recognition of appropriate forms of masculinity. It is thus impossible to view the archetypical German pictured here without also registering both the raced and gendered processes of subject formation that produced him as such.

This collection of photographs raises important questions about the implications of how we see race and blackness and its indexical registers in the photography of Black Germans in this period. For example, does light skin color

Figure 4.10. Hauck, army photo, circa 1945 (USHMM).

erase African heritage? Does gender, by way of masculinity and the military uniform, elide or disguise race? In what ways is racial visibility muted or overwritten by gender in the images of Black German boys and men as masculine members of both the nation and the family? Lastly, does the emergence of this Black German photographic subject in both everyday German contexts and in hyper-German/masculine organizations like the *Wehrmacht* erase their racial heritage in relation to their identification as Germans?

On some fundamental level, these images of extremely if not almost uncomfortably German subjects, albeit of African heritage, make us both *question* and at the same time *confirm* their relationship to the African diaspora. In this way, they urge us to consider the imbrications of race, gender, and nation in constituting diasporic subjects. The indexicality of race in this photographic archive challenges us to think about the differential visibility of European communities in the African diaspora by posing difficult questions about who counts as diasporic, who gets seen in this formation and who does not, and what or whose criteria of representation and definition are operative at implicit and explicit levels of our understanding of what constitutes diasporic membership and belonging. This visual archive in this way helps us to think through some of the underlying assumptions that structure how we see race, how it relates to skin color, how it is produced as always already gendered, and in what ways race and gender both color (and at times appears to not to color) our everyday interactions. For regardless of whether we *see* them, or if they *register* to us as "Black" or not, as individuals who fit neither the racially pure fiction of Germanness nor, for that matter, the archetypically mobile or cosmopolitan construction of a Black diasporic, these picture-perfect German national and diasporic subjects were and will at some level remain unsettled and inappropriate in profoundly productive and transgressive ways.

Acknowledgments

This essay and the larger project that has emerged from it are indebted to the influence of a group of individuals who were instrumental in helping me access the images at its core. I am grateful to Dieter Kuntz and U.S. Holocaust Memorial Museum for recovering and making available to me the remarkable collection of photographs reprinted here with the permission of the Museum. Keith Piper and Nicola Laure al Samarai initiated me into this exploration of the status of visual culture in Black German history during our collaborative work together on the "Historical Sounding Gallery" in Berlin, Germany. Peter Seel and the House of World Cultures in Berlin provided the resources and the institutional framework for that initial project. Yara-Colette Lemke Muniz de Faria offered me valuable advice and critical commentary. Above all, the late Hans Hauck has remained with me throughout this process as an active, persistent, and probing interlocutor regarding all questions of race and gender in the African diaspora in Europe.

References

Bechhaus-Gerst, Marianne, and Reinhard Klein-Arendt, eds. 2003. *Die (koloniale) Begegnung: AfrikanerInnen in Deutschland 1880–1945—Deutsche in Afrika 1880–1918.* Frankfurt/Main: Peter Lang.

———. 2004. *AfrikanerInnen in Deutschland und schwarze Deutsche—Geschichte und Gegenwart.* Münster: Lit., 197–210.

Brown, Jacqueline Nassy. *Dropping Anchor, Setting Sail: Geographies of Race in Black Liverpool.* Princeton: Princeton University Press, 2005.

Burleigh, Michael, and Wolfgang Wippermann. *The Racial State: Germany 1933–1945.* New York: Cambridge University Press, 1991.

Campt, Tina. *Other Germans: Black Germans and the Politics of Race, Gender, and Memory in the Third Reich.* Ann Arbor: University of Michigan Press, 2004.

Campt, Tina, and Pascal Grosse. "Mischlingskinder in Nachkriegsdeutschland: Zum Verhältnis von Psychologie, Anthropologie, und Gesellschaftspolitik nach 1945." In *Psychologie und Geschichte* 6, no. 1–2 (1994): 48–78.

Campt, Tina, Pascal Grosse, and Yara-Colette Lemke Muniz de Faria. "Black Germans and the Politics of Imperialist Imagination, 1920–1960." In Sara Lennox, Sara Friedrichsmeyer, and Susanne Zantop, eds., *The Imperialist Imagination: German Colonialism and Its Legacy.* Ann Arbor: University of Michigan Press, 1998, 205–29.

El-Tayeb, Fatima. *Schwarze Deutsche: Der Diskurs um "Rasse" und nationale Identität, 1890–1933.* Frankfurt: Campus Verlag, 2001.

Friedländer, Henry. *The Origins of Nazi Genocide: From Euthanasia to the Final Solution.* Chapel Hill: University of North Carolina Press, 1995.

Fusco, Coco. "Racial Time, Racial Marks, Racial Metaphors." In *Only Skin Deep: Changing Visions of the American Self.* Ed. Coco Fusco and Brian Wallis. New York: International Center of Photography/Harry N. Abrams, 2003, 13–15.

Grosse, Pascal. "Zwischen Privatheit und Offentlichkeit: Kolonialmigration in Deutschland 1900–1940." In Birthe Kundrus, ed., *Phantasiereiche: Zur Kulturgeschichte des Deutschen Kolonialismus.* Frankfurt/Main: Campus, 2003, 91–109.

Heyden, Ulrich van der, and Joachim Zeller, eds. *Kolonialmetropole Berlin: Eine Spurensuche.* Berlin: Berlin Edition, 2002.

Hirsch, Marianne. *Family Frames: Photography, Narrative, and Postmemory.* Cambridge, Mass.: Harvard University Press, 1997.

Kesting, Robert. "Forgotten Victims: Blacks in the Holocaust." *Journal of Negro History* (Winter 1992): 30–36.

Lebzelter, Gisela. "Die 'Schwarze Schmach': Vorurteile-Propaganda-Mythos." *Geschichte und Gesellschaft* 11 (1985): 37–58.

Lemke Muniz de Faria, Yara-Colette. *Zwischen Fürsorge und Ausgrenzung: Afrodeutsche "Besatzungskinder" im Nachkriegsdeutschland.* Berlin: Metropol, 2002.

Lusane, Clarence. *Hitler's Black Victims: The Historical Experiences of Afro-Germans, European Blacks, Africans, and African Americans in the Nazi Era.* New York: Routledge, 2003.

Marks, Sally. "Black Watch on the Rhine: A Study in Propaganda, Prejudice, and Prurience." *European Studies Review* 13 (1983): 297–334.

Mirzoeff, Nicholas. "The Shadow and the Substance: Race, Photography, and the Index." In *Only Skin Deep: Changing Visions of the American Self.* Ed. Coco Fusco and Brian Wallis. New York: International Center of Photography/Harry N. Abrams, 2003, 111–28.

Nelson, Keith L. "'The Black Horror on the Rhine': Race as a Factor in Post-World War I Diplomacy." *Journal of Modern History* 42 (1970): 606–27.

Oguntoye, Katharina. *Eine Afro-deutsche Geschichte: Zur Lebenssituation von Afrikanern und Afro-Deutschen in Deutschland von 1884 bis 1950.* Berlin: HoHo, 1997.

Pommerin, Reiner. *Sterilisierung der Rheinlandbastarde: Das Schicksal einer farbigen deutschen Minderheit, 1918–1937.* Düsseldorf: Droste Verlag, 1979.

Proctor, Robert. *Racial Hygiene: Medicine under the Nazis.* Cambridge, Mass.: Harvard University Press, 1988.

Reed-Anderson, Paulette. *Eine Geschichte von mehr als 100 Jahren: Die Anfänge der Afrikanischen Diaspora in Berlin.* Berlin: Ausländerbeauftragten des Berliner Senats, 1994.

———. *Rewriting the Footnotes: Berlin and the African Diaspora.* Berlin: Ausländerbeauftragten des Berliner Senats, 2000.

Reinders, Robert. "Racialism on the Left: E. D. Morel and the 'Black Horror on the Rhine.'" *International Review of Social History* 12 (1968): 1–28.

Tagg, John. *The Burden of Representation: Essays on Photographies and Histories.* Minneapolis: University of Minnesota Press, 1993.

Willis, Deborah. *Picturing Us: African American Identity in Photography.* New York: New Press, 1996.

5

The Conundrum of Geography, *Europe d'outre mer,* and Transcontinental Diasporic Identity

T. SHARPLEY-WHITING AND
TIFFANY RUBY PATTERSON

> Because of its systematic negation of the other person . . . colonialism forces the people it dominates to ask themselves the question constantly: "In reality, who am I?"
>
> —Frantz Fanon, *The Wretched of the Earth*

> The Europeans in general and the French in particular, not satisfied with simply ignoring the Negro of the colonies, repudiate the one whom they have shaped into their own image.
>
> —René Maran, Un homme pareil aux autres

There is, in our usual study of Europe, the tendency to explore its borders on a West-East axis. And despite former French president Valéry Giscard d'Estaing's declaration that its inclusion would spell "the end of Europe,"[1] the hotly debated membership of Turkey in the European Union would extend Europe in an even more easterly direction. That Europe is also located on a North-South axis with its furthest reaches where the Atlantic Ocean meets the Caribbean Sea and the Indian Ocean and the Atlantic are separated by the vast continent of Africa would also seem to trouble the contours of this apparently fixed geographical entity. As we contemplate the trajectory of the emergent field of inquiry called Black European studies and/or African diaspora studies in Europe, questions of national identity, citizenship, location, and geographical boundaries move quickly to the forefront, particularly with respect to France and the citizens of its overseas departments (*d'outre mer*). We can certainly add to that list "race" even though in France the official policy is that "race" does not exist. Talk of multiculturalism and identity politics are handily dismissed as polarizing U.S. imports. Nation-state metaphors of mosaics, melting pots, mixing bowls, and colorful salads are, as a matter of course, anathema to that universal document penned in 1789, *La Déclaration des droits de l'homme et du citoyen.* Socialist author Jacques Attali suggests in a special report from the European edition of *Time* that "the centralizing French state created one French citizen. It killed the local languages. It created equality between French citizens. It avoided the danger of different, competing communities."[2] One is either French or not. But just because the French state would like to wash away "race" and dismiss multiculturalism as the "implosion of social microgroups"[3] does not mean that racial hierarchies and lived experiences of race that authenticate group identification do not exist.

Unlike Great Britain, Germany, Spain, and Portugal, who during their heydays as European colonial powers followed principally a philosophy of "might is right," France's philosophical inclinations regarding conquest, assimilation, and the beneficent and beatific force of its culture present bumpy terrains in our attempts to interrogate the multiple mapped meanings of a unified Europe. There is perhaps no one who has so deftly summed up France's civilizing and assimilative inclinations than the historian Jules Michelet in his *L'Introduction à l'histoire universelle:*

> The Frenchman wants above all to imprint his personality on the vanquished, not as his own, but as the quintessence of the good and the beautiful; this is his naïve belief. He believes that he could do nothing more beneficial for the world than to give it his ideas, customs, ways of doing things. He will convert other peoples to these ways sword in hand, and after the battle, in part smugly and in part sympathetically, he will reveal to them all that they gain by becoming French. Do not laugh; those who invariably want to make the world in their image, finish by doing so. . . . Each one of our armies, upon retreating, has left behind a France.[4]

At the height of its power in the 1920s and 1930s, France possessed a colonial empire twenty times its size, which extended from the Americas (North and South) to the Antilles, French Indochina and the Pacific Ocean, and Africa and the Indian Ocean. And in its darkest hours of partition, indemnities, Vichy collaborators, and the German occupation during World War II, such was the "fondness" of the French for the colonies that they staunchly believed that above all else France should defend and maintain the overseas empire.[5]

The close of the second world war ushered in organized mass unrest in French Indochina and Algeria that would challenge variations of the prevailing French mentality regarding "L'Algérie," or "L'indochine"—"C'est la France!" Efforts to shore up the cracks in the declining empire took the form of globetrotting hat in hand, rather than "smugly" and "sympathetically" with the ever-menacing sword in tow, proffering independence or all that the colonies would gain by becoming France *d'outre mer.*[6] Prior to World War II, the practices of republican citizenship were disbursed unevenly throughout the colonies. Parts of Senegal (Gorée Island and Saint-Louis, for example) had citizenship status, while others were subjects, leading to the well-known protests in the aftermath of the Great War by Senegalese and Malagasy soldiers. In the French Atlantic world, slavery had been abolished since 1848, thus elevating the Antillean slave to citizen within a colonial formation. Hence such citizenship was freighted with all the inequality, domination, and oppression that colonialism implied.

The 1946 "oui" of the old colonies in the Americas, specifically Martinique, Guadeloupe,[7] and French Guiana, and Réunion in the Indian Ocean, cast on the referendum was an overwhelmingly one that moved these islands from the colonial matrix to "departmentalization." According to poet-politician Aimé Césaire, who led the charge on the island of Martinique, departmentalization was a "fool's bargain."[8] He continues in the interview in *Le Monde:*

> Every political decision is situated historically and is taken in answer to quite precise aspirations. In 1945 all the subjects of the former French empire wanted to become citizens and to stop being subjects. . . . No law has ever been more popular in the French West Indies than the one that brought Departments into being. For West Indians that measure put an end to arbitrary administration. . . . Departmentalization was intended, naively perhaps, but sincerely to ensure equality under the law. But France was reticent to apply the law it had voted into being . . . departmentalization was only a new form of domination. If it was an error, it was a collective error.[9]

Departmentalization was intended to augment the standard of living on the island, afford access to salaries and benefits on par with those in Europe, and provide improved health care and social services. Though the debate rages on about the efficacy of the move politically, that it was a mere sleight of hand, shifting "the old colonies" from colonial status to a neocolonial template, the geopolitical reality is that Martinique, Guadeloupe, French Guiana, and Réunion are at once island-nations and France—and by extension Europe.

In what follows, we will briefly explore how geography and nonwhiteness restricted and continues to impede access to Frenchness and citizenship despite the rhetoric of French republicanism. Using Frantz Fanon as a point of departure, we contend that a transnational (French) and transcontinental (European) understanding of Black diasporic identity opens up our engagements with the idea of Europe, Black Europeans, and Black European studies. Indeed, it is the combined prevailing ideology of "French but not quite" and of geographical dissonances that foreclose the inclusion of the departments *d'outre mer* in our scholarly explorations of the emergent field of Black European studies and/or research unified under the rubric African diaspora studies in Europe.

Anxious Identities and Black European Diasporic Subjectivity

And so in 1961 when Fanon wrote in *The Wretched of Earth* of the probative and negative methods that are part and parcel of colonialism, mechanisms that require the questioning of who one is, the revolutionary psychiatrist had at that moment firmly laid claim to a national identity as Algerian. But we want to suggest that this maneuvering, this rupture with Frenchness undergirded by revolutionary zeal, also points to the becoming and belonging that characterizes Black diasporic subjecthood, the multiple locations and adopted and imposed identities that lead one to belong simultaneously here and there.

Indeed, Fanon clearly grappled with this conundrum as a result of colonialism's cultural impositions in 1952, six years after the promises of departmentalization, in *Black Skin, White Masks,* a grappling that gives life to Michelet's boastful proclamations regarding France and Frenchness: "Martinique [is] a European country . . . The Martinican is a Frenchmen, he wants to remain part of the French Union. . . . I can imagine myself lost, submerged in a white flood composed of men like Sartre and Aragon, I should like nothing better. . . . What is all this talk of a Black people, of a Negro nationality? I am a Frenchman. I am interested in French culture, French civilization, the French people. We refuse to be considered 'outsiders,' we have full part in the French drama . . . I am personally interested in the future of France, in French values, in the French nation. What have I to do with a Black empire?"[10]

Part of the conundrum of diasporic identity in the context of France was that Fanon knew full well that the Martinican situation had everything to do with blackness *and* Frenchness. It was the constant denials of full access to Frenchness, of recognition in the Hegelian sense as a consequence of blackness, of an "*in*equality between French citizens" that Attali wistfully denies that serve as the prima facie evidence for the poetically brooding *Black Skin, White Masks.* And Fanon takes to task with razor-like analytical precision the writers Mayotte Capécia and René Maran, his Martinican compatriots,[11] who boldly give voice to anxieties about being not quite French enough because of their racial difference.

Fanon diagnoses Mayotte Capécia, winner of the Prix littéraire des Antilles for the novel *Je suis martiniquaise,* as experiencing racial overcompensation and inferiority: "At the fifth year of her age and the third page of her book: 'She took her inkwell out of the desk and emptied it over his head.' She quite soon recognized the futility of such attempts. Since she could no longer try to . . . [negrify]

the world, she was going to try in her own body and in her own mind, to bleach it."[12] Criticisms of Fanon's diagnosis have entered into the broad panoply of feminist writing.[13] That Fanon's criticisms were not especially original have not. That Capécia's first novel is in fact a collaboratively written work orchestrated by the French publisher Éditions Corrêa to assure the metropolitan French reading public that racial and sexual hierarchies in the French West Indies in the aftermath of the "oui" to departmental status were still firmly intact is little known.[14] Martinican Jenny Alpha subjects Mayotte Capécia and the novel *Je suis martiniquaise* to an equally rigorous critique in a review published originally in 1948 in *Présence africaine*. Alpha's earlier undertaking in some parts reads interestingly similar to Fanon's when she suggests, "Pour punir ses petits camarades blancs, elle rétablit l'equilibre épidermique avec de l'encre. Dans son esprit elle leur inflige ainsi cette 'infériorite' qui l'obsède. . . . Le diagnostic: 'Souffre d'un terrible complexe d'infériorité'" (In order to punish her white schoolmates, she reestablishes an epidermal equilibrium with ink. In her mind she inflicts them with the very inferiority that obsesses her. . . . The diagnosis: "Suffers from a terrible inferiority complex").[15]

In overlooking this review in the otherwise meticulously footnoted *Black Skin, White Masks,* where *Présence africaine* is heavily cited to substantiate claims concerning culture, literature, psychiatry, and psychoanalysis, is it possible that Fanon deliberately erased another Martinican woman's scholarship to bolster his diagnosis or that his failure is mere oversight? That Femi Ojo-Ade's *Analytic Index of Présence Africaine* (1947–1972) did not index the review also merits further examination. But these are topics for another day.

Despite the ghostwritten aspects of *Je suis martiniquaise,* the publisher's ruse represents something that is endemic to the colonial experience. Capécia becomes an assuring stand-in for French superiority and Antillean inferiority. With her mangled French—a veritable litmus test for French citizenship in parts of the colonial world—she represents the native's incapacity for wholly achieving the status and responsibility of Republican citizenship. Fanon may have been annoyed by Capécia's closing remarks in *Je suis martiniquais*—"I should have liked to be married, but to a white man. But a woman of color is never altogether respectable in a white man's eyes. Even when he loves her. I knew that"[16]—but it was the exchanges leading up to those concluding remarks, in broken French no less, that got at the crux of the colonial drama around race, national identity, and citizenship: "Je suis F'ançaise tout comme aut'" ("I am Frenchwoman like any other").[17] The retort from the (white) French commandant is that she has forgotten that "you are a woman of color."[18] It is Capécia's status as a *femme de couleur* that prevents her access to Frenchness (read "whiteness"). Her claim to Frenchness is no different than Fanon's. In eagerly making the "effort" to "slaughter" another "lamb,"[19] Fanon sets his sights on the Prix Goncourt-winning author, negritude forefather, and salonist Rene Maran's Jean Veneuse from the 1947 novel *Un homme pareil aux autres*. In Veneuse, Fanon finds a doubling as well: "Jean Veneuse is a Negro. Born in the Antilles, he has lived in Bordeaux for years; so he is European. But he is Black; so he is a Negro. There is the conflict."[20]

With the 1955 publication in *Revue Esprit* of "Antillais et Africains," and the 1958 and 1959 appearance of "Aux Antilles, naissance d'une nation," and "Cette Afrique à venir," in *El Moudjahid* and Fanon's journal notes, Fanon had become Black, African, Algerian, Antillean, Martinican. He cannot help still being French and thus European, despite his rhetorical renunciation of that national/continental identity. And his belonging here and there at once manifests itself with verve even in death: his burial in Algeria (Africa) and the amphitheatre, street, and library bearing his name in *Europe d'outre mer* (France overseas), the lesser Antilles, that is, Martinique.

Europe d'outre mer: Transcontinental Citizenship and Disciplinary Dilemmas

Given this backdrop, it is important to acknowledge then how the particularity of the French departments complicate the boundaries of Europe, and more specifically, the idea of a Black Europe. While the Black European experience in what we have come to understand as Europe defined on a West-East axis may be one centrally studied via colonialism, in the framework of the French Atlantic and Réunion, the transatlantic slave trade and departmentalization too are equally relevant to explaining how certain black bodies arrived in territories deemed French, hence becoming extensions of Europe or, more explicitly, the southernmost parts of France. Europeanness, and more specifically Black Europeanness, courtesy of the French colonial legacy, is unequivocally a transcontinental identity.

The overseas departments of France are bound by the EC treaty. That is the treaty that

> [D]etermine[d] to lay the foundations of an ever closer union among the peoples of Europe,
>
> [R]esolve[d] to ensure the economic and social progress of their countries by common action to eliminate the barriers which divide Europe,
>
> [Are] anxious to strengthen the unity of their economies and to ensure their harmonious development by reducing the differences existing between the various regions and the backwardness of the less favoured regions,
>
> [I]ntend[s]to confirm the solidarity which binds Europe and the overseas countries and desir[es] to ensure the development of their prosperity.

Hence the Euro is the legal tender of the French West Indies and Réunion, and these four areas are depicted beneath the map of Europe on Euro banknotes. As we think about the trajectory of the field of Black European studies, we would like to close therefore by posing a series of methodological, pedagogical, and historical questions. Will our interrogations of Europe and the emerging field of Black European studies rest primarily on geography rather than historical processes? To move in this direction would tacitly exclude Europeans from Martinique, Guadeloupe, French Guiana, and Réunion from the very notions of citizenship (in the European Union), nationhood, and identity that departmentalization provided. How should the field accommodate the history of Europe in all of its gnarled configurations? Should perhaps a category of Black Europeans *d'outre mer* be on the table? Would such a delightfully integrative and novel construct necessarily detract from the need to have a "Black Europe" unified by already porous borders?

Notes

1. BBC News World Edition, Nov. 8, 2002.

2. Thomas Sancton, "Special Report: Mixing Bowl," *Time Europe,* June 12, 2000, n.p.

3. Sancton, "Special Report," n.p.

4. Jules Michelet, *L'Introduction á l'histoire universelle* (Paris: Libraire Armand Colin, 1962), 64.

5. Film historian Pierre Sorlin discusses the importance of the colonies to the French, particularly as they related to the birth of a French national cinema, in "The Fanciful Empire: French Feature Films and the Colonies in the 1930s," *French Cultural Studies* 2, no. 5 (June 1991): 135–51.

6. By 1946 and 1952, respectively, France found itself nonetheless embroiled in brutally savage wars in both Africa and Asia attempting to maintain the empire.

7. Guadeloupe is an archipelago of nine inhabited islands, including Basse-Terre, Grande-Terre, Marie-Galante, La Desirade, Iles des Saintes, Saint-Barthelemy (St. Barts), Iles de la Petite Terre, and Saint-Martin (shared between the Netherlands—St. Martin and France—Saint Martin).

8. Phillipe Decraene, "Aimé Césaire: Black Rebel," *Callaloo* 17 (1983): 68, originally published in French in *Le Monde,* dimanche (1981), translation by James Arnold.

9. Decraene, "Aimé Césaire," 68.

10. Frantz Fanon, *Black Skin, White Masks* (New York: Grove Press, 1952), 202–3.

11. Maran was born in Martinique though his parents were French Guyanese and he was educated in Bordeaux.

12. Fanon, *Black Skin,* 45.

13. Gwen Bergner, "Who Is That Masked Woman? Or, The Role of Gender in Fanon's *Black Skin, White Masks,*" *PMLA* 110, no. 1 (1995): 75–88; Mary Anne Doane, *Femmes Fatales: Feminism, Film Theory, Psychoanalysis* (New York: Routledge, 1991); Clarisse

Zimra, "A Woman's Place: Cross-Sexual Perceptions in Race Relations, The Case of Mayotte Capécia and Abdoulaye Sadji," *Folio* (August 1978): 174–92.

14. Christiane Makward, *Mayotte Capécia, ou l'Alienation selon Fanon* (Paris: Éditions Karthala, 1999).

15. Republished in *L'Echo des Antilles* 2 fevrier (1949), n.p.

16. Mayotte Capécia, *Je suis martiniquaise* (Paris: Corrêa, 1948), 202.

17. Ibid., 178.

18. Ibid., 181.

19. Fanon, *Black Skin,* 76, 80, 66.

20. Ibid., 64.

SECTION 2

Race and Blackness in Perspective: France, Germany, and Italy

6

"Black (American) Paris" and the French Outer-Cities: The Race Question and Questioning Solidarity

TRICA DANIELLE KEATON

There are countless reasons to love Paris . . . As an African-American, I have always touted the city's, and indeed France's ethnic diversity and tolerance. After all, African Americans have a long and loving history with the French . . . I have embraced and believed in the French model of integration because I myself am living it. I speak their language, respect their culture and share their values. I have not been hampered professionally or socially by the color of my skin or the ring of my name . . . France is not perfect. And yes, the world has seen the shadowed underbelly of the City of Light [a reference to the "riots" of 2005]. But I believe that the French have gotten their wake-up call and will do what it takes to make "Liberté, Egalité, Fraternité" a reality.

—Janet McDonald, "NOTEBOOK, Feelings Tested in Paris," *Newsday*

They [Europeans] use other minorities as auxiliaries to create a fiction that race does not matter and that culture is, in essence, what sets subjects apart from citizens, victims from victimizers.

—Ch. Didier Gondola, "'But I Ain't African, I'm American!' Black American Exiles and the Construction of Racial Identities in Twentieth-Century France"

To accuse Black American expatriates in Paris of indulging in privileged status is both to ignore the very real differences in racial oppression on different sides of the Atlantic and to deny people the option of achieving liberation through flight that has been a primary means of agency for Blacks in both France and the United States over the years.

—Tyler Stovall, "No Green Pastures: The African Americanization of France"

On December 13, 2005, the *International Herald-Tribune* published an instructive op-ed about the "riots" in France that was written in such a way as to beg interrogation. Titled "France's Rift: Culture, Not Color" and penned by a self-identified "young black male who has lived in both France and the United States," this essay appeared not only in a widely read international daily but also circulated on the Internet and within "U.S. expatriate communities" in Paris.[1] What makes this piece, the opening epigraph, and similar essays instructive (and intriguing) has less to do with the actual uprisings[2] and more with how they exemplify the power of interpellation—as narratives of inclusion—narratives that foster the perception of a color-blind or race-free France. Here, interpellation derives from sociologist Louis Althusser's analysis of ideology as an inculcated system of dominating ideas and representations that "hail" or "interpellate" individuals and groups to them, rendering them an effect of that ideology in which they participate and consequently perpetuate.[3] Thus, there is an element of complicity at work in this formulation upon which the ideology relies.

These contemporary intertextual narratives of migration coalesce past celebratory texts, anecdotes, and echoes of Black American expatriate lore with Black Americans' recent positive accounts of life in Paris. What emerges from this mélange, however, is a problematic, enduring, and deceptive—though ever alluring—(mis)representation of Paris and France as sites of a paradoxical Black American inclusionism, the basis of which I seek to question in this paper. In so being, these narratives also dismiss and/or deny the social realties of race in French society while making those interpellated by inclusion narratives seemingly complicit with the nation-state at its most racist moments, a point that I also take up briefly relative to so-called "model minorities" in the U.S. Nowhere is social race more apparent than in places that I refer to elsewhere as the "other France," those wretched public housing projects in the French outer-cities or suburbs, such as Clichy-sous-Bois, where the 2005 uprisings began.[4] These uprisings were both a signpost and a watershed in the politics of "color-blindness" in French society, politics coupled with a complex race consciousness that conjugates with gender and class in this "other France."

In this essay, which derives from a broader project on Black relations and the politics of Black (im)migration, I seek to upset what I will call here "Black migration narratives of inclusion." In many ways, these narratives foster the fallacy of color-blindness and the denial of a "race question" in French society, despite France's own inglorious history of race-making, points to which I will return.[5] In the French context, such narratives derive from transnational migration, thus are fashioned and (in)formed by accounts of a fetishized France wherein Black Americans have experienced a celebrated positive reception, most notably in Parisian society.[6] Rooted in a well-traced history of U.S. Blacks' transnational migration and settlement in France, these narratives spur continued Black American (im)migration to Paris, as do they inhere in a variety of fascinating popular commodities, such as heritage tourism, that frequently draw from scholarship on "Black Paris." In her illuminating study "Black Paris: Touristic Simulations," sociologist Bennetta Jules-Rosette examines how Black diaspora tourism "involves the conversion of a physical site . . . into a touristic spectacle, attraction, or cultural marker," and as she reasons further, "Black Paris" tourism "may have the capacity to regenerate and transform the very communities that it constructs as symbolic ideas."[7]

Ultimately, these narratives, often sincere in their projections, wind up rationalizing and justifying those ideals of Black inclusion that have been readily challenged by the social realities of race suffered by France's racialized "others," in particular those perceived and self-identified as Black or "Noir," and/or Arab. To illustrate the social potency of race in French society, in opposition to such narratives, I will draw from previous research in the French outer-cities and recent fieldwork conducted in Clichy-sous-Bois.

In a piece such as this, self-location performs a certain clarifying labor. That is, as a Black American woman of racial slavery to U.S. shores and one who has had an over twenty-year-long ambivalent relationship with France, I have been complicit with and seduced by the very narratives that I seek to dissect. And while I recognize that uses of "Black" are necessarily unsettled—even as they define lived experiences—they are saturated by the assumptions, provocations, significations, sublimity, and weight of a blackness always present, understandings destined to be unnamed and transformed in shifting projects and politics of defiant and (un)desired belonging. To self-understand as Black is a political act, in keeping with the perspective of scholars such as sociologist Pedro Noguera, who compellingly writes in his controversial article, "Anything but Black: Bringing Politics Back to the Study of Race," itself informed by Toni Morrison's "On the Backs of Blacks," "I have learned from experience that to identify as [B]lack in America is an inherently political act, because in so doing one links oneself to a group that continues to be despised and maligned in American society,"[8] the election of President Barack Obama and post-race discourses notwithstanding.

Clearly, Noguera's observation holds beyond U.S. shores, as the wealth of scholarship and activity on "Black Europe" or the Black presence in Europe patently demonstrates in ways evocative of Aimé Césaire's ardent reply to a European questioner—following his conference paper at the First International Congress of Black Writers and Artists organized in Paris in 1956—who asked him of what consisted his Négritude and why he deemed it important. Césaire was reported to have said by James Baldwin who was chronicling the event: "We do not choose our cultures; we belong to them . . . We are not [B]lack by our own desire, but, in effect, because of Europe."[9] And yet, this self-representation can perpetuate what it seeks to transcend, that is, pregiven or preconstituted "identities" predicated on solidarity formations that are all too frequently presumed and/or based on skinship. The questions of blackness and belonging are, nevertheless, integral to these migration narratives, themselves fashioned by the type of rejection that racism, indeed anti-blackness—whatever the source—produces.

Black Migration Narratives of Inclusion

In the *Tribune* op-ed cited in the opening paragraph, its impressively credentialed author argues with aplomb that "France's problem isn't about race," again in reference to the 2005 uprisings.[10] Rather, as he and his title aver, these revolts were indicative of "a more insidious problem," culture, or what has been called in the United States "culture wars."[11] The use of culture to evade race is not without its logic and is not entirely invalid when placed within the genealogy of the resistance to racial classification in France. Nevertheless, what convinced this author and those of his perspective that culture trumps race in the French context is best expressed in his own words and the intertextual migration narrative that they weave. He is worth quoting at length:

> I had my first interaction with the French police on a December night in 1991. I had recently moved to Paris, and was strolling back to my tiny apartment in an exclusive neighborhood. I probably looked scruffy in my old army jacket and jeans. Suddenly two unmarked police cars pulled up. Four officers climbed out, asked where I was going, and demanded to see my "papers." But when I began speaking French, one of the officers heard my accent. "Oh, you're American? Please excuse us. Have a great evening." I was stunned. Americans had warned me that the French didn't welcome people of color and constantly harassed Arabs and Africans. But I soon learned that being an African American in France is wonderful. I was generally treated better than I would have been treated in the States. I was treated well elsewhere in Europe too . . . Seldom did I encounter prejudice. Usually I was made to feel special . . . Paris, in particular, has been a second home for intellectuals such as Richard Wright and James Baldwin. I have inherited that legacy. Europeans associate me with the aspects of America they embrace, especially African American art and music, and the historical struggle for freedom and civil rights—exotic, but not threatening . . . In America, prejudice has long been a question of color. In Europe, it's not about color; it's about culture. France doesn't have a race problem. It has a problem embracing the culture and customs of its immigrants and their children.[12]

The cultural read of the uprisings in France by the author resides in his positive reception as a "young black male," read "American," in situations where the master status of race[13] would have typically defined both him and the terms of engagement, as he acknowledges. Gender, status, nationality, and social location all serve in this context to authenticate the author's views, themselves seemingly legitimized by the broader forum in which they are published and disseminated, the international press and Internet. Consequently, the prevailing ideology of a race-free France remains intact because "race" is removed from the equation by dint of the "race," class, and gender of the author himself and the legacy of inclusion upon which his argument is built. Thus the uprisings become not about "race" but rather about what is readily left at hand, culture, which in France is frequently a code word for "race."

These narratives have historical antecedents, some of which are well documented in an impressive variety of critical, scholarly works on or related to Black Americans in Paris too lengthy to identify here. More to the point, Black migration narratives of inclusion draw upon these texts and owe their continued vitality to transnational social networks formed from the practice of "Black American Paris" in myriad formations, practice defined as the site of the dialectic of structure and the structures of the habitus.[14] Implicit in this understanding is the question of how practice is constituted toward, hopefully, revealing the traces of its formation, traces which are not readily apparent, are taken for granted, and thus go unquestioned. In this light, it is equally important to acknowledge that some formations are more fascinating and significant than others, and I would argue that the practice of "Black American Paris" falls within that realm as an object of study, precisely because of the narratives that it has generated and regenerated. And, as much as these narratives rely on race terror in the United States to explain the causes of migration—legitimately so I might add—they must equally depict a tolerant, liberal, and racially utopic France, again, to rationalize being in a country where other African and Asian descended peoples have clearly not been well received, as a plethora of postcolonial literature aptly demonstrates.[15]

A common feature of such inclusion narratives is the infamous "identity check" (contrôle d'identité), which can entail literally being stopped in one's tracks with demands to see one's identification papers by the French police, as the aforementioned op-ed highlights. A classic example from the annals of Black expatriate lore, and one often alluded to in other writings about "Black American Paris," has become the stuff of urban legend, indeed an interpellative moment specific to Black Americans. It concerns James Baldwin's encounter on the Seine in that very situation, and woe to the hapless person of color today who tries what he did: "One evening when the French police were checking papers as usual, Baldwin found he had forgotten his carte de séjour [residence permit]. But he had a copy of his book and hesitantly showed it to the agent; it was accepted as proof of his identity, and the policeman said respectfully: 'Oh, vous êtes écrivain monsieur!' [Oh, you are a writer, sir.] Not only was Baldwin not treated patronizingly, as Arabs and Africans were, but he sensed that in France the man in the street revered artists. . . . This greatly endeared France to him."[16]

It is worth noting here that an identity check would play decisively in the 2005 uprisings, as it has become an act of racial profiling and violence for youth in the "other France." Moreover, it is not only outer-city youth who are subjected to the uglier side of these checks, as scholar Manthia Diawara illustrates in his poignant memoir, *We Won't Budge,* who was riding in a taxi in Paris when he was stopped and subjected to humiliating treatment by the French police. Despite obvious counter examples, the identity check story is a recurring theme in the repertoire of migration narratives, used to exemplify not exclusion but inclusion in a color-blind/race-free France. And no narrative is more compelling than that by the icon of icons of "Black American Paris," Richard Wright, who in his 1951 essay, titled "I Choose Exile," states, "There is no Black Belt in which a Negro must confine his domicile. Paris is racially a free city."

While we may judge such sentiments as naïve today, it is, nonetheless, important to acknowledge that the causes of migration to Paris were quite real, as the violence from the Red Summer of 1919 and the legacies and vestiges of Jim Crow apartheid illustrate. While an abundant literature attests to this lived violence, one in particular, for me, that is salient in this context comes from the collection of short stories written by Langston Hughes, who was also a Black expatriate in Paris. In *The Ways of White Folks,* Hughes recounts in vivid detail the insanity of race and racism in the United States in a short story that he titled "Home." In it, the main character, Roy Williams, a cosmopolitan native son, is lynched in Jim Crow Missouri for "forgetting he wasn't in Europe" where he had lived as a classically trained musician, forgetting the codes of deference between those raced black and whites, especially women, that Williams unconsciously fails to display and for which he is subsequently beaten and lynched.

My point is that narratives of inclusion, as I have described them, remain robust, having the unintended consequence of further fetishizing the "City of Light" as "Black American Paris," owing largely to the ante-narratives of those now apotheosized. This fact was driven home to me in an e-mail disseminated by an impressively credentialed Black American whose immigration to Paris was greatly fueled by migration narratives replete with the adventures of Black Americans in Paris in search of a dream. She now organizes successful tours on "Black Paris," drawn from scholarly texts, which journalists have showcased in articles disseminated in various print and virtual media, thus becoming their own Black American migration narratives of inclusion in a race-free France. I do not begrudge her for identifying an industry to exploit in a country where that is rare, particularly one recognized by France. However, she invites necessary critique when circulating e-mails about her tours to an international list that conclude by expressing her joy over now living in a country (France) "without racism at its core." Already, a Google search of the term "Black Paris" yields thousands of hits, though it is left to be determined how many of those items qualify as Black American migration narratives of inclusion in a race-free Paris, France.

It should not be overlooked that Black Americans, especially Baldwin or William Gardner Smith, and Maya Angelou, for example, have challenged that representation, indeed from the inception of what I'm describing as "Black American Paris." However, even as Black expatriates denounced forms of exclusion, they were also inspired by and/or ambivalent about their positive reception. Scholar Werner Sollors picks up on the positive reception aspect in his article titled "African American Intellectuals and Europe between the Two World Wars." Sollors avers, "There has been a 'European theme' in Black American writing, in which Europe was typically stylized as the haven for Black and mixed-race Americans, where there were whites who did not share white American prejudices, and where interracial couples and their descendants could live happily ever after."[17] Further, as Tyler Stovall compelling argues in *Paris Noir: African Americans in the City of Light* and his examination of postwar Black Americans in Paris, titled "The Fire This Time: Black American Expatriates and the Algerian War," Black American expatriates were "caught up in the heady feeling of being accepted, even sought after, by whites in a glamourous foreign capital, [so] it was easy for Blacks in Paris to pay little attention to racism directed against another minority group."[18] The Algerian War, with all its violence that spilled onto French shores, would ultimately belie that race-free image among Black expatriates, as Stovall documents. While not as all-consuming as the Algerian War, the 2005 uprisings (and those yet to come) have not achieved similar ends, as the epigraph and op-ed at the onset of this paper suggest.

Howard University professor and U.S. ambassador Mercer Cook well articulates this ambivalence in his 1938 address delivered at Atlanta University, titled "The Race Problem in Paris and the French West Indies," in which he prefaced his remarks: "France is no utopia." However, he went to add, "For many years France has enjoyed—and rightly so, I believe—the reputation of being the most liberal country in Europe . . . In the final analysis the whole question in France is more definitely one of class than of caste."[19] Although Cook presciently identifies the importance of class and its intersection with race, other modes of domination become overshadowed by the representation of a "liberal" France writ large. The limitations of this essay preclude an exhaustive listing of those persons who rejected the race-free/color-blind image of Paris and France. Nonetheless, such observations along with narratives of inclusion would render complex the popular representation of Black Americans in Paris toward demystifying Paris as an exceptional, color-blind site in the African diaspora.

It bears noting that U.S. Blacks are not the only ones implicated in these narratives, as theorists Tracy Sharpley-Whiting and Brent Edwards show through their analysis of and writings by prominent figures, including Blaise Diagne and Marcus Garvey during the interwar years.[20] In her analysis of race in France in *Negritude Women,* Sharpley-Whiting draws light not only to Diagne's—the first Black African deputy in the National Assembly—but also to W.E.B. Du Bois's "political idealism toward France" as well as eventual tensions that would jeopardize their solidarity, due to differing responses to race and racism in French society. This is another area ripe for further mining, particularly in contemporary Paris, that is, migration narratives of inclusion by or about non-U.S. Blacks that assert a color-blind image of Paris and France. Edwards's own critique of the color-blindness to French racism in *The Practice of Diaspora: Literature, Translation, and the Rise of Black Internationalism* illustrates the possible costs and stakes of that position when drawing from Claude McKay's critique of the "Negro intelligentsia": "This blindness allowed the 'Harlem Renaissance' intelligentsia to bask in its own vanguardist myths, as it employed the putative universality of the French 'Rights to Man' to decry U.S. racism. In effect, transnational Black solidarity is traded in for a certain kind of national currency, an anti-racism in one country," as the price of the ticket.[21]

"Black American" as "Auxiliary Minority"

For as long as Black migration narratives of inclusion have existed, so, too, have critiques of that trope, often caustic ones, along with both subtle and overt denunciations of Black Americans in Paris, owing to such inclusionism. Claude McKay's acclaimed novel *Banjo* puts these issues in sharp relief, from his harlequin portrayal of the main character, a Black American after whom the book is titled, to his antithesis, the intellectual Ray, for whom Marseille, the setting of this narrative, is, "ever reminiscent of his own Caribbean."[22] In one memorable scene, Ray verbally undresses a French student during a conversation at their local café for his unmitigated praise of the benefits of "French civilization" and France's tolerance toward "colored people," as the student exclaims. While Ray's riposte is intended to denounce this clearly troubling view, it cannot do so without acknowledging a differential inclusion that, in a moment of prescience, augurs what is now a lived reality, a truly Black Paris, and a France unprepared for it:

> You're right when you say you're more tolerant toward colored people in your country than the Anglo-Saxons in theirs. But from what I have seen of the at-

titude of this town toward Negroes and Arabs, I don't know how it would be if you Europeans had a large colored population to handle in Europe . . . The student abruptly left the table . . . He was just crammed full of the much-touted benefits of French civilization, especially for colored people. His acquaintances, from workman to students, always parroted that, *though he missed the true spirit in their attitudes.* The cocotte was strikingly conscious of it, newspapers were full of it, and certain clever writers insisted that Paris was the paradise of the Aframerican.[23]

That "large colored population" indeed troubles the representation of Paris as the "Aframerican paradise" in a city where the stigma of blackness transcends nationality and where transcultural cross-fertilizations make it difficult to know who is whom, and from which part of the diaspora people hail. It is precisely for this reason that linguistic distinction has been a means of self-differentiation and identification—speaking English or French with an "American accent" for example—of which the op-ed essayist's encounter with the police is but one illustration, which parallels the uses of accent in the U.S. context and elsewhere as a strategy of distinction.

Disparate views of French liberalism and racial tolerance has engendered a type of transnational "call-and-response" between diaspora Blacks occupying Parisian space that continues to this day. And while the pull factor of desired color-blindness in France and/or the push factor of racism in the United States offer some insight into the causes of Black American migration to Paris, they do not fully explain what accounts for Blacks' differing reception in Paris and France. Nor do they capture why migration narratives of inclusion persist for Black Americans as an exceptional, imagined community, unlike any other population of the African diaspora in French society.

In the United States, the discourse of "African and West Indian model minorities" has become a theory through which the paradoxical inclusion of Black immigrants is articulated and apprehended, such that their perceived socioeconomic successes serve to confirm color-blindness against U.S. "home-grown" Blacks' claims of racism. Ultimately, this speaks to the need to theorize more the interrelationality of the subjectivity and objectivity of Black inclusion in transnational and comparative ways.

In France, during certain key historical moments, Black American inclusionism has been very much the object of critique. For example, in *Negrophilia: Avant-Garde Paris and Black Culture in the 1920s,* historian Petrine Archer-Straw filters the positive reception of Black Americans through the trope of "negrophilia," a deviant and defiant love of "Black culture." Black Americans, perceived as noble primitives in negrophiliac relations, provided the Parisian avant-garde of the 1920s with the means to rebel against prevailing social norms predicated on a bourgeois modernity that demonized intimacy with those perceived as ignoble savages, namely colonial Africans. However superficial, there was a degree of reciprocity to this relationship, argues Archer-Straw, which can also be read as utilitarianism. That is, Black Americans whose self-esteem and self-worth had been eroded by U.S. racism found a certain validation in the negrophiliac embrace. Parisian avant-gardists, on the other hand, could bask in blackness without assuming any of the burden of being "black," while having Black Americans serve as proxies for a primitivism possible only at a distance or projected onto Black women's bodies both repulsed and desired, as Tracy Sharpley-Whiting cogently documents in *Black Venus: Sexualized Savages, Primal Fears, and Primitive Narratives in French.*[24]

Historian Ch. Didier Gondola offers an alternative perspective of Black American inclusion in terms of "auxiliary minorities" in his polemical article, "But I Ain't African, I'm American!: Black American Exiles and the Construction of Racial Identities in Twentieth-Century France." While Gondola's analysis of Black Parisian expatriates, such as Josephine Baker and Richard Wright, has been praised by some and read by others as typifying anti-Black Americanism, I find that his article as a whole captures the idea of "call-and-response" within the Black diaspora, as does it reflect persistent tensions in Black/Afro relations. It is also reminiscent, in flavor, of the heated, transatlantic exchange between René Maran and Alain Locke in the September 1924 edition of the journal *Opportunity* that focuses on competing interpretations of Black inclusionism in France. The debate that Gondola invites merits intellectual critique and is one from which we must not retreat or be dismissive of its author, if any formation of solidarity is a goal, for he is not a lone voice on this topic. Drawing upon theories of exoticization, Gondola argues, "The preferential hospitality accorded Black Americans in France served an officially sanctioned discourse proclaiming the absence of race discrimination and negrophobia" during the inter- and postwar years.[25] "France" he continues, "had something tangible to offer [Black Americans]—liberty. Even if millions of colonized people in the French empire were deprived of it . . . Few Black Americans have excoriated this double-standard treatment meted out to Blacks."[26]

The notion of "auxiliary minorities" differs in one significant way from the "model minority" construct typically reserved for Black immigrants in the U.S. since economic incorporation is not a critical element in this model, although both auxiliary and model minorities serve, again, to support color-blind ideologies. The "auxiliary minority" need not be economically successful, upwardly mobile, or even perceived as such, as is implied by "model minorities." Rather, as sociologist Mary Waters explains, in drawing from the foresight of Malcolm X in her study on Black identity and relations in the U.S., persons or groups so (mis)recognized need only be a face of color that does not mirror back a country's history of race relations, thereby creating what she calls a "comfort factor."

As Waters reasons, such persons or groups, often linguistically distinguishable by their lilt or accent put, "whites at ease, and a cycle of expectations is created," one in which strained relations are not expected and are largely met.[27]

At micro and more intimate levels of society, this idea seems to apply to the French context as well, as it supports the notion of a "paradox of liberty": the social inclusion of Black Americans and the exclusion of other diaspora Blacks and people of color, especially Arabs. However, this claim of Black inclusion must be questioned in a country wherein those fleeing race terror in the United States were knowingly and unknowingly subject to deportation back to those conditions should they question or criticize, especially publicly, France's atrocities committed on French soil and in its colonies. Agence France-Presse journalist and writer William Gardner Smith vividly documents this fact in his novel, *The Stone Face,* which turns around the main character's ambivalence about and critique of Black American inclusionism, though the novel is itself a migration narrative of inclusion.[28] Scholar Hazel Rowley recounts in her controversial biography of Richard Wright, titled *Richard Wright: The Life and Times,* a private conversation between Wright and then executive editor of *Ebony* magazine, Ben Burns, whose own critique of the "paradox of liberty" and Black American inclusionism appears to be confirmed by Wright when responding to Burns's queries about the silence from expatriate sectors over the treatment of Arabs in France: "Suddenly Wright was talking in whispers that contrasted immensely with his usual loud, sure tone. 'You can say or write just about anything you want over here, but don't get started on France's colonies,' he admitted. 'Whoop, the police will be on your neck and out you go in forty-eight hours. There's no explanation—just out you go!'"[29]

During the postwar years, crafted by the Marshall Plan, relations between the United States and France increasingly soured with the prominence of the United States as a world power that ultimately supplanted the position of authority that French once enjoyed. A general disgust for and resistance to Americanization taking hold in France rendered it fertile ground for anti-Americanism during that period. Black Americans escaping U.S. racism became, then, a means to attack what the French identified as U.S. hegemony. Thus, the seeming positive reception of U.S. Blacks can be read politically or interest-based at macro-social levels, that is, as a means to buttress the idea of French cultural superiority in terms of racial tolerance vis-à-vis racial intolerance in the United States.

Accordingly, one must question the notion of the "paradox of liberty" because Black American expatriates are rendered utilitarian in this context, though indeed perceivable as auxiliary minorities. More importantly, the interpellation of Black American migration narratives of inclusion that seduce and compel us to acquiesce to and/or consume the ideas that they advance wind up legitimizing a universal color-blind, race-free image of France that simply has never been true.

Inclusion has been conditional at best, an observation well illustrated by scholar Terri Francis in "Embodied Fictions, Melancholy Migrations: Josephine Baker's Cinematic Celebrity," when noting that "Paris was in no way an uncomplicated freedom zone for African-American[s] . . . Americans traveling to European cities found themselves in a hall of mirrors, in which they negotiated their self-perceptions and ideas about America and about Blacks in the diaspora that were projected on to them,"[30] perceptions both rejected and embraced, even as the mirror cracked.[31]

In truth, both model and auxiliary minority constructs in the United States, France, or elsewhere, and those "hailed" by them, render diaspora Blacks complicit with the false claims of nation-states, again, when they are most racist. These claims are exemplified by racial slavery, apartheid, and colonial wars for independence of the past, in addition to the Hurricane Katrina tragedy with its "hidden race war"[32] and the 2005 and subsequent uprisings of the present, along with the criminalization of the undocumented and poor people worldwide. The migration narrative of Black American inclusion, when mediacized, becomes evidence of a race-free, consumable France, indeed a commodity both packaged for and purchaseable by a broader public. Ultimately, when left uninterrogated and excised from domination as a particular form of power, such narratives become seized as an expression of so-called African American hegemony. This provocative assertion, examined elsewhere in this volume, necessarily invites broad public debate, greater clarity and varied evidence to support it, and epistemological excavation relative to the use of the concept of hegemony that implies that Black Americans exercise domination over ideological institutions in the U.S. and within U.S. academies wherein power asymmetries leave many Black Studies departments and programs under-resourced and non-degree granting, while marginalizing its scholarship, despite visible gains. And, in light of its multiple interpretations, this discourse can foment false antinomies and antagonisms between African descended peoples, even as it reveals issues of importance that necessitate examination and critique, if solidarity is a shared pursuit and not simply the joy of the circle without a goal.

Returning, then, to the views expressed in the op-ed at the beginning of this essay, it becomes understandable that a race-read of the 2005 uprisings would seem unimaginable in light of the narratives that informed it. Yet, once contextualized, it is clear that France has long entertained the idea of race as biology, and it is the social reality of race that is painfully lived by those in the "other France."

The Social Reality of Race and Racism

That France does not officially categorize its populations according to racial categories, as occurs in the United States and Britain, does not preclude the existence of race in the French context nor its social potency. Here, the Thomas theorem resonates: "If men define situations as real, they are real in their consequences." Although the construction of French "national identity" is premised on cultural and political unity, race and racialist doctrine are nevertheless a well-documented sociohistorical fact in French thought and practices. Philosopher Tzvetan Todorov's analysis of the development of "popular racialism" in France is instructive in this context, which he elaborates in his critical study of race, *On Human Diversity: Nationalism, Racism, and Exoticism in French Thought.* Effectively, Todorov elucidates how influential thinkers such as Renan, Le Bon, Gobineau, and Taine advanced ideas of "the division of humanity into several major races—white, yellow, and black—and the hierarchization of this division," as were they adherents of polygenesis. Todorov argues further that "the idea of the inequality of the human races is a constant in Renan's thinking," as illustrated in Renan's *Philosophical Dialogues and Fragments:* "The negro, for instance is made to serve the great enterprises that have been willed and conceived by the white man."[33] While Renan is also held to have rejected a descent-based formation of a French nation-state, his view represents a break with prevailing humanist thought, itself one formidable barrier to the salience of race in French society.

The Enlightenment becomes pivotal in the archeology of race in France, as Enlightenment doctrines of universal humanism would structure France's Jacobin heritage and thereby the belief in cultural assimilation as the means to achieve this end. Yet, similar to historian Barbara Fields' illuminating examination of the dual formation of race as biology and democracy (and its inalienable rights) in the United States, historian Sue Peabody argues that the notion of humanism in France would ironically produce racial hierarchies and racism. That is, it would become necessary to legitimize and explain slavery and other social inequalities that patently violated the absolute rights of men advanced by humanist thought, ideas produced by thinkers in the Enlightenment pantheon, some of whom were unabashed racists.[34] The fundamental question of who was fully human would be critical to such theorizing, for can there be slaves without masters, if the determining criteria are derived from what one is measured against, not what or who one is?

The idea of race would legitimize increased territorial occupation and expansion into a number of countries, and in France the principal architect of this was the celebrated statesman Jules Ferry. The influential and well-educated men of Ferry's time believed firmly that theirs was a modern, industrial society, a democratic society, and a superior society in which the "higher races" were presumed to have the clear and righteous "duty to bring science and industry to the inferior races and raise them to a higher level of culture."[35] Indeed, Frantz Fanon passionately critiqued these sentiments in his writings, including his critical essay, "Culture and Racism," delivered at the 1956 First International Congress of Black Writers and Artists in Paris in which he argued that the very act of colonization rests on delegitimizing the human worth of the colonized in being a racist formation of psychological violence. Moreover, scholars such as Etienne Balibar, David Berris, Mamadou Diouf, Paul Gilroy, Stuart Hall, Maxim Silverman, Michel Wieviorka, and Michelle Wright effectively argue that "culture" is made a proxy for "race" in the French context. In other words, what gets constituted as "culture" is in fact racialized and in so being does the work of "race" in the absence of a so-named discourse.[36] "Race" here is understood as a social construction, a concept that still has purchase for its recognition that "race" is a human-made idea or set of ideas (which is why those ideas evolve and transform) about assigned social meanings of inferiority and superiority to observable and perceived differences. Nonetheless, as critical race theorist Kimberlé Crenshaw rightly observes, the fact that race is constructed does not mean that it lacks social significance.[37] Racial classification (as a system of division/domination), the narratives spun in societies about the meanings of differences, differences deployed to rank human worth, and the cultural, social, psychological, and physical violence that "race" and racism inflict (as products of power/politics), all make race a social, not biological, reality.

France, as political scientist Fred Constant writes in this volume is "colorblind in theory but not practice," which creates the conditions for "new racisms" or "culture wars." In these culture wars, racial hierarchy is dismissed, targeting instead the presumed cultural differences of undesired groups that are deemed a threat to the dominant culture, its narratives, and representations. The symbiotic dimensions of relations from populations flows in both literary and lived texts become effaced in this discourse, as scholar Dominic Thomas illuminates in *Black France: Colonialism, Immigration, and Transnationalism.*[38] And in referencing the "immigration complex," philosopher Etienne Balibar further complicates the race question in France in arguing that there is "a racism without races . . . It is a racism whose dominant theme is not biological heredity but the insurmountability of cultural differences, a racism which, at first sight, does not postulate the superiority of certain groups or peoples in relation to others but only the harmfulness of abolishing frontiers, the incompatibility of lifestyles and traditions."[39] Again, culture becomes a code word for race, and thus does its work in a "racism without races."

The putative markers of "race"—skin color, hair, features, language varieties, and by extension family name, religion, in short, people's ways of being and knowing—have long-standing social meanings in France, underpinned and enlivened by ideologies and policies acting on them. Scientific racism, which legitimized chattel slavery and colonization, is the most obvious historical example, while the outer-cities themselves are the contemporary manifestation.

Currently, efforts are underway to test the palatability of producing data on ethnicity and race in France in order to document and battle racism through statistical evidence of its existence since lived realities prove insufficient in countering race-blind discourses in these culture wars.[40]

Migration narratives of Black American inclusion in France become salient in this context because they rely on the dismissal of the potency and reality of race in order to sustain the message and representation of belonging that they project. This only works if the society is color-blind and race-free, and France, clearly, is not. What is left is a twist on a critical observation advanced by Frantz Fanon who has effectively shown how deeply the idea of race and racism are inscribed in French institutions that reduce human beings to the condition of a "thing," a "thingification" as Aimé Césaire so eloquently put it in *Discourse on Colonialism,* a dehumanization that persists to this day. Without interrogating the trope of inclusion, Black Paris becomes a Bourdieuian vision through division or a binary of blackness, which, to borrow from Fanon, leaves only the so-called "Dirty nigger/*sale nègre!*" Or simply a Negro!"[41]

Racial oppression is maintained by the central institutions of a society, as sociologist Stephen Small argues in his critical analysis of race, "Racisms and Racialized Hostility at the Start of the New Millennium." These "racialized structures" refer to "the normal, recurrent, and routine procedures of institutions that shape and constrain our daily lives, from politics (voting and political representatives), economics (business, employment), education (universities, schools), health (hospitals), and other spheres of social life (family, media, music, sport). The practices of key institutions shape and determine who succeeds and who fail, who is rewarded and who is punished."[42]

These structures are clearly represented in the neighborhood where the uprisings occurred, an area officially associated with intergenerational, concentrated poverty and crime. According to the last French census, such barriers include segregated housing (38 percent of which is substandard projects whose visible majority population is of color), secondary schools (wherein over 30 percent of those over fifteen do not have meaningful diplomas—those left in the school system are largely tracked into dead-end vocational studies and taught predominately by white teachers who may fear them), the labor market (wherein unemployment is over 30 percent for those between the ages of fifteen and twenty-four, and over 50 percent have been unemployed for more than one year), the judicial system (curfews targeting outer-city youth of color, racial profiling—especially identity checks—and the deportation of youth who, though raised most of their lives in France, may not be acceptably documented).[43]

Finally, ongoing anti-delinquency initiatives and legislation reflect the continued and normative penalization of the conditions of poverty in France. When speaking of his support for such legislation in the National Assembly, Nicolas

Sarkozy stated, "We must be tougher on crime because *to excuse violence is to encourage barbarism.* Punishment is the first step towards prevention."[44] Here, violence is understood unidirectionally, not in terms of the lived violence of outer-city life *on* so-called delinquents who are the legacies, not the architects, of statist violence. Further, a racialized image of the French outer-cities is not a new phenomenon in France, nor is the stigmatization of those who live there. Historically, France has always shunned those deemed to be "barbarians" at its gate. The racialized classification today is "jeune de banlieue"(youth from the suburbs) whose differing ethnonational origins are less relevant than the categorical and phenotypic group that they constitute, youths doubly excluded by their racialized outsider class status.[45]

Fanon, however, also theorized subaltern resistance to such domination, which returns us to the 2005 uprisings as a watershed in the politics of race. For as much as social race is denied in France, the media-driven faces that dominated the so-called riots were stigmatized youth of color, publicly insulted, (mis)represented as "scum," and wrongly accused of being thieves by Nicolas Sarkozy before he knew the facts. And while "whites" were well represented at those events, the racialization of outer-city youth supported other interests, namely Sarkozy's bid for the presidency at a moment in the country when visible difference matters, difference that is both feared and disdained. The criminalization of the conditions of poverty, to borrow a powerful expression from sociologist Loïc Wacquant, and I would add its racialization in the outer-cities, serve to deflect attention from the fact that neither Sarkozy nor France have viable solutions to the intergenerational misery that has become naturalized in those neighborhoods.

What was additionally lost in the rush to report the thousands of cars set aflame by this so-called scum was the act that precipitated those uprisings. This was not only the horrific deaths of two teenagers, fifteen-year-old Bouna Traoré and seventeen-year-old Zyed Benna, but also the searing realization of delegitimized human worth, of life less valued, if at all, for those categorized as social problems. These young people needlessly died and their friend (seventeen-year-old Muhittin Altun) was seriously injured fleeing an identity check that is underpinned by race in French society in terms of the cumulative, inferiorizing social meanings attached to (sub)urban youths' observable and perceived differences.

As I have argued elsewhere, these revolts are going to continue, as the March 2007 eruption of violence in the subway at Gare du Nord—a central gateway to and from the French outer-cities—aptly illustrates, another signpost to the future and one rooted in the ongoing practice of racial profiling in the metro. Indeed, the recent round of unrest in November 2007[46] is a stark reminder that the underlying causes of youths' reaction have not been clearly identified, and therefore go unaddressed. As the 2005 uprisings effectively disrupt notions of color-blindness in French society, how might they, when set against Black American migration narratives of inclusion, offer us some insight into the social realities of race, race consciousness, and the certitude of future uprisings?

Voices from the “Other France”: “As Long as You Don’t Have Their Color, You Don’t Fit Their Image!”

On Thursday, October 27, 2005, during Ramadan, ten boys from Clichy-sous-Bois, who had spent their afternoon playing soccer in a neighboring area, were heading home to break the fast and enjoy the evening meal with their family. Visibly of color and not from that neighborhood, by definition for some, they did not belong. The manicured homes of the area where the soccer field was located stand in stark distinction to the housing project, just minutes away, where the boys actually lived. Thirsty and hungry after a day of fasting, Bouna and his friends were rushing back home not only to eat but also because their parents would admonish them for being late, parents known to be strict disciplinarians. While en route, it was reported that a security guard at a construction site in that area had called the police because several boys whom the guard believed were thieves were allegedly “lurking” about a shed on that site. Next came the sirens from the “anti-crime” squads that have become fixtures in the outer-cities. These squads are known to profile youth from the “other France,” typically those of North and West African origins.[47]

For young people, perceived as criminals and terrorists in the making in French society, sirens have come to signify a police harassment that has become all too routine. As they describe it, and as research supports, this treatment begins with random, often unwarranted stops and searches by the police, punctuated by physically aggressive, often violent demands for their identity papers. It ends at the police station where they are held for several hours amid accusations and humiliation, if they don’t have their papers or if they resist. After years of witnessing this treatment, outer-city kids learn to run, not *to* but *from* the police. As Bouna’s older brother shared in an interview, “Today, the identity checks are more physical,” which his friend picks up on, in highlighting what could be called a counterinterpellative moment to the “Black American narrative of inclusion”:

> Today we’re faced with a type of police that inspires fear. It’s always the same people who do identity checks, sometimes several on the same day . . . When it’s bad, they insult you and make all kinds of insinuations. They speak to you disrespectfully, and you wind up at the police station, if you don’t have your papers. So, kids grow up with an obsessive fear of the police . . . [with a combination of

> frustration and agitation, he continued:] This story didn't start on October 27, 2005! Not that specific date, no! To understand why they ran, you need to go back five years, even six, seven or ten years back because in Bouna and Zyed's minds, they already knew how things go down: people taken to the police station for no reason, others beaten up. To really know what happened on October 27th, you have to understand what they were thinking, and what they've already experienced in their lives.

Relations with the police are such that young people expect mistreatment or violence at the hands of law enforcement, behavior I have witnessed personally throughout my research and years in France. However, the police only represent part of the threat, as youths must also face angry, economically strapped parents who risk losing their social allowances if their children become juvenile offenders, per existing French laws. In the worst-case scenario, those without French nationality can be deported to their parents' countries of origin, to countries that the children may not know nor speak the language. Some parents make similar threats to send their children *au bled,* as is said, and in so doing, they unconsciously equate their home countries with punishment in their children's minds, thus making them the last place on earth where they want to be. On that day in October, the boys did not have their identity papers on them since they were just going to play football. It should not be overlooked that these papers are precious in France, important documents, not something one carries when playing sports.

Upon hearing sirens and with harassment scenarios in mind, fueled by other fears, these boys took off running in multiple directions again, not to but from the police. Some ran behind cars and to any refuge they could find. Three ran blindly onto a grassy knoll and in a panic scaled a fence, not aware of signs and the warnings they screamed: "Stop! Electricity is stronger than you!" "Stop! Don't Risk Your Life!" Once in the power substation and still in a panic, Bouna and Zyed ran to a transformer, not knowing what it was. Several thousand volts later they both lay dead. Muhittin, who was just a bit slower getting to their hiding place, survived with serious injuries from the ball of fire that engulfed him as it took his friends' lives. At 6:12 p.m., there was an electrical outage throughout the neighborhood. Bouna's brother was getting dressed at that moment to go buy bread for dinner; his younger brother would not make it home to share that meal. The police denied having chased the boys but later recanted this story. However, they were in violation of French law for failing to come to the assistance of someone in danger that is supposed to apply to all in France.

Epilogue

U.S. notions of hypodescent (the "one drop rule," according to which any traceable African ancestry makes one black) do not obtain in a France that eschews categories defined and described in terms of race. Nevertheless, the social reality of race intersects with class, gender, and real and imagined religion in the "other France" where race, as I have defined it, has social potency. One telling illustration of that point emerges from Bouna's brother, Siyakha, whom I met shortly after the uprisings and whom I asked to write an open letter to France so that those most directly affected could give voice to their perspective so glaringly missing at the time. Social race is quite present in his poignant message, the note on which I conclude this essay. But let me add first that if we, as Black Americans, expect Black (im)migrants and others to acknowledge the multiple forms and formations of race and racisms in the United States that we suffer, let us do the same wherever we may (im)migrate. Let us acknowledge, too, that inclusion in or a blind love of Paris and France is at best double-edged, at worse illusory. Finally, we must see and hear the offspring of France's legacies of race who reside in its outer-cities for whom burning cars, as they shared, is a way to be heard. Bouna's older brother captures the fallacies and weaknesses in the Republic's color-blind model in that open letter to France:

> People are quick to point out Black and Arab kids from the suburbs as the ones who are rioting and looting, but they never talk about blue-eyed white kids looting. People never talk about them. Anyway, we all know the routine by now—take a Black and white person with same background; in the beginning everything starts out fine. But after we graduate from school, things fall apart. When both apply for a job, that's when discrimination comes into play. It's supposed to be about competency, not color. Whites are confident about their futures, but for Blacks, even if they have good grades, people only see the color of our skin, and that is a serious problem in France . . . People always talk about Liberté, Egalité, Fraternité, and yes, there is freedom, but not everywhere and for everyone. Remember, we're French; we were born here. Our grandparents fought in wars to defend France. Back then, they were considered unsuitable, and today so are we.[48]

Acknowledgments

My profound thanks first and foremost to Darlene Clark Hine for her visionary insight, genuine kindness, and generosity in welcoming me into what is fondly referred to among scholars as a "Clark Hine production." I extend that thanks to Allison Blakely, Manthia Diawara, Mamadou Diouf, Roderick Ferguson, Abiola Irele, Bennetta Jules-Rosette, Ousmane Kane, Stephen Small, and Tyler Stovall for their illuminating comments on drafts of this document. Special thanks go to Fatimata Wane Sagna, Maboula Soumahoro, and Franck Poupeau for their critical participation in the fieldwork conducted in Clichy-sous-Bois. I especially thank Siyakha Traoré and Samir Mihi whose words and lived experiences breathe life into this work. I would be remiss if I did not mention the next generation of scholars who are doing exciting work in this field, including Vanessa Agard-Jones, Laila Amine, Jovonne J. Bickerstaff, Rashida Braggs, Niambi Cacchioli, Crystal M. Fleming, Nadine Golly, Njideka Stephanie Iroh, Kennetta Hammond Perry, Araba Evelyn Johnston-Arthur, Laurie McIntosh, Dena Montague, Victoria Robinson, and Claudia Unterweger.

Notes

The first epigraph is from Janet McDonald's article titled "NOTEBOOK, Feelings Tested in Paris," *Newsday,* November 20, 2005, A.49/Opinion. Also see her *Project Girl* (Berkeley: University of California Press, 2000). On Apr. 11, 2007, Janet joined the ancestors after losing her battle with cancer, a battle that she braved in silence and unbeknownst to many of us who knew her. Her love of Paris is sincere and understandable given her own trajectory documented in *Project Girl.* Moreover, the views expressed in this writing should not be regarded as an "attack" of any particular individual or group. Rather, it is my desire to examine a sensitive issue that is underdiscussed in public forums, one that inheres in serious tensions and antagonisms between Blacks in the African diaspora.

1. Spencer P. Boyer, "France's Rift: Culture, Not Color," *International Herald Tribune,* Dec. 13, 2005.

2. I prefer to use the term "uprisings" instead of "riots" to describe the revolts in the French suburbs, which reflect a long-standing French tradition of resistance to oppression. That tradition is reflected in such harbingers as Article 35 of the 1793 version of the Declaration of the Rights of Man and Citizen, a product of the French Revolution, which has inspired revolt in and beyond France and has been part of the constitution of every French republic since 1789. Article 35 reads, "When the government violates the rights of the people, insurrection is, for the people and for each portion of the people, the most sacred of rights and the most indispensable of duties." Contemporary events also exemplify those traditions from May 1968 to the 2006 uprisings against "Le Contrat Première Embauche" (CPE), which, broadly, would have given employers the right to fire "French" workers under the age of twenty-six without offering a reason.

3. Louis Althusser, "Ideology and Ideological State Apparatuses," in *Lenin and Philosophy and Other Essays* (New York: Monthly Review Press, 1971).

4. For my previous fieldwork on the French outer-cities, see Trica Danielle Keaton, *Muslim Girls and the Other France: Race, Identity Politics, and Social Exclusion* (Bloomington: Indiana University Press, 2006).

5. For instructive perspectives on "race" and racialization in French society, see Didier and Eric Fassin, *De la Question Sociale à la Question Raciale? Représenter la Société Française* (Paris: La Découverte, 2006); and Loïc Wacquant's *Parias Urbains: Ghetto, Banlieues, Etat* (Urban Outcasts: Towards a Sociology of Advanced Marginality) (Paris: La Découverte, 2006). See also Bennetta Jules-Rosette's *Black Paris: The African Writers' Landscape* (Urbana: University of Illinois Press, 1998) and *Josephine Baker in Art and Life: The Icon and the Image* (Urbana: University of Illinois Press, 2007); Dominic Thomas' *Black France: Colonialism, Immigration, and Transnationalism* (Bloomington Indiana University Press, 2007); and Pap Ndiaye's *La Condition Noire: Essai sur une*

minorité française (Paris: Calmann-Lévy, 2008). for analyses of the impact of the Black diaspora in France.

6. My use of "positive reception" draws from migration theories advanced by sociologists Alejandro Portes, Min Zhou, and Rubén Rumbaut as part of their analysis of immigrant incorporation. The context of reception, or how they are received, can range from positive to hostile, making a community of welfare-maximizing co-ethnics critical in the latter case. See Alejandro Portes and Min Zhou, "The New Second Generation: Segmented Assimilation and Its Variants," *Annals, AAAPSS*, no. 530 (1993): 74–96; and Rumbaut and Portes, *Ethnicities: The Children of Immigrants in America* (Berkeley: University of California Press, 2001).

7. Bennetta Jules-Rosette, "Black Paris: Touristic Simulations," *Annals of Tourism Research* 21, no. 4 (1994): 679–700. On "Black Paris" tours, see Ervin Dyer, "Passage to Paris: A New Wave of Black Americans Is Calling the French Capital Home," *Crisis*, Jan./Feb. 2006, 30–33; and Belva Davis, "Black Paris: A Tour Highlighting the Parisians' Celebration of African Americans," *San Francisco Chronicle*, Mar. 16, 2003. There are virtual counterparts and corresponding Web sites for these and other related tours.

8. Pedro Noguera, "Anything but Black: Bringing Politics Back to the Study of Race," in *Problematizing Blackness: Self-Ethnographies by Black Immigrants to the United States*, ed. Percy C. Hintzen and Jean Muteba Rahier (New York: Routledge, 2003), 200.

9. In particular, see projects by scholars Peggy Piesche, Fatima El-Tayeb, and other colleagues at the helm of Black European Studies (BEST) events in Europe, an impressive array of scholars involved in the Collegium for African American Research (CAAR), in addition to the work by contributors to this volume. James Baldwin, "Princes and Powers" in his collection titled *Nobody Knows My Name* (New York: Vintage Books, 1961), 52–54. Baldwin uses the term "Negros" in the quote, though Césaire is likely to have said "Négre."

10. Spence Boyer is a fellow at the Center for American Progress.

11. The notion of "culture wars" emerges from meritocratic and color-blind/race-free discourses. It refers to the tendency to use cultural differences as explanation of racial inequalities and poverty typically attributed to the putative "cultural pathologies" of Black people and other stigmatized groups of color. Commonsense reasoning holds, then, that the failure of poor people of color to lift themselves out of poverty is cultural and specifically rooted in their behavior, supposed moral deficiencies, and "poor choices," as opposed to structural barriers.

12. Boyer, "France's Rift: Culture, Not Color," 9.

13. "Master status" refers to sociologist Robert Merton's notion that while any sociocultural diacritic could be used in society to identify people, race—in societies where it is a social reality—becomes a defining feature. See Robert Merton, *Social Theory and Social Structure* (New York: Free Press, 1967), and Mary Waters, *Black Identities: West Indian Dreams and American Realities* (Cambridge: Harvard University Press, 1999).

14. Pierre Bourdieu, *The Logic of Practice* (Stanford: Stanford University Press, 1990), 52.

15. Also see documentaries by Pascal Blanchard, including *Paris Couleur*, which explores the historical presences of people of color in the French capital, as well as the

2007 French reality show, "*Dans le peau d'un Noir,*" modeled after its U.S. counterpart, "Black. White," which focuses on "race swamping" to promote "race" sensitivity. See, too, Sue Peabody and Tyler Stovall, eds., *The Color of Liberty: Histories of Race in France* (Durham: Duke University Press, 2003), particularly in that volume, "Sambo in Paris: Race and Racism in the Iconography of the Everyday," by Leora Auslander and Thomas C. Holt.

16. Michel Fabre, *From Harlem to Paris: Black American Writers in France, 1840–1980* (Urbana: University of Chicago Press, 1991).

17. Werner Sollors, "African American Intellectuals and Europe between the Two World Wars," *GRAAT* 27 (2003): 41–57.

18. Tyler Stovall, "The Fire This Time: Black American Expatriates and the Algerian War," in *The French Fifties,* ed. Susan Weiner (New Haven: Yale University Press, 2000), 190.

19. Mercer Cook, "The Race Problem in Paris and the French West Indies," *Journal of Negro Education* 8 (1939): 673, 678.

20. Also see Eslanda Goode Robeson article published in *Challenge* in 1936 titled "Black Paris," Babacar M'Baye, "Marcus Garvey and African Francophone Political Leaders of the Early Twentieth Century: Prince Kojo Tovalou Houénou Reconsidered," *The Journal of Pan African Studies* Vol.1, No. 5 September 2006, and Zinsou, Émile Derlin and Luc Zouménou, *Kojo Tovalou Houénou Précurseur, 1887–1936: Pannégrisme et Modernité.* (Paris: Maisonneuve & Larose, 2004).

21. Brent Edwards, *The Practice of Diaspora* (Cambridge: Harvard University Press, 2003), 6.

22. Ibid for Edwards' insightful analysis of McKay's *Banjo.*

23. Claude McKay, *Banjo* (London: X Press, 2000), 55, 237; emphasis added.

24. Also see: T. Denean Sharpley-Whiting, *Negritude Women* (Minneapolis: University of Minnesota Press, 2002), and "Engaging Fanon or Reread Capecia" in *Fanon: A Critical Reader,* eds. Lewis Gordon, T. Denean Sharpley-Whiting, and Renée T. White (New York: Blackwell, 1996).

25. Gondola, "But I Ain't African, I'm American!" *Blackening Europe: The African American Presence,* ed. Heike Raphael-Hernandez (New York: Routledge), 209.

26. Ibid., 205, 207.

27. Waters, *Black Identities,* 172. See also Elliott P. Skinner, "The Dialectic between Diasporas and Homelands," in *The Global Dimensions of the African Diaspora,* ed. Joseph E. Harris (Washington, D.C.: Howard University Press, 1993); Winston James, *Holding Aloft the Banner of Ethiopia: Caribbean Radicalism in Early Twentieth-Century America* (New York: Verso, 1998); Milton Vickerman, *Crosscurrents: West Indian Immigrants and Race* (Oxford: Oxford University Press, 1999), and Percy Hintzen, *West Indian in the West: Self-Representations in an Immigrant Community* (New York: New York University Press, 2001).

28. Stovall, "The Fire this Time," for a compte rendu of Gardner Smith's novel.

29. Hazel Rowley, *Richard Wright: The Life and Times* (New York: Holt, Owl Books, 2001), 473. See also Henry Louis Gates Jr. and K. A. Appiah, eds. *Richard Wright: Critical Perspectives Past and Present* (New York: Amistad Press, 1993). Also see Madison D.

Lacy's 1994 documentary, *Richard Wright—Black Boy* and James Campbell's *Exiled in Paris: Richard Wright, James Baldwin, Samuel Beckett, and Others on the Left Bank* (Berkeley: University of California Press, 2003).

30. Terri Francis, "Embodied Fictions, Melancholy Migrations: Josephine Baker's Cinematic Celebrity," *Modern Fiction Studies* 51, no. 4 (2005): 842.

31. See also Auslander and Holt, "Sambo in Paris: Race and Racism in the Iconography of the Everyday."

32. A. C. Thompson, "Katrina's Hidden Race War," *Nation*, Dec. 17, 2008.

33. Tzvetan Todorov, *On Human Diversity: Nationalism, Racism, and Exoticism in French Thought* (Cambridge: Harvard University Press, 1993), 106–7, 110.

34. Sue Peabody, *"There Are No Slaves in France": The Political Culture of Race and Slavery in the Ancien Régime* (New York: Oxford University Press, 1996). See also Emmanuel Eze, *Race and the Enlightenment: A Reader* (Cambridge, Mass.: Blackwell, 1997), and Robert Bernasconi and Tommy Lee Lott, *The Idea of Race* (Indianapolis: Hackett, 2000).

35. Michel Wieviorka. *The Arena of Racism* (London: Sage, 1995), 6.

36. Etienne Balibar and Immanuel Wallerstein, *Race, Nation, Class: Ambiguous Identities* (London: Verso, 1988); David Beriss, *Black Skins, French Voices: Caribbean Ethnicity and Activism in Urban France* (Boulder, Colo.: Westview Press, 2004); Mamadou Diouf, "Recompositions Historiques et Cityoyennes dans les 'Territoires Perdus de la République Française'" (Historical Reconstructions and Citizenship in the "Wastelands of the French Republic"), in *Black France—France Noire: The History and Politics of Blackness*, eds. Tyler Stovall, Trica Keaton, Tracy Sharpley-Whiting (forthcoming); Paul Gilroy, *The Black Atlantic: Modernity and Double Consciousness* (Cambridge: Harvard University Press, 1993); Stuart Hall, "Formations of Modernity" and "The West and the Rest: Discourses and Power," in *Modernity: An Introduction to Modern Societies*, ed. Stuart Hall, David Held, Don Hubert, and Kenneth Thompson (Oxford: Blackwell, 1996); Maxim Silverman, *Deconstructing the Nation: Immigration, Racism, and Citizenship in Modern France* (London: Routledge, 1992); Michel Wieviorka, "The Development of Racism in Europe," in *A Companion to Racial and Ethnic Studies*, ed. David Theo Goldberg and John Solomos (Malden, Mass.: Blackwell, 2002); and Michelle Wright, *Becoming Black: Creating Identity in the African Diaspora* (Durham: Duke University Press, 2004).

37. Kimberlé Crenshaw et al., eds., *Critical Race Theory: The Key Writings that Formed the Movement* (New York: New Press, 1995).

38. Thomas, *Black France*, 5.

39. Etienne Balibar, "Is There a 'Neo-Racism'?" in *Race, Nation, Class: Ambiguous Identities*, ed. Etienne Balibar and Immanuel Wallerstein (London: Verso, 1988), 21.

40. For illuminating work on this topic, see Daniel Sabbagh's policy brief from the Equality of Opportunity Program of the French-American Foundation, titled "The Collection of Ethnoracial Statistics: Developments in the French Controversy," http://www.frenchamerican.org, and his coedited volume with Shanny Perry of *French Politics, Culture, and Society* 26, no. 1 (Spring 2008), which features a number of critical readings, in particular, Louis-Georges Tin, "Who Is Afraid of Blacks in France? The Black Question: The Name Taboo, the Number Taboo," and Patrick Simon, "The Choice of Ignorance: The Debate on Ethnic and Racial Statistics in France."

41. Frantz Fanon, *Black Skin, White Masks* (New York: Grove Press, 1961), 109.

42. Stephen Small, "Racisms and Racialized Hostility at the Start of the New Millennium," in *The Blackwell Companion to Race Relations,* ed. David Theo Goldberg and John Solomos (Malden, Mass.: Blackwell, 2001), 259–82.

43. See the French press for the story of nineteen-year-old high school student, Aminata Diallo, who was deported to Bamako, Mali, although she had been born and spent her entire life in France, and nineteen-year-old Abadallah, who was deported to Morocco.

44. Nedjma Bouakra, "Why Change the Code Regulating Society? France's Domestic Law," in *Le Monde Diplomatique* (April 2007), http://mondediplo.com/2007/04/; emphasis added.

45. See Tyler Stovall, "From Red Belt to Black Belt: Race, Class, and Urban Marginality in Twentieth-Century Paris," in *The Color of Liberty: Histories of Race in France;* Loïc Wacquant, "Banlieues ouvrières françaises et ghetto noir américain: de l'amalgame à la comparaison," in *Parias Urbains,* and Trica Keaton, "Structured Exclusion: Public Housing in the French Outer-City," in Keaton, *Muslim Girls and the Other France.*

46. On Nov. 27, 2007, two teenage boys of African origin were killed in the outer city of Villiers-le-Bel, north of Paris, following a collision with a police car. Accounts differ of the police response to the accident, as some residents have accused them of fleeing the scene while others stated that the police attempted to resuscitate the teens to no avail. Given the already hostile relations between outer-city youth and the police, the belief that the police fled does the work of "truth," irrespective of what that "truth" may actually be.

47. Interview with Siyakha Traoré, elder brother of Bouna, on May 19, 2006, at the fast-food restaurant "Beurger Muslim King" in Clichy-sous-Bois. Details of the uprisings derive from ethnographic methods that were also informed by a revealing book written by the lawyers of the families concerned: Jean-Pierre Mignard and Emmanuel Tordjman, *L'Affaire Clichy: Morts pour rien* (Paris: Éditions Stock, 2006).

48. Following my return from fieldwork in this area, I asked Siyakha to dictate this open letter to France 24 journalist Fatimata Wane Sagna, who had introduced me to him. I presented this letter, along with the background information described here, at the inaugural lecture at the Museum of the African Diaspora (MoAD) in April 2006 devoted to the topic: "Paris Is Burning (Again). See: http://www.moadsf.org/visit/parisburning.html. Also see Fatimata Wane Sagna's interview with Siyakha, recorded shortly after the uprisings, titled "Morts pour que rien ne change?" in *Africa Internationale France* (Dec. 2005): 8–10. Also see Franck Poupeau's "French Sociology Under Fire: A preliminary diagnosis of the November 2005 "urban riots" (June 11, 2006) retrieved at: http://riots-france.ssrc.org/Poupeau, and Maboula Soumahoro, "On the Test of the French Republic as Taken (and Failed)," *Transition* 98 (2008): 42–66.

7

Black Italia: Contemporary Migrant Writers from Africa

ALESSANDRA DI MAIO

Convergent Boundaries, Shifting Landscapes: Africa Begins in the Alps

Although Italy lies on the European continent and politically belongs to Europe, from a geological point of view it is part of the African continent. Once, several million years ago, the Italian peninsula was part of Africa's continental plate, from which it gradually detached itself. The Alps were the result of its collision with the Eurasian continent. In fact, according to the theory of plate tectonics, the entire African plate is slowly converging towards Europe, so geologists hypothesize the possible formation of a Euro-Asian-African supercontinent in the far future (Mayer 1999). Italy and Africa have always been close, not only geographically or geologically, but also culturally, in times of both war and peace. Through the centuries, historical and fictional characters of African descent have been an integral part of Italian culture and imagery at large—Hannibal, Othello, Alessandro de' Medici (see Brackett 2005), and *Faccetta nera*[1] are but some of them. Yet their presence in the national landscape has often been marginalized, considered episodic if not entirely overlooked by Italy's dominant discourse.

The recent arrival of a plethora of migrants from the four corners of the world, many from African countries, has lately urged Italians, or at least some of them, to recuperate their African past as a fundamental, knotty component of their national identity.[2] This phenomenon has inscribed Italy as a site of the African diaspora, offering new perspectives and directions to the field of Black diaspora studies, especially to its latest developments, Black European studies, which, if on the one hand sprout from analyses of diaspora at large and on the

African diaspora in particular, on the other hand borrow methods and instruments from European studies—this, too, an emerging multidisciplinary field, focusing on the economic, political, and cultural formation of a new European identity that simultaneously includes and transcends nation-state borders.

Among these African migrants are a number of emerging writers whose increasingly flourishing literary production has been reshaping Italy's contemporary letters, but whose voices, more often than not, have been excluded by the dominant literary discourse in ways that seem to reproduce the social marginalization to which the African Italian community has generally been subjected. However, these writers' narratives offer an original, multifaceted, and complex portrait of contemporary Italy, where the African community is becoming larger in number, while providing insights into the ways in which migrants express their feelings of belonging, loss, and possible aspirations towards the nations from which they or their parents come. Their stories provide more textured details about these issues than are usually provided by sociologists or anthropologists, and by the nation's dominant discourse on immigration, mostly led by the media and legal texts. They are new voices in the discourse on an Italian multicultural identity and point out that the nation's alleged homogenous identity is nothing but a deliberately constructed myth. Moreover, they demonstrate, and indeed highlight, that Italy, too, has multiple facets to offer to the African European community and a variety of artistic expressions to contribute.

Little has been written about the Black diaspora in Italy, especially from a literary or cultural studies perspective. In general, the African diaspora in Italy has not been the subject of attention in ways that it has been in many other European nations, such as Britain, France, and the Netherlands, which have come to be considered paradigmatic for Black European studies. Most of the ancient states and city-states that later formed Italy were not major players in the slave trade—Venice is the most notable exception—and the modern nation, in spite of its colonial past, did not attract larger numbers of former colonial immigrants after World War II. Yet there is a "postcolonial" community from the Horn of Africa that adds to the growing African Italian community. Indeed, some of the most powerful voices from the younger generation in Italian contemporary letters belong to Somali Italian women writers, whose spectrum of voices offers a choral representation of Italy's oldest and youngest connections with Africa—more specifically with East Africa. By lending an ear to these and other voices, I intend to offer a glimpse of Italy's contemporary literary production, see how it represents the nation's fast-changing social and cultural texture, reflect on how migration has marked national identity, and contribute from a divergent perspective and with little-known data to an assessment of a present-day Black Europe.

Emigration and the Construction of Italy's National Identity

Since Unification in 1861, Italy has struggled to define its own national identity in a way that takes into account what Pasquale Verdicchio concisely calls its "indigenous cultural diversity" (1997, 156). Italy resulted from the political union of a number of relatively small, contiguous states that, although connected by the semi-isolation of the geographic territory, similar histories, frequent intermarriages, and the power of the Papacy, had developed autonomous cultural identities throughout the centuries. Their unification was challenging, and gave rise to a wide range of issues, the aftermath of which the contemporary Italian nation is still facing. An economic disparity exists between the *Mezzogiorno*—the Italian south and the two major islands, Sicily and Sardinia—and the rest of Italy, especially if one compares it to the wealthiest regions of northern Italy. This disparity was apparent at the time of Unification and became more pronounced afterwards when the north became increasingly industrialized and urban whereas the economy of the south remained largely agricultural. This vexed relationship between north and south Italy is generally referred to as the "Southern Question" and has shaped the nation's political, social, and cultural life. Umberto Bossi's *Lega Nord* (Northern League), for instance, which emerged in the 1990s and won unprecedented success in the 2008 national elections, is only one of the most recent aspects of the unresolved Southern Question, which last century Antonio Gramsci, among others, recognized as being one of the nation's central concerns (see Gramsci 2006). However, the "Italianness" recognized throughout the world in the country's arts, fashion, food, and so forth derives from this unique century-long, dynamic, often problematic, but extremely fertile syncretism.

The amalgam characterizing Italy's national identity is not only endogenous, but also exogenous. For nearly a century after Unification, Italy was an emigrating country. Roughly from the 1860s until the 1960s, masses of Italians left their country in search of a better life. Most settled in the New World, some went as far as Australia and New Zealand, while many others traveled north to countries as close as Switzerland, France, and Germany. There also were smaller flows to other countries. Moreover, during Fascism's expansionistic years, groups of colonists settled in Italy's colonies in Africa—Libya, Eritrea, Ethiopia, and Somalia—and the Balkans—Albania, former Yugoslavia, and the Dodecanese.

Although the dominant discourse has long tended to remove from the national psyche Italy's history of emigration, as well as its "weak" colonial era (Calchi Novati 1999), a "horde" of Italians indeed dispersed to the four corners of the world (Stella 2002), where their offspring in many cases still reside. Today the time of the "great migrations" is well over and Italy is one of the G8 nations, but a different kind of exodus, smaller in proportion and concerning a specific target, persists and has, for that matter, regularly increased over the last few years: a brain drain has sent abroad younger and not so young professionals and researchers from virtually every field in search of the opportunities, support, and structures they cannot find in their native country. Emigration in all its forms, in other words, has been a constant for Italy, and "rethinking nationalism through the Italian diaspora" (Verdicchio 1997) seems to be imperative. Today the Italians in diaspora—people of Italian origin, not necessarily Italian by birth or citizenship, but also the children and grandchildren of Italian emigrants—are estimated to be a few million more than those living within the borders of the nation-state.[3] A growing number of descendants of Italians worldwide are applying for Italian citizenship—which is regulated by *ius sanguinis,* namely, it is transmitted "by blood"—hoping thereby for an open door to Europe as well. Such "new Italians" have proliferated, if not always on the boot and its major islands, where birth rates have dropped, unquestionably throughout the world (Turco 2005; Richards 1994). Their hyphenated cultures add up to Italy's distinctive syncretism.

Immigration, Europe, and Globalization

During the last decades a further, variegated layer has been added to Italy's already multilayered society, contributing to redefining its migrant identity in new directions. Traditionally a source of emigrants, the country has recently become a hub for immigration. The Second National Conference on Emigration, held in Rome in 1988, reported that for the first time since Unification, the number of people entering the country exceeded that of those leaving. People have been arriving in great numbers, following different routes (see Corneli 2005) from various regions of the world: many, if not most, from Africa—the Maghreb as well as sub-Saharan Africa; but also from the Middle East, Eastern Europe, Southeast Asia, and South America.[4]

Initially considered transitory by both the newcomers and the host country, immigration to Italy soon tended to assume a permanent status. The "immigrant question" was immediately regarded by Italy as a European question, not only because some newcomers were arriving from adjacent countries—former Yugoslavia, for example—but especially because immigration inscribed itself within the broader context of a migratory trend that concerned the European Union as a whole. The increasing presence of immigrants from multiple sites of origins imposed a reconsideration of European community discourse, raising issues of borders, nationality, ethnicity, race, and civil tolerance. Umberto Eco has observed that this massive, diversified immigration toward Western Europe was a far more significant phenomenon for the formation of a new European identity than the crisis of communism in the former Eastern bloc (1990). One might argue that the two phenomena are in fact closely related, if considered in a global frame.[5]

As Saskia Sassen suggests in her study *Guests and Aliens,* "Migrations do not simply happen. They are produced. And migrations do not involve just any possible combinations of countries. They are patterned. . . . Although it may seem that migrations are ever present, there are actually distinct phases and patterns over the last two centuries" (Sassen 1999, 155). Comparing the large transatlantic migrations in the second half of the nineteenth century to the contemporary mass movement to Europe, she explains that migratory waves are "bounded in space, time, and scale" and that the contemporary flows to Europe involve the entire world and its global market, and are characterized by new forms of economic, political, and cultural "transnationalization" (Sassen 1999, 133). Hence she emphasizes the necessity of a transnational migration policy, remarking, "National governments still have sovereignty over many matters, but they are increasingly part of a web of rights and regulations that are embedded in other entities—from EC institutions to courts defending the human rights of refugees" (133). Sassen's words resonate with those of Jan Karlsson, cochair of the Global Commission on International Migration,[6] who advocates the necessity of "multilateral, joint action," by virtue of which nation-states would abdicate their autonomy in migratory matters in favor of international law in order to manage and regulate global migrations—the most complex case of which, according to the Commission, is presented by Europe—and in order to actively protect what can be considered one of the most unprotected groups of people worldwide—migrants (Karlsson 2005). Thus, if on the one hand migratory fluxes warrant considerations in a "global framework" (Karlsson 2005), on the other hand they must be studied in their peculiarity. Sassen concludes, "There is only one enlightened road to take for Europe today: that is to work with settled immigrants and refugees toward their full integration, and to do so through frameworks that ensure cultural and religious diversity will be part of civil society, that is, part of what binds us rather than what segregates us" (Sassen 1999, 133).

A New Nation: New Laws, New Language

Italy gradually discovered that it was playing a new role in the global picture and that it was far from prepared for this responsibility. Although an active participant in the frameworks outlined above—transnational entities, an international code of laws, a transversal civil society, the global market, and so forth—it nonetheless found itself unprepared to receive such a plethora of people whose presence called for prompt regulation. As an emigrating nation, Italy had neither laws nor social policies nor yet a language in which to address its new immigrant reality. Everything had to be invented. Social and political controversy quickly arose. Concurrent with an attempt to promote a culture of acceptance and solidarity was a relapse of nationalism or, in the best case, bewilderment. Multiculturalism was countered by racism. Newcomers were more often than not forced to the margins by the "welcoming" Italian society. However, they have increasingly interacted with, and added to, the composite social, political, economic, religious, intellectual, and even aesthetic Italian texture. From an initial alleged invisibility, their presence has become progressively more apparent in major urban centers as well as in the countryside, in the north and in the south, in schools, factories, the media, sports, politics, and the arts. As a result, the Italian landscape has changed, in some cases, literally: along with St. Peter's Basilica and the imposing synagogue on the opposite bank of the Tiber, Rome now boasts the largest mosque in Europe (see Richards 1994, 233–56).

The Italian language has undergone concomitant changes in view of the need to invent a new vocabulary. The media have promoted new terms and definitions, not infrequently revealing racialist overtones. Neologisms have flourished in newspapers and on TV, and are now used in everyday conversation. Many epithets have been invented to refer to the newcomers: *extracomunitari* (literally, people, individuals from outside the European Community), *vu cumpra'* (literally, would you like to buy something?),[7] *scafista* (refers to the people involved in human trafficking by sea, derived from *scafi,* boats), *badante* (home nurse, from *badare,* to look after), and many others.[8] The semantic field of other terms has expanded. For instance, particular nationalities have become the repository of associated characteristics. *Marocchino* is not only somebody from Morocco, but every immigrant with a darker complexion. *Filippina* refers not only to a woman from the Philippines, but to any maid who is not a native Italian. Even the term *immigrato*—by far the most frequent appellative in the media—whose English translation "immigrant" I have often used so far, has been subjected to a semantic shift, referring to every newcomer, independent of their juridical status. Thus, refugees, asylum seekers, seasonal migrant workers, and naturalized citizens are frequently and indiscriminately referred to as *immigrati.* In fact, the immigrant is not a juridical figure in Italy, but rather a socially, and, one might say, mass-media-constructed *persona*—or, more accurately, what sociologist Alessandro Dal Lago refers to as a *non-persona* (1999). There are no immigration laws in Italy, strictly speaking. There are laws—relatively recent laws—concerning *stranieri* (foreigners, strangers) who reside in Italy. When I use the term "immigrant," therefore, I do not intend to refer to a specific legal status, as yet absent; rather, my intent is to propose a re-semanticization of this word, favoring the idea of "migration" over that of "strangeness" implied by the legal term *straniero,* and indicating with the prefix "im-" a patterned direction, a destination, and a sense of location in this discourse: namely, the convergence in Italy of newcomers from different parts of the world.

The first legal text that attempted to regularize the "immigrant question" in Italy—or "emergency immigration," as media started to label it—dates back to 1986, and refers to *extracomunitari.*[9] It regulates migrant work but does not deal with norms of residence. The second half of the 1980s, when entries to Italy—especially from North and West Africa—were increasing in number and becoming more visible to society, was a period of rapid transformation in the country. The economy was flourishing, anti-mafia movements seemed to be more successful than ever before, and *Tangentopoli*—a neologism, translated as "Bribegate" by the Anglophone media—appeared to be finally putting an end to corruption. Immigration, among other things, was a motor of change. It was both a cause and an effect of a new economic status. However, it was kept invisible and silent for years mainly by remaining an illegal phenomenon. The fact that "immigrants" were individuals with an autonomous power of expression, and the right to exercise it, seemed to be ignored. The narration of immigration, when it began to be articulated, was an exclusive prerogative of legislators and the media.

This was true until 1989, when a young South African, Jerry Masslo, was murdered by a group of thugs in Villa Literno, an agricultural town not far from Naples, in the Campania region, where he worked as a tomato picker. In the predominantly rural south, immigrants have been primarily employed in farms and greenhouses. The assassination of Jerry Masslo, who had fled the apartheid regime of South Africa for democratic Italy only to encounter a racially motivated death, made the headlines and stirred public opinion. Above all, it changed the narration of the Italian immigration, opening it up to different voices. Immigrants began to speak up, especially those coming from Africa like Masslo. The first major law legalizing the status of the many "strangers" residing in Italy was hastily promulgated in 1990. Granting *in situ* individuals (those who had entered the country prior to December 1989) a *permesso di soggiorno* (literally, a permit to stay), the Martelli Law, as is commonly called after the name of its proponent, was in fact an amnesty.[10] A major step in the regularization of immigrant flows and living conditions was later provided by the Turco-Napolitano Law, in 1998, the first that tried to address systematically the issue of immigration to Italy.[11] A turning point—considered by many, especially by "immigrants," a drawback—in this kind of legislation was the Bossi-Fini Law (2002), which has made fingerprinting compulsory for every non-Italian residing in Italy.[12] In August 2006, in a new political climate, Interior Minister Giuliano Amato's bill proposing that citizenship be granted to those who have been legally resident in Italy for at least five years—not ten as is the case at present—was approved by the government. Amato also proposed a long-term plan aimed at reconsidering other citizenship laws, including one that introduced the principle of *ius soli* (birthright citizenship), which would grant a right to Italian citizenship to all children born in Italy. However, when in April 2008 Italy's sixty-second government—and Silvio Berlusconi's third—was formed, the bill had not yet passed, and soon thereafter new Interior Minister Roberto Maroni introduced additional punitive measures against immigrants.

From Africa: The Birth of an Italian Multicultural Literature

In 1990, when for the first time foreigners were allowed to come out of illegality, Senegalese-born Pap Khouma, Moroccan-born Mohammed Bouchane, and Tunisian-born Salah Methnani published autobiographical fictions in which they recounted their experiences as African immigrants in Italy. As Khouma explained, "One can consider 1990 the year one of African legal immigration to Italy" (Khouma in Parati 1995, 116).

Methnani's novel, *Immigrato* (Immigrant), written in first person but coauthored by writer Mario Fortunato, narrates the experience of a young Tunisian who travels Italy from South to North, finding out that the country of his dreams more often than not is that of his nightmares. Bouchane's *Chiamatemi Alì* (Call me Ali), edited by Carla De Girolamo and Daniele Miccione, is a first-person narrative about a young Moroccan man who, after joining a group of migrant laborers, decides to change his name—Abdullah—to Alì, so that Italians can pronounce it without difficulty while he can retain his Muslim identity. Khouma's *Io, venditore di elefanti* (I, the elephant seller), also written in first person in collaboration with journalist Oreste Pivetta, tells the story of a Senegalese street vendor who, after having briefly resided in France, tries to make a life in Italy, where his expectations are met and proven wrong at one and the same time. Among these three book-length narratives, the latter has perhaps been the most successful: a best seller since its publication, it has been used as a textbook in many high schools nationwide and is now its eighth reprinting.[13]

It is worth noting that all three texts contain references to the 1986 laws. Moreover, one might argue that the narratives published by Khouma, Bouchane, and Methnani in 1990 indirectly responded to the Martelli Law promulgated the same year. This law was what in Italian legal jargon is referred to as a *sanatoria*—an amnesty, in this particular case aiming not only to regularize the position of the considerable number of clandestine immigrants but also possibly to prevent further illegal entry into the country. The word *sanatoria* derives from the verb *sanare,* meaning "to heal," to restore one's health. Graziella Parati notes the negative connotations of this metaphor: this terminology, borrowed from the rhetoric of sickness, assumes that becoming a nation of immigration involves a contamination of the body of the country, which in this legal text is narrated as diseased (Parati 1997a, 119). Parati suggests that the malady, according to the legislation, should be cured and further contagion prevented. Yet, she concludes, in "narrating the multiracial nation through the legal text, Italy has attempted, and failed, to 'practice safe text'" (1997a, 119). Methnani, Bouchane, and Khouma offer their interpretation of the aching Italian sociopolitical, legal, and narrative body in their works. Claiming for themselves the right to speak with their own voices, to tell their stories from their own standpoints, and to write the history to which they have been contributing participants, these writers re-manipulate and revolt against the narratives created on and about them. With the force of their own creative imaginations, they portray their own experiences as African migrants to Italy, thereby appropriating the reins of the nation's discourse on immigration. From narrative objects, they have made themselves narrative subjects. Asked what he intended to demonstrate with his book, Khouma answered, "I did not start writing because I wanted to demonstrate something. What I wanted to do was take the floor. Because Italians were talking about us, but they were asking questions and answering them, all by themselves. That's why we took the floor: to interrupt their monologue and establish a dialogue. This was the goal of my book" (Khouma in Parati 1995, 115–16; my translation).[14]

The fact that the first extended Italian immigrant narratives are all written by Africans, who recount, through the prism of fiction, their personal experiences, is worth particular attention. Recently, millions of Africans have settled all over Europe, not only in the former colonial nations, fleeing civil wars, famine, and poverty. Italy, perhaps largely thanks to its geographic position, has been a prime destination, in the beginning especially for North Africans but soon also for those from the sub-Saharan regions. In the 1990s, in particular, migration from Africa was far larger than that from other continents.[15] Together with Spain, Italy is the European country with the highest number of migrants from Africa, most entering the country illegally and becoming "regularized" only later (Karlsson 2005). Despite what is advocated by the recent, xenophobic, myopic discourses on the "defense of the West" by the former president of the Italian senate, Marcello Pera (2005), and, even more recently, by former prime minister Silvio Berlusconi—who claims to be in favor of economic migration but says, "although the Left envisions a pluri ethnic, pluri cultural country, Italy must *remain* Catholic and *belong* to Italians" (2006; my italics)—the nation is heading rapidly towards a multicultural future where borders and ethnicities will increasingly be crossed, and where Africa will be present more than ever before. Khouma, Methnani, and Bouchane are among those African diasporic writers who have contributed to telling the story—and the history—of their people's recent migrations to Europe, as well as of Italy's changing social landscape and cultural texture. As writers, they belong to a plurality of traditions: they are part, and constitute a turning point, of the Italian literary tradition, first and foremost because they write in Italian; they participate in and expand the literary traditions of their native countries and mother tongues, which are often more than one and are embedded in their Italian texts; they contribute to the development of a transnational literature of migration; and they are a new addition to the literature of the African diaspora, to which they contribute with their African Italian voices and offer specific, lesser known perspectives on contemporary Black Europe.

The example set by Khouma, Bouchane, and Methnani marked the beginning of a trend in Italian letters that has been flourishing ever since.[16] Their texts were soon followed by others, different in form, genre, linguistic choice, style, and perspective, but sharing the same intent: narrating the experience of African migration to Italy, writing back, as it were, to the nation's dominant discourse about it, or, as Parati phrases it, "talking back in a destination culture" (2005). Among these, Saidou Moussa Ba's *La promessa di Hamadi* (Hamadi's promise), which chronicles the life of two Senegalese brothers in Italy, was published in 1991; in 1992, Mohsen Melliti's novel *Pantanella, canto lungo la strada* (Pantanella, a song along the road), about an abandoned pasta factory in Rome in which a heterogeneous group of immigrants settles but is eventually forced by police to leave; in 1993, *Volevo diventare bianca* (I wanted to become white), one of the first extended narratives by an African Italian woman, Nassera Chohra, born in France of Algerian parents, who recounts in this loosely autobiographical text the various stages of her journey through Europe as a black woman; and in 1994, Fernanda Farias de Albuquerque's *Princesa* (Princess), the autobiographical story of a Brazilian transvestite who works the streets in Italy. The list becomes richer as years go by.

As is clear even in some of the above titles—*I, the elephant seller; I wanted to become white*—many of the earliest narratives by African Italian writers use a first-person narrator and protagonist. The autobiographical element has been essential to the development of the African Italian literature of migration. However, although several of the earliest works are written in the first person, they are the product of collaboration between the migrant authors and native Italian writers—journalists, authors, editors, transcribers, interviewers, and translators. The controversial question of authorship has been crucial to the birth of every ethnic literary tradition, especially to much literature from the African diaspora. In particular, as Alessandro Portelli remarks, "The complex structure of the authorial role is one of the most significant analogies between Afro-Italian and Afro-American literary productions, although authorial collaboration is stated much more explicitly in the former than in the latter" (Portelli 2004). In the earliest African American texts, Portelli continues, "The names of the white editors appeared only in the paratextual materials, with the exclusive scope of authenticating the narrative. So the Black protagonist's discourse was kept separate from that of the white sponsor, in a pretense of authenticity." On the contrary, in the recent African Italian texts, collaboration is made explicit, becoming visible even on the cover, where multiple names appear, "with the intent of being both a procedure of authentication and a mechanism of composition of the text as a dialogic discourse" (Portelli 2004). However, Portelli concludes, these contemporary African Italian "migrant writers share with their African American forefathers a similar uncertainty towards their co-authors" (2004).

The literary collaboration between an African migrant and a native Italian fictionalizes and symbolizes the actual encounter between Africa and Italy, between the host society and the newcomers. In much the same way as social encounters, these artistic experiences have been extremely positive at times, laying the bases for professional relationships and personal friendships, while in other instances they have proven to be problematic and conflictual. For instance, whereas Nassera Chohra lamented that her editor pressed her to reforge her narrative materials, Saidou Moussa Ba, who wrote both *La promessa di Hamadi* and *La memoria di A.* (A.'s memory) with the collaboration of Micheletti, remarked, "Our books assume political meaning, because the immigrant and the native worked together, tried together. Therefore, these are books of encounter, dialogue, and culture" (quoted in Colace 1995, 87B).

Monuments or Documents? The Risk of Marginalization

Collaborative authorship, the autobiographical theme, the sociopolitical subject, and the plainspoken style and often explicit language shared by these books determined that many readers—including literary critics and writers—regarded these narratives as "pre-literary experiences with mere sociological value" (Fortunato in Polveroni 1995). My argument is that in order to fully appreciate the importance of these recent works, their profound anthropological, sociological, and historical implications, they should be read in the first place as conscious, individual pieces of literature, without thereby denying their valuable social testimony. These African migrant texts are literary pieces, written in Italian, produced by, and within, a society—the Italian, first of all, but also the European—in a process of rapid transformation. Reading these texts as mere "documents" rather than as "monuments" hides an otherwise clear attempt of marginalization.[17] In the introduction to Tahar Ben Jelloun's collection of Italian stories *Dove lo stato non c'è* (State of absence)—a text that challenges national boundaries from multiple perspectives and occupies a special place in the contemporary African European literary production—Volterrani claims, "In this book, we recognized the fundamental status and essential function of literature, which is to create fiction with the materials of reality" (1991, vi). Far from being an element of disruption, or of dishonoring the composite Italian literary tradition, the African migrants' works add to it and offer alternative models and modes to its canon.

This point can be easily proven by looking more closely at Khouma's *Io, venditore di elefanti* as an example. The metaphoric quality of the title is made explicit in the first of the book's thirty-one chapters, "Vendere" (Selling). After an apology for the importance of resistance in order to survive street life, the first-person narrator clarifies that, however, "selling is not only a question of resistance. . . . You will understand what I mean, if you follow me while I tell my story. You will see that selling elephants, framed butterflies, or bone vultures is an *art*" (Khouma 1990, 12; my emphasis). The elephant in the title is first of all an artifact—one that comes from a region, West Africa, that boasts a major tradition in arts and crafts, especially sculpture. But in the Italian imagery the elephant also represents, and is a metaphor for, an entire continent: Africa. If selling in general requires conviction and endurance, selling artifacts in particular necessitates a special kind of competence in that it demands aesthetic skills. The elephant seller of the title is not only a migrant turned illegal merchant; he is also, and especially, an *African* and an *artist*. More specifically, he is primarily a storyteller in the tradition of his people, the Wolof, who have a saying which he reports in the conclusion of his narrative: "As we say in my country, if you can tell a story, it means it brought you good luck" (Khouma 1990, 143). The protagonist/narrator of *Io, venditore di elefanti* can tell his story because he has had the good fortune to survive it. Eventually, he can look back and recount it—in Italian, the chosen language of *invention*. "After some time and a number of adventures, I arrived in Milan, where I have been an *inventor*, because I was the first to put up mini-markets in the subway stations, together with three friends. . . . By *selling*, I have also learned *Italian*. Some people make an effort to change their job, hoping to live an easier life, to find a home, to put back together a family. And that is fine. But selling is a great trade. There is no reason to be ashamed of it" (Khouma 1990, 13; my emphasis). Art in this text—be it elephant selling or storytelling—constitutes the main form of resistance. Its possibilities of reinvention assure survival. The elephant seller's story offers a counternarrative to that proposed by the legal narration of immigration and provides the possibility of a happy ending. It makes mediation possible and a dialogue plausible.

The African Italian literature of migration is the result of individual and social "acts of mediation" through various cultural, national, and linguistic planes (Parati 1997b, 174). These acts of mediation, which are also ultimately acts of translation from one culture into another, imply inclusion and connection among people and across a plurality of spaces and languages, which they open and connect in an effort to establish a dialogue. Much of the postcolonial literary jargon, althought it has the merit of challenging the binarism of Western discourse and reverting relationships of power, does not seem particularly relevant to these texts and their protagonists, eliciting its reconsideration from new perspectives. Upon being asked whether he felt that he occupied "spaces in-between cultures and literatures," Moussa Ba explained, "First of all, I consider myself a man who has had the chance to transmit something. Then, I want to struggle to conquer *one* space in this world. But there are still obstacles to overcome. There are walls impeding the dialogue among subjects of different cultures. The common goal is speaking with one another without frontiers" (Moussa Ba in Parati 1995, 106; my italics). To the same question, Khouma replied, "I have never thought about it in this way. First of all, I am an African. I am more African than Senegalese. . . . I am not afraid of confronting myself with other cultures. If one is open-minded, one can give and take. In the process of exchanging cultures, people transform themselves. In Senegal, we live in a multicultural, or rather multi-ethnic society. In Dakar, for example, we speak Wolof, with some French, English, Portuguese, Spanish, and other local languages. If you speak with a man from Dakar who lives in Milan, he will throw in Italian too" (Khouma in Parati 1995, 118).

From Twoness to Plurality

The risk of marginalizing literary production deriving from the contact of two or more worlds is not new. In his interesting comparison between the beginnings of an emerging African Italian literary tradition and African American literature, Portelli exhorts Italians to be less myopic than Americans were in appreciating from the start their ethnic literature. He wonders, "It took us two centuries to recognize that Phillis Wheatley, the first African-American woman poet, was an artist and not a freak. Are we supposed to wait another two hundred years before acknowledging the embedded difference peculiar to the figures and creative processes of the Italian literature of migration?" (Portelli 2004).

In an analysis of some African Italian texts, Portelli remarks that, although the experience of slavery is obviously altogether different from that of migration, "twoness"—a concept that he borrows from W.E.B. Du Bois—constitutes the central organizing textual principle in both literary traditions. Twoness, Du Bois declared in 1903, is "double consciousness, this sense of always looking at one's self through the eyes of others, of measuring one's soul by the tape of a world that looks on in amused contempt and pity." The history of the African American people, Du Bois explains, is based on this strife (Du Bois 1903, 5).

My argument is that the metaphor of twoness, masterfully used by Du Bois at the dawn of the twentieth century to describe a very specific historical context, can be fragmented and amplified into one of plurality at the onset of the millennium, when concepts such as migration, multiculturalism, transnationalism, and globalization have become so pivotal not only to the literary but also to the historic and economic discourses of many traditions, challenging the conventional philosophical relationships self/other, host/guest, native/stranger, which now call for a reconsideration from a post-postmodern, global perspective. If at the core of American epics is a twoness primarily founded on the contrast black versus white, mirroring the process of essential racialization that was fundamental to the construction of an American national identity, then plurality constitutes the organizing textual principle, as well as one of the privileged themes, of the contemporary Italian literature of migration whether it is written by authors coming from Africa or the diaspora. In their own ways, the Italian migrant artists are exploring new ways of expressing their experience of plurality by inverting, revising, revaluing, and eventually expanding not only cultural binary oppositions but the ideologies that propose them. Khouma says, "I could have introduced the immigrant in a negative light, or vice versa; I could have said nice things about Italians, or I could have said nasty things about them. What I did, instead, was gather actual facts and let readers judge for themselves" (Khouma in Parati 1995, 115).

The poem "Prigione" (Prison), written by the Cameroonian Italian poet Ndjock Ngana, also known by the Italian name of Teodoro, clearly illustrates how plurality can become an organizing textual principle. This poem, which has become a sort of a manifesto of the Italian literature of migration, is included in the collection *ÑindôNero* (1994), where it appears, like the other pieces in the book, *en-face* in Baasa and Italian. Significantly, the title is made up of the words that mean "black" in each language, retaining an original African identity together with the possibility of translating it into different cultures and languages. Beside its Italian side, I here propose a third version of the poem—my English translation—confident that I will remain faithful to its spirit.

Vivere	Living
Amare	Loving
Conoscere	Knowing
Avere	Having
una sola cosa	one thing only
è prigione.	is prison.
Vivere una sola vita,	Living only one life,
in una sola città,	in one town only,
in un solo paese,	one country only,
in un solo universo,	one universe only,
vivere in un solo mondo	living only in one world
è prigione.	is prison.

Amare un solo amico,	Loving only one friend,
un solo padre,	one father only,
una sola madre,	one mother only,
una sola famiglia,	one family only,
amare una sola persona	loving only one person
è prigione.	is prison.
Conoscere una sola lingua,	Knowing only one language,
un solo lavoro,	one craft only,
un solo costume,	one custom only,
una sola civiltà,	one civilization only,
conoscere una sola logica	knowing only one logic
è prigione.	is prison.
Avere un solo corpo,	Having only one body,
un solo pensiero,	one thought only,
una sola conoscenza,	one knowledge only,
una sola essenza,	one essence only,
avere un solo essere	having only one being,
è prigione.	is prison.

One-ness, in Ngana/Teodoro's poem, is prison. Only plurality—of voices, places, bodies, thoughts—would then be equated with freedom. By celebrating multiplicity in his poem-manifesto, Teodoro/Ngana claims for himself and his peer African migrant artists a broad, unrestricted artistic space that includes and yet transcends the conventional boundaries imposed by national and cultural constructions. More generally, the migrant—at once immigrant and emigrant—can translate his/her African identity—*ñindô* and *nero*—and represent the free person par excellence, because s/he is the one who can freely move across names, spaces, languages, and traditions. Indeed, as one of the most eminent contemporary migrant writers, Salman Rushdie, suggests, in the era of multiculturalism and globalization the migrant becomes the ultimate metaphor for man/woman (Rushdie 1991, 277–78).

Multiplicity is not only the artistic principle of composition but also the central theme of Fernanda Farias de Albuquerque's autobiographical novel *Princesa* (1994), one of the most intense and superb stories of the new Italian literature of migration. *Princesa* is a trans-story. It is the account of how Fernandinho, born in the Brazilian Nordeste, one of the main destinations during the slave trade, becomes first Fernanda, a prostitute transvestite, and then Princesa, not quite a transsexual but no longer exactly a man. Young Princesa undertakes a transatlantic journey to Europe. After spending a short time in Spain, she reaches Italy, where she works the street with the other *viados*—Brazilian transvestite and transsexual streetwalkers—and develops an addiction to heroin, experiencing some of the most violent aspects of illegal immigration. Princesa is eventually arrested and imprisoned in Rebibbia, Rome's all-male jail, where she finds out that she has contracted AIDS.

In *Princesa,* names, sexual identities, bodies, nationalities, and even languages are multiple. While in prison, Farias de Albuquerque—who after a period of probation was deported to Brazil where she died in 2000—told her story in a peculiar mixture of Portuguese and Italian to Giovanni, a Sardinian shepherd jailed for life. Giovanni, whose first language was Sardinian, translated, transcribed, and then passed the story on to Maurizio Jannelli, a former member of the Red Brigades,[18] who ultimately wrote its final draft in Italian—an Italian which, as he states in his introduction to the novel, resulted from the chemistry of the three inmates' native tongues. This plurality of authorial voices, in Jannelli's words, "opened a space for an encounter, and for mutual knowledge" that "proved crucial to resist the devastating act of seclusion" (Jannelli in Farias de Albuquerque 1994). To the imprisonment enforced by the law, the three authors respond with their collective writing. Yet if the narration was made possible by a multiple act of translation, the protagonist experiences multiplicity—of bodies, genders, love affairs, streets, homes, and so on—as fragmentation, alienation, suffering, isolation, and, eventually, imprisonment. While providing textual organization, multiplicity appears as both a condemnation and an act of liberation in *Princesa.* By reading the novel against Teodoro/Ngana's poetry, one can discern two opposite faces of the same metaphor: the prison and the theme of migration. While the poem is an optimistic plea for inclusion and celebrates unity within plurality, *Princesa* denounces the irreconcilable yearning of a fragmented human being and of the pain of becoming in a Black body (in fact Farias de Albuquerque was mestizo).

Plurality is also at the center of Tahar Ben Jelloun's short story "Pietro il matto, Pietro il saggio" (Peter the fool, Peter the wise), included in the Moroccan French author's collection of Italian stories *Dove lo stato non c'è* (1991, 177–89), which also includes the tale "Villa Literno," a fictionalized reconstruction of the murder of South African immigrant Jerry Masslo. The protagonist of "Pietro il matto, Pietro il saggio" is a Sicilian *cantastorie* (literally, a story singer, a traditional popular figure whose function was to travel to towns and villages and spread the news of the day) with a peculiar disability: every time he is interrupted while he is speaking, he begins to stutter. Pietro travels through the squares of Italy to tell people "the truth," because, he suggests, "Truth is not what you see. Truth is not what it is; truth is what you tell. I tell my stories without interruption, so that the truth can come out."[19] Nonetheless, he recommends, "If the truth is stuttering in my mouth, be ready to catch it, and hold on to it; put its pieces together." (Ben Jelloun 1994, 183). Only storytelling, which implies the active collaboration of both authors and audiences, can turn fragments into significant plurality. Only a storyteller can tell the truth in an area—southern Italy—where, as the title suggests, the state, its laws, and institutions are absent.

Plurality entails brotherhood in Ben Jelloun's story. Pietro has two brothers: Cicciu, his Sicilian maestro, who "proclaims the truth while singing" (Ben Jelloun 1994, 185), and Moha, his Moroccan double, a ventriloquist storyteller who can hear, understand, and repeat without hesitation the stories of all those people—women, children, young militants—whose voices history has tried to silence. Sometimes, Pietro imagines that his Moroccan brother—the protagonist of Ben Jelloun's celebrated novel *Moha le Fou, Moha le Sage* (1978), which opens a plurality of resonances and establishes a further dialogue among literary traditions—now lives in Italy; in Sicily, specifically, which is geographically, historically, and culturally the region closest to Africa, where immigration from the Maghreb has reached its peak; more precisely, in Mazara del Vallo, a major fishing port town facing the north coast of Africa, host of the largest Tunisian community in Europe. "Often, I think I may meet [Moha] in Sicily. I can't find him, but I imagine him. Once I even believed that I saw him in Mazara del Vallo's *Kasbah,* in a café full of Tunisian fishermen. They were all there, around him, listening to the latest stories from their country. The Tunisians were watching and listening to him. They were sturdy young men, who had long left their villages, and had recreated their original place in Mazara; but they still lived in sadness" (Ben Jelloun 1994, 184–85).

In Pietro, Moha, and Cicciu, migrant, wise, and mad storytellers of the Mediterranean, one may recognize a glimpse of their ventriloquist creator and his desire—akin to that of his fellow African Italian migrant writers—to break the transnational walls of silence by "telling the truth." The voices of the three storytellers merge into a chorus that can be heard all over the Mediterranean basin, offering itself as an alternative to the media.

It has been said that Ben Jelloun's text should not be considered within the frame of Italian migrant literature by virtue of the fact that its author was an established "francophone" writer well before his Italian book was published. I believe this is a moot point. First of all, a number of immigrant authors had already written in one or more languages before learning Italian; indeed, some were established writers before migrating to Italy.[20] Moreover, by choosing to set *Dove lo stato non c'è* in southern Italy ("Italian Stories" is the explicative subtitle of the book) and to write it directly in Italian, with the assistance of Egi Volterrani—a well-respected journalist who is his Italian translator but appears as a coauthor in this text—Ben Jelloun meant to make a precise statement: he wanted to offer his own vision of Italy, one of the countries that he often visits, for whose press he writes regularly. But the Italy he describes in his stories is often far from flattering. In his view, in spite of its beauty, Italy is a divided nation, corrupt and even diseased. One might hypothesize that this unflattering portrait of Italy may be one reason why *Dove lo stato non c'è* has been received negatively. Perhaps many Italian readers refuse to recognize themselves in Ben Jelloun's portrait, in which he argues that the perennial negligence of the state, and certainly not the relatively recent presence of immigrants, has been the main cause of the socioeconomic and political problems of the south. Whatever the case, by writing his "Italian Stories," Moroccan writer Ben Jelloun has established new connections among literary traditions from both Europe and Africa, further expanding and making ever more visible the "open" space of the African migrants' literature.

Postcolonial Writing: Somali Italian Literature

A form of immigration that Italy has not much discussed, having tried to suppress it by assimilating it to the more general migratory trend involving the nation, is that from its former colonies and occupied territories in Africa. Since the 1960s, relatively large numbers have arrived in Italy from Eritrea, Ethiopia, and Somalia, most fleeing brutal dictatorships or civil wars. In spite of the fact that it has a historical responsibility towards these people, after a first effort in 1981—when a law was promulgated granting them a temporary permit to stay[21]—Italy has offered them no form of asylum, whether legally or in terms of specific social policies. Somalis, for instance, as Nuruddin Farah points out in the Italian section of his book *Yesterday, Tomorrow,* should be considered refugees, having escaped either Siyad Barre's wicked regime or the civil war that followed and precipitated the nation's collapse (Farah 2000). But Italy has never fully enforced the 1951 Geneva Convention on refugees and asylum; the Italian media consider Somalis "immigrants," and the laws treat them as regular "strangers." Nevertheless, there is a large Somali community in Italy. Moreover, there is a group of Somali Italian writers, many of whom are women, who have used their powerful voices to tell their often inconvenient stories.

Among them are Ubax Cristina Ali Farah and Igiaba Scego. Although both were born in Italy in the 1970s, their relationship with Somalia, their personal stories, and their poetics differ from each other. Scego was born in Rome, where she was brought up and still resides, to Somali parents who fled their country after Barre's coup d'état. She has visited Somalia but never lived there for any extended period of time. Ali Farah, born in Verona to an Italian mother and a Somali father, was raised in Mogadishu, where her family moved while she was still a baby, and returned to Italy as a young adult, via Hungary, to escape Somalia's civil war. With Shirin Ramzanali Fazel and Sirad S. Hassan, also from Somalia, Maria Abbebù Viarengo and Gabriella Ghermandi from Ethiopia, Erminia Dell'Oro and Ribka Sibhatu from Eritrea, and several others, these women writers have created what can be considered an Italian postcolonial literary production. Their works are read mainly within the migratory literary context, but a more detailed analysis shows that although they share some of the preoccupations of other migrant writers, they also present some peculiarities that connect them to the specificity of the Italian postcolonial experience and, by extension, to postcolonial texts in other languages. In fact, these texts suggest a reconsideration of the entire concept of postcoloniality by highlighting, first and foremost through their very existence, what Sandra Ponzanesi, in her comparative study on contemporary women's writing from the Indian and African Italian diasporas, describes as one of the most evident paradoxes of the postcolonial condition: the implicit assumption that most postcolonial literature is expressed in English, the global dominant language, which results in a marginalization of all other postcolonial traditions, such as those in Dutch, French, Portuguese, Italian, and other "minor" languages (Ponzanesi 2004). Ponzanesi suggests that the emerging literature by African Italian migrant women offers itself as a unique, largely unknown site to explore the contradictions and "dissymmetrical relationships" that inform postcolonialism, besides contributing to the revival of "an obscure chapter of Italian history: that of colonialism" (Ponzanesi 2004, xiv). The very existence of this literature prevents further reproduction of homogenizing and totalitarian theoretical discourses, on the contrary favoring the historical, political, and linguistic complexity of the postcolonial condition by bringing "to the fore a set of asymmetric relationships in which language, hegemony, and diaspora play a crucial role" (Ponzanesi 2004, 3).

One of the aspects that set the African Italian postcolonial texts as distinctive within the frame of a general migratory context is their use of language. For most, if not all, of these writers, Italian is a mother tongue—usually not the only one, but one nonetheless. In contrast to the Italian migrant writers' earliest works, the more recent works are written without the support of a native speaker—although now most authors have given up coauthorship and write their texts autonomously. As a consequence, the result is often more experimental. A specific example is, for instance, some Somali terms that are borrowings or calques from the Italian that are discernible in many of Ali Farah's narratives and poems, such as those in the short story "Madre piccola" (Little Mother),[22] a poetic reflection of the Somali diaspora in Europe from an all-female perspective: *farmascio* (from the Italian *farmacia,* pharmacy), *restauranti* (from Italian *ristorante,* restaurant), *olio olivo* (from Italian *olio d'oliva,* olive oil), and *guersce* (from Italian *guercio,* blind in one eye).[23] But what all these texts have primarily in common is an artistic agenda. They portray a nation where Africa and Italy's colonial past and postcolonial present are central, proposing a dialogue that challenges those who are partial to monologue, historical revisionism, and persevere in believing in a monolithic national identity. The protagonists of these texts, as disparate as they are, all show major concern in the construction of an individual identity that takes into consideration the totality of their life's experience.

It is not unusual for these writers to shape the form of the monologue to their own ends. Ali Farah's short story "Madre piccola" was conceived as a monologue and has been more than once performed as such by its author. Scego wrote the humorous short story "Salsicce" as an interior monologue in the aftermath of the promulgation of the Bossi-Fini Law. The story tells in first person of a fictional, young Somali Italian woman from Rome who, in spite of her Muslim religion and the mid-August heat in the city, goes to the closest butcher and buys "a large quantity of sausages" (Scego 2005, 214). The story is built on the suspense of whether the protagonist/narrator will eventually eat these sausages and whether eating them can help her feel more Italian. Feeling threatened by the new law, the protagonist believes that she must find new ways to assert her Italian self, which in fact she had not doubted until that point but rather negotiated with her Somali identity. She makes this point clear:

> My worries all began with the announcement of the Bossi-Fini Law. "All non-ECC immigrants who wish to renew their permits must be fingerprinted as a preventive measure." Where did I stand in all this? Would I be considered a non-ECC immigrant and therefore a potential criminal, to be fingerprinted by the government to prevent a crime that had not yet been committed (but which they supposed that I would sooner or later commit)? Or would I be considered a revered, cosseted Italian given the benefit of the doubt by the government even if it showed that I had a long police record?
>
> Italy or Somalia?
>
> Doubt.
>
> Fingerprints or no fingerprints?
>
> Horrendous doubt.
>
> My beautiful passport was burgundy red and it proclaimed to all intents and purposes my Italian nationality, but did that passport speak the truth? Deep down was I truly Italian? Or was I supposed to be fingerprinted like so many others? (Scego 2005, 216; translation by Bellesia and Poletto)

The protagonist compiles an exhilarating list itemizing the moments when she feels Somali and when Italian (Scego 2005, 219–20). But she is not able to solve the puzzle of her double sense of national belonging. A further dimension adds to her already composite identity: the awareness of being Black and therefore connected to other diasporic Africans worldwide. Plurality is her way of living and feeling; it is part of her daily life. She is reading the newspaper when she says, "I go on reading and what do my eyes see? A short article, 'African-American community in uproar over beating of Black youth by white policemen.' I am fed up with news like this! Why the heck are they always beating us up? And besides, this is not helping me forget about the sausages! And most of all it isn't helping me forget about the fingerprinting!" (Scego 2005, 222).

However, as her skin color constantly reminds her and everyone else of her Africanness, the protagonist's main concern in this story is to affirm her Italianness as well, as a constitutive and non-eliminable part of her multifaceted individuality. The all-Italian *concorso*—a state contest for a job in the civil service—for which she has sat and whose results she is still awaiting—which constitutes the other thread of the narrative—seems to serve this purpose. When the protagonist finally tries to eat the sausages, she vomits on them and throws them into the garbage—and then she receives a phone call from a friend announcing that she has indeed passed the exam and will be given the position she applied for. Obtaining this unexpected state job—the reasons she considers her chances slim are sarcastically outlined, providing a bittersweet social commentary (Scego 2005, 218)—helps her accept her Italianness as part of her complex identity. If earlier she complained about others' desire to see her divided—"I had never 'fractioned' myself before, and besides in school I always hated fractions. They were unpleasant and inconclusive (at least for yours truly)" (Scego 2005, 219)—after the good news concerning the *concorso,* she admits to "starting to like fractions" (Scego 2005, 225). Tension is released when she concludes, "I roll up my sleeves. I must clean up the vomit in the kitchen" (Scego 2005, 225). The protagonist tidies up her home, enjoying its reestablished, albeit transformed, order.

Final Considerations

As noted at the beginning of this study, Italianness is the result of a long, complex, and fertile syncretistic process, to which Africa has offered its contribution in the past as well as in the present with the current phenomenon of mass migration. The emerging corpus of African Italian literature which I have presented inscribes Italy in the global mapping of the African diaspora while recounting how contemporary Italy is changing, how it is rewriting its national identity, and how it is contributing to a better understanding of the Black diaspora in Europe and elsewhere.

Notes

I wish to thank the John D. and Catherine T. MacArthur Foundation and the Italian Academy for Advanced Studies in America at Columbia University for having supported this research. I also wish to thank the directors and the first-year fellows of the UCLA Mellon Postdoctoral Program in the Humanities "Cultures in Transnational Perspective" for having provided precious feedback to an earlier version of this essay.

1. *Faccetta nera* (literally, "little black face") is the title of a fascist song whose lyrics were written by Giuseppe Micheli in 1935, referring to an episode during the war between Italy and Ethiopia (1935–1936). The occasion for the song was the discovery and adoption by the Italian troops—Mussolini's "black shirts"—of a young Ethiopian girl whose mother had just been killed, to whom "freedom" (*libertà*) and "hope" (*aspetta e spera,* "wait and hope," is the imperative invocation of the refrain) are promised, mainly

in the form of "other laws" (*un'altra legge*) and "an another king" (*un altro re*). One of the best-known songs of the fascist era, *Faccetta nera* has marked Italy's collective imagery (see Pinkus, *Bodily Regimes,* 56–58), and its title and refrain still resonate even among the youngest generations.

2. The recent, renovated interest in Italy's colonial past in East Africa by a number of scholars from Italy and abroad seems to prove this statement. Among the most recent publications, the following have particularly informed my work: Calchi Novati (1994; 1999); Labanca (2002); Palumbo (2003); Ben-Ghiat and Fuller (2005); Andall and Duncan (2005); Triulzi (2006); and, above all, Del Boca (1999; 2002; 2005).

3. According to the estimates of the Italian National Institute of Statistics (ISTAT), the population of Italy, as of July 2008, is well over 59 million people, while Italians and the people of Italian descent living in diaspora are estimated to be around 62,000 (see Italian National Institute of Statistics, http://demo.istat.it/index_e.html, last accessed January 29, 2009).

4. The 2008 report from ISTAT (Italian National Institute of Statistics) states that, as of January 2008, there are 3,432,651 foreigners resident in Italy, 1,701,817 men and 1,730,834 women (see http://www.istat.it/popolazione/stranieri/, last accessed January 29, 2009). This census does not take into consideration nonresident seasonal workers or illegal immigrants. The most reliable dossier on the state of immigration to Italy is provided yearly by Caritas. The data in this paper refer to Caritas/Migrantes 2008. Reliable data are also provided by ISMU (Initiatives and Studies on Multiethnicity Foundation, http://www.ismu.org, last accessed January 29, 2009).

5. During the past few years, many studies have been conducted on the causes, effects, and dynamics of immigration both in Italy and in the rest of Europe. The following have been particularly relevant to the development of my discourse: Calavita 1994; Bolaffi 1996; Papademetriou 1996; Papademetriou and Hamilton 1996; Bonifazi 1998; Sassen 1999; Dal Lago 1999; Pugliese 2002; Macioti and Pugliese 2003; Corneli 2005; and Turco 2005.

6. The Global Commission on International Migration was launched by the United Nations secretary-general and a number of governments on Dec. 9, 2003, in Geneva, Switzerland, and closed on Dec. 31, 2005. Cochaired by Jan O. Karlsson and Mamphela Ramphele, it was composed of nineteen members from various regions of the world and was given the mandate to formulate a coherent, comprehensive, and global response to the issue of international migration. The final report is available at http://www.gcim.org/en/finalreport.html, last accessed May 16, 2008.

7. This expression is used as a noun, hypothetically deriving from a corruption of the French *vous* (second person plural pronoun, also used for the courtesy form) and the Italian *comprare* (to buy), referring to the line with which foreign street vendors, mainly francophone Senegalese, would call for the attention of eventual clients; by extension, the epithet refers to every immigrant, independent of their nationality or job.

8. A dictionary of terms concerning the Italian lexicon of immigration is Bolaffi, Gindro, and Tentori 1998.

9. Law n. 943, Dec. 30, 1986.

10. Law n. 39, Feb. 28, 1990, proposed by Claudio Martelli, a former member of the now defunct PSI (Italian Socialist Party).

11. Law n. 286 (1), July 25, 1998, proposed by Livia Turco and Giorgio Napoletano, both from the former PCI (Italian Communist Party), now DS (Democrats of the Left). Napoletano, who was then minister of the interior, became the president of the Italian republic in 2006.

12. Law n. 189, July 30, 2002, proposed by Umberto Bossi (founder of the Northern League) and Gianfranco Fini (of AN, National Alliance, Italy's principal right-wing party).

13. Khouma's latest novel, *Nonno Dio e gli spiriti danzanti* (Grandfather God and the Dancing Spirits), was published in 2005.

14. All translations from Italian in this chapter are mine, unless otherwise noted.

15. See the data provided by ISMU (Initiatives and Studies on Multiethnicity Foundation, http://www.ismu.org) and by the yearly Caritas dossiers.

16. Graziella Parati and Armando Gnisci have been the two pioneering scholars of Italian migrant literature, which they have analyzed following different approaches. For a list of their most representative titles in this field, see "References" below.

17. My perplexity concerning the dichotomy monuments vs. documents is explained in Esposito 2006, 303.

18. The Red Brigades (*Brigate Rosse* in Italian) were a militant left-wing terrorist organization active in Italy in the 1970s that gained notoriety for kidnappings, murders, and sabotage. Their self-proclaimed aim was to undermine the Italian state through armed struggle and pave the way for a Marxist upheaval led by a revolutionary proletariat.

19. The translation of this and the following passages from Ben Jelloun's *Pietro il Matto, Pietro il saggio* is mine. However, the book containing the short story "Dove lo Stato non c'è" is the title of the entire book, which has been translated into English by James Kirkup with the title "State of Absence" (London: Quartet 1994).

20. One of the most notable examples is provided by Gëzim Hajdari, a respected Albanian poet (winner, among other prizes, of the Montale Prize in 1997) who moved to Italy in 1992 and who writes in both Italian and Albanian.

21. Law n. 763, Dec. 26, 1981.

22. Cristina Ali Farah is also the author of a novel entitled *Madre Piccola* (2007), loosely based on the short story with the same title.

23. For a reflection on Ubax Cristina Ali Farah's poetics, see Di Maio 2006.

References

Ali Farah, C. *Madre piccola*. Milan: Frassinelli, 2007.

Ali Farah, U. C. "Madre piccola." In *Lingua madre Duemilasei: Racconti di donne straniere in Italia* (Mother Tongue 2006: Short Stories by Foreign Women in Italy). Turin: Seb27. (English translation by Giovanna Bellesia and Victoria Offredi Poletto, "Little Mother.") In T. Pandiri, *Metamorphoses*, 281–85.

Allen, B., and M. Russo, eds. *Revisioning Italy: National Identity and Global Culture*. Minneapolis: University of Minnesota Press, 1997.

Andall, J., and D. Duncan, eds. *Italian Colonialism: Legacy and Memory*. Oxford: Peter Lang, 2005.

Bellucci, S., and S. Matteo, eds. *Africa Italia: Due continenti si avvicinano*. Santarcangelo di Romagna: Fara, 1999.

Ben-Ghiat, R., and M. Fuller, eds. *Italian Colonialism.* New York: Palgrave Macmillan, 2005.

Ben Jelloun, T. *Moha le Fou, Moha le Sage.* Paris: Éditions du Seuil, 1978.

Ben Jelloun, T., ed. (Preface by E. Volterrani). *Dove lo Stato non c'è. Racconti italiani.* Turin: Einaudi, 1991.

Berlusconi, S. Opening Speech: Meeting dell'amicizia di Comunione e Liberazione. Rimini, Italy, 21 August 2006.

Bolaffi, G. *Una Politica per gli Immigrati.* Bologna: Il Mulino, 1996.

Bolaffi, G., S. Gindro, and T. Tentori, eds. *Dizionario della diversità.* Florence: Liberal Libri, 1998.

Bonifazi, C. *L'Immigrazione Straniera in Italia.* Bologna: Il Mulino, 1998.

Bouchane, M., with C. De Girolamo and D. Miccione. *Chiamatemi Alì.* Milan: Leonardo, 1990.

Brackett, J. K. "Race and Rulership: Alessandro de' Medici, First Medici Duke in Florence, 1529–1537." In T. F. Earle. and K.J.P. Lowe, *Black Africans in Renaissance Europe.*

Brinker-Gabler, G., and S. Smith, eds. *Writing New Identities: Gender, Nation and Immigration in Contemporary Europe.* Minneapolis: University of Minnesota Press, 1997.

Calavita, K. "Italy and the New Immigration." In W. A. Cornelius, J. F. Hollifield, and P. L. Martin, eds. *Controlling Immigration: A Global Perspective,* 303–29.

Calchi Novati, G. *Il corno d'Africa nella storia e nella politica. Etiopia, Somalia e Eritrea fra nazionalismi, sottosviluppo e guerra.* Turin: SEI, 1994.

———. "L'Italia e il corno d'Africa: l'insostenibile leggerezza di un colonialismo debole." In S. Bellucci and S. Matteo, *Africa Italia,* 1999, 100–116.

Caritas/Migrantes, eds. *Immigrazione. Dossier statistico 2007. XVII Rapporto.*

Chohra, N., with A. Atti Di Sarro. *Volevo Diventare Bianca.* Rome: E/O, 1993.

Colace, G. "Nascita di una scrittura meticcia. Gli immigrati africani in Italia." In *Linea d'Ombra* 13, no. 106 (1995): 87–89.

Corneli, A. *Flussi migratori illegali e ruolo dei paesi di origine e di transito.* Soneria Mannelli: Rubbettino, 2005.

Cornelius, W. A., J. F. Hollifield, and P. L. Martin, eds. *Controlling Immigration: A Global Perspective.* Stanford, Calif.: Stanford University Press, 1994.

Dal Lago, A. *Non-Persone: L'esclusione dei migranti in una società globale.* Milan: Feltrinelli, 1999.

Del Boca, A. *Gli italiani in Africa Orientale,* 2 vols. Milan: Mondadori, 1999.

———. *L' Africa nella coscienza degli italiani. Miti, memorie, errori e sconfitte.* Milan: Mondadori, 2002.

———. *Italiani, brava gente?.* Venice: Neri Pozza, 2005.

Di Maio, A. "A Poetics of Passage: The Prose of Ubax Cristina Ali Farah" (with an interview with the author). In T. Pandiri, *Metamorphoses,* 241–68.

Du Bois, W. E. B. *The Souls of Black Folk.* Chicago: A. C. McClurg, 1903.

Earle, T. F., and K. J. P. Lowe, eds. *Black Africans in Renaissance Europe.* Cambridge: Cambridge University Press, 2005.

Eco, U. "L'Africa e l'Est: migrazione e liberazione." In *L'Espresso,* Apr. 15, 1990.

Esposito, C. "Of Monuments and Documents." In T. Pandiri, *Metamorphoses,* 302–7.

Farah, N. *Yesterday, Tomorrow: Voices from the Somali Diaspora.* New York: Cassell, 2000.

Farias de Albuquerque, F., with Jannelli, M. *Princesa.* Rome: Sensibili alle Foglie, 1994.

Gnisci, A. *Il rovescio del gioco.* Rome: Carucci, 1992.

———. *Creolizzare l'Europa. Letteratura e migrazione.* Rome: Meltemi, 2003.

Gnisci, A., ed. *Nuovo planetario italiano. Geografia e antologia della letteratura della migrazione in Italia e in Europa.* Troina: Città Aperta, 2006.

Gramsci, A. *The Southern Question* (translated by P. Verdicchio). Toronto: Guernica, 2006.

Karlsson, J. "A Global Framework for International Migration." Lecture delivered at the Secretary General's First Annual Global Colloquium of University Presidents, Columbia University, 18 January 2005.

Khouma, P., with Pivetta, O. *Io, Venditore di Elefanti.* Milan: Garzanti, 1990.

Khouma, P. *Nonno Dio e gli spiriti danzanti.* Milan: Baldini Castoldi Dalai, 2005.

Labanca, N. *Oltremare. Storia dell'espansione coloniale italiana.* Bologna: Il Mulino, 2002.

Macioti, M. I., and E. Pugliese. *L'esperienza migratoria. Immigrati e rifugiati in Italia* (The Migratory Experience: Immigrants and Refugees in Italy). Rome-Bari: Laterza, 2003.

Mayer, L. "L'Africa incomincia alle Alpi. Terremoti italiani del passato e previsioni per il futuro." In Bellucci, S. and S. Matteo, *Africa Italia,* 1999, 26–33.

Melliti, M. (transl. by M. Ruocco). *Pantanella: Canto lungo la Strada* (Pantanella: A Song along the Road). Rome: Edizioni Lavoro, 1992.

Methnani, S., with Fortunato, M. *Immigrato.* Rome–Naples: Theoria, 1990.

Moussa Ba, S., with Micheletti, A. *La Memoria di A.* Novara: De Agostini, 1995.

———. *La Promessa di Hamadi.* Novara: De Agostini, 1991.

Ngana, N. (Teodoro). *ÑindôNero.* Rome: Anterem Edizioni Ricerca, 1994.

Palumbo, P., ed. *A Place in the Sun. Africa in Italian Colonial Culture from Post-Unification to the Present.* Berkeley and Los Angeles: University of California Press, 2003.

Pandiri, T., ed. *Metamorphoses.* Special Issue: *Other Italies/Italy's Others* 14, no. 1–2 (Spring-Fall 2006).

Papademetriou, D. G. *Coming Together or Pulling Apart? The European Union's Struggle with Immigration and Asylum.* Washington, D.C.: Carnegie Endowment for International Peace, 1996.

Papademetriou, D. G., and K. A. Hamilton. *Converging Paths to Restriction: French, Italian and British Responses to Immigration.* Washington, D.C.: Carnegie Endowment for International Peace, 1996.

Parati, G. 1997a. "Looking through Non-Western Eyes: Immigrant Women's Narratives in Italian." In G. Brinker-Gabler and S. Smith, *Writing New Identities.*

———. 1997b. "Strangers in Paradise: Foreigners and Shadows in Italian literature." In B. Allen and M. Russo, eds. *Revisioning Italy.*

———. 2005. *Migration Italy. The Art of Talking Back in a Destination Culture.* Toronto: University of Toronto Press.

Parati, G., ed. *Margins at the Centre: African Italian Voices*. Special issue of *Studi d'Africanistica nell'Africa Australe/Italian Studies in Southern Africa* 8, no. 2 (1995).

———. *Mediterranean Crossroads. Migration Literature in Italy*. Madison, N.J.: Fairleigh Dickinson University Press, 1999.

Pera, M. "Democrazia è libertà? Difesa dell'Occidente." Opening Speech, Meeting dell'amicizia di Comunione e Liberazione, Rimini, Italy, Aug. 21, 2005.

Pinkus, K. *Bodily Regimes: Italian Advertising under Fascism*. Minneapolis: University of Minnesota Press, 1995.

Polveroni, A. "L'immigrato racconta in italiano. Intervista con Mario Fortunato." In *L'Unità* (Apr. 27, 1995).

Ponzanesi, S. *Paradoxes of Postcolonial Cultures: Contemporary Women Writers of the Indian and Afro-Italian Diaspora*. Albany: State University of New York Press, 2004.

Portelli, A. "Le origini della letteratura afroitaliana e l'esempio afroamericano." In *El Ghibli. Rivista online di letteratura della migrazione* (http://www.el-ghibli.provincia.bologna.it) 0, no. 3 (2004).

Pugliese, E. *L'Italia tra migrazioni internazionali e migrazioni interne*. Bologna: Il Mulino, 2002.

Richards, C. *The New Italians*. London: Michael Joseph, 1994.

Rushdie, S. *Imaginary Homelands*. London: Granta, 1991.

Sassen, S. *Guests and Aliens*. New York: New Press, 1999.

Scego, I. "Salsicce." In Capitani, F. and E. Coen, eds., *Pecore nere*. Rome-Bari: Laterza. English translation by Giovanna Bellesia and Victoria Offredi Poletto, "Sausages," in *Metamorphoses* 13, no. 2 (2005): 214–25.

Stella, G. A. *L'orda. Quando gli albanesi eravamo noi*. Milan: Rizzoli, 2002.

Triulzi, A. "Displacing the Colonial Event: Hybrid Memories of Postcolonial Italy." In *Interventions: International Journal of Postcolonial Studies* 8, no. 3 (2006): 430–43.

Turco, L., with Tavella, P. *I nuovi italiani. L'immigrazione, i pregiudizi, la convivenza*. Milan: Mondadori, 2005.

Verdicchio, P. *Bound by Distance: Rethinking Nationalism through the Italian Diaspora*. Cranbury, N.J.: Associated University Press, 1997.

8

Talking Race in Color-Blind France: Equality Denied, "Blackness" Reclaimed

FRED CONSTANT

During the last few months, the pace of events in the long-troubled field of ethnic relations in France has been both extraordinary and contradictory. On the one hand, the Paris suburbs in flames, the *banlieues,* moved back to center stage critical issues—such as "race,"[1] "Islam," "integration," "colonial past," "memory of slavery"—in ways that would have been unthinkable scarcely a decade ago. On the other hand, the violence of the social explosion that shook up France's race-neutral model did not lead to significant changes—carving out innovative measures—on the ground. The emphasis on maintaining law and order rather than focusing on underlying problems such as a lack of political representation and economic empowerment postponed badly needed corrective measures. At the same time, there have been some accelerating changes—driven by the pressure of events—both in political rhetoric and at a lower extent in policy choices. Let's mention some recent developments:

In June 2005, Nicolas Sarkozy, then the interior minister and president of UMP,[2] broke one of the last great taboos of French republicanism by calling for a policy of *discrimination positive* (preferential treatment) in favor of minority ethnic groups while Prime Minister Dominique de Villepin publicly rejected his rival's option as incompatible with France's color-blind traditions (de Montvalon 2005).

President Chirac, who took in 2004 a sledgehammer to crack the nut of the Islamic headscarf through a law that many consider to be discriminatory, set up an independent equal opportunity authority, HALDE, while opposing any attempt by his interior minister to change French 1905 law about *laicité.*[3]

Sarkozy stigmatized youngsters of a Parisian suburb by calling them scum as he called for the violent flushing out or purging of the *banlieues.* President

Chirac opposed strongly his minister's statement, advocating once again for equality for all, regardless of ethnic, religious, or social origin.[4]

President Chirac endorsed the passing of a law emphasizing France's colonial legacy in North Africa while taking, a month later, a strong statement in favor of a national day celebrating in France the abolition of slave trade and slavery. The two brought up almost simultaneously the battle over France's colonial past and the memory of slavery.[5]

Civil society gave birth to the first ever Council of Associations of blacks living in France and to never-before-seen initiatives such as *Appel des indigènes de la République, Collectif Devoir de Mémoire,* and *Appel contre les ratonnades Anti-Blancs.*[6] Again, the specter of race haunted the public debate without correcting either the national phobia against anything that smacks of American-style affirmative action or the widespread faith of French elite in the republican mantra of equality.

Does this mean that France's policy decisions are less a response to current events than a consequence of attitudes shaped by past experiences? Or does this suggest that the pressure of events may be strong enough to shake up inherited policy frames?[7] Whatever the right prospect is, it is now necessary to clarify the concept we designate as "race," which has a different use and meaning in the French and the American contexts. While the term "race" is widespread in the latter, it is not so in the former where its conceptual status remains problematic even to Black French people.[8] David Beriss (2000) rightly reported that "culture" has become in France a convenient gloss—a euphemism—for something that looks like race. Contrary to the United States, where race has been located at the center of the political and social organization (Omi and Winant 1994), in France culture has been at the center of the political and social fabric. Here, my argument is twofold. On the one hand, culture in France takes on some characteristics of race. On the other hand, race cannot be treated only as a mere manifestation of culture. As a result, as Fogarty and Osborne put it, "French racial attitudes in general were and remain based on a mixture of biological and cultural factors" (2003, 206).

I would like to engage in a discussion of race in France by breaking from widely held political assumptions in two ways. First, the French race-neutral model has been far more an ideal than an empirical model: color-blind in theory, it has always been race-coded in practice. This major contradiction between principles and reality has unsurprisingly generated the emergence of an Afro-French activism. Second, there has been a reinforcement of the color-blind model at the level of rhetoric while the state, sometimes in contradictory moves, has tolerated a kind of multicultural policy in an attempt to incorporate visible minorities and at the same time maintain social order. Focusing on the Black experience in France, this short essay highlights the national political debate over such critical issues as "Frenchness," identity and difference, belonging, and membership.[9]

Taking Race Seriously: Breaking through Color-Blind Rhetoric

Whatever really happened in the burning *banlieues* in October 2005, it has given the French mass media a rare opportunity to drop partially the taboo on the sensitive subject of race, acknowledging that there is a *question noire* (a Black question) in the country that has always prided itself on being the birthplace of human rights.[10] Here, I will look first at how race happened to be covered in the media and discussed in the political arena. Then, I will attempt to set up a new framework to address properly the issue.

OVERCOMING THE FRENCH PRISM

In the aftermath of the social explosion in the suburbs, race has been openly debated in public circles, television, magazines, newspapers, and radio shows in ways that would never have taken place a couple of years ago. No longer silenced, race came out, making big news in the mass media. The creation of CRAN did help, and France appeared to be suddenly a more race-conscious society than ever before (Wieviorka 2005).

Yet race was addressed through a French prism that made it hard to fully acknowledge the reality in a country that is home to *liberté* and *égalité:* the growing presence of a Black France, separate and unhappy (Richburg 2005). Unsurprisingly, the meaning of the earthshaking events in the *banlieues* remained trapped in the predictable ideological straightjackets of the dominant political views on minorities' incorporation in France. They all share a tendency to reduce race to a manifestation of other supposedly more fundamental social and political relationships such as class and culture. Instead of exploring how groups become racially identified over time and how racial conflicts shape French polity and society, mainstream approaches tend to deny race any explanatory powers, instead acknowledging problems of policy, of social engineering, of state management. The leftists (Hollande 2005) might have put the emphasis on more government programs (housing, schooling, jobs, welfare) while the rightist (Sarkozy 2005) might have sought law and order,[11] calling for a change in the moral behavior of poor Black urban adults and restless youths. In both cases, these views still confine discussion about race in France to the "problems" of making "them" more like "us," seeing Blacks (as well as Arabs, popularly known as *Beurs*) as "problem people" rather than as fellow French citizens (or residents) with problems (West 1994). Both views focus on the "problems" that Black people pose for the white majority rather than consider what this view of Black people reveals about France as a nation (Stovall 2003).

Therefore, the tenants of these widespread viewpoints also reject any attempt to break—even temporarily and partly—from the color-blind model in order to tackle the problems of racial discrimination (Diamond and Magidoff 2005). Such proposals are considered *communautarisme*, which is held to run counter to the French tradition of assimilation (Bleich 2003). At the same time, those who resist any official change of policy—such as Interior Minister Sarkozy, who was the first French politician to promote *discrimination positive*—fail to fulfill the promises of *liberté, égalité, fraternité* to those who are surely more deprived of it among the French citizens. Moreover, the emphasis on law and order prevents them from conceiving *intégration* as a two-way process (Sayad 1999), from acknowledging that the presence and predicaments of black people in France are, to put it in Cornell West's words, "neither additions nor defections from *French* life, but rather constitutive elements of that life" (1994, 6).

Here again emerges the critical question about Frenchness that "implies a perception of race as visual difference from some preconceived notion of who is French" (Beriss 2004, 7). The implication is that only a category of French can define what it means to be French—and the rest must simply fit in or remain never truly French. Does it also suggest that "culture in France has taken on some of the deterministic qualities of race?" (Beriss 2004, 8). These are some of the questions guiding my attempt to carve out a new approach on that old controversy that is urging France to come to terms with itself as an increasingly diverse society.

PROMOTING AN ALTERNATIVE FRAMEWORK

To set up the proper terms for discussing racial issues in France, my argument is threefold. In the first instance, it is necessary to stop viewing black people as a "them" who are to be perpetually "integrated" into France's (white) society and culture. Secondly, it is important to break from the widely held sociological assumption in France that gives class (ascription) primacy over ethnicity (prescription). Thirdly, it is critical to rethink the French model of *intégration* that silences race matters (Calvès 2003; Constant 2004). It is absolutely necessary to stop viewing black people as a "them" who must become "like us." In fact, although most black French people are citizens born in mainland France, blacks of African or Caribbean descent are still referred to as immigrants, as if the status of immigrant were hereditary. How often, for example, are black Frenchmen—along with other members of visible minorities such as French Arabs—asked questions about their color or origins, such as "How long have you been in this country?" Or, in the same vein, "How wonderful your French is: where did you learn our language?"[12] Or, more aggressively, "Why don't you go back home if you are unhappy here?" (Badiou 2005). Even educated people often share this almost unbelievable ignorance about the ongoing anthropological transformation of the population of France. Of many examples, consider this salient one: Hélène Carrère d'Encausse, a distinguished French historian internationally known for a prescient book on the collapse of USSR, and currently *secrétaire perpétuelle de l'Académie Française,* was asked on prime-time television to comment on the October 2005 social explosion in the *banlieues.* She said, "I am not surprised at all: how could young Blacks, coming directly from their African villages, adapt to the French way of life?" (Millot 2005). Somehow, blacks in France do not look "French" to many white nationals; the color of their skin makes them perpetual outsiders in their native country.[13] The average life of white French citizens bears little resemblance to the average life of the *banlieusards,* the Arabs and black children of mostly Muslim immigrants. Therefore, most French politicians, journalists, and average citizens have never really acknowledged that being French is today very different from being white and Catholic (Weil 2005; Keaton 2006).

It is also important to break from the common view held in France that gives ascription (class) primacy over prescription (ethnicity). Faith in the model of assimilation runs so deep that it is frequently held that, similar to previous waves of immigrants, assimilation will also work with the young French Africans and French Arabs "rioting" in the *banlieues.* "We need them to speak French like the French," is often said by politicians, who invariably add, "If they go through the French school system, they'll be fine" (Slama 2005). But the young blacks and Arabs are different in many ways from Portuguese, Italians, or Spanish who came to France in the last century. Their religion—most are Muslim—sets them apart from earlier Christian immigrants. They are in France at a time of high unemployment and economic stagnation, if not recession. Moreover, there is the unacceptable truth of racial discrimination. Their appearance is different. Egalitarian principles are not always enforced when it comes to relations with nonwhite French fellow citizens (Beaud and Noiriel 2004; Keaton 2006). Here, prescription tends to prevail over ascription. Somehow hidden or discreet, the color bar is present not only at the top management of major private companies, but also (un)surprisingly in French high civil service. Of the many instances, consider two of the most obvious cases: (1) nonwhite French graduates from elite universities—*Grandes écoles*—have an average of 25 percent less chance of obtaining a job in the private sector than their white counterparts (Zappi 2004), and (2) there has been no black French ambassador ever appointed anywhere in one of the 156 French embassies around the world. In both cases, the potential applicants speak French "like the French," have gone through the French school system like any other French person and yet, they remain excluded or on the fringes of these social spheres (Bernard 2004).

Finally, engaging in a serious discussion over race invites us to rethink the so-called *modèle français d'intégration.* It is no longer possible to have such a narrow but widely shared sense of the past—a history that has viewed Frenchness strictly in terms of European ancestry. Contrary to the concept of nation that France prides itself on having given birth—emphasizing the nation as a legal, contractual entity, open to anyone ready to embrace its core values and "culture"—it has always carried the same ambivalence between civil and cultural constructs, intertwining race and nation from its inception.

While different from the United States, race has inhered in the creation of a French national identity, in a "France" defined as "white." The perniciousness of the racial bias in the construction of Frenchness is such precisely because it has been rendered invisible or recast as "culture" through the official discourses that constitute France's history (Vergès 2005). But France has been racially diverse since its inception, and this reality is increasingly becoming visible. For that reason, our model of integration must evolve from one that emphasizes assimilation to one that welcomes racial and cultural diversity. It is no longer possible, nor has it ever been tenable, to demand that nonwhite French people born in France fit in a predominantly white society that keeps them outside the mainstream. Inclusion implies a two-way process. If not, it remains a fallacy.

Black Skins, French Voices

Over the last few years, France's slowness to act against color-based racism and to promote ethnic diversity in society at large has made the case for a growing black activism in a supposedly color-blind country.[14] For the first time, people of African or Caribbean descent have been taking up the challenge to invent themselves both as French and Black in postcolonial France. How are we to interpret these recent, almost unbelievable developments? Does it mean that race-neutral France is becoming a race-conscious country? I have two answers. First, I think that there is a close relationship between broken republican promises and the rise of Black activism. Secondly, I argue that the current situation requires less, theoretically, rhetoric of diversity and more practically sound actions.

BROKEN REPUBLICAN PROMISES AND THE RISE OF BLACK ACTIVISM

In Europe, France is probably one of the few countries that has not really come to terms with the fact that its society is becoming more multiracial and multicultural (Constant 2000). To be precise, the French state is clearly ambivalent in dealing with issues of race. At once, the state acknowledges, if not encourages, ethnic-based organizations, while the idea of group rights is alien to French law. Despite the recurrence of *diversité* in political rhetoric, visible minorities are still tragically invisible in practice: on television, in corporate board rooms, in political parties, in academic circles (Constant 2004). France's unique model of inclusion, which stresses the individual over his community or race and considers it unlawful to keep statistics by origin, religion, or ethnicity, is ill-equipped to acknowledge or address racial discrimination, from police harassment to racial bias in jobs, housing, even in leisure activities. In short, racial discrimination is more rampant than commonly acknowledged (CNCDH 2005). France's weak will to live up to its egalitarian principles, when confronted by its visible minorities, resulted in the growth of ethnic activism among nonwhite people. Initially confined to cultural militancy, it rapidly became politicized. If it were possible to identify key dates in the political awakening of Black France, I would suggest the following five:

In 1998, commemoration of the 150th anniversary of the abolition of slavery in the French colonies;
In 2001, passing of the law acknowledging the slave trade and slavery as crimes against humanity by the French Parliament;
In 2002, French presidential elections and first ever participation of a black female candidate (MP Christiane Taubira);
In 2005, public statement on 18 January 2005 by *Les Indigènes de la République,* followed on 23 November by the creation of CRAN, the council of black associations that battle anti-black discrimination;
In 2006, President Chirac's decision on 31 January to commemorate in France's mainland every year the abolition of the slave trade and slavery.

Following the rise in consciousness among French Arabs two decades ago, the growing awareness among Blacks culminated with the 2005 launching of CRAN, which asserts its identity not in national origin or cultural but rather *racial* terms. This apparently surprising event has completed France's range of "ethnic and religious" lobbies that emerged around the contradictions surrounding issues of citizenship, ethnicity, equality, and membership (Geisser 1997; Constant 1998).[15] Citizenship shortcomings and a growing feeling of rejection have led to the emergence of an Afro-French reclamation of the self in a France that is supposed to be race-neutral (Beriss 2004).

In this perspective, what happened recently in the Paris suburbs was neither a "race riot" nor a religious rebellion. Rather, it was the result of core frustrations and grievances accumulated over many years of hardship and neglect. For all its violence, self-destruction, and apparent nihilism, the reaction clearly illustrated the sense of social despair and powerlessness in French society (Beck 2005; Glucksmann 2005). Therefore, attempts to put the emphasis on restoring law and order rather than taking necessary corrective measures missed the mark: a riot is always the language of the unheard (Bernard 2005). It might look racial at the surface; it is not so in substance. In France, reclamation of blackness is proving a more powerful equality-driven force than an ethnic/separatist-oriented movement. However, one cannot claim that there is a complete consensus among black activists concerning the question of race in France (Netter 2006). Recent discussions on strategy emanate from two different camps.[16] On the one hand, there is a small minority of those who believe that unjust discrimination will be more effectively overcome by the provision of *group rights* (in addition to individual rights) attached to the status of citizen. They recommend asserting themselves in terms of a community representing the group's views. On the other hand, there is a large majority of those who are convinced that a group seemingly defined innocuously as "Blacks" in France will be better served by a system of individual rights. They recommend playing down differences.[17] In other words, while those in the first camp demand specific rights for blacks as members of a national minority—one both disadvantaged and discriminated against—those in the second camp refuse to recognize any form of minority rights, preferring instead to promote practices defined in individual terms, that is, independently of whether other members of the groups are or are not involved. Both camps agree that inclusion in the mainstream goes far beyond equal access to rights, individual or not. It requires tackling issues related to the subjective feeling of full membership in society at large.

BEYOND EQUALITY IN THEORY: GRASPING THREE UNDERLYING PROBLEMS IN PRACTICE

In order to avoid a further racial fragmentation, French policy makers must break through the rhetoric of equality in theory toward grasping three interrelated problems in practice: the Frenchness of nonwhite French people, the economic empowerment of non-European minorities, and the political representation of the Afro-French population.

First, let's consider the Frenchness of nonwhite French citizens. Here, we must begin with a frank acknowledgement of the extraordinary diversity of France, which is becoming obviously more multiracial and multicultural. People of Arab and African descent make up more than 10 percent of the population, by most estimates.[18] Despite their numbers, most French—politicians, journalists, and average citizens—have not yet fully acknowledged that they are part of the diverse national community that France has become. France is long overdue in recognizing this diversity, recognizing more precisely its populations of color as unconditional members of French society, history, and culture. Indeed, Frenchness can no longer be defined as white, Catholic, and European since, for some time now, being French has also meant being black, Muslim, and of African descent; the national population's true colors are on vivid display in its urban centers, such as Paris, Lyon, and Marseille. Thus, while color-blind in theory, Frenchness should be color-blind in practice, which, until now, has not been the case officially.

On the question of economic empowerment, French Africans offer another insightful illustration of activism. On the one hand, there has been a political move to increase the struggle against racial discrimination in public and private sectors (Bleich 2003b). On the other hand, there has been the same reluctance in official circles to drop the taboo on the sensitive subject of race in order to achieve political and social incorporation. Here again, the problem is not recognized partly because of France's entrenched model of inclusion that makes it impossible to tell how well represented French Blacks are in business in the absence of racial statistics documenting such representation. Therefore, *status quo ante* prevails over any attempt of change while racial bias increases in job market and in corporate life. Sound measures are needed on the ground that fail to materialize, owing to such contradictions that French authorities have thus far failed to address. Whatever it is called *(traitement préférentiel, discrimination positive, préférence territoriale, action positive),* the outcome should be clear: the French labor force, irrespective of its level, must look like France, and if vigorous actions are not taken, then ethnic fragmentation will unsurprisingly amplify, reinforcing the very entity that France claims it rejects—group-based identity politics and demands for inclusion based upon them.[19]

It is ironic to note that diversity, which is becoming a widespread slogan across the political spectrum, is at once so badly implemented in French politics where it is most evident.[20] Consider that of the 577 members of the National Assembly, the handful of twenty nonwhite faces represent France's overseas territories. Among the 331 members of the Senate, there is not even one nonwhite senator elected in France's mainland; the 14 senators of non-European descent are representatives of *France d'outre mer,* again, its overseas departments. Over the last few years, there have been a couple of ministers of non-European descent out of about thirty-five ministers appointed in government. In political parties, the situation remains the same, that is, with rare exception, not one political figure of non-European descent has become a prominent leader.[21] The left wing and the right wing share the same poor record. They resist anything in practice that would result in the diversity they call for in theory, which sends a clear message about belonging in French society to people of color, especially the most socially excluded. Therefore, young political activists of non-European descent have decided to create their own political clubs, maintaining the practice of race coding.[22] What is to be done? First of all, political parties must acknowledge that there is a problem, and a racial one. According to their ideological positions, they have to admit that the present state of affairs is unacceptable. In this regard, a wonderful initiative from their current leaders would be to commit themselves publicly to take action, in practice not merely in theory.[23] Consequently, they should actively recruit people of color at every level of the hierarchy (from the bottom up to the top positions) and give the promising members prominent places on their electoral lists of candidates vying for political offices in the country. French political parties must look like France. At the moment they do not.

Conclusion

Racial and cultural fragmentation is the price France is paying for its inability or unwillingness to incorporate into its society French Arabs and Afro-French—along with white, working-class, post-Christian French—as it has similarly incorporated so many other groups. The *banlieues* riots of 2005 served as a dramatic reminder for much of the nation of the continuing economic marginality, social decay, and racial stigmatization of the low-income housing districts on the periphery of the capital and other urban centers (that is, Lyon, Marseille, Strasbourg). French authorities must decide now whether France will be a site of opportunity, united in a vision of a just society as a whole, one with a comprehensive definition and protection of individual rights. However, there will be little prospect to realize such a happy state of affairs as long as appropriate measures are neither clearly identified nor taken. The first step is recognizing—in theory and in practice—the Frenchness of nonwhite French people like French white citizens. It is time to drop the taboo on race, color, and complexion that fosters the idea that non-European phenotypes do matter in every day life. Here, sound statements have been largely missing from the national discourse, even from President Chirac's rival Nicolas Sarkozy.

Moreover, it is critical that France ceases to define its Black populations as problems to be managed rather than fellow French citizens with problems to be addressed. It must be remembered that the Paris "riots" were not an intifada but a spectacular demonstration of deprived French kids who wanted to make themselves heard (Dyer 2005). Here, we need a comprehensive equal opportunity plan to raise the standard of living in the suburbs where the old white working class shares the same poor social conditions as French Arabs and Afro-French people.[24] Empowering the deprived segments of the national population is key to the battle for socioeconomic inclusion. However it may be identified, there is a dramatic need to embrace methods that bring more people of color into the mainstream. In the elite schools, corporate boards, entrepreneurial circles, mass media, political parties, high civil service, and government, France's population's true color range should be on full display. As Mitsuye Yamada once phrased it, "To finally recognize our own invisibility is to finally be on the path toward visibility" (1983).

Notes

1. A definition of the concept of "race" in the French context is provided below.

2. *Union pour un Mouvement Populaire (UMP)* is the leading political party in France. Nicolas Sarkozy ran for the presidency in 2007 and took every occasion to challenge

both President Chirac and Prime Minister De Villepin. Since the last general elections, UMP members are 364 out of the 577 members of the National Assembly, 155 out of the 331 senators. There is a lively debate on *discrimination positive,* which is far from being a consensual issue. On December 17, 2008, President Sarkozy gave an important speech at Ecole Polytechnique, one of the finest French Grandes Ecoles, in which he unveiled a set of actions for equal opportunity. If none of these actions are race-based, all are indirect strategies of affirmative action. In early January, 2009, President Sarkozy appointed Yazid Sabeg, a successful French entrepreneur of Algerian descent, as junior minister for "diversité" and equal opportunity.

3. High Authority for the Fight against Discrimination and for Equality *(Haute Autorité de Lutte contre les Discriminations et pour l'Egalité),* HALDE, created in June 2005; statement by President Chirac on the occasion of the setting up of the High Authority for the Fight against Discrimination and for Equality, Paris, June 23, 2005 (Présidence de la République, http://www.elysee.fr/elysee/elysee.fr/francais/interventions/discours_et_declarations/2005/juin/discours_du_president_du_president_de_la_republique_lors_de_l'installation_de_la_haute_autorite_de_lutte_contre_les_discriminations_et_pour_l'egalite). The French tradition of *laicité* rests upon a demarcation between the Church and the State. The 1905 law redefined the realm of the Catholic Church, out of public education and public influence. Public subsidizing of religious institutions is forbidden. Yet the right of everyone to practise their own beliefs is ensured by the law.

4. Sarkozy used the word "racaille," which has become a controversial word in the political arena. Accused of pouring fuel on the flames, Sarkozy responded, "For too long politicians have not used the right words to describe reality" (Dyer 2005). "Purging": Sarkozy used "nettoyage au Kärcher." By such a provocative stand, Sarkozy seeks to appear the toughest on crime and on immigration. He regularly conflates these two issues as if non-European immigrants and their children born in France were "enemies within" France's land of plenty. Statement by President Chirac in the aftermath of the social turmoil in Paris and other big cities' suburbs, Paris, Nov. 14, 2005 (http://www.elysee.fr/elysee/elysee.fr/francais/interventions/discours_et_declarations/2005/novembre/allocution_du_president_de_la_republique_sur_les_violences_urbaines).

5. Under the growing pressure of many lobbies in the French mainland and the overseas territories, President Chirac felt compelled some months later to submit the "problematic" law to the Constitutional Council; keynote address by President Chirac on Jan. 30, 2006 (http://www.elysee.fr/elysee/elysee.fr/francais/interventions/discours_et_declarations/2006/janvier/allocutions_du_president_de_la_republique_lors_de_la_reception_du_comite_pour_la_memoire_de_l'esclavage); Dulucq Zytnicki 2005; Constant 2006, 2007.

6. Conseil Représentatif des Associations Noires (CRAN) was created Nov. 26, 2005; movement was launched on Jan. 16, 2005, by several associations of French Arabs or Afro-French, mostly left leaning. Its core statement denounces France as a colonial and postcolonial state and calls for the decolonization of the French republic; association of activists opposed to the silencing of France's colonial past and struggling against racial discrimination in daily life (Collectif Devoir de mémoire, http://collectifddm.free.fr, last accessed May 16, 2008); in March 2005, some (white) teens demonstrating against reform of the school system were violently attacked and robbed by alleged (black and

Arab) youth gangs coming from the Paris suburbs. In the aftermath, a call to denounce so-called racism against whites was launched and backed up by several French intellectuals (Claris 2005).

7. Here defined as "sets of cognitive and moral maps that orient actors within a policy sphere" (Bleich 2003:169).

8. In French social sciences, there is a tendency to minimize the importance of race in understanding France's political history. Race has been theoretically understood by relying on one of the three central categories: class, ethnicity, or culture. There are no such initiatives as the Black European Studies Project (BEST) in Germany. For a recent assessment of black studies in Europe, refer to the proceedings of "African American and Diasporic Research in Europe: Comparative and Interdisciplinary Approaches," symposium organized by W.E.B. Du Bois Institute for African and African American Research (Harvard University), Paris, Université de la Sorbonne Nouvelle, Dec. 15–18, 2004.

9. Here the black experience falls into two main categories. First is the situation of black nationals who are French citizens like any other, in theory. The second is black immigrants or residents who are not French citizens. Attempting to gauge the significance of race as related to citizenship and Frenchness, I decided to focus on the first of these experiences, even if there is little difference between the two in practice for the average white French person.

10. Mass media commentators tend to divide into two main camps. Those in the first camp put the emphasis on (under) class (Colombani 2005; Mauduit 2005; Taubira 2005; Mekaoui 2006)—however (under) class is also defined by race. Those in the second camp focus on race, religion, culture (Finkielkraut 2005; Luca 2005; Millot 2005)—however these parameters are interrelated with class in practice.

11. The two exceptions were Azouz Begag, minister of equal opportunity, and Léon Bertrand, minister of tourism, who voiced their disagreement.

12. In her latest book (2006), Anna Moï, a French novelist of Vietnamese descent, criticizes the concept of *francophonie* in literature, which separates the "true" French white authors, known worldwide, from the other nonwhite French writers, who will never be brought into the mainstream.

13. For a useful report of French stereotypes about Africans, read Philippe Dewitte's paper "Questions d'images: Contributions pour une réflexion sur la place des Africains noirs en France." Paris, 2004 (unpublished).

14. This section was named after David Beriss's book (2004), to which it pays homage.

15. Among others, Representative Council of Jewish Institutions of France *(Conseil Représentatif des Institutions Juives de France),* French Council of the Muslim Cult *(Conseil Français du Culte Musulman).*

16. Most European—if not French—minority politicians carry on this debate regularly with themselves.

17. Several associations of West Indians living in France opposed the creation of CRAN, which is accused of racializing demands for equality, in practice (Netter 2006).

18. Patrick Simon, "Les politiques anti-discrimination et les statistiques: paramètres d'une incohérence." *Sociétés Contemporaines* 53 (2004): 57–84.

19. In France, Africagora is today the leading ethnic business club dedicated to the social promotion of young professionals of African and Caribbean descent. It was created in 1999 on the assumption that ethnic lobbying was the only way to make it past broken promises. Seven years later, it has generated several branches in major French cities and holds every year a national event to promote *La France des talents et de la diversité.*

20. It is also important to note that France played a critical role in the adoption of UNESCO's Universal Declaration on Cultural Diversity in October 2005.

21. With the exception of Christiane Taubira, first ever black female candidate to 2002 French presidential elections (Stovall 2003).

22. Among others (*Club Averroes, Conférence Périclès*), the *Club du XXIe siècle* gathers the finest French elite of non-European descent—mainly born in France with a North African background—around issues surrounding citizenship, equality and Frenchness. Created in 2004 by Hakim El-Karoui, then affiliated with Prime Minister Raffarin's office, it was named after the very select *Club Siècle* whose recruitment remains largely traditional (white and Catholic).

23. French political parties were submitted in early January 2006 a draft on diversity in politics *(Charte de la diversité politique)* by several associations. It is still under consideration.

24. French Parliament voted on March 2006 for an equal opportunity bill. One of the key components of the First-Job Contract (CPE) simplified the process by which employers could dismiss or fire employees, typically young adults, during the two years of their probationary period. It was strongly opposed by trade unions and movements of students. Still, the law offers a set of three additional measures to combat discrimination: (1) establishing a National Agency for Social Cohesion and Equal Opportunity, (2) strengthening the powers of the High Authority for the Fight against Discrimination and for Equality, and (3) legalizing testing as a means to reveal discrimination in relation to employment, housing, and leisure activities.

References

Badiou, A. "L'humiliation ordinaire" (Ordinary Humiliation). *Le Monde,* Nov. 15, 2005.

Beaud, S. and G. Noiriel. "Les nouveaux parias de la République" (The New Parias of the Republic). *Le Monde,* Sept. 12, 2004.

Beck, U. "Banlieues: la dignité blessée des insurgés" (The Wounded Dignity of Rebels). *Le Figaro,* Nov. 18, 2005.

Beriss, D. "Culture-as-Race or Culture-as-Culture." *French Politics Culture and Society,* vol. 18 (3) Fall 2000, 18–48.

———. *Black Skins, French Voices: Caribbean Ethnicity and Activism in Urban France.* Boulder, Col.: Westview Press, 2004.

Bernard, P. *La Crème des beurs: de l'immigration à l'intégration* (*The Cream of the Arabs: From Immigration to Integration*). Paris: Seuil, 2004.

———. "Banlieues: la provocation coloniale" (*The Suburbs: Colonial Provocation*). *Le Monde*, Nov. 18, 2005.

Bertrand, L. "La République, l'affaire de tous" (The Republic: Everyone's Concern). *Libération*, Nov. 17, 2005.

Blauner, B. *Still the Big news. Racial Oppression in America.* Philadelphia: Temple University Press, 2001.

Bleich, E. *Race Politics in Britain and France: Ideas and Policymaking since the 1960s.* Cambridge: Cambridge University Press, 2003a.

———. "Histoire des politiques françaises antidiscrimination: du déni à la lutte" (History of French Antidiscrimination Politics: From Denial to Struggle). *Hommes et Migrations,* 1245, 2003b.

Calvès, G. "Il n'y a pas de race ici: le modèle français à l'épreuve de l'intégration européenne" ("There's No Race Here: The French Model Tested by European Integration"). *Critique Internationale,* 17, 2003: 173–86.

Claris. "La dérive ethnique" (The Ethnic Drift). *Libération,* Apr. 5, 2005.

Colombani, J. "Après le choc." *Le Monde,* Nov. 28, 2005.

Commission Nationale Consultative des Droits de l'Homme (CNCDH). *Rapport 2005 sur la lutte contre le racisme, l'antisémitisme, et la xénophobie* (*The 2005 Report on the Struggle against Racism, Anti-Semitism, and Xenophobia*). Paris: La Documentation Française, 2005.

Constant, F. "La République Française, l'identité nationale et la couleur de la peau" ("The French Republic, National Identity, and Skin Color"), forthcoming.

———. *Le Multiculturalisme* (*Multiculturalism*). Paris: Flammarion, 2000.

———. "Les Noirs sont-ils solubles dans la République? Notes sur l'invisibilité des minorités visibles en France" ("Is There a Black Solution in the Republic? Notes on the Invisibility of Visible Minorities in France"). Occasional paper, 2004, www.capdiv.org.

———. *La Citoyenneté* (*Citizenship*). Paris: Montchrestien, 1998.

———. "Le débat public autour de l'esclavage: conflits de mémoires et tensions sociopolitiques" ("The Public Debate about Slavery: Contested Memory and Socio-political Tensions"). *Cités* (25) 2006, 174–79.

———. "Pour une lecture sociale des revendications mémorielles victimaires." *Esprit* (2) 2007, 105–17.

Diamond, A., and J. Magidoff. "A gauche, le racial impensé" ("To the Left, Racially Unthinkable"). *Libération,* Nov. 30, 2005.

Dulucq, S. and C. Zytnicki. "Penser le passé colonial. Entre perspectives historiographiques et résurgence des mémoires." *Vingtième siècle. Revue d'histoire* (86) (Apr.-June 2005): 59–69.

Dyer, G. "Not the Paris Intifada." Nov. 4, 2005 (unpublished).

Finkielkraut, A. "J'assume." *Le Monde,* Nov. 26, 2005.

Fogarty, R. and M. A. Osborne. "Constructions and Functions of Race in French Military Medicine, 1830–1920." In Sue Peabody and Tyler Stovall, eds., *The Color of Liberty: Histories of Race in France.* Durham and London: Duke University Press, 2003, 206–37.

Geisser, V. *Ethnicité Républicaine.* Paris: Presses de Sciences Po, 1997.

Glucksmann, A. "Les feux de la haine." *Le Monde,* Paris, 2005.

Hollande, F. "Banlieues. Hollande demande la levée de l'état d'urgence" (Suburbs: Holland [a French politician] demands a lifting of the state of emergency), Nov. 28, 2005 (http://www.parti-socialiste.fr).

Luca, Lionel, cited by Vanessa Schneider. "Colonies: un député UMP tacle les ministres trop bronzés." *Libération*, Dec. 13, 2005.

Keaton, Trica Danielle. *Muslim Girls and the Other France: Race, Identity Politics, and Social Exclusion.* Bloomington: Indiana University Press, 2006.

Mauduit, Laurent. "Les nouvelles métamorphoses de la question sociale" ("New Metamorphosis of the Social Question"). *Le Monde*, Apr. 6, 2005.

Mekaoui, Adam. "Quand il s'agit de cohésion nationale et non plus d'intégration" ("When it's about national cohesion and no longer integration"). *Le Figaro*, Jan. 4, 2006.

Millot, Lorraine. "Hélène Carrère d'Encausse dérape à la télévision" (Hélène Carrère d'Encausse goes awry on television). *Libération*, Nov. 15, 2005.

Moï, Anna. *Espéranto, désespéranto. La Francophonie sans les Français.* Paris: Gallimard, 2006.

de Montvalon, Jean-Baptiste. "Le premier ministre se prononce contre la discrimination positive" ("The Prime Minister Weighs in on Affirmative Action"). *Le Monde*, July 2, 2005.

Netter, Sarah. "Louis-Georges Tin ou l'émergence d'une conscience noire" ("Louis-Georges Tin or the Emergence of a Black Consciousness"). *Antilla*, 1185, 2006, 12–16.

Omi, Michael, and Howard Winant. *Racial Formation in the United States.* New York: Routledge, 1994.

Peabody, Sue, and Tyler Stovall, eds. *The Color of Liberty: Histories of Race in France.* Durham: Duke University Press, 2003.

Richburg, Keith. "The Other France, Separate and Unhappy." *Washington Post*, Nov. 13, 2005.

Sarkozy, Nicolas. "Discours aux Préfets" (Speech to the Prefects). Nov. 18, 2005 (www.interieur.gouv.fr).

Sayad, Abdelmalek. *La Double Absence. Des Illusions de l'émigré aux souffrances de l'immigré* (Dual Absence: From Emigrant Illusions to Immigrant Suffering). Paris: Seuil, 1999.

Slama, Alain-Gérard. "Le communautarisme, un danger pour la France?" (Communitarianism, a danger for France?). *Le Figaro magazine*, Dec. 5, 2005.

Stovall, Tyler. "From Red Belt to Black Belt: Race, Class and Urban Marginality in Twentieth-Century Paris." In Sue Peabody and Tyler Stovall, eds., *The Color of Liberty: Histories of Race in France.* Durham: Duke University Press, 2003: 351–71.

Taubira, Christiane. "La République comme Horizon" (The Republic as the Horizon). *Le Monde*, Dec. 2, 2005.

Vergès, Françoise. "Les troubles de la mémoire. Traite négrière, esclavage et écriture de l'histoire" (Memory Disorder: Slave Traffic, Slavery and Historiography). *Cahiers d'études Africaines*, 179–180 XLV (3–4) 2005: 1143–79.

Weil, Patrick. *Qu'est-ce qu'un Français? Histoire de la Nationalité française depuis la Révolution.* Paris: Grasset, 2002.

———. *La République et sa diversité. Immigration, intégration, discriminations.* Paris: Seuil, 2005.

West, Cornell. *Race Matters.* New York: Vintage Books, 1994.

Wieviorka, Michel. "Ghettoïsation: un cran d'arrêt" (Ghettoization: A Stopcock). *Libération,* Dec. 19, 2005.

Yamada, Mitsuye. "Invisibility Is an Unnatural Disaster: Reflections of an Asian-American Woman." In Cherrie Moraga and Gloria Anzaldùa, eds., *This Bridge Called My Back: Writings by Radical Women of Color* (New York 1983) quoted by Ronald Takaki 1993: 426.

Zappi, Sylvie. "Les jeunes diplômés issus de l'immigration ont des difficultés à trouver un emploi" (Youth of immigration with diplomas have difficulty finding a job). *Le Monde,* Apr. 24, 2004.

9

My Volk to Come: Peoplehood in Recent Diaspora Discourse and Afro-German Popular Music

ALEXANDER G. WEHELIYE

> The exoticization of Western thought [must result from the examination of] this thought itself from the landscape or perspective of the *blues* people—and therefore from the perspective, not of the-people-as-*Volk*, but as in the *popular* aspect of the [1960s black liberation] movements, of the people as the movements of people who are logically excluded . . . from our present order.
>
> —Sylvia Wynter

The recent prominence of diaspora discourse in Black studies has supplanted the emphasis on African American identity that defined the field for some time with the interrogation of U.S. Black life within and against the context of other diasporic groups. The nominal passage from Black studies to African American studies and now diaspora studies sets some of the groundwork for querying the conceptual underpinnings of these developments.[1] Replacing the designation *black* with *African American* signals foremost a turn away from a primarily political category towards an identitarian marker of cultural and/or ethnic specificity, while *diaspora* suggests a concurrent deemphasizing of specificities in the embrace of transnational frames of reference and a return of said particularities via the comparison of Black populations that differ in nationality. The turn to the diaspora concept in the history of Black studies frequently positions the nation as a dialectical stepping-stone toward a supranational sphere that appears as more desirable than its national shadow. Still, these discourses often replicate and reify the nation-form they are seeking to escape in their comparison of different national literatures, cultures, languages, and so forth.

The appeal and success of diaspora as a concept within critical discourse lies in its reframing of rigid national precincts. Instead of focusing on the bounded historical continuity of the nation-state, *diaspora* offers pathways that retrace layerings of difference in the aftermath of colonialism and slavery, as well as the effects of other forms of migration and displacement. Thus, diaspora enables the desedimentation of the nation from the "interior" by taking into account groups that fail to comply with the reigning definition of the people as a cohesive political subject due to sharing one culture, one race, one language, one religion, and so on, and from the "exterior" by drawing attention to the movements that cannot be contained by the nation's administrative and ideological borders.

We might sum up diaspora's promise as that of a virtual technology of collectivity, or at least as a formation that highlights its virtuality in more acute ways than the nation. Of course, nations are also virtual, but their virtuality tends to be actualized in sovereign territories and the states that rule over and through them. Diasporas, in contrast, generally do not follow the same patterns of actualization as the nation, although they are forced to exist within and between nation-states. The severing of collectivity from territory and the state marks diaspora's virtuality and the concept's radical potential vis-à-vis the theorization of Black cultures. But this decoupling also represents a danger, since cultural and/or ethnic peoplehood frequently emerge as defining traits of community when the state and its concomitant geographical terrain have taken a leave of absence.

While many commentators have censured the intermural sameness smuggled in through the back door in the idea of a seamless continuity between various African-descended populations around the globe, these critiques oftentimes assume stable, if not coherent diasporic populations. Thus, despite the thoroughgoing problematization of the homeland conundrum, what remains largely uninterrogated thus far is the particular shape of Black collectivity within diasporic groups. There exists a basic assumption in much diaspora discourse that diasporic groups are indeed communities, and that these communities, if not better than national ones, are at least more open; otherwise the very invocation of the D-word would be moot.

Some recent statements from the bourgeoning field of Black European studies have shifted the emphasis from conceptualizing the African diaspora as a semi-homogeneous field to a malleable space marked above all by difference. Although this modification is in many ways laudable, the insistence on difference as the defining attribute of diaspora leaves the door open for the hushed entry of peoplehood as the principal mode of articulating not the African diaspora tout court, as in prior conceptions of this field, but specific national diasporas. Following the groundwork laid by Paul Gilroy, the recent work of Jacqueline Nassy Brown concerning the black British diaspora in Liverpool, Tina Campt's writings on Afro-Germans during the Third Reich, and Brent Edwards's analysis of the history of the term/concept diaspora in black cultural contexts, all focus on interdiasporic diversity rather than arguing for or assuming a common thread that magically unites various African-descended groupings around the world.[2] Campt writes of the oftentimes unequal "intercultural address" that marks the dialogue between diasporic groups, Brown ruminates on the "margins of the African Diaspora," and Edwards highlights the necessary but impossible linguistic and cultural translation in transnational Afro-diasporic conversations. All three authors have done much to draw our attention to the multiple vectors of interdiasporic differentiation and the specificities of Black groupings beyond the United States. Yet in their albeit differently pitched insistence on the variable multiplicity of black life, these authors still maintain the discrepancy between African Americans and other diasporic formations as *the* measuring device to calibrate the radical differences between individual diasporas defined by national or linguistic borders.

Brown, Campt, and Edwards are careful to distance themselves from previous progressivist narratives that construe black European and other diasporas as nascent versions of the African American "community." Yet by only taking in the divergences between this arrangement and British, French, and German configurations, these authors tend to reinscribe African America as the model for the African diaspora, perhaps not its Platonic ideal but a category through which European diasporas are qualified and circumscribed nonetheless. Brown, for instance, in invoking "the margins of 'the African Diaspora'" asks, "when does the unrelenting presence of Black America actually become oppressive, even as it inspires?" (2005, 297).[3] Similarly, in his discussion of Léopold Senghor's notion of *décalage,* Edwards accents the "changing core of difference" found "among African Americans and Africans," describing *décalage* as "the received biases that refuse to pass over when one crosses the water" (65). Finally, Campt, who draws heavily on the previous two critics, suggests "'intercultural address' . . . encourages us to reflect on the status of Black America in relation to other Black populations in the process of articulating their own experiences and constructing alternative forms of Black identity and community" (207). Despite my agreement with much of these analyses, the pesky question remains as to why Black America appears as the solitary point of comparison, especially given that all three critics explicitly reject African American "vanguardism" (Edwards), "cultural imperialism" (Brown), and "hegemony" (Campt). Thus, European diasporas materialize as differently constituted only by virtue of their analytic localization in the comparative context of Black America.

This is especially evident in the use of "margins" (Brown) and "alternative" (Campt) to describe non-African American diasporic populations. The perspective from which Black Europeans appear at the "margins of diaspora" or as "alternative forms of Black identity and community" runs counter to the political organizing and critical theorizing of Afro-European diasporas, particularly since these are generally more concerned with their marginalization within the nation-states in which they dwell as opposed to their supposed divergence from U.S. models of racial identity and community. Consequently, we should pause to query the conceptual work done by invoking terms/concepts such as hegemony, imperialism, vanguardism, margins, and alternative. If the task of recent diaspora discourse has been to aerate the putatively dominant position of African America within the African diaspora, then we need to ask why the scent of center and periphery still lingers so heavily in the comparative framework of Black European studies.

Furthermore, by so determinedly stressing the disparities between these different nationally located communities, these inquiries run the risk of interpellating individual African diasporas, whether in Europe, the United States, or the Caribbean, as primordially constituted beacons of racial kinship. Instead of a transnational ethnic notion of peoplehood that unites all African-descended subjects around the globe, national boundaries, or linguistic differences that often help define the national ones, become the ultimate indicators of differentiation. In this process, national borders and/or linguistic differences are in danger of entering the discursive record as ontological absolutes rather than as structures and institutions that have served again and again to relegate Black subjects to the status of the western modernity's nonhuman other.

My point is that the turn away from envisioning the African diaspora as a transcendental racial bond to series of radical differences can unwillingly lead to the importation of what Etienne Balibar calls the "nation form" into diaspora discourse. Balibar describes the process by which collectivities are transformed into "the people" in the following fashion: "social formations . . . [are] represented in the past or in the future *as if* they formed a natural community, possessing of itself an identity of origins, culture and interests which transcends individuals and social conditions."[4] This "natural community" also constitutes a spectral grammar of current diaspora discourse. Given that peoplehood represents the foremost mode of imagining, (re)producing, and legislating community, and thus managing inequality in the intertwined histories of capitalism and the nation-state, peoplehood sneaks in as the de facto actualization of diasporas in the national context, especially when we avoid specifying how Black collectivity might be codified in the absence of this category.

Witness, for instance, the following statement by Anne Adams about the recent history of Afro-German culture, which spells out what often remains tacit in writings about diaspora. In this passage, Afro-Germans paradoxically emerge as a *Volk* as a result of being incorporated into the folk of the African diaspora: "African diaspora as condition *resolves* any 'contradiction' or 'oxymoron' in 'Afro-German'; African diaspora as process *resolves* the DuBoisian 'twoness' in the souls of Afro-German Black Folk/*Volk*."[5] The Volk appears here both in terms of the particularities of being Afro-German and the sublatory muscle of the African diaspora. This notion of community or peoplehood is precisely what diaspora discourse set out to avoid and reformulate by dislocating the nexus of people and territory.

In contrast to other critics, who see the category of the people as a unitary body politic, Giorgio Agamben locates a fundamental breach within this domain: "Any interpretation of the political meaning the term *people* ought to start from the peculiar fact that in modern European languages this term always indicates also the poor, the underprivileged, and the excluded. The same term names the constitutive political subject as well as the class that is excluded—de facto, if not de jure—from politics."[6] Still, diaspora discourse at times elides the unitary political subject with the excluded. While this does not occur at the level of the nation per se, it does so in terms of individual national diasporas by virtue of stressing their radical particularities and mutual cultural and linguistic incompatibilities; as a result, diaspora discourse reproduces the nation-form by staging individual African diasporas in the idiom of peoplehood as cohesive culturo-political formations.[7] Agamben continues his ruminations by noting the particularities of the German designation *Volk* vis-à-vis the duality of the people: "We ought to understand the lucid fury with which the German *Volk*—representative par excellence of the people as integral body politic—tried to eliminate the Jews forever as precisely the internecine struggle that divides *People* and *people*. With the final solution . . . Nazism tried to obscurely and in vain to free the Western political stage from this intolerable shadow so as to produce finally the German Volk as the people able to heal the original biopolitical fracture."[8]

Since the German word Volk simply designates *people* in the English-language sense and does not necessarily evoke Nazism in the same way as the term *Völkisch*, a distinction should be made between *das* Volk, which signifies the people as an undifferentiated mass of humans, including the oppressed, and *ein* Volk as a specific and supposedly homogenous ethnic, cultural, and/or linguistic group. This contrast corresponds roughly with Agamben's distinction between the people with a capital *P* and those with a lowercase *p*. Hence, the biopolitical project of Nazism was to transform *das* Volk into *ein* ethnically pure Volk.

Given the history of the term Volk, it seems surprising that Adams would invoke it so lightly and link to the folk, which is both another name for the people with a lowercase p and the group abjected by the very idea of the Volk as it was defined and practiced during the Third Reich. Since African diasporas generally tend to populate "the intolerable shadow," to use Agamben's phrase, within different nation-states, whether as prisoners in the United States or as victims of racial violence in contemporary Germany, Belgium, Austria, and

Russia, diaspora discourse should claim and use this banishment rather than attempting to heal western modernity's constitutive biopolitical fracture by knowingly or inadvertently rendering the folk as *ein* Volk. I will now turn my attention to contemporary Afro-German musical practices in order to show how, in a similar vein to diaspora discourse, these sonic formations, as hard as they try, cannot move away from imagining collectivity through the form of peoplehood and return to diaspora discourse in the closing section.

Brother Volk

Recent years have seen the materialization of two divergent yet intertwined forces within Afro-German popular music. On the one hand, black musicians have shown an increasing politicization. The most prominent examples of this trend are two not-for-profit hip-hop projects, Brothers Keepers and Sisters Keepers, that consist of a large group of well-known Afro-German hip-hop, R&B, and reggae artists formed in 2001 to protest neo-Nazi terror and to publicly perform a collective black presence in Germany. On the other hand, there has been a proliferation of Afro-German R&B by artists such as Joy Denelane, Vanessa Mason, Chima, Bintia, Mic, Nadja Benaissa, J-Luv, Glashaus, and Xavier Naidoo that does not construe German blackness in terms of the identitarian narratives often found in hip-hop or seek recognizably political goals as in the case of Brothers and Sisters Keepers. I will focus on these two musical formations in order to analyze how they ostensibly imagine black collectivity differently but in the final instance fall back on community as primordial kinship: peoplehood surfaces again and again as the chief modality of inventing racial and/or religious collectivity.

The will to peoplehood is clearly exhibited in Brothers Keepers's grainy black and white video for their hit "Adriano (Letzte Warnung)" (Final Warning) that shows the collective of Afro-German rappers and lead singer Xavier Naidoo traversing public spaces in Berlin. Both the lyrics of the song and the demeanor of the men stage the Afro-German Volk as a physical and symbolic threat to the German nation-as-Volk. Naidoo sings the following lines in the chorus, which highlight both the unity of the Brothers and their warlike posture vis-à-vis the mainstream German Volk:

> This is something like a final warning
>
> Because our counterattack has been in planning for a long time. . . . We'll finally stop your brown shit. . . . [9] We offer clenched fists and not open hands. Your downfall forever, and we'll hear your sobbing and moaning . . .

Fortified by the militaristic lyrics, the images of the men forming an Afro-

German phalanx as they move through Berlin are intercut with iconic figurations of neo-Nazi violence against which the masculine unity of Brothers Keepers serves as bulwark. While a few women are featured in the final shots of this video, female musicians are completely absent, drawing attention to the constitutive (female) outside of this mode of racial unity. When Brothers Keepers were asked in interviews about the visible and audible absence of women from this group, the organizers responded that all the eligible female performers were either pregnant or on maternity leave.[10] Though women are needed to both literally and figuratively reproduce the Afro-German Volk, they remain absent from the Afro-German Volk envisioned by the Brothers, and they do not pose a threat to the whiteness of the German nation. In other words, Afro-German women are not needed to fight neo-Nazi violence but to bear children and to play the role of the consoling counterpart to Brothers Keepers' aggressive stance.

Sisters Keepers' song and video "Liebe und Verstand" (Love and Understanding), which was released months after "Adriano" and was not nearly as successful in terms of sales and video airplay, bears this out in its can't-we-all-get-along vibe. As opposed to "Adriano," which features a sung chorus interspersed with rapped verses, "Liebe und Verstand" is almost exclusively sung and the lyrics are much more conciliatory. Where the Brothers refuse to shake hands, offering clenched fists instead, the Sisters tell their audience, "Come on, give us your hand, we can change things with love and understanding." The video is shot in sumptuous color, imaging a harmonious Germany virtually devoid of white people. Even the Sisters' ostensibly "female" space in the guise of a Black Germany is framed by a male viewpoint, plus several of the Brothers Keepers have cameos in the video. In fact, before the female performers come into view in the video, we hear a snippet of "Adriano" on a car radio and see a close-up of Brothers Keeper Tyron Rickets. Then rapper Meli—who in her other public appearances favors a masculine look that consists of heavy Timberland boots, baggy jeans, and cornrows—appears sporting a flowing haircut, full makeup, and tight-fitting clothing that partially reveals her stomach. In order to be a Sisters Keeper, Meli is forced to visually conform to hegemonic codes of femininity. While Sisters Keepers are excluded from the Afro-German Volk interpellated by the Brothers Keepers video, they also do not constitute their own Volk: Brothers Keepers' previous success and overbearing presence in the video gives birth to and authorizes this "female" version of Afro-Germaneness.[11] By relegating female performers and feminism to the margins, or rather the delivery room, Brothers Keepers runs counter to the strong presence of women and feminism in the history of Afro-German political organizing.[12]

Apocalypse Now

In contrast to Brothers and Sisters Keepers, German R&B does not feature explicit sociopolitical messages about racial identity, projecting a version of the collective that is not based on a racialized notion of peoplehood. I will focus on Xavier Naidoo and Glashaus, whose lyrics prominently feature pan-religious themes that combine Christianity, Islam, and Rastafarianism, providing a utopian model for life and political change in ways that secular politics seemingly cannot offer. Xavier Naidoo's first album *Nicht von dieser Welt* (Not of This World, 1998) remains one of the all-time best-selling German language albums, and Naidoo is the most well-known and successful popular musician in Germany today. Naidoo's arrival on the German music scene was remarkable not only because of his stratospheric rise to fame as a hyphenated German but also due to his melismatic singing style and devout lyrics; Naidoo takes the homonymic resonances between *Xavier* and *savior* very seriously. His lyrics are steeped in the Old Testament, oftentimes vis-à-vis the coming, or rather already-in-place apocalypse. The group Glashaus consists of chanteuse Cassandra Steen, producer and rapper Moses Pelham, and pianist/producer Martin Haas. The latter two also form Pelham Power Productions (3P) and were responsible for the sonic architecture of Naidoo's first album. Although comparable in some respects to Naidoo, especially in the biblical librettos and the German-language singing, Glashaus's sound largely lacks the pathos and pomp so central to the aesthetic of *Nicht von dieser Welt,* replacing it with a minimalist aural tapestry that better suits Steen's restrained intonation. What unites these two projects, besides the same team of producers, is the creation of a uniquely (Afro-) German form of R&B, a genre hitherto absent from this musical landscape.[13]

The forms of R&B performed by Xavier Naidoo and Glashaus espouse minoritarian instantiations of being Black and German, since neither Naidoo nor Steen address their Afro-German identity in their lyrics. But both are members of the Brothers Keepers collective, so their politicized racial identities infiltrate their musical output, even if not expressly figured in the text. Naidoo and Glashaus draw on and reformulate diasporic musical traditions (spirituals, gospel, hip-hop, soul, and reggae) that have used spirituality, especially Christianity and Rastafarianism, to imagine worlds beyond the immediate and as culturo-political modes of worldly resistance against racism and oppression. Even so, there exists no precedent for these artists' sonoric piousness in modern Germany, since spirituality has not been a component of German popular music; the only forms of religious music hitherto available were explicitly tied to the church. In fact, Naidoo, who rejects organized forms of religion, is both credited with and maligned for introducing religion to contemporary German popular culture, especially among young people. While open proclamations and discussions of faith were largely an anathema in German public discourse, now they are (grudgingly) accepted.[14]

One of the striking aspects about Naidoo's and Glashaus's religious imaginary is the turn away from the state as a guarantor of social justice, or even the primary location of the political. Instead a supranational and cross-denominational spiritual community of like-minded people replaces an immediately racialized collectivity as it might be recognized by the state. This circumvention of state power appears very clearly in the lyrics for Naidoo's "Seine Strassen" (His Streets), where he sings the following lines: "His streets from the mountains to the sea . . . You're throwing parties on the streets approved by the wrong authority. I hope you're all done with your foolishness. Are you ready for the final dance?"

Naidoo believes that this combat between the worldly and spiritual can only be won by the higher powers; the government is misguided in its attempt to legislate His streets. Naidoo stages his censure of the worldly fools via the state's usurpation of powers proper only to the Lord, since the urban party locales are part of His dominion, one that extends from the mountains to the sea. The lyrics continue: "His lanes, because the Lord is leading his army and your badly constructed trails hinder the arrival of his throne-chariot." Drawing on the Old Testament Book of Ezekiel, Naidoo envisions the metaphysically deficient trails hindering both the march of the Lord's army and the entrance of his throne-chariot.[15] The juxtaposition of His streets and profane paths illustrates Naidoo's resolve to negate the secular world. Naidoo is not after a peaceful coexistence of religious and secular forces because God's higher authority both supersedes and displaces the political rule of the state. Instead, he calls for a complete reversal of the current situation in which politics is firmly rooted in the spiritual domain.[16]

This antistatist stance also appears in the music video for this song, where we see Naidoo and his producer at the time, Moses Pelham, on a night drive toward one of Germany's borders. The clip illustrates the chasm between the spiritual and the secular already so prominent in the lyrics through an extreme close-up of the two men's German passports on the dashboard of their Porsche. The passport functions as an important signifier of citizenship for people of color in Germany because they are positioned as de facto non-German by the national imaginary and therefore frequently have to prove their belonging by showing their identification papers. In their classic 1992 track "Fremd im eigenen Land" (Stranger in My Own Country), pioneering Afro- and Italian hip-hop group Advanced Chemistry use the passport as a political tool for claiming and occupying public space.[17] In addition, this form of official identification makes a brief appearance at the end of Sisters Keepers's video "Liebe und Verstand." In an ironic reversal of the balance of power, one of the few white people in the video is forced to present his passport, as legal proof of his Germanness, to two black German police officers. For Naidoo and Pelham, however, any form of identification issued by the state represents a barrier to full membership in the kingdom of God. The passports on the dashboard symbolize the hubris of the state in legislating national boundaries. There should only be "His streets," and all subjects who are a part of his flock should have equal access to these roads. Although these images, especially when contrasted with the lyrics, represent a forceful critique of the restrictive immigration policies that are a core feature of the modern nation-state, they still dwell in the domain of peoplehood; only here God administers belonging and membership rather than state institutions. The people-as-Volk remain an absent presence here in the decisive rift between the blind dupes on the street who only see the territory mapped by the state and God's flock, which exceeds both the nation-state's territorial grasp and its legislation of peoplehood via citizenship.

While Naidoo at least brings to the fore the tension between the spiritual and the secular, Glashaus generally eschews secular politics altogether. Both their first and most recent records feature a number of songs with religious content, but often not overtly so; the paeans to peace and redemption could also reference a worldly love object. The group's second album, *Jah Sound System,* however, concretizes the group's otherwise hazy devout agenda. Conjuring the Rastafarian name for God derived from Jehovah (Jah), the title of the record positions the group as God's sonic messenger by alternately emphasizing Armageddon and utopian divine salvation: they are, after all, Jah's sound system. Unlike the rest of Glashaus's oeuvre, which features mainly piano-heavy ballads, this album also includes several up-tempo tracks with hip-hop beats and ominous interludes spoken by Moses Pelham.

Pelham makes many more vocal appearances on this album than on the rest of the group's oeuvre, which insinuates that the more explicit politico-religious content needs to be accompanied by a masculine voice that counteracts the seeming femininity of R&B as a musical genre, especially when contrasted with hip-hop. Steen frequently sings about peace and love, whereas Pelham warns us about the impending Judgment Day. This is further underlined by the fact that the male voice performs the traditionally aggressive and masculine tasks, while the female voice provides solace, both lyrically and sonically. In the song "NAL (Nix als Liebe y'all)" (Nuttin But Love Y'all), for instance, Steen dreams of a higher spot enshrined only by love:[18]

> I saw that there was no place for retaliation and vengeance in this glorious [*herrlich*] thing.[19] Hate did not exist, blood did not flow there, and there were no tears.
>
> I saw it when my eyes closed, who of us here doesn't want to go there.
>
> Then tell me why aren't we just like that.

Steen projects a utopian scenario that also serves as a political injunction to actualize her dream of a superior realm by emulating this place of infinite love. Conversely, Pelham recites the following biblical verses in the spoken "Prelude zu Bald" (Prelude to Now): "And ye shall hear of wars and rumors of wars: see that ye be not troubled: for all *these things* must come to pass, but the end is not yet. For nation [*ein Volk gegen ein Volk*] shall rise against nation, and kingdom against kingdom: and there shall be famines, and pestilences, and earthquakes, in diverse places. All these *are* the beginning of sorrows" (Matthew 24: 6–8).

The contrast to Steen's loving vociferations could not be any starker in their invocations of a coming holy war. However, some fissures in the lyrical and musical text counteract these traditionally masculine and feminine vocal performances by disassociating this process from the gendered body. The gendering of the male and female voices is recast in the recitation of a well-known spiritual poem "Footprints in the Sand," where Pelham shows some humility (not something he does very often in his music or public persona) by putting himself in the role of a child carried by the Lord in times of need:

> "But I have noticed that during the most troublesome times in my life there is only one set of footprints. I don't understand why when I needed you most, you would leave me."
>
> The Lord replied, "My precious, precious child I love you and would never leave you during your times of trial and suffering. When you see only one set of footprints in the sand, it was then that I carried you."

Steen leaves behind demure womanhood when she exhibits a more confrontational posture vis-à-vis the audience, for instance, singing of a "Jetzt" (Now) in which she chastises the worldly herd for failing to decipher God's coded messages: "These secret messages are supposed to reach you. Their worldly author doesn't get them, because he only writes what the powers want. They are supposed to encourage you to finally get up; it could happen in a few seconds."[20]

Still, just as with Pelham's humbleness, Steen's hostile vociferations are only authorized by the Lord's otherworldly power, which renders the two positions closer than they initially seem. Consequently, the dispersal of the gender roles needs to be heard in a different light, since the powers inherent in Steen's and Pelham's voices are literally drawn from another world. Moreover, this gendering is further complicated by the fact that Pelham wrote all the lyrics for Glashaus's first two albums, even those sung by Cassandra Steen.

Put differently, in Glashaus's universe, Armageddon and salvation are two sides of the same coin, as the former is the precondition for the latter. Accordingly, the differing gendered voices meld into a placeless totality that erases the material world to supplant it with a smooth holy realm of existence. And on this plane, Pelham's and Steen's gendered positions do not register in the same way as they do in the secular sphere; on this plane, both will not only be subject to a higher power but also, and more importantly, be one with God. In Glashaus's cosmology, this religious utopia denotes a genderless space of minoritization, where dyads such as woman/man or black/white seemingly become irrelevant. Since worldly identities no longer play a constitutive role in the drama of collectivity, there appears to be no pressing need for the people-as-Volk. Thus, the combination of R&B and an ecumenical religious discourse aids Naidoo and Glashaus in creating a different mode of collectivity, one that ostensibly avoids the masculinist and identitarian traps of Brothers and Sisters Keepers.

Nonetheless, the quotes from Matthew explicitly draw on the language of the Volk by pitting one group against another, as well taking this clash as the launch of a catastrophic temporality. In addition, the Volk surfaces in an offbeat way as the central trope of the Glashaus song, "Eine Hymne für mein Volk" (An Anthem for My Volk). In this song, the group suggests that the community envisioned by these sacred discourses does not so much interpellate a formation already in existence but a people to come that accentuates the positive, productive, creative, and provisional aspects of spiritual Volk-building. The song's chorus proceeds, "This song is an anthem for my Volk that doesn't yet exist, but my Volk now has a voice and is united in this song." Glashaus's song sounds a future people not yet actualized that, nevertheless, comprises a unified voice within the confines of this musical work. The paradoxical nature of this Volk is accentuated further by a series of oxymora in the verses that describe its manifold properties; Glashaus has no problem dwelling in the realm of paradox: "We are mighty speakers and don't say a word. We are acrimonious adversaries and immediately love each other." Accordingly, this Volk represents everything and nothing. The Volk can contain multitudes precisely because it has no actual existence, which is to say that futurity represents its defining trait insofar as this people remains perennially lodged in the domain of the "to come."

The lines from the chorus cited above are not a literal translation, since the German adverb *so* (*mein Volk, das es so noch nicht gibt*), which forms a crucial part of Glashaus's formulation, cannot not be easily rendered in English. A more literal translation would read thus: "my Volk that does not yet exist that way (or in this particular manifestation)." It would seem that the Volk already exists, just not in the way Glashaus desires. In order to secure its futurity, then, Glashaus's Volk has to figure as a continuation of a previous formation rather than a new sighting. As with the verses from Matthew in "Prelude zu Bald," the article used in conjunction with Volk specifies the contours of this community. Instead of "ein Volk" as in "Prelude," here Glashaus insists on "*mein* Volk," which couples *ein* Volk (People with a capital P) with belonging and ownership. The possessive pronoun *mein* both stages the Volk as homogeneous and intimates a strong sense of predetermined inclusion because Steen vocalizes her connection to a group that has yet to make an appearance on the empirical corner: the Volk is not present thus far but Steen's belonging to it is a given. For this automatic integration into an invented religious community is exactly what unites all the opposing forces Glashaus ascribe to this Volk and creates the gender- and race-less sphere of existence. In other words, the Volk's futurity is established in the face of an a priori membership, a chosenness, anchoring it in the primordial swamps of peoplehood we know all too well, and which severely curtails the utopian dimensions of this cosmology. In the glasshouse, the fluids happen to be of the holy variety, but in other quagmires they are populated by culture, race, language, and so forth.

Despite the impulse to think and perform collectivity not along strict identitarian lines, as with Brothers and Sisters Keepers, the religious dimensions do not shield Glashaus and Xavier Naidoo from being entrapped by peoplehood, since they posit a previous and seemingly natural connection as the unifying trait of community. These attempts to refashion collectivity as a future people have to resist the seeming naturalness that flows from peoplehood for a variety of complicated historical, epistemological, and cultural reasons. Instead of waiting for my Volk to come, perhaps, the time has come to let my people go. On the whole, the strong desire to envisage collectivity beyond peoplehood and simultaneous failure to do so in Afro-German popular music and diaspora discourse underlines the nagging pervasiveness of this category and the pressing need for some alternatives.

The People

As opposed to constructing Black Germans as ein Volk via their connection to the African diaspora, poet and theorist May Ayim contends that Afro-German subjectivity unearths the radical possibility found in the interstitial abyss of "die Zwischenwelt als Chance" (the in-between world as potential), which echoes W.E.B. Du Bois's thinking of double consciousness not only as cumbersome hindrance to full subjectivity but also, and more importantly, as the gift of black people to the world. Ayim writes, "In those instances in which Afro-Germans do not accept the externally imposed ostensible contradiction between being both African and German, a self-awareness can emerge that does not necessitate this particular limitation."[21] According to Ayim, Afro-Germans cannot form ein Volk precisely because they inhabit both German and Black worlds, which belies the mutually exclusive logic of western racial formation and launches modalities of being and belonging not reducible to mere amalgamation. Following Ayim's footsteps, we need to formulate and imagine nonempirical and visionary versions of blackness and/as collectivity. This undertaking seems especially imperative in light of diaspora studies's institutional ascent to a catchall clearing house for various (minority) discourses, which, paradoxically, not only turns down the volume on colonialism and slavery, but, in the context of black studies, blunts the radicality of blackness's working within and against western modernity. For what gets lost in the traces of peoplehood qua unified political subject that trail the idea of diaspora, whether explicitly articulated or not, is precisely Du Bois's doubleness or Ayim's in-between world of blackness. By deserting these important nonempirical and visionary formulations of blackness and/as collectivity, we abjure the promise to undo the Afro and the Euro and concomitantly ruin their very conditions of possibility.

In order to impair these foundations, blackness should not be defined as primarily empirical, as occurs so frequently in recent diaspora discourse by virtue of comparatively enumerating the minute differences between African Americans and other diasporic constellations. Situating blackness and Black subjects in the jurisdiction of the epiphenomenal simply continues the work of white western hegemony, which invented and continues to circumscribe blackness as its nonhuman other. Once we take into account how blackness figures and materializes ontologically, we can practice a politics of being that, rather than succumbing to the brutal facticity of blackness, introduces invention into existence, as Sylvia Wynter states in the footsteps of Frantz Fanon. She writes, "The struggle of our new millennium will be one between the ongoing imperative of securing the well-being of our present ethnoclass (i.e., Western bourgeois) conception of the human, Man, which overrepresents itself as if it were the human itself, and that of securing the well-being, and therefore the full cognitive and behavioral autonomy of the human species itself/ourselves."[22] This is a battle to supplant the current instantiation of the human as synonymous with the objective existence of white, western Man and his various damned counterparts, especially black subjects, offering in its stead new styles of human subjectivity and community that are no longer based on the glaring rift between the folk as the nonhuman other and ein Volk as the most extreme version of the immaculately homogenous political subject.

Coda

Glashaus's "Eine Hymne für mein Volk" ends with a sample of James Brown's Civil Rights anthem "Soul Power" that repeats the phrase "power to the people"; in fact, Brown's voice is the last thing we hear. The recurring loop of "power to the people" fades into Brown chanting "soul power."

This particular sample, which stands at the crossroads of people and soul power and might be said to conjure the blues people, puts Glashaus and their Volk-to-come in an Afro-diasporic lineage of political struggle motored among other things by religious impulses, particularly the Civil Rights movement. Not only does this establish a precedent for Glashaus's messianic quest for social justice, as does the use of the spiritual domain to make decidedly worldly demands in spirituals, gospel, and reggae, but it also disrupts the notion of peoplehood promulgated by the earlier lyrics in its addition of *das* Volk (people power, soul power) as a sanctuary of the excluded and oppressed to the collective mix of "mein Volk, das es so noch nicht gibt." Thus, Glashaus juxtaposes *mein* Volk and *das* Volk rather than endeavoring to heal the fracture that segregates them, sounding for us listeners the *Zwischenwelt* below and beside these categories.[23] Glashaus dwells in the glasshouse, the interspatial location in which Cassandra Steen's restrained voice blurs the line between singing and everyday speech, where Moses Pelham's lyrics as sung by Steen veer from biblical grandiosity to pithy and at times devastating everyday observations. This (non)place has no walls just so that it can radically transform the grand piano from the sign for western classical music and its concomitant projection of bourgeois individualism into a rhythmic, melodic, and textural instrument in the service of a black musical idiom, while the engineering and production emphasize expansive space and melodic restraint so as to remind us that we have traveled beyond the borders of traditional architectural structures. Glashaus's sound, which manages to perform fragility and robustness in chorus and verse, constructs a contemporary version of the Kunstlied,[24] albeit syncopated by R&B singing, hip-hop beats, and cinemascope sonic spaces that gesture towards other universes in which "to live in a glasshouse is a revolutionary virtue par excellence."[25] This cosmos, rather than being populated by *ein* Volk or a consortium of different Völker, shelters weary travelers May Ayim, Walter Benjamin, Octavia Butler, and W.E.B. Du Bois on their long journey *daheim unterwegs.*

Notes

1. See Sylvia Wynter, "On How We Mistook the Map for the Territory."

2. Brown, "Black Liverpool"; Campt, *Other Germans;* Edwards, "The Uses of Diaspora."

3. In her recent book, Brown comes to an analogous conclusion: "We might begin by inquiring into the way particular Black communities outside the United States are affected by the global dominance of American culture. Britain is surely more inundated with things American than the reverse" (*Dropping Anchor,* 41). While this statement surely carries some validity, the presence of (African) American cultural artifacts in the global domain is not tantamount to political, cultural, or economic hegemony per se. In addition, this discussion is partially a response to an emergent consensus—among both U.S. and European scholars of the African diaspora—at several recent conferences about an "African American hegemony" vis-à-vis other black populations. Frequently, the long histories of black studies in the United States—and the lack thereof outside the United States—and the global circulation of African American cultural artifacts are summoned as the grounds for said hegemony. Even though I'm not disputing these two

points, I would strongly caution against the invocation of hegemony for the reasons I mention above, as well as the underfunded and embattled status of many U.S. black studies departments and the mass impoverishment, criminalization, and incarceration of so many people of African descent in the United States.

4. Balibar, *Race, Nation, and Class*, 96.

5. Adams, "Souls of Black Volk," 230–31.

6. Agamben, *Means without End*, 29. Recently Michael Hardt and Antonio Negri have pitted the concept of the people against that of the multitude. The former stands for a traditional notion of a unified and closed collectivity, where the latter signifies immanent openness. See their *Multitude*, xiv, 99, and 242–43. Ernesto Laclau, on the other hand, places "the people" at the center of politics. Noting a similar fracture within "the people" as Agamben, he distinguishes between *populus* as "the body of all citizens" and *plebs* as "the underprivileged." Laclau asserts that this category becomes political when "a *plebs* claims to be the only legitimate *populus*—that is, a partiality which wants to function as the totality of the community." *On Populist Reason*, 81.

7. In her discussion of Edwards's work, Michelle Stephens makes a comparable point about the recurrence of difference as the central figure of diaspora in contemporary criticism when she states, "Whether or not a project of diaspora such as Edwards defines it, and the projects of black internationalism . . . may be moving in fundamentally different directions: one toward the reification of difference that actually maintains, theoretically, the borders between black nationalities, the other toward alternative unities and articulations that threaten to erupt and confront those of empire, that radicalize notions of blackness by revealing the limits of nationality." Stephens, "Disarticulating Black Internationalisms," 105.

8. Agamben, *Means without End*, 34.

9. In this context, the color brown is a reference to Nazism or neo-Nazism and derives from the color of SA uniforms worn during the Third Reich. Unless noted otherwise, all translations from German are mine.

10. Daniel Bax and Joshua Aikins, "Wir sind stolz, Deutsche zu sein."

11. In her discussion of the gender politics of Afro-German hip-hop, including Brothers and Sisters Keepers, Fatima El-Tayeb points out that the masculinist tendencies of these two groups should be seen in relation, and perhaps also in reaction, to the defining role of women and feminist discourse within the history of Afro-German critical theorizing. See El-Tayeb, "If You Cannot Pronounce My Name."

12. Nicola Lauré al-Samarai has observed that black German theorizing is unique, since feminism has been the defining force of Afro-German discourse over the last twenty years, which has resulted in a brand of feminism that does not take gender as its sole category of analysis but focuses on race in its complex intermingling with gendered subjectivity. See Lauré al-Samarai, "History, Theory, Experience." This becomes especially pertinent when contrasted to the recent and rapid institutionalization of gender studies as the only form of minority discourse in the German university system. According to Eske Wollrad, by positing gender as the meta-category (i.e., white women) of analysis, the German variant of gender studies institutes yet another way to displace discussions of race in the German context and erase the multifarious contributions of German women of color to feminist theorizing. See Wollrad, *Weißsein im Widerspruch*.

13. Another version of German R&B, known as R'n'Besk, has developed recently. Performed by Turkish Germans, R'n'Besk combines German language R&B singing, hip-hop beats, and melodic elements, both in the instrumentation and vocal phrasing from the Turkish and Arabic genre Arabesk. R'n'Besk's most visible figure, Muhabbet, who has had several top twenty hits in Germany, cites Xavier Naidoo as his main influence.

14. See Braun, "Oh Herr, Alles wird Dein!" and Winkler, "Deutscher Pop entdeckt religiöse Inhalte."

15. The Book of Ezekiel, especially the prophet's vision of a fiery chariot in the sky, has exerted a marked influence of Jewish and Christian mysticism, modern UFO mythology, and the founding narratives of the Nation of Islam.

16. In an interview in *God Is a DJ,* a collection of conversations with musicians about their relationship to religion and spirituality, Naidoo explicitly uses the term "Gottes-Volk" (God's people) to describe his vision of community, and he also makes clear that his vision of salvation is squarely located in the here and now and not in the afterlife. Schröder, *God Is a DJ,* 122.

17. See Weheliye, *Phonographies,* 145–97, for a more extensive treatment of the symbolic function of the passport for Advanced Chemistry and nonwhite Germans in general.

18. Here, the sample of a Buddhist monk reading from the Dhammapada, which opens Glashaus's track "Erhalte meine Liebe," is also pertinent: "For in this world, hate never yet has dispelled hate. Only love dispels hate. This law is ancient and will last forever." In an interview I conducted with Moses Pelham, he cites this statement as closely echoing his own philosophy. See Weheliye, "Ich will mich nicht ausgrenzen."

19. The German word *herrlich* contains an explicit reference to the Almighty, as in "der Herr."

20. Here Walter Benjamin's notion of a "Jetztzeit" (nowtime) serves as pertinent echo, both in terms of Glashaus's messianic desire and their insistence on both apocalypse and redemption as categories of the present and not the future. Benjamin writes, "The nowtime, which, as a model of messianic time, comprises the entire history of mankind in an enormous condensation, coincides exactly with *the* place the history of humanity occupies in the universe." "On the Concept of History," 396.

21. Oguntoye et al., *Farbe Bekennen,* 141.

22. Wynter, "Unsettling the Coloniality," 260.

23. Similarly, Fred Moten cites a statement by Duke Ellington that beautifully blends *my* people and *the* people so that the distinction between them becomes moot: "Oh but I have such strong influence by the music of the people—*the people!* that's a better word, *the* people rather than *my* people, because *the* people *are* my people." Ellington cited in Moten, *In the Break,* 261, n. 2.

24. The German term *Lied* as used in the English language refers to the works of classical and romantic composers such as Franz Schubert, Robert Schumann, and Johannes Brahms that also made extensive use of the piano as the counterpoint to the human voice. In German, *Lied* refers to any musical work with a song structure, and the genre referenced here is known as *Kunstlied* (art song).

25. Benjamin, "Surrealism," 209.

References

Adams, Anne V. "The Souls of Black Volk: Contradiction? Oxymoron?" In *Not So Plain as Black and White: Afro-German Culture and History, 1890 2000*. Ed. Patricia Mazon und Reinhild Steingröver. 215–31. Rochester: University of Rochester Press, 2005.

Agamben, Giorgio. *Means without End: Notes on Politics*. Trans. Vincenzo Binetti and Cesare Casarino. Minneapolis: University of Minnesota Press, 2000.

Balibar, Etienne. "The Nation Form: History and Ideology." In *Race, Nation, Class: Ambiguous Identities*. Eds. Etienne Balibar and Imanuel Wallerstein. 86–106. New York: Verso, 1991.

Bax, Daniel, and Joshua Aikins. "Wir sind stolz, Deutsche zu sein." *Die Tageszeitung*, July 12, 2001. http://www.taz.de/pt/2001/12/07/a0153.1/text (accessed July 29, 2006).

Benjamin, Walter. "Surrealism: The Last Snapshot of the European Intelligentsia." Trans. Edmund Jephcott. *Selected Writings, Volume 2: 1927–1934*. 1929. Ed. Michael Jennings, Howard Eiland, and Gary Smith. Cambridge, Mass.: Belknap Press of Harvard University Press, 1999. 207–21.

———. "On the Concept of History." Trans. Harry Zohn. *Selected Writings, Volume 4: 1938–1940*. Cambridge, Mass.: Belknap Press of Harvard University Press, 2003. 389–400.

Braun, Christoph. "Oh Herr, Alles wird Dein! Im Land der Pop-Propheten." 18 Aug. 2003.

http://www.fluter.de/look/article.tpl?IdLanguage=5&IdPublication=2&NrIssue=20&NrSection=12&NrArticle=2140. 11 Aug. 2006.

Brothers Keepers. *Adriano (Letzte Warnung)*. Nitty Gritty Music (Warner Brothers), 2001.

Brown, Jacqueline Nassy. "Black Liverpool, Black America, and the Gendering of Diasporic Space." *Cultural Anthropology* 13, no. 3 (1998): 291–325.

———. *Dropping Anchor, Setting Sail: Geographies of Race in Black Liverpool*. Princeton: Princeton University Press, 2005.

Campt, Tina. "The Crowded Space of Diaspora: Intercultural Address and the Tensions of Diasporic Relation." *Radical History Review* 83 (Spring 2002): 94–113.

Edwards, Brent Hayes. "The Uses of Diaspora." *Social Text* 66 (Spring 2001): 45–73.

El-Tayeb, Fatima. "'If You Cannot Pronounce My Name, You Can Just Call Me Pride': Afro-German Activism, Gender, and Hip Hop." *Gender and History* 15, no. 3 (2003): 459–85.

Glashaus. *Glashaus II (Jah Sound System)*. 3P (Mercury-Universal), 2002.

Hardt, Michael, and Antonio Negri. *Multitude: War and Democracy in theAge of Empire*. New York: Penguin, 2004.

Laclau, Ernesto. *On Populist Reason*. New York: Verso, 2005.

Lauré al-Samarai, Nicola. "History, Theory, Experience: Aspects of Diaspora in Black German Feminist Thought." Presentation at "Challenging Europe—Black European Studies in the Twenty-first Century." Mainz, Germany, November 2005.

Moten, Fred. *In the Break: The Aesthetics of the Black Radical Tradition*. Minneapolis: University of Minnesota Press, 2003.

Naidoo, Xavier. *Seine Strassen.* 3P (Sony BMG), 2000.

Oguntoye, Katharina, May Opitz (Ayim), and Dagmar Schultz, eds. *Farbe bekennen: Afro-deutsche Frauen auf den Spuren ihrer Geschichte.* 1986. Frankfurt am Main: Fischer Taschenbuch Verlag, 1992.

Schröder, Matthias. *God Is a DJ: Gespräche mit Popmusikern über Religion.* Neukirchen-Vluyn: Aussaat Verlag, 2000.

Sisters Keepers. *Liebe und Verstand.* Nitty Gritty Music (Warner Brothers), 2001.

Stephens, Michelle Ann. "Disarticulating Black Internationalisms: West Indian Radicals and the Practice of Diaspora." *Small Axe* 17 (2005): 100–111.

Weheliye, Alexander G. *Phonographies: Grooves in Sonic Afro-Modernity.* Durham, N.C.: Duke University Press, 2005.

———. "'Ich will mich nicht ausgrenzen': Alexander G. Weheliye im Gespräch mit dem HipHop-Pionier Moses Pelham." http://www.migration-boell.de/web/integration/47_924.asp.

Winkler, Thomas. "Deutscher Pop entdeckt religiöse Inhalte." October 2003. http://www.goethe.de/ges/rel/thm/de61704.htm. 11 Aug. 2006.

Wollrad, Eske. *Weißsein im Widerspruch: Feministische Perspektiven auf Rassismus, Kultur und Religion.* Königstein: Ulrike Helmer Verlag, 2005.

Wynter, Sylvia. "Unsettling the Coloniality of Being/Power/Truth/Freedom: Towards the Human, after Man, It's Overrepresentation—An Argument." *CR: The New Centennial Review* 3, no. 3 (2003): 257–337.

———. "On How We Mistook the Map for the Territory and Re-Imprisoned Ourselves in Our Unbearable Wrongness of Being, of Désêtre: Black Studies toward the Human Project." In *Not Only the Master's Tools: African-American Studies in Theory and Practice.* Ed. Lewis R. Gordon and Jane Anna Gordon. Boulder, Colo.: Paradigm Publishers, 2006.

10

No Green Pastures: The African Americanization of France

TYLER STOVALL

In 1951, the African American journalist Roi Ottley published a book, *No Green Pastures,* which stands as a landmark text in the history and historiography of the African diaspora. In this book, Ottley explored the lives of Blacks and other minorities in a wide variety of countries. He concluded from this survey that no country he had visited was free of racism; that, in contrast to the perspective of many African American intellectuals upon life abroad, exile abroad offered "no green pastures," no escape from the vicissitudes of bigotry so familiar to blacks in the United States.[1]

For those interested in modern France, Ottley's book seems particularly relevant after the widespread uprisings that struck French suburbia in the fall of 2005. The French have long cherished an image of themselves as a nation free from racial prejudice, a color-blind society par excellence. A crucial part of France's republican heritage from the great Revolution, the idea that all citizens were equal both juridically and socially, has constituted a key aspect of what it means to be French in the modern era. Racial identities and conflicts might trouble other, less happy, lands, but they had no place in French life.[2] The riots of November 2005 frontally challenged this cozy consensus. The specter of thousands of young people of color burning cars, attacking schools, and in general giving violent expression to their fundamental alienation from French society made it a lot more difficult to claim that race had no place in France. By forcing the nation to confront the conditions of its marginalized postcolonial suburban belt, the uprisings of the fall of 2005 underscored a new vision of France, one in which colonial legacies and racial difference constituted the heart of national identity.

November 2005 had a particular significance for the place of Black Americans in French life and culture. During the course of the last century, Blacks from the

United States have played complex roles in France's racial imaginary. African American expatriates in Paris in particular have often been held up as proof of French tolerance and rejection of racism, especially in comparison to American bigotry. At the same time, postcolonial communities and cultures in contemporary France have borrowed freely from Black American cultural models, most notably hip-hop music but also including cinema, dance, and language (for example, the widespread use of the English-language term "Black").[3] When the youth of the *banlieues* rose up in revolt during the fall of 2005, commentators on both sides of the Atlantic compared these events to race riots in America, especially those that struck Los Angeles in 1992. An eminently plastic symbol, the African American could represent both color-blind France and the agonies of the postcolonial republic at the same time.[4]

Given this contrast, what do French views of Black Americans reveal about their own racial history and contemporary condition? How do the glamorous tales of famous expatriates like Josephine Baker and Richard Wright speak to the gritty realities of crumbling *HLMs*, police harassment, and job discrimination on the outskirts of Paris and other French cities?[5] Could it be that African Americans who come to Paris today in search of the legendary color-blind paradise might only find a world very similar to the one they left behind? Such questions, which concern the global nature of race in general and Black American culture in particular, prompted me to attempt a comparative overview of the black histories of the United States and France. In doing so, I will pursue two primary themes. The first is that since the mid-twentieth century there has been a certain convergence between the Black life of the two nations. Another way of considering this is the idea that the communities of Blacks in France have moved from resembling the life of African American expatriates to a greater similarity to Black life back at home in the United States. This convergence has not been one-dimensional, since aspects of African American life have also come to resemble more closely the condition of Blacks in France. Finally, I will briefly compare Black America and France as a whole. Comparisons between France and the United States, the two great modern republics, are legion. My specific purpose here is to consider the ways in which contemporary France in general, not just its peoples of color, has manifested traits reminiscent of the Black American experience.

This contrast between upscale and ghetto centric French images of Black American life has existed for over a generation, yet the events of November 2005 underscored it graphically. They not only suggested the truth of Roi Ottley's conclusion half a century earlier, but at the same time emphasized the staying power of the African American as an iconic figure in French life. In both regards, they indicate new dimensions of the relationship between blackness and French identity at the dawn of the twenty-first century.

Intersecting Histories

Comparing the Black histories of France and the United States is a bit like trying to compare a mouse with an elephant. Not only has metropolitan France had a much smaller population of African descent than the United States, but African Americans have generally received much more popular and scholarly attention than their counterparts across the Atlantic.[6] In spite of this major difference of scale, however, the two diasporas do share many traits, as well as having some important differences.

At the heart of the histories of both Black France and Black America stand the transatlantic slave trade and the slave societies it produced. Both France and the United States not only practiced slavery but share conflicted histories that placed into dialogue slavery and republicanism. Since both nations have viewed themselves as beacons of liberty to the world as a whole, this contrast between freedom and slavery goes to the heart of what it has meant to be French and American in the modern era. For France, the political form of the republic constituted the historical demarcation between absolutist slavery and modern freedom. The nation's two abolitions of slavery, in 1794 and 1848, were both carried out by insurgent republics, and the rebel slaves of Saint-Domingue fought for the republic and liberty against the forces of Napoleon, whose imperial regime had restored slavery in the French Caribbean.[7] Unlike France, the United States has a history as a slave republic, creating a strange hybrid polity in the antebellum era whose contradictions were only resolved by the Civil War.[8]

The slave heritage of both nations also included the division of the national territory into slave and free zones, a division enshrined in legal theory yet malleable in practice. Both metropolitan France and the American North increasingly defined themselves as lands of liberty, but the same flag that flew over them also flew over slave territories. This has often been interpreted as a major distinction between the two nations' Black histories: whereas the United States had a large population of African descent on its national soil, in France slavery was reserved for the colonies in the modern era.[9] Yet if we think of France and its colonies as one integral unit, or alternately view the antebellum U.S. South as a kind of semicolonial periphery, this difference largely disappears. To put it another way, slave and free territories were divided by the Mason-Dixon Line in America and by the Atlantic Ocean in France.

A much more salient contrast between the Black histories of France and the United States is the role of nonslave African migrants. Until very recently, virtually all blacks in the United States descended from slaves brought to the New World as a part of the Middle Passage, either those brought directly to America or migrants from the Caribbean with their own heritage of slavery. The United States never had any African colonies or significant involvement in the affairs of that continent. Africa and African migrants have played a much more prominent role in black life in France. Thanks in part to its belated efforts to stamp out the slave trade, France established a huge formal empire in sub-Saharan Africa in the late nineteenth century. Even after the rapid decolonization of the 1960s, France retains a significant political, cultural, and military influence in francophone Africa. One consequence of this has been a sizeable African migration to France, starting with the *tirailleurs sénégalais* of World War I and becoming a mass phenomenon after 1945. Whereas the American Black population has been almost entirely a product of the Atlantic diaspora, that of France is divided between descendents of Caribbean slaves and African immigrants. Among other things, this distinction has made it much harder to speak of a single Black "community" in France than in America, and even to a certain extent called into question the idea of blackness itself as a social identity.[10]

If the heritage of slavery both unites and differentiates the history of Black America and Black France, so does the post-slave period. Emancipation was an incomplete affair in both the French Caribbean and the American South. In both cases, the former slave-holding elites managed to retain decisive political and economic power, and to preserve the plantation system of agricultural production. Crucially, in both cases postemancipation regimes refused to break up the plantations and distribute the land to the former slaves, ensuring the continuation of poverty and powerlessness whose legacy remains with both nations to this day. Although both Black Americans and Blacks in the French Caribbean became citizens after emancipation, their citizenship was in many ways in name only.[11]

The late nineteenth century also witnessed the rise of racialized versions of democracy and imperial expansion in both France and the United States. American scholars of whiteness have demonstrated how increasingly in the 1800s democracy and liberty were racially coded, so that white racial status became an essential requirement for full citizenship. The massive waves of immigration from Europe that peopled nineteenth-century America gradually forced an expansion of the nation's democratic polity, but only to the extent that the new immigrants could claim to be white, and their claims rested above all on establishing distinctions between themselves and peoples of color in general, Blacks in particular.[12] In France, the achievement of universal male suffrage under the Third Republic went hand in hand with the creation of a new republican empire based upon the principles of assimilation and universalism.

Both the United States and France, and essentially those two countries alone, became imperial republics by 1900. Empires without an empress or emperor, this strange and contradictory political formation rested upon racial distinctions. In both countries, a nation of citizens ruled over an empire of subjects, and in both the citizens were mostly white, the subjects mostly black and brown.[13] The

Black citizens of the United States and France occupied a paradoxical position in these racial empires: largely deprived of democratic rights at home, they were often used as soldiers of empire abroad. France made widespread use of Caribbean soldiers and administrators in Africa, and the United States used Blacks both in the conquest of the Indians in the West and in imperial campaigns in Cuba and the Philippines.[14]

Perhaps the most salient difference between Black America and Black France in the postemancipation era concerned the level of violence directed against the former slaves. Whereas the brutality of France's slave colonies in the Caribbean was unparalleled, after 1848 the French Caribbean did not know the level of violence experienced by the Blacks of the American South. The post-Reconstruction governments of the South were established by and survived thanks to a reign of racial terror symbolized by the Ku Klux Klan and other white vigilante organizations.[15] Since in the French Caribbean Blacks represented the overwhelming majority of the population, whites could not successfully undertake the kinds of lynchings, beatings, and wholesale assaults on entire black communities that became a regular feature of life in the American South after the Civil War. The minority status of African Americans was reinforced by a greater level of social isolation than in France. The successful imposition of rigid racial categorizations, notably the famous "one drop" rule, which made anyone with any discernable African ancestry at all officially Black, emphasized the harsh, immutable distinction between whites and Blacks in American society, rendering theoretically impossible the kind of *métissage* that created a much more Creolized Black population in France and its empire.[16]

One potent reaction of blacks to the perils and disappointments of postemancipation society in both the United States and France was migration. In both cases, however, this primarily took the form not of exile from their country of origin altogether but rather a move within the nation from formerly slave to traditionally free territories. In the United States, the first great black migration brought hundreds of thousands of African Americans from the South to the North, establishing large new Black communities in cities like New York and Chicago. These migrants produced a vibrant Black urban culture, one that reached its apogee with the Harlem Renaissance and shaped seminal musical forms like jazz and blues.[17] French Blacks also migrated to the metropole in the early twentieth century, if not in such large numbers. For many Caribbean Blacks in particular, the metropole represented the "good" France of republicanism and emancipation as opposed to the "bad" France of the white plantation owners and colonial administration.[18]

World War I played a central role in both migrations. The needs of the American war economy and the temporary cessation of immigration from Europe opened up jobs in the North for American Blacks.[19] In France, the desperate need for both military and industrial manpower led the government to enlist African and Caribbean soldiers to fight in the European war, bringing to the metropole the first mass population of color in French history.[20] The *tirailleurs sénégalais* in particular had a major impact on French views of Blacks and of Africa, as the history of the famous Banania ads showed. Modern warfare required the social and economic mobilization of all sectors of the national population, and the ideology of the war portrayed it as a struggle for liberty and popular sovereignty. In promoting Black migration from Black colonies and former slave states to the heart of national territory, the Great War undermined the distinction between these different regions. Although not fully realized until after 1945, the roots of the postcolonial era in France and of the civil rights movement in the United States go back to the first world war.

World War I also brought the first significant African American migration to France, a movement that embodied different aspects of the histories of both Black France and black America, and put the two Black cultures into dialogue. Although blacks had traveled from the United States to France since the eighteenth century, World War I marked the first time that a critical mass of African Americans settled there, establishing a permanent Black community. The war itself brought 200,000 Black soldiers and laborers to France from America, and also powerfully reinforced the perception of the French as a people without color prejudice, in stark contrast to white Americans. The interwar taste for exoticism and black culture, plus the popularity of jazz, made Paris in particular a center for hundreds of African American performers, artists, and writers. Josephine Baker's triumphal Parisian debut with the *Revue nègre* in 1925 cemented the idea of France as a land open to Black talent.[21]

This rosy portrait of African American life in Paris contrasted sharply, of course, with the experiences of most French Blacks. Like African Americans, many French Caribbean and African soldiers returned home after the war demanding full citizenship only to be disappointed by the durability of the colonial order of racial inequality. In francophone Africa, the new emphasis on the economic development of the colonies led to a massive increase in forced labor, often under brutally exploitative conditions. While Blacks in the French Caribbean and Africa did not suffer the kind of violence that afflicted American Blacks during the race riots of the 1919 "Red Summer," neither did they achieve full acceptance as French citizens during the years after World War I.[22]

The experience of French Blacks in the metropole, like that of African Americans in Paris, constituted a partial exception to this rule. Although many of these Blacks were unskilled laborers, a solid core of students and intellectuals also came to France in the 1920s and 1930s. As a counterpart to the world of Black American jazz in Montmartre, musicians from the Caribbean established a lively performative culture in Montparnasse, centering around nightclubs like the *Bal nègre.* The rise of negritude in the 1930s brought young students like Léon Damas, Léopold Senghor, and Aimé Césaire together in Paris to explore the global nature of Black culture. This dialogue between francophone Blacks from the Caribbean and Africa constituted a seminal moment in the creation of a Black French culture. Moreover, its many interactions with African American intellectuals underscored the parallels between the two Black experiences. Langston Hughes, Countee Cullen, and other Americans frequented the weekly salon of the Nardal sisters in the Paris suburbs, and Claude McKay's novel *Banjo* became must reading for Black students in France. Both negritude and the Harlem Renaissance thus exemplified a new Black consciousness, emphasizing the African roots of Black cultures and their signal contributions to the human experience as a whole.[23]

Towards Full Citizenship?

If the history of African American expatriates in France reflected a certain confluence of the conditions of Blacks on both sides of the Atlantic in the interwar years, the aftermath of the second world war saw it become more a symbol of the difference between these two national experiences. At the same time, the situation of French Blacks came to resemble that of American Blacks more than ever before. One example of this is the parallel histories of civil rights in America and decolonization in France. In both cases, Blacks asserted, more powerfully than ever before, demands for full inclusion into the national community. The parallel is strongest between Black America and the French Caribbean: both black communities overwhelmingly rejected the idea of separation from the national community, instead achieving a recognition of their rights as citizens. The end of de jure segregation and the granting of voting rights to Blacks in the United States strongly resembled the granting of departmental status to Martinique, Guadeloupe, and Guyana in 1946. In contrast, France's sub-Saharan African colonies chose formal independence, but usually in a way that ensured continued close ties to France. In both the United States and France, therefore, the twenty years after the end of World War II brought at least the promise of full equality for these nations' Black populations.[24]

These years also brought unprecedented levels of Black migration to national heartlands. This happened most dramatically in France: during the 1960s in particular, France brought hundreds of thousands of Caribbean laborers to the metropole, placing them in both public and private sector employment. Mass migration from Black Africa took longer to develop, but by the end of the 1960s one could frequently encounter Africans in the streets of Paris and other French cities. In the United States, the second world war initiated what has been called the second Great Migration, even larger than the first, of Blacks from the South to the North.[25] The great urban uprisings that shook America during the 1960s illustrated the fact that, for the first time in the nation's history, a majority of its Black population lived outside the South. In both cases, large new Black populations helped reshape urban structures and society in general. Both France and the United States invested heavily in urban public housing after the war, building the (usually horrendously ugly) high-rise towers known as "housing projects" and *habitations à loyer modéré*. Over time, these would become centers of Black settlement and culture as well as symbols of the limits of migration as a strategy for racial liberation and the failures of societies to integrate fully their Black citizens into the life of the nation.[26]

This of course brings us to one of the greatest contrasts of all between Black America and Black France. African Americans confronted the limits of civil rights with a widespread series of urban uprisings and the development of new ideological forms (that is, Black Power, Black nationalism) that harshly criticized American society and championed Black culture and Black unity.[27] At the same time, blacks were able to use their numerical weight and political mobilization to push successfully for a number of state practices, ranging from voting rights and antidiscrimination legislation to affirmative action, that brought the dream of full equality much closer to reality, in particular creating a sizeable Black middle class. In contrast, the much smaller Black communities of France, lacking the dense institutional networks and political power of African Americans, remained much more quiescent. In the francophone worlds of Africa and the Caribbean, black protest was similarly muted. Political movements for independence developed in the French West Indies, but for the most part lacked mass support or political impact.[28] Francophone Africa became a classic case of neocolonialism, with the French military intervening in the political affairs of the continent more than thirty times from 1960 to the end of the twentieth century.[29] Paradoxically, while Black France and Black America resembled each other more than ever, these growing similarities also underscored the very real differences between the two nations' Black cultures.

The last quarter of the twentieth century brought further shifts that in some ways pointed to a possible convergence of communities of African descent on both sides of the Atlantic. From the late 1970s on, Black Americans faced a growing wave of racist activism that sought to undo the social and political achievements of the civil rights and Black Power eras. The election of Ronald Reagan as president ushered in a series of attacks on all programs, notably school integration and affirmative action, intended to improve the Black condition in America and reaffirmed the intention of the Republican party to use white racism for political gains. The dawn of the new century witnessed repeated attempts to disenfranchise Blacks, not only the electoral chicanery that ensured the election and reelection of George W. Bush as president in 2000 and 2004, but also the imprisonment of huge numbers of Black men that has deprived them of, among other things, the right to vote. This climate of racist backlash has threatened to silence African Americans and reverse some of the key gains of the civil rights revolution.[30]

Whereas the full integration of Blacks into American society has begun to seem more and more like a dream deferred, during the same period Blacks in France began to enjoy more of a presence in national life. The nation's Black population has continued to grow, spurred largely by undocumented immigration from sub-Saharan Africa. The rise of the National Front during the 1980s certainly threatened this population, but it also prompted an unprecedented level of antiracist organizing and public activism by Black and other minority communities. The most prominent antiracist organization, SOS-Racisme, chose as its head a young Black man named Harlem Désir. Blacks also became much more prominent culturally in France. The rise of hip-hop culture from its African American roots to global prominence during the 1980s and 1990s had a particular impact upon France, which soon became the second largest producer of rap music in the world after the United States. French Blacks were intimately involved with hip-hop both as musicians, integrating into it musical traditions from Africa and the Caribbean, and as producers. The first TV show in France ever hosted by a Black man, Sydney Duteil, was a dance show entitled *Hip Hop.* The trendy use of the English-language term "Black" in France also reflected a new awareness of blackness as a social and cultural fact.[31]

If African and Caribbean life in France moved gingerly toward a greater sense of blackness, African American life began also to exhibit some of the traits of French communities. By the end of the century, the United States was experiencing a small but noticeable immigration from the African continent. Many leading Senegalese musicians divided their time between Dakar, Paris, and New York, and one could buy the exact same trinkets from African street merchants in American and French cities.[32] Increasingly like France, Black life in the United States was no longer exclusively the product of the transatlantic slave trade.

Another similarity was what one might call the growing "Creolization" of African American society. Although privilege and light skin had often gone together, racial traditions like the "one drop" rule and powerful currents within the black community emphasizing social and political unity largely rendered the idea of a separate Creole elite unworkable in the United States. Moreover, interracial sexual relationships had traditionally been far less acceptable than in France, as African American soldiers discovered during World War I. Over the last few decades, however, the number of marriages and other sexual liaisons between blacks and whites in the United States has risen sharply and has become much more accepted in American culture. One consequence has been a newly assertive mixed race population, many of whose members have insisted on claiming both black and white identity and distinguished themselves from African Americans as a social and racial group.[33] The fact that this has been primarily a middle-class phenomenon further underscores the similarity with racial patterns in France and the French West Indies.[34]

These patterns of convergence between Black France and Black America have changed the significance of African American expatriates in France. The dual impact of decolonization in France and the civil rights movement in the United States cast into question the traditional opposition between a tolerant France and a racist United States. As the French population became increasingly multicultural, often with its own patterns of racial segmentation and discrimination, France began to seem more like the country many expatriates sought to escape. Moreover, the makeup of the expatriate population itself shifted. The rise of a large Black middle class in the United States meant that increasingly the African Americans who came to France were less likely to be artists, musicians, and writers, and more likely to be students, tourists, and people in international business, just like Americans as a whole. Many of these visitors had a strong cosmopolitan interest in Black cultures overseas, and were as likely to visit Dakar, Jamaica, or Bahia as Paris. Finally, the rise of mass transatlantic air travel in the 1960s meant that settling abroad no longer represented the definitive rupture that it did in the 1920s. As one expatriate commented, when one could breakfast in Paris, take a jet across the ocean, and then dine in New York the same day, the idea of exile no longer had the same meaning. By the end of the twentieth century, therefore, the Black expatriate colony in Paris had become less a separate community and more an extension of the educated African American middle class overseas.

By the beginning of the new millennium, therefore, Black France and Black America had come to resemble each other more closely, in ways that rendered the transatlantic link historically constituted by African American expatriates less important in effecting a connection between the two. The French suburban uprisings during the fall of 2005 made this clear. One could discern strong parallels between them and the urban riots that shook the United States in the wake of the 1992 beating of Rodney King. Both arose out of feelings of the exclusion of minority citizens in general and of police harassment and brutality in particular. Both highlighted the particularly difficult conditions of poor young men of color. Both illustrated strong sentiments of frustrated consumerism, as Americans looted stores for goods they could not buy and French people burned cars they could not afford.[35]

But the events of November 2005 also showed the strong differences between black France and the United States. Blacks were not nearly as central to the uprisings as were African Americans in Los Angeles and other U.S. cities. There was much less violence against people in France than in the United States, and many fewer deaths. Finally, the events in France had a much greater political impact than the Rodney King protests in the United States: the latter occurred in the middle of a presidential campaign and were completely ignored by all the major candidates, whereas the suburban riots in France dominated that nation's political discourse for weeks if not months. Paradoxically, given the prevalent contrast between a multicultural America and a color-blind France, the fall 2005 disturbances showed that the French people were beginning to grapple with fundamental questions of race, power, and citizenship, whereas the 1992 events (and subsequent racial conflicts as well) have underscored the near-impossibility of straight talk about race in mainstream American political discourse.

The events of the fall of 2005 also underscored a rising sense of black consciousness that had been developing in France since the 1990s. In 1998, France celebrated the 150th anniversary of the final abolition of slavery in its empire. This became an opportunity for West Indians in both the metropole and the Caribbean to mobilize around the question of the memory of slavery and to press their perspectives as a Black community within France.[36] They forced their country to confront its history as a slave nation, a process that culminated in the government's formal apology for its historic involvement in the slave trade and the slave system in general.[37] The 1990s also brought a new wave of activism on the part of Africans in France, in particular undocumented immigrants. In 1992, for example, hundreds of Malians camped out in front of the Chateau de Vincennes outside Paris to dramatize the plight of African immigrants, and in 1996 police expelled 300 Africans seeking sanctuary in the city's Saint-Bernard church.[38] By the beginning of the twenty-first century, Black Frenchmen and women began creating a series of Black communal associations, culminating in November 2005 with the foundation of CRAN (the Representative Council of Black Associations) representing some sixty African and Caribbean groups in France.[39]

In a France shaped by concerns over race riots and rising Black consciousness, what is the significance of African American expatriates, or more broadly, how do black Americans outside the United States illustrate and shape the politics of blackness? Have Richard Wright and even Afrika Bambaata been displaced by Colin Powell and Condoleezza Rice as prototypical Black Americans in the eyes of the world? Whereas most African Americans in Paris reacted with concern to the suburban disturbances of 2005, they demonstrated no special relationship to them or to the world they inhabited. Most Black expatriates live in Paris, not the suburban housing projects. When I talked to one friend, a leading member of that community, last November, he said that he knew little about what was going on "out there." Thanks to the Internet, which allowed people around the world to read the French press and a wide variety of relevant blogs online, I could learn as much about the events in the *banlieues* from my home in California as could many residents of Paris.

Nor, I would argue, did the specter of race riots in France lead many black Americans there to reconsider their reasons for staying, since few today believe in the old notion of color-blind France. The November riots in France suggest a view of African American expatriates as people attracted to life overseas for a number of reasons ranging from personal and family ties to a feeling that a black American can receive more respect and encounter less racism directed toward him or her by leaving the United States. To accuse Black American expatriates in Paris of indulging in privileged status is both to ignore the very real differences in racial oppression on different sides of the Atlantic and to deny people the option of achieving liberation through flight that has been a primary means of agency for Blacks in both France and the United States over the years.[40] As many Caribbean and African immigrants to the United States have also found, blackness somehow becomes more acceptable when it speaks with a foreign accent. Theorists and celebrants of diaspora should thus also consider the ways in which migration can bring both greater freedom and greater privilege, and the relationship between the two.

Finally, the uprisings of the fall of 2005 also crystallized a new image of France that bears more than a little similarity to traditional views of Black America. The most obvious symbol is the huge popularity of hip-hop among young French people of all colors. However, if this alone symbolizes a similarity with American blackness, then the whole world is African American (including much of the United States). More significant in the case of France are the difficulties in social, economic, and political life that the riots highlighted. For decades now, France has been portrayed as a land in crisis, economically stagnant and unwilling to abandon the welfare state of the late twentieth century in favor of neoliberal orthodoxies.[41] The idea of France as overdependent on the welfare state resembles the classic idea of Black Americans as dependent on welfare and lacking entrepreneurial drive. Both the suburban upheavals of the fall of 2005 and the disturbances provoked by the government's attempts to change youth employment laws in early 2006 played into this idea of France as socially troubled and economically retrograde.

Foreign policy, surprisingly enough, constitutes another area of similarity. Ever since the start of the second Iraq war, the Bush administration and its allies, notably Tony Blair's Britain, have tended to regard France as politically out of step with the "war on terror" and its assertion of neoimperialist global hegemony.[42] Only in the summer of 2006 did the congressional cafeteria in Washington drop the name "freedom fries" in favor of the traditional "French fries."[43] Just as American Blacks have continued to resist neoliberal politics domestically, voting overwhelmingly for the political opposition, so has France come to symbolize a rejection of those policies internationally. The fact that two leading proponents of the Bush administration's foreign policy, Colin Powell and Condoleezza Rice, are Black underscores this similarity, since their opposition to the French replicates their isolation from the political views of the vast majority of African Americans. The uprisings in fall 2005 were widely interpreted in the American media and elsewhere as ominous manifestations of the new Muslim Europe, a kind of European intifada, and were often blamed erroneously on Islamic fundamentalism.[44] The idea of France as a land of social and political danger in the heart of the Western world resonates with the view of Black American ghettos as the haunts of the underclass at the center of the imperial United States.

A final similarity between France and Black America arises from this view of France as a center of opposition to neoimperialist hegemony. A key theme of the African American experience has been the contrast between blacks as socially and politically excluded from American life in general, and their central role in American culture. From food to music to political ideology, the black experience has been so central to what it means to be American that one simply cannot imagine the United States without it. Yet Blacks have also remained marginal to the opportunities offered by American society, and to America's view of itself: witness the difficulty of integrating an analysis of slavery into the dominant image of the United States as a beacon of freedom. Strikingly, American views of France seem to be replicating this paradox. For all the condemnations of French society and politics, the elite role of French culture in American life remains unquestioned. The best restaurants in any American city invariably serve French cuisine (in fact, traditional peasant foods like cassoulet often benefit from a transatlantic status upgrade), and those who turn up their noses at French fries happily indulge in bistro fare or French-inspired nouvelle cuisine. The same is true of cultural production in the arts and humanities. Even those American conservatives who snub French culture do so by portraying it as a symbol of cultural elitism, in contrast to their own jingoist populism. In short, on a global scale the French seem to be experiencing what African Americans have long known: people can love what you do while ultimately hating who you are.[45]

The crisis of the fall of 2005 in France did not constitute the first time that African American expatriates had to confront the limits of French tolerance; the Algerian war and the rise of a multicultural population in France during the second half of the twentieth century had already done so. It did, however, highlight important similarities and convergences between Black France and Black America, and underscore the importance of a dialogue between the two. On the one hand, these convergences and increased opportunities for dialogue undercut the historically seminal role of African American expatriates in bridging the two experiences: African American culture is everywhere today, and television and the Internet render it immediately accessible to people around the world. On the other hand, this process of convergence suggests a new role for Black Americans in France, one that showcases the possibilities of a diasporic Black community, exploring its advantages and limitations. Since French Blacks also travel and live abroad, to the United States and elsewhere, such a role speaks to another kind of transatlantic convergence. The triangular diaspora of Senegalese musicians between Dakar, Paris, and New York is a case in point. One may say, in conclusion therefore, that the history of Black American expatriates in France may be entering a new phase, one marked less by American exceptionalism and more by integration into the tradition of Black diasporas as a whole. In this spirit, Paris may no longer constitute a refuge from racism, but rather the front line of diasporic and global debates about what it means to be Black.

Notes

Earlier versions of this paper were presented at the Museum of the African Diaspora in San Francisco, Stanford University, and Northwestern University. I would like to thank Waldo Martin, Trica Keaton, Elizabeth Mudimbe-Boyi, and Louis Chude-Sokei for their kind and helpful comments.

1. Roi Ottley, *No Green Pastures* (New York: Scribner, 1951).

2. On questions of race and republicanism in France, see among many works, Sue Peabody and Tyler Stovall, eds., *The Color of Liberty: Histories of Race in France* (Durham: Duke University Press, 2003); Herrick Chapman and Laura Frader, *Race in France: An Interdisciplinary Approach to the Politics of Difference* (New York: Berghahn Books, 2004); Maxim Silverman, *Deconstructing the Nation: Immigration, Racism, and Citizenship in Modern France* (London: Routledge, 1992); Michel Wieviorka, *Une société fragmentée? Le multiculturalisme en débat* (Paris: La Découverte, 1996).

3. Alec Hargreaves and Mark McKinney, eds., *Post-Colonial Cultures in France* (New York: Routledge, 1997); Paul Silverstein, "'Why Are We Waiting to Start the Fire?' French Gangsta Rap and the Critique of State Capitalism," in Alain-Philippe Durand, *Black, Blanc, Beur: Rap Music and Hip-Hop Culture in the Francophone World* (Lanham, Md.: Scarecrow Press, 2002), 45–67; "Black: Africains, Antillais . . . Cultures noires en France," special issue of *Autrement*, no. 49 (Apr. 1983).

4. Colin Nickerson, "Youths' Poverty, Despair Fuel Violent Unrest in France," *Boston Globe*, Nov. 6, 2005.

5. Trica Danielle Keaton, "An Open Letter to France from the 'Other France,'" unpublished paper presented to the conference "Paris Is Burning," Museum of the African Diaspora, San Francisco, April 2006. On contemporary African American tourism in Paris, see Tyler Stovall, "Paris Soul," *African American Travel* (Fall 1997); Bennetta Jules-Rosette, "Black Paris: Touristic Simulations," *Annals of Tourism Research* 21, no. 4 (1994); Ervin Dyer, "Passage to Paris: A New Wave of Black Americans Is Calling the

French Capital Home," *Crisis,* January/February 2006; Christiann Anderson and Monique Y. Wells, *Paris Reflections: Walks through African American Paris* (Blacksburg, Va.: McDonald and Woodward, 2002).

6. This is of course reflected in the historiographies of the two subjects. A comprehensive listing of major texts on African American history would take up far more space than that available for this entire article, whereas the number of studies of black France is relatively limited. For the former, some key texts are John Hope Franklin, *From Slavery to Freedom: A History of African Americans* (New York: McGraw Hill, 1994); Manning Marable, *Living Black History: How Reimagining the African American Past Can Remake America's Racial Future* (New York: Basic Civitas, 2006); Evelyn Brooks Higginbotham, ed., *The Harvard Guide to African American History* (Cambridge, Mass.: Harvard University Press, 2001), 22–26; see also the brief but stimulating essay by Thomas Holt, "From Slavery to Freedom and the Conceptualization of African American History," *Journal of Negro History* 785, nos. 1, 2 (Spring 2000). On the history of black France, see Shelby McCloy, *The Negro in France* (Louisville: University of Kentucky Press, 1961); Pascal Blanchard et al., *Le Paris Noir* (Paris: Hazan, 2001); Pap Ndiaye, "Pour une histoire des populations noires en France: Préalables théoriques," *Mouvement social* (Fall 2005); Mar Fall, *Les Africains noirs en France: Des tirailleurs sénégalais aux . . . blacks* (Paris: Harmattan, 1986); Philippe Dewitte, *Les mouvements nègres en France, 1919–1939* (Paris: Harmattan, 1985).

7. Louis Sala-Molins, *Dark Side of Light: Slavery and the French Enlightenment* (Minneapolis: University of Minnesota Press, 2006); C.L.R. James, *Black Jacobins: Toussaint L'Ouverture and the San Domingo Revolution* (New York: Random House, 1963); Carolyn Fick, *The Making of Haiti: The Saint Domingue Revolution from Below* (Knoxville: University of Tennessee Press, 1990); Laurent Dubois, *Avengers of the New World: The Story of the Haitian Revolution* (Cambridge, Mass.: Harvard University Press, 2004); Lawrence Jennings, *French Anti-Slavery: The Movement for the Abolition of Slavery in France* (Cambridge: Cambridge University Press, 2000).

8. David Brion-Davis, *Inhuman Bondage: The Rise and Fall of Slavery in the New World* (New York: Oxford University Press, 2006); George M. Frederickson, *The Arrogance of Race: Historical Perspectives on Slavery, Racism, and Social Inequality* (Middletown, Conn.: Wesleyan University Press, 1988).

9. Sue Peabody, *"There Are No Slaves in France": The Political Culture of Race and Slavery under the Ancien Régime* (New York: Oxford University Press, 1996).

10. Félix German, "Dangerous Liaisons: The Lives and Labor of Antilleans and Sub-Saharan Africans in 1960s Paris" (PhD diss., University of California, Berkeley, 2007).

11. Frederick Cooper, Thomas C. Holt, and Rebecca Scott, *Beyond Emancipation: Explorations of Race, Labor, and Citizenship in Postemancipation Societies* (Chapel Hill: University of North Carolina Press, 2000); Leon Litwack, *Been in the Storm so Long: The Aftermath of Slavery* (New York: Knopf, 1979); Auguste Cochin, *L'abolition de l'esclavage* (Paris: Désormeaux, 1979); Mickaëlla L. Périna, "Construire une identité politique à partir des vestiges de l'esclavage? Les department français d'Amérique entre heritage et choix," in Patrick Weil and Stéphane Dufoix, *L'esclavage, la colonization, et après . . .* (Paris: Presses Universitaires de France, 2005), 509–32; Kim D. Butler, "Abolition and

the Politics of Identity in the Afro-Atlantic Diaspora: Toward a Comparative Approach," in Darlene Clark Hine and Jacqueline McLeod, eds., *Crossing Boundaries: Comparative History of Black People in Diaspora* (Bloomington: Indiana University Press, 1999), 121–33.

12. On whiteness theory, see David C. Roediger, *The Wages of Whiteness: Race and the Making of the American Working Class* (London: Verso, 1991); Roediger, *Colored White: Transcending the Racial Past* (Berkeley: University of California Press, 2002).

13. Alice Conklin, *Mission to Civilize: The Republican Idea of Empire in France and West Africa* (Stanford: Stanford University Press, 1997); Ann L. Stoler, ed., *Haunted by Empire: Geographies of Intimacy in North American History* (Durham: Duke University Press, 2006);

14. Willard B. Gatewood, *Black Americans and the White Man's Burden, 1898–1903* (Urbana: University of Illinois Press, 1975); Véronique Hélénon, "Les administrateurs coloniaux originaires de Guadeloupe, Martinique et Guyane dans les colonies françaises d'Afrique, 1880–1939" (PhD thesis, Ecole des Hautes Etudes en Sciences Sociales, Paris, 1997).

15. C. Vann Woodward, *The Strange Career of Jim Crow* (New York: Oxford University Press, 1965); Leon Litwack, *Trouble in Mind: Black Southerners in the Age of Jim Crow* (New York: Vintage, 1999).

16. F. James Davis, *Who is Black? One Nation's Definition* (University Park: Pennsylvania State University Press, 1991); David A. Hollinger, *Cosmopolitanism and Solidarity: Studies in Ethnoracial, Religious, and Professional Affiliation in the United States* (Madison: University of Wisconsin Press, 2006); Owen White, *Children of the French Empire: Miscegenation and Colonial Society in French West Africa, 1895–1960* (Oxford: Oxford University Press, 1999); Emmanuelle Saada, *Les enfants de la colonie. Les métis de l'empire français entre sujétion et citoyenneté* (Paris: La Découverte, 2004).

17. Alain Locke, *The New Negro* (1925; reprint, New York: Atheneum, 1989); George Hutchinson, *The Harlem Renaissance in Black and White* (Cambridge, Mass.: Harvard University Press, 1989); David Levering Lewis, *When Harlem Was in Vogue* (New York: Oxford University Press, 1989); James R. Grossman, *Land of Hope: Chicago, Black Southerners, and the Great Migration* (Chicago: University of Chicago Press, 1989).

18. Michel Giraud, "Les enjeux presents de la mémoire de l'esclavage," in Weil and Dufoix.

19. William Trotter Jr., *Black Milwaukee: The Making of an Industrial Proletariat, 1915–1945* (Urbana: University of Illinois Press, 1985); Trotter, ed., *The Great Migration in Historical Perspective: New Dimensions of Race, Class, and Gender* (Bloomington: University of Indiana Press, 1991).

20. Joe Lunn, *Memoirs of the Maelstrom: A Senegalese Oral History of the First World War* (Oxford: James Currey, 1999); Gregory Mann, *Native Sons: West African Veterans and France in the Twentieth Century* (Durham: Duke University Press, 2006); Marc Michel, *L'Appel à l'Afrique: Contributions et Réactions à l'Effort de Guerre en A.O.F. (1914–1919)* (Paris: Publications de la Sorbonne, 1982).

21. Tyler Stovall, *Paris Noir: African Americans in the City of Light* (Boston: Houghton-Mifflin, 1996); Jody Blake, *Le Tumulte Noir: Modernist Art and Popular Entertainment*

in Jazz-Age Paris (University Park: Pennsylvania State University Press, 1999); Petrine Archer-Shaw, *Negrophilia: Avant-Garde Paris and Black Culture in the 1920s* (New York: Thames and Hudson, 2000); Brett Berliner, *Ambivalent Desire: The Exotic Black Other in Jazz-Age France* (Amherst: University of Massachusetts Press, 2002); Phyllis Rose, *Jazz Cleopatra: Josephine Baker in Her Time* (New York: Doubleday, 1989); Elizabeth Ezra, *The Colonial Unconscious: Race and Culture in Interwar France* (Ithaca: Cornell University Press, 2000).

22. Conklin, *Mission to Civilize;* Gary Wilder, *The French Imperial Nation-State: Negritude and Colonial Humanism between the Wars* (Chicago: University of Chicago Press, 2006); Tony Chafer and Amanda Sackur, eds., *French Colonial Empire and the Popular Front: Hope and Disillusion* (New York: Palgrave, 1999); Martin Thomas, *The French Empire between the Wars: Imperialism, Politics, and Society* (Manchester: Manchester University Press, 2005).

23. Lilyan Kesteloot, *Black Writers in French: A Literary History of Negritude* (Washington, D.C.: Howard University Press, 1991); Brent Hayes Edwards, *The Practice of Diaspora: Literature, Translation, and the Rise of Black Internationalism* (Cambridge, Mass.: Harvard University Press, 2003); T. Denean Sharpley-Whiting, *Negritude Women* (Minneapolis: University of Minnesota Press, 2002); Claude McKay, *Banjo: A Story without a Plot* (1929; reprint, New York: Harcourt, Brace, and Jovanovich, 1957).

24. On the American civil rights movement, see Taylor Branch, *Parting the Waters* (New York: Simon and Schuster, 1988); David Garrow, *Bearing the Cross: Martin Luther King, Jr., and the Southern Christian Leadership Conference* (New York: Vintage, 1986). On departmentalization in the French West Indies, see Richard D. E. Burton, *La famille coloniale: la Martinique et la mere patrie, 1789–1992* (Paris: Harmattan, 1994); Armand Nicolas, *Histoire de la Martinique,* vol. 3 (Paris: Harmattan, 1998).

25. Nicholas Lemann, *The Promised Land: The Great Black Migration and How It Changed America* (New York: A. A. Knopf, 1991).

26. Elizabeth Huttman et al., *Urban Housing Segregation of Minorities in Western Europe and the United States* (Durham: Duke University Press, 1991); Thomas Sugrue, *The Origins of the Urban Crisis: Race and Inequality in Postwar Detroit* (Princeton: Princeton University Press, 1996); Mehdi Lallaoui, *Du bidonville aux HLM* (Paris: Diffusion Syros, 1993).

27. Stokely Carmichael and Charles V. Hamilton, *Black Power: The Politics of Liberation in America* (New York: Vintage, 1967); Peniel E. Joseph, ed., *The Black Power Movement: Rethinking the Civil Rights-Black Power Era* (New York: Routledge, 2006); Jeffrey Ogbonna Green Ogbar, *Black Power: Radical Politics and African American Identity* (Baltimore: Johns Hopkins University Press, 2005).

28. Richard D. E. Burton, *Assimilation or Independence? Prospects for Martinique* (Montreal: McGill University, 1978); Alain Blérald, *La question nationale en Guadeloupe et en Martinique: Essai sur l'histoire politique* (Paris: Harmattan, 1998).

29. Patrick Manning, *Francophone Sub-Saharan Africa, 1880–1995* (New York: Cambridge University Press, 1998); Tony Chafer, *The End of Empire in French West Africa: France's Successful Decolonization?* (New York: Berg, 2003).

30. Thomas Byrne Edsall and Mary D. Edsall, *Chain Reaction: The Impact of Race, Rights, and Taxes on American Politics* (New York: Norton, 1992).

31. Harlem Désir, *Touche pas à mon pote* (Paris: B. Grasset, 1985); Fred Constant, "Talking Race in Colorblind France: Equality Denied, 'Blackness' Reclaimed," paper presented at the conference "Black Europe and the African Diaspora," Northwestern University, April 2006; Andre Prevos, "Postcolonial Popular Music in France: Rap Music and Hip-Hop Culture in the 1980s," in Tony Mitchell, ed., *Rap and Hip-Hop Outside the USA* (Middletown, Conn.: Wesleyan University Press, 2001), 39–56.

32. James Winders, *Paris Africain: Rhythms of the African Diaspora* (New York: Palgrave Macmillan, 2006).

33. Naomi Zack, ed., *American Mixed Race: The Culture of Micro-Diversity* (Lanham, Md.: Rowman and Littlefield, 1995); Jon Michael Spencer, *The New Colored People: The Mixed-Race Movement in America* (New York: New York University Press, 1987); David A. Hollinger, *Postethnic America: Beyond Multiculturalism* (New York: Basic Books, 2000).

34. Michel Giraud, *Races et classes à la Martinique* (Paris: Editions Anthropos, 1979).

35. Jewelle Taylor Gibbs, *Race and Justice: Rodney King and OJ Simpson in a House Divided* (San Francisco: Jossey-Bass, 1996); Min Hyoung Song, *Strange Future: Pessimism and the 1992 Los Angeles Riots* (Durham: Duke University Press, 2005).

36. Catherine Reinhardt Constant, "Slavery and Commemoration: Remembering the French Abolitionary Decree 150 Years Later," in Alec Hargreaves, ed., *Memory, Empire, and Postcolonialism: The Legacies of French Colonialism* (Lanham, Md.: Lexington Books, 2005), 11–36.

37. "France Pays Homage to Victims of African Slave Trade," *San Francisco Chronicle*, May 11, 2006, A19.

38. Winders, *Paris Africain*, chapter 4.

39. Constant, "Talking Race in Color-blind France."

40. Here I disagree with Ch. Didier Gondola; see his "'But I Ain't African, I'm American!': Black American Exiles and the Construction of Racial Identities in Twentieth-Century France," in Heike Raphael-Hernandez, ed., *Blackening Europe: The African American Presence* (New York: Routledge, 2004), 201–16.

41. Timothy Smith, *France in Crisis: Welfare, Inequality, and Globalization since 1980* (New York: Cambridge University Press, 2004).

42. Daniel Levy et al., *Old Europe, New Europe, Core Europe: Transatlantic Relations after the Iraq War* (London: Verso, 2006).

43. "Au Revoir, Freedom Fries!" *New York Times*, Aug. 4, 2006.

44. See, for example, "War on Terror—Battleground France," *National Review*, Dec. 5, 2005; "Falluja-sur-Seine," *Daily Standard*, Nov. 8, 2005.

45. Greg Tate, ed., *Everything but the Burden: What White People Are Taking from Black Culture* (New York: Broadway Books, 2003).

SECTION 3

Theorizing, (Re)presenting, and (Re)imagining Blackness in Europe

11

Black Europe and the African Diaspora: A Discourse on Location

JACQUELINE NASSY BROWN

The most abused term in the study of Black folks here and there is the very term that describes them: diaspora. The term's ostensible inclusiveness is the source of its potential to negate. The association of diaspora with worldwide Black kinship, as it were, can actually render certain kinds of Black subjects, experiences, histories, and identities invisible. Black Europe's recent inclusion into the African diasporic framework sets it up to represent the newest item in a global catalogue that aspires to exhaustiveness.[1] The danger is that the newly included entity might be made to fit into an already existing structure rather than presenting new challenges to it. In a related critique, Khachig Tololyan has provocatively suggested that diasporas are created in the academy (1996). While I am not quite that cynical, I do seek a meeting ground between the academy, which should indeed continue to theorize diaspora, and the ordinary people who are the academics' ostensible concern. Rather than assuming that we know what the nature and basis of the connections and/or differences between Black Europe and the larger diasporic world are, students of Black Europe might adopt a diasporic approach focused on the situated encounters in which people actually express some form of desire for connection. Presumably, desire for such would not exist were it not for the recognition of an operative and meaningful—even if perceived—difference. The proposal advanced in this essay is reflective of my own investment in the ethnographic project and is animated by the view that the failure to theorize diaspora open-endedly and through the totally subjective and amorphous yet historically and culturally specific thing called desire runs the risk of turning Black Europe into the newest entry in the encyclopedia of the global Black experience.

Where is Black Europe? I recently encountered it in New York City, where I live. Black Europe arrived in the form of some folks I met at the historic, first-time-ever reunion of the Nassy family. In what follows, I want to use the Nassy family reunion as well as some ethnographic material from Liverpool, England, to show how Black Europe might be theorized diasporically. I develop the point, also elaborated elsewhere, that diaspora should be understood not as an existential condition of displacement and dislocation but as a kind of relation, one between and among counter/parts (Brown 2005). This means that diasporic subjects recognize themselves as being of like kind—as sharing some basis of identity—even if they express distinct, sometimes contrary, histories and experiences in relation to it. In the present case, the counter/part relation is mediated through "relations"—that is, through kinship. Place and kinship are interwoven both as bases of difference and as objects of desire, shaping the tenor and significance of the encounter between Black folks here and Black folks there.

Nassy is my mother's maiden name, one that I adopted years ago as my middle name. For all of my life, my mother and her siblings have spoken of the Nassys as an important family from Surinam. My mother's father, Alwin Nassy, was one of nine children born to Adolf and Caroline. No one of Alwin's generation survives today, and indeed there is little or no information about four of his siblings. The reunion, held in New York City, consisted of Alwin's descendents (or the American Nassys) and the children of two of Alwin's siblings. The Nassy family reunion was a small affair in terms of participants but a large one in terms of the oceans that were bridged.

The children of Alwin's siblings (like Alwin himself) were born in Surinam, but had emigrated from there long ago, well before independence in 1975. These children—who range in age from their mid-sixties to early eighties—are now settled in Curacao, Aruba, and the Netherlands. Their own children—my generation—are in their forties, and are similarly spread out across these countries, plus Canada. This was the first time that I had met all but one of the Nassys who had come from abroad. I didn't know, for example, that in a little town outside of Amsterdam lives my cousin David, aged eighty-two (who, for his age, we younger Nassys called Uncle), and another cousin Sophie, aged forty-eight. And although many of the Dutch Nassys weren't in attendance, it became clear that there are many more where these two came from. In both generations, the international Nassys have moved back and forth between the Netherlands and other countries. What they have in common is not their origins in Surinam—especially since the Nassys of my generation were born elsewhere—but the Netherlands, which is where most of the international Nassys of both generations were educated.

The Nassys are mostly middle class, owing in part to the wealth my great-grandfather amassed in Surinam. Alwin's father was a very successful businessman, which enabled him to send his children to Holland for their education.

And Alwin's uncle—my mother was always proud to tell me—was an important doctor in Surinam. A street in the capital city of Paramaribo is named after him. That point received several iterations at the reunion. Two of the visiting Nassys, including Uncle David, are physicians—a bit of knowledge that prompted one of the American Nassys to observe that the Nassys have always been doctors. Whether they chose to stay in the Netherlands or not, that country was the springboard of upward mobility for all but the American Nassys, who were educated in the United States. Even my grandfather, Alwin, who settled in New York and never actually achieved middle-class status, went from Surinam to Holland for university education, and honed the ability to speak six languages. Because my grandfather died when I was an infant, I never knew him. But my mother, always so proud of her father, did make sure I knew this about him: he spoke six languages. But I vaguely remember a racial commentary always preceding that fact: he worked as a janitor and doorman—even though he spoke six languages.

Holland, for being the site of the Nassys' education, is the touchstone of Nassy pride. The colonial roots of class formation for the Nassys are further evidenced in the choices and parameters of their various travels—their locations and relocations. The Nassys' collective trajectory has largely followed Dutch imperial routes: Surinam, Curacao, Aruba, and, most significantly, the Dutch metropole. Otherwise, Nassy history is a history of travel, not only in the form of settlement and resettlement but in the pursuit of intellectual goals at all cost. We see this in the life trajectory of a man who is the real pride of the family, Josef, Alwin's brother. Born in Surinam in 1904, Josef Nassy trained as a painter in Belgium, where he was when the Nazis invaded. Undeterred by their dangerous presence, he stayed on in Belgium and wound up being interned as a suspicious alien (having the wrong citizenship) and for having a Jewish last name. During his three-year internment, Josef Nassy painted the portraits of other internees as well as a series of landscapes. His collected works, numbering some two hundred paintings, provide a rare visual record of the experience of internment.[2]

The Nassy family reunion inspired the present effort to theorize diaspora through encounters between Black *kin*folk from here and there. Here, in a hotel in the heart of New York City's Times Square, the crossroads of the world, international kinship bonds were being forged among the European, Caribbean, and American contingents of the Nassy clan. Black Europe exists, then, not only in the place called Europe, or more particularly in the Netherlands, but also in the United States, in the form of the desires of the Nassys to rehearse and reproduce Nassy-ness. Holland is important to the Nassys not for reasons related to Dutch society and culture writ large, nor for its historical role in the colonial politics of race, but because it plays host to a substantial part of Nassy family history.

As the weekend-long event was coming to a close, I found myself chatting with one cousin, in her sixties, whom I had not spent much time with. Our brief conversation sparked my recognition that diasporic encounters are defined by translation, or perhaps mistranslation. I asked her to characterize what life is like for Black people in Holland. How is it to be Black in Holland these days? A woman of few words, she responded, "It's getting worse. It didn't used to be as bad as it is now." I asked her, "What would you attribute the change to?" I expected to hear something about post-9/11 xenophobia in a country renowned for being more open to immigrants than other European countries. Her answer surprised and disturbed me. She explained that she immigrated to Holland in the 1940s, before Surinam achieved independence. Blacks were accepted back then. Later, with the advent of independence, Surinamers immigrated to Holland en masse. But they were poor and uneducated. I interpreted her analysis—perhaps wrongly—to imply that these folks' presence marked the beginning of Dutch racism against Blacks.

In light of the counter/part relation I described earlier, in which people of "like" identity nevertheless invoke and negotiate distinct if not contrary histories and experiences in relation to it, my cousin's invocation of colonial history distinguishes—I think, critically—pre-independence Surinamers from the postcolonial ones who immigrated to Holland. Surinam's colonial versus postindependence relationship to Holland is an index of class difference, separating a sizable population of poor and less educated Blacks from a tiny educated Black middle class.[3]

A similarly disturbing class dynamic unfolded in a series of exchanges that I had with Uncle David, the physician who lives near Amsterdam. Over the course of the weekend, he kept asking me about everyone's profession. And what is your brother's profession? What is your sister's profession? "Profession" is a term with strong middle-class connotations. I was happy to be able to report about myself that I was a college professor. Uncle David's last such question concerned my grandfather, Alwin, whom he never knew. What was your grandfather's profession? I found myself in the position of being embarrassed about a man whom I had been raised to revere. I heard myself mimicking my mother: despite speaking six languages, he was a doorman. I felt compelled to bring my mother's racial analysis to bear. This was, after all, America in the 1940s, and my grandfather was still Black, no matter how many languages he spoke. I felt the strong desire to protect the progenitor of the American Nassys by translating for Uncle David, which would require me to rehearse the history of race and racism in America.

Throughout this essay, I have been using the late St. Clair Drake's diasporic phrase, "black folk here and there," which is the title of his last book (1987). That title, of course, is an allusion to W.E.B. Du Bois's *Black Folk Then and*

Now (1939). Both phrases are useful in theorizing diaspora as a form of desire that is premised on difference and that is, in the present analysis, expressed in terms of place and kinship. Diaspora is invoked—sometimes literally, sometimes metaphorically—as a form of racial kinship consisting of Black folks across time *and* space—in this case, family members in Holland, Curacao, Aruba, the United States, and in different historical epochs. What it means to be Black in these distinct national and historical contexts requires explanation, or perhaps translation. Tina Campt refers to such translations as "intercultural address," which she states "point . . . to the discrepancies we encounter . . . understanding our respective experiences of race in the diaspora." They also point to "the insistent need for the translation of these differences . . . the modes of diasporic interpellation enacted in these exchanges" (2004, 207). In view of the thousands of African and Caribbean families that have experienced dispersal through international migration over the course of generations, I would suggest that reunions can be a rich site of investigation in postcolonial diaspora studies.[4] Diaspora manifests within the historical narratives that construct family identities. As Catherine Nash observes in a related context, "Genealogy is about significant places—family homes and 'origins'—and complex global networks of travel, desire, and imagination" (2002, 29). The family reunion, I would suggest, lays bare the networks of significant places and the multiplicity of homes for the (ostensibly) single family in question, while also providing the staging ground for the rehearsal of narratives that constitute, at one and the same time, genealogical and diasporic identities.

Place, in the foregoing, derives its meaning from within narratives of family, and more specifically in terms of one particular family's preoccupation with social mobility. That mobility was contingent on place, the Netherlands. The process of class formation in this case study warns against treating place as static, as a geographical dot on a map. Instead, place is constituted through movement and the possibility it affords. Black Europe's constituent locales articulate with other, extra-European locales through family. The travels and trajectories of its members are affected by larger historical processes of racism, colonialism, and independence. Individual Black European places are not isolates, then, but nodes and points of comparison. Encounters among differently located Black subjects, including those from Europe, reveal the utter necessity of translating Black experiences rather than assuming them. In that process, we see how the networks constituted by those nodes take shape. People make sense of place—and race—relatively, through its connection to other places. This view of diaspora counters approaches that would render Black Europe—even in its many parts—as another entry in a worldwide catalogue. A focus on place, as I am advocating here, might seem to invite the catalogue approach to diaspora; it might also seem to preclude a focus on movement—one of the common, and in my mind, mistaken starting points of diaspora studies (Brown 2005). But as the case of Liverpool, England, further shows, movement can be definitive of place.

Liverpool was, in its heyday, an international seaport of tremendous national and global importance. That city's Black population descends largely—but not exclusively—from West African seamen hired by Liverpool shipping companies, beginning in the mid-nineteenth century. While there are many histories that account for the Black presence in that city, most notably post-World War II immigration from the Caribbean, contemporary Blacks ascribe a primary role to the city's history as a seaport. Black people are especially proud that their African fathers and grandfathers were so very central to Liverpool's defining tradition, seafaring.

I began conducting ethnographic fieldwork among Blacks in Liverpool in 1989. The material that follows is based on research I conducted on my last trip to the city, in 1999. At that time, it was my great pleasure to make the acquaintance of a Nigerian man named Frank. He belonged to a group that my Black informants loosely referred to as "The Old Africans." Frank spent most of his working life as a seaman. After retiring from the sea, he worked as a barman at the Nigerian Club in the Black part of Liverpool. When I met him, he was completely retired—and, he admitted to me, a bit bored. So Frank was thrilled to be asked about his life. When I first met him, he even suggested that I interview him while he prepared an authentic Nigerian meal for me. I was to return to his home the following Sunday. What follows are some field notes I wrote about the evening.

> I had dinner at Frank's house. He made dinner for me. He said I would later forget it, but I promised I wouldn't. He played that awful radio station that played British pop rubbish. I commented on the station, and he says he listens to it faithfully every day.
>
> When he first got here, he met Africans who had been here for fifty years. His response was, "Fifty years! Bloody hell, what have you been doing here so long?!" He never expected that he would stay that long, but the years started ticking away. Now that his kids are grown, he could go back, but he's better off here. He has a little bungalow, a pension, and he's taken care of in terms of social services that would be precarious in Nigeria. He'd have to work there; it doesn't matter about his age.
>
> When his father died, he was working a ship on its way to Japan. He got a wire informing him of the news. Frank wanted to fly to Nigeria from Japan, but the captain wouldn't allow it. Talked about a Nigerian friend he met on the way to his mother's funeral, who helped him out when he got there. This prompts another memory: his sister criticized their mother for offering his children land, saying, "Why would she offer those children from Europe land before her own

> kid?" [He] said that the connection between [Britain] and his home and family in Nigeria is made through letters. If you don't write, they forget you, he said. When his parents died, he lost the connection.

Frank's mobile existence is emblematic of place—that is, Liverpool. But that mobility leads to the classic diasporic situation. His relation to "the homeland," which is conventionally understood as the object of diasporic desires, is severed due to the loss of kinship. He expressed that sense of loss in two ways: first, while his mother is alive, she is cajoled into denying Frank's children land because they're over in Europe, and second, he does not maintain his relationship with his family through letters. He can scarcely get to Nigeria when his parents die. Failing to have meaningful, sustained connections or reunions with his family, he ultimately disavows Nigeria itself. Nigeria gets displaced as his home in favor of Britain, whose policies and resources assure him a reasonably comfortable life in retirement. Frank's life trajectory illustrates the sense of loss that is most often taken as the paradigmatic diasporic sensibility. But the next bit of narrative shows the actualization of diaspora in ways that are neither dependent on homeland nor indicative of loss. This is a diasporic relation in which difference is mediated through desire among racial kin—or counter/parts, Black folk here and there. The following passage is lifted directly from my field notes:

> He talked about how the Black Americans he met in the United States (in Norfolk and Newport News) used to love to talk to him about Africa. This was second world war time, '50s and '60s. They were made up [elated] when he would tell them what certain words were in his own language. He imitated Black American speech for me. Said that the Black Americans were confused to see how well he could dance—and he said, are you kidding? These dances you do here all came from Africa; jiving and jitterbugging came from Africa!
>
> Said he traveled on busses in the South during the era of segregation, and he and his friends would feign ignorance of Jim Crow laws by feigning ignorance of the English language. He would sort of wink to the other Blacks on the bus, who were amused at their game. The Africans would sit right up front. They would respond in their own language to the bus driver's demands to get to the back of the bus.
>
> Spent a long time in NY. Went to clubs there. Went to Harlem, where he said he saw Blacks wearing a lot of African garb. Would make money in NY in the restaurants washing dishes.

Place has a central, mediating role in the layers of diasporic experience that come to bear in Frank's life, travels, and encounters. The very premise of my interest in Frank was shaped by the meanings and salience of place. He is one of the Old Africans—a group that defines not only Black Liverpool but Liverpool itself. His is a diasporic narrative of kinship—or missed kinship—as we saw in the first excerpt about his family in Nigeria. His is also a diasporic experience created in the context of encounter. Black Liverpool, historically, was not defined by stability in place, but by travel and by the connections and dis/connections among Black folks here and there that travel and its vicissitudes produce. And Frank's narration of his life is affected by the circumstances of its iteration: an encounter with a Black American (me) who is primarily interested not in his settled life, per se, but in his life as an African seaman. His maritime life is a sign of authenticity in Liverpool, even as that life has entailed travels among places. His travels led, alternately, to the making and missing of kinship connections with Black folks in a myriad of *there*s.

Meanwhile, on another street in the Black part of that city, my good friend Veronica offers a libation to the ancestors before pouring afternoon rounds for the rest of us sitting at her kitchen table. Veronica, then thirty-three years old, is the daughter of a Nigerian man, now deceased, and a white English woman. Veronica had had a tense relationship with her father. She spent the better part of her childhood trying in vain to please him, for which purpose she found herself a Nigerian boyfriend, tried to learn Yoruba, and made a pilgrimage to her father's village in Nigeria. Veronica recognized me as racial kin even in our manifest differences. Chief among these differences was not the fact that she was Black British and I Black American, but the fact that I did not know the exact location of my African origins. On this score, Veronica seemed to regard me as a person with two heads, an alien from another planet. Despite her many heartbreaking stories of being disavowed by her own father, who disparaged Veronica and her sisters for being light-skinned, Veronica actually and explicitly pitied *me* for not knowing, as she did, the exact spot on the continent of Africa from whence my people hailed. Claiming exact, place-based knowledge of my ancestral heritage in Surinam (there is even a street in Paramaribo named after my great-uncle!) did not work.

Back at Frank's house, and after such a wonderful dinner, I was moved to accept his invitation to the Rob Roy, a pub that was popular at the moment. I was to meet him there the next night. Yet with Frank being my senior by about forty years, I was a bit wary of this arrangement, so I prevailed upon Veronica to accidentally bump into us there. Dutiful friend that she is, Veronica showed up right on schedule. When Frank and Veronica got a gander of each other, sparks of recognition flew around the room.

Frank was elated to see her, and she him. She was really sweet with him, shaking his hand longingly and soaking him up with her eyes. He asked her name, and she gave not her first name, but her family name, which immediately placed her as a Nigerian—Yoruba, at that. In the thrill of the moment, she paused to explain to me that he was one of her father's old friends. And he explained to me that her father was a shipmate of his. When, a bit later, Frank excused himself momentarily, Veronica quizzed me seriously: "*What's* his name again?" "Frank," I said. She looked at me as if I were the world's biggest idiot. "No, what's his real name!?" "I just know him as Frank," I responded. A few minutes later, she asked me yet again, and she was again disappointed that I was clinging to the same stupid answer. Veronica, it turned out, once knew him by his African name. In pursuit of it, she finally decided to ask him. Frank seemed taken aback. How could she have forgotten it so quickly? "Frank," he said. Veronica responded a bit sharply, "Don't give me that! What's your *real* name?!" In this rich little exchange, *she* was the one trying to get an African cultural connection going, while he was happy being Frank. Her response was consistent for a woman who had spent years trying, in her own words, to be the good little Nigerian girl for her father. For her, meeting Frank was tantamount to a family reunion with the father who never fully accepted her. Her deepest desire was to overcome the difference between her and her father. Frank became a conduit for the expression of a larger set of kinship-cum-diasporic desires for Veronica. Asked for her name, her impulse was to provide just her decidedly African family name.

Attention to the question of place should prompt the question, where is Black Europe? Black Europe is not locatable; it is a *discourse* on location. Black Europe, like Europe before it, points outward in many ultimately unmappable directions. If Europe has never stayed within its own geographic boundaries, why should we expect Black Europe to do so? Black Europe is a racialized geography of the imagination even for *non-European* Blacks. Family history and identity are expressed and contested through networks, consisting of all sorts of routes, colonial and otherwise. In terms of conceptualizing diaspora, I would argue for an approach that not only appreciates Black Europe's reach into other worlds but also one that discourages the expectation that Black European histories, experiences, and perspectives will map neatly onto each other, or onto their American or Caribbean or African counter/parts. Further, if we are to avoid reducing diaspora to a catalogue of the global Black experience, we might pay more attention to situated encounters between specific members of Black communities. What we see in the foregoing ethnography, for example, are relations between Black Liverpudlians on the one hand, and Africans and Black Americans on the other; we see the effects of non-encounters and non-reunions between a Nigerian in Britain and his family in Nigeria; we see an encounter between that same Nigerian and a Black American, and finally between Blacks from Surinam, Curacao, Holland, Aruba, and the United States. None of the foregoing stories should be taken as exemplary of the Black experience in Europe. Rather, in their utter variety, the encounters described above represent a collective warning about treating Black Europe—wheresoever that imagined geography happens to get momentarily concretized—as an isolate.

Let me close by paying brief homage to St. Clair Drake, a pioneer both in the study of Blacks in Europe and in diaspora studies. I had the pleasure to know Professor Drake when I was a graduate student in anthropology at Stanford University. Although he had long since retired, he happily met with me to chat about his work and to give me advice on mine. How I wish I had taken a picture with him and recorded the lengthy lesson he gave me on his rich and fabulous life and career. I was so in awe of him that it is a wonder that I heard a single word he said. He told me about the politics of his choice to do his doctoral fieldwork, back in the 1940s, on a Black seafaring community in Cardiff, Wales. Europe was such an unorthodox field site for an ethnographer, he told me, that he had spent the better part of his career making up for that work—work which, for political and ethical reasons, he never published as a monograph. And so, in view of all this, I asked what he thought my career prospects were, given my own interests in Britain. He pondered my question seriously for maybe a minute. Finally, he looked me in the eye and asked, "Have you given any thought to Brazil?"

Notes

1. While it would be foolish to suggest that the study of Blacks in Europe is in any way new, "Black Europe," as a scholarly object, has achieved an unprecedented currency and cachet.

2. The collection is owned by the United States Holocaust Memorial Museum in Washington, D.C. Josef Nassy is profiled in the film *Hitler's Forgotten Victims*, by David Okuefuna and Moise Shewa, and in Paul Gilroy's *Between Camps*.

3. For more on the relationship between recent Surinamese immigrants to Holland and the longer-settled Surinamese and Black Dutch community, see Wekker, *The Politics of Passion*.

4. Catherine Nash in "Genealogical Identities" usefully theorizes the production of family identities in terms of diaspora by focusing on the process that precedes family reunions: genealogical research that identifies ancestors in other countries of origin as well as the selective tracing of family lines.

References

Brown, Jacqueline Nassy. *Dropping Anchor, Setting Sail: Geographies of Race in Black Liverpool.* Princeton: Princeton University Press, 2005.

Campt, Tina. *Other Germans: Black Germans and the Politics of Race, Gender and Memory in the Third Reich.* Ann Arbor: University of Michigan Press, 2004.

Drake, St. Clair. *Black Folk Here and There: An Essay in History and Anthropology.* Los Angeles: Center for Afro-American Studies, University of California, 1987.

Du Bois, W.E.B. *Black Folk Then and Now: An Essay in the History and Sociology of the Negro Race.* New York: Octagon Books, 1973 [1939].

Gilroy, Paul. *Between Camps: Race, Identity and Nationalism at the End of the Colour Line.* London: Penguin, 2000.

Nash, Catherine. "Genealogical Identities." *Environment and Planning D: Society and Space* 20, no. 1 (2002): 27–52.

Tololyan, Khachig. "Rethinking Diaspora(s): Stateless Power in the Transnational Moment." *Diaspora* 5, no. 1 (1996): 3–36.

Wekker, Gloria. *The Politics of Passion: Women's Sexual Culture in the Afro-Surinamese Diaspora.* New York: Columbia University Press, 2006.

12

Theorizing Black Europe and African Diaspora: Implications for Citizenship, Nativism, and Xenophobia

KWAME NIMAKO AND STEPHEN SMALL

Changing definitions of who is Black in Europe, who is a bona fide member of the African diaspora, including suggestions that would expand the idea of who is in the diaspora, are currently taking place in Europe and in Africa. This is happening in a context in which Blacks in Europe now reveal far more diverse national origins and citizenship status than ever before. At the same time, a dramatic increase in the membership of the European Union (from six nations in 1957 to twenty-seven in 2007) alongside expanding notions of who is European, pose several challenges and opportunities for the future of Blacks in Europe, and indeed the world.

One problem for those who probe Black Europe and the African diaspora is that they must decide whether to confront the issues of *periodization* and *subordination* or circumvent them. The issue of periodization deals with the general and specific histories of migration and of the diasporic existence. While migration tells us about movement and settlement, it does not tell us about citizenships, nor about belongings. This is all the more relevant since early migrants from the Caribbean and Africa to Europe were legally citizens of different European countries; however, from the point of view of nativism, they were viewed, and in most cases treated, as foreigners partly because of skin color and the history of subjugation. The notion of Black Europe therefore implies an implicit knowledge of the existence of an Other Europe of color. But in African diaspora discourse, we analytically, and perhaps consciously and deliberately, distinguish between voluntary and forced migration, which brings us to the issue of subordination. Clearly subordination is associated with transatlantic slavery and colonialism and, as an extension, neocolonialism. Subordination also draws our attention to the position and status of Black Europe and the

African diaspora in Europe, and their relation to the phenomena of exclusion, racism, and discrimination.

Traditionally, state-sponsored research in EU member states emphasizes immigration or periodization and plays down subordination and its racist variants (Essed and Nimako 2006). Thus observing the status and position of Black Europe and the African diaspora as a descriptive category is one thing, but articulating Black Europe at the analytical and explanatory levels is another matter. Not only does officially sanctioned research tend to place emphasis on migration, but also it generally focuses on the *description* of the status and position of "migrants" and social mobility. This translates into integration policy and restrictive immigration policy (Essed and Nimako 2006). Early Black researchers, predominantly in Britain, went a step further and looked critically at the nature of subordination by taking factors such as history and race as analytical categories, and notions of struggle and resistance as explanatory variables. They were quick to establish that "race as a socio-cultural category has appeared historically to be relatively independent of class" (Mullard 1980, 7). Flowing from this analysis, issues of equal opportunity, antiracism, antidiscrimination, and social mobility remained at the core of Black scholarship.

This in turn raises the question as to which aspect of Black European existence should be articulated as struggle and resistance in relation to social mobility. Whereas the issue of subordination breeds a brand of scholarship that can analyze and explain social mobility and inequality in the framework of struggle and resistance, it is doubtful if the same method can be used to analyze and explain violence, criminality, and drug abuse in Black Europe, since struggle and resistance is not the prerogative of the "wretched of the earth," be they Black, oppressed, poor, or powerless, and for that matter any particular class. Thus whether we consider *struggle* in the context of "building strength through weakness" along the thoughts of Amilca Cabral and *resistance* in the context of antiracist struggle against ethnic hierarchy, or in Mullard's formulation, *etharchy,* we should bear in mind that the privileged and the powerful also struggle and resist (Mullard 1988, 360). The privileged and the powerful resist change that is not beneficial to them and struggle to accumulate wealth and protect material and moral interest on a daily basis. Whether we confront or circumvent them, we will be confronted with the following question. Are the dynamics of black Europe and the African diaspora in Europe dependent on there own internal dynamics and logic or on the status and position assigned to them in the European Union? Put differently, what makes Black Europe a community of its own within the EU and its member states?

Viewed against the backdrop of the above question, a lot has happened with the Black community (in Europe) and the African diaspora (in Europe) and the European community since the publication of Sivanandan's *Here to Stay,* and Chris Mullard's *Black Britain* (Mullard 1973). *Here to Stay* suggested that a certain phase had come to an end or there was an "end to particular history"; "We are here because you were there" was an effective slogan, anchored in periodization and migration (Sivanandan 1982). *Black Britain* reminded us that a new generation of Black Europe had come of age; namely, those who were born in Britain, and for that matter in Europe, who knew no other country than the countries in which they were born. In turn, Stuart Hall drew our attention to a new culture that was unfolding as a consequence of these developments (Hall 1978). It is worth mentioning that these publications were produced at a time when the veto power of President De Gaulle of France within the European Economic Community (EEC) kept Britain out of the EEC. Since then, not only has Britain become part of the European community but also the community has been enlarged and become a union.

We shall return to these issues below. For the moment, this chapter is based on three broad observations. First, the broader classification of the Black community—which in the 1960s and 1970s referred to Africans, Asians and Caribbeans from former British colonies—has narrowed. Not only has there been a distinction between the African diaspora, Asians, and others but also the notion of the Asian community has been unpacked since the 1980s. There is now less reference to the Asian community and more reference to the Muslim community, Hindu community, Sikh community, and others. These developments are a consequence of internal dynamics (including self-identification), official state classifications for political purposes, and political, economic, and cultural developments in Asia and other parts of the world (Runneymede Trust 1980). Thus these days it is not sufficient to speak of Black British of Caribbean origin; one can be reminded that there are also Black British of Afro-Caribbean origin. It is also not sufficient to use the blanket term Creoles to describe people of Surinamese descent in the Netherlands; some consciously define themselves as Afro-Surinamese instead. This implies that apart from history and color, official classifications and self-identification have become a defining feature of black Europe. This broader notion of Black community never gained broader usage in continental Europe and seems extremely unlikely to do so in the future.

The second observation is that whereas the notion of black Europe has been narrowed, the narrow classification of the African diaspora, which used to refer to Caribbeans of African descent, has been broadened to include peoples from postcolonial Africa. This is compounded by the recent African Union (AU) classification of Africa's diaspora as its sixth regional grouping (for further details, see the Foundation for Democracy in Africa and Western Hemisphere Africa Diaspora). The AU notion of Africa, which refers to the fifty-three African countries in continental Africa, is at variance with the definition of Africa used by the European Union. The EU deals with Africa at three levels, namely, North Africa, sub-Saharan Africa, and South Africa. Even more, the AU's notion of the African diaspora challenges the conventional wisdom of African diaspora. This raises the question as to whether the African Union's claim is based on history, race, or citizenship, especially since many, if not most, Black Europeans and members of the African diaspora in Europe are actually citizens of particular European states.

Thirdly, the collapse of the Soviet Union and the end of the cold war has given rise to the enlargement of the European Union. This has reinforced the position of Black Europe as "enclaves" in the EU. Traditionally the distribution of Blacks in Europe was tied to a given European country's role in the transatlantic slave trade, slavery, and colonialism. Thus not only is Black Europe confined to a few EU countries, but Blacks are concentrated in a few EU cities and a few occupations. Two important European Union projects, namely, Corporate Europe and Fortress Europe, hardly have space, if any, for Black Europe and the African diaspora. This raises the question whether we can use the EU as the unit of analysis of Black Europe and the Africa diaspora in Europe, especially since there is no European citizenship but rather citizens of European countries.

This issue is addressed next, where we consider the enlargement of the EU in relation to the notion of Black Europe. We argue that Black Europe is not a major player in the shaping of the EU. Rather, the EU is shaped by "stakeholders" from within and global forces from without; on the stakeholder continuum, Black Europe is not a strong stakeholder. The second section addresses the issue of nativism, national interest, and Black Europe. We argue that there is a thin line between notions of nativism and national interest; this operates to the disadvantage of Black Europe. Finally, the third section deals with the African diaspora as ongoing process of migration from Africa to Europe and its implications for transnationality and xenophobia.

Stakeholders, Black Europe, and Citizenship

Emerging from the ruins of World War II, the six founding states of the EEC, Belgium, West Germany, France, Italy, Luxembourg, and the Netherlands, made security concerns fundamental in the architecture of the subsequent European Union project. But whereas the security component tells us where the EU came from, it does not tell us where it is heading. Examples are the 2005 rejection of the EU draft constitution by the citizens of France and the Netherlands in a referendum and the objection of some EU member states to allow other states to join the EU; both developments have influence on the pace and direction of the EU project. The EU project, like national projects, is partly determined by activities of *stakeholders* within the EU and partly by global economic, political, social, and cultural forces beyond the EU. Within the EU project, member states serve as stakeholders and *constituencies* and thus send people to represent, promote, and protect "national interests" through institutions such as the European Parliament and the European Commission.

ON STAKEHOLDERS AND THE EUROPEAN PROJECT

Like member states who act as stakeholders to represent, protect, and promote their interests, various stakeholders within member states, strong and weak, also attempt to or do influence national policies, which in turn influence EU policies and direction. These national stakeholders range from strong transnational corporations (TNCs) through farmers' associations, trade unions and women's groups to weak Black European and African diaspora and migrant groups and organizations. Interest groups organized within the workplace (social partners) and those organized outside the workplace (civil society) engage in social and civil dialogue (Obradovic 2005). It is not clear if Black Europe and the African diaspora in Europe constitute a social partner or civil society. Suffice it to say that as a project, economic integration has been one of the major driving forces at the level of policy. As one of the strongest stakeholders in the EU, the TNCs have been influential in shaping economic policy. As a consequence, some authors have coined the term *Europe, Inc.*, to indicate the influence of TNCs on policy making within the EU project. The authors of *Europe, Inc.* noted, "The massive resources which TNCs and their lobby groups have at their disposal for lobbying decision makers and manipulating perceptions through PR campaigns is one key factor behind corporate influence in the political realm. Additionally, the political power held by TNCs is connected to their privileged access to politicians and civil servants in national and international political institutions. Finally, the current elite consensus around the expediency of a global economy dominated by TNCs provides fertile ground for corporate lobbying" (Balanya et al. 2003, 177).

The authors also refer to the EU as a corporate lobbyist's paradise: "The accelerated process of European unification has resulted in a fundamental democratic gap, which provides an ideal environment for corporate lobbying. The powers of the European parliament remain far too limited to compensate for the loss of democratic control created as more and more decision-making power shifts from national capitals to Brussels." The complex and opaque institutional setup of the EU makes it almost impossible to track who is lobbying whom on which issues and with what effect (Balanya et al. 2003, 177–78).

Though unintended, the interest and influence of Corporate Europe is held in check by, among others, Fortress Europe, which regulates immigration. As we shall see below, Fortress Europe is tied to nativism, which in turn influences the status and position of black Europe. Unlike Corporate Europe and other interest groups, Black Europe and the African diaspora have been one of the weakest stakeholders in the EU project. Apart from the fact that the notion of Black Europe never gained wide public usage in continental Europe, the exclusion of Britain in the initial formation of the EU also implied the exclusion of Britain's *race* debate in continental Europe, and for that matter in the construction of the EEC in its initial stages. Thus despite the upsurge of racist events in Britain between 1958 and 1963, the EU project was constructed as if Blacks were not yet present. In the formulation of Stuart Hall, "Western Europe did not have, until recently, any ethnicity at all. Or didn't recognize it had any" (Hall 2004, 256).

Nevertheless, in order to understand the position of the African diaspora in Europe, one has to understand the construction of the EU. Of the six founding members of the EEC, only two, West Germany and Luxembourg, did not carry a major colonial burden at the time its formation. The initial references of the EU to Black Europe and the African diaspora were tied to colonialism. Through the colonial project, the founding members were aware of the existence of Black Europe and the African diaspora in Europe, but colonialism was not even mentioned by name. In fact Articles 131 through 136 of the European Economic Community Treaty of 1957, also referred to as the Treaty of Rome, provided for *association* of non-European countries and territories with which EEC member states had "special relations," that is, their colonies. The Treaty of Rome further states that the purpose of such an association was to "promote the economic and social development of the countries and territories and to establish close economic relations between them and the Community as a whole" (Article 131; see Mullard et al. 1997).

Section 4 of Article 132 is explicit on the issue of equality among the EEC member states, noting, "For investments financed by the [European Economic] Community, participation in tender and supplies shall be open on equal terms to all natural and legal person who are nationals of a [EEC] Member State or of one of the countries and territories." In other words, the EEC member states without colonies were allowed to share the spoils of the colonies with those who had them.

It was against this backdrop that the Yaounde 1 Convention was signed on July 20, 1963, between eighteen African states (Associated African States and Madagascar—AASM) and six EEC member states and overseas departments and territories (ODTs), namely the Dutch Antilles and Suriname and the French overseas territories and departments.

The infamous role of Nazi Germany in World War II gave France the moral high ground in the formative period of the EU project, especially under the leadership of President De Gaulle. Political initiatives from France were complemented by financial contributions from Germany. With regard to race relations, this implied that the "assimilation policy" of France, which argued in favor of citizenship and the assumed color blindness of the dominant groups in France, also led to the denial of racism in institutions and in society. In practice, this implied emphasis on France's relation to ACP and less on black Europe.

It is worth noting that the upsurge of racist events in Britain between 1958 and 1963 went almost unnoticed in continental Europe. Paradoxically, these events gave the United Kingdom the oldest and the most extensive antiracism and antidiscrimination legislation in the European Union; the British Race Relations Act of 1965 was adopted before the United Nations Convention on the Elimination of All Forms of Racial Discrimination on December 21, 1965 (UN document 27, 1965; see also UN Resolution 1904 [XVIII]). In continental Europe, white middle-class social upsurge in the form of university student revolts in May 1968 in Paris gained more attention; these were followed by similar developments in Amsterdam and elsewhere which in turn facilitated the democratization of the universities, gender "equality," and democratization of lifestyle. Antiracism and antidiscrimination regulations entered continental Europe via the United Nations. In response to the United Nations Convention on the Elimination of All Forms of Racial Discrimination, antiracist legislation was adopted in France in 1972 forbidding discrimination in housing, employment, and the provision of goods and services. Italy enacted laws in 1975 to conform to the UN Convention. Belgium enacted legislation on racism and discrimination on July 30, 1981. However, unlike the British Race Relations Act, the Belgian legislation did not contain provisions for equal opportunity for all irrespective of race. In Ireland, the Hatred Act of 1989 derives from the implementation of the International Covenant on Civil and Political Rights (Mullard et al. 1997).

In other words from the point of view of race relations and social forces (or stakeholders), UK policy was a consequence of improvement of indigenous policy, whereas in Europe the new policy was a consequence of domestication of international law. Apparently in the context of color-blind discourse, it was taken for granted that national constitutions are perfect documents to protect every citizen whereas international humanitarian laws protect everybody. Britain's approach to the EEC went hand in hand with tight immigration controls. This took the form of the Commonwealth Immigration Act of 1962, the Commonwealth Immigration Act of 1968, and the Immigration Act of 1971 (Miles and Phizacklea 1984). By the time Britain joined the EEC in 1973, it had harmonized its immigration policy with EEC member states, which in turn made aliens of the British Commonwealth aliens in Europe as well; the exception to this rule was British Commonwealth nationals from Canada, Australia, and New Zealand, nearly all of whom are white, and whom many British politicians referred to as "our kith and kin" (Miles and Phizacklea 1984).

When the UK joined the EEC, it brought its former weak colonies in line, but left out former strong colonies such as India. Nevertheless the inclusion of the former British colonies into the ACP arrangement led to the replacement of the Yaounde Convention with the Lome I Convention, signed on February 28, 1975, in Lome, Togo, between forty-six ACP countries (thirty-seven African, six Caribbean, and three Pacific) and nine EEC member states; Lome I represented a transformation and expansion of the provisions of Yaounde II. Not only was it established on the basis of "partnership" instead of "association," but also it "resolved to establish a *new model* for relations between developed and developing States, compatible with the aspirations of the international community towards a more just and balanced economic order."

By the end of 1995, the ACP states numbered seventy and the EU states fifteen, making the Lome IV Convention the largest development partnership in the world outside the United Nations. At the time of writing the EU consists of twenty-five member states, with two more, Bulgaria and Romania, joining on January 1, 2007. This brings us back to the issue of periodization, namely, black presence in Europe. Though the presence of ACP migrants in Europe was no secret to the signatories of the Lome I Convention, the issue of their status and conditions in the EEC did not feature at the meetings until December 1977, when the joint committee adopted a declaration on the protection of the rights of migrant workers (Mullard et al. 1997).

The Organization of United African Trade Unions (OUATU) had informed the Confederation of European Trade Unions of its desire that the status of ACP migrant workers should be incorporated in the future Lome Convention. Thus as stakeholders, African trade unions depended on the solidarity and goodwill of their European counterparts to get their message across in Europe. Following this, a Joint Working Group was set up to make proposals on the issue of ACP migrants in the EEC. Furthermore, the Pan-African Conference on the Lome Convention held in Brazzaville in December 1978 called for the creation of a joint committee of EEC/ACP trade unions and the recognition and respect of the rights of ACP workers in the EEC.

These initiatives led to the Bordeaux Declaration of 1979, the Kingston Resolution of 1983, the Berlin Resolution of 1983, and the Arusha Resolution of 1987 (ACP-EEC Resolutions 1991 in Mullard). In a nutshell, the Bordeaux Declaration agreed to develop an ACP-EEC convention to protect the rights and improve the conditions of ACP migrant workers resident in the member states of the EEC. The Kingston Resolution called on the EEC to ensure that the EEC member states lift all discriminating measures against students who are nationals of ACP countries. This was repeated in the Berlin Resolution. The Arusha Resolution called upon the EEC to act in accordance with International Labor Organization (ILO) provisions.

However, the result of these declarations and resolutions was that Annex V of Lome IV Convention stated, "Each Community Member State and each ACP

State will, in the framework of and in compliance with its respective general legislation, grant workers who are nationals of the other Party legally carrying out an activity in its territory, and the members of their families residing with them, the fundamental freedoms as they derive from the general principles of international law" (Lome Convention IV, Annex V, Articles 1 and 2, 1992).

Annex V of the Lome IV Convention also states, "The Community will develop measures to support Member States' nongovernmental organizations (NGOs) endeavoring to improve social and cultural facilities for workers who are ACP nationals (such as literacy campaigns and social welfare)" (Lome Convention IV). Apparently Black Europe and the African diaspora in Europe did not exist as independent stakeholders and constituencies within the EU project: African trade unions had to go through EU trade unions to seek recognition of the rights of ACP nationals in the EEC and through European Union NGOs to seek their welfare. Compared to other stakeholders, not only is Black Europe weak but also it is an *enclave* at several levels. First, though clearly visible in certain parts of Europe, demographically Black Europe is less than 5 percent of EU population (Eurostat 1996), confined mainly to a few member states with a colonial past. For historical, cultural, and legal reasons, 99.8 percent of Surinamese in the EU live in the Netherlands; 93 percent of francophone ACP nationals and 93 percent of anglophone nationals in the EU reside in France and the United Kingdom; 86 percent of the Portuguese-speaking ACP nationals reside in Portugal while 54 percent of Spanish-speaking ACP nationals live in Spain. Exceptions to the rule are nationals from the Horn of Africa, such as Somalia, Ethiopia, and Eritrea, who entered the EU as refugees. The larger EU states such as Italy and Germany have also attracted ACP nationals since the 1980s. In absolute terms, ACP nationals in the EU reside predominantly in France (31 percent), the United Kingdom (29 percent), Italy (9 percent), Germany (9 percent), the Netherlands (8 percent), and Portugal (5 percent). This means that 91 percent of ACP nationals in the EU reside in six EU member states (Eurostat 1996).

Secondly, Black Europe is also confined to few cities in these member states, to a few neighborhoods in these cities, and to a few occupations in society at large. Neighborhoods of primarily Black residents are real and imagined dangerous places. One of the major concerns of Black Europe is racism, discrimination, and xenophobia and how they impact on education and employment, expressed in underachievement in schools and unemployment in the labor market. Thus, thirdly, in this context, there is an occupational enclave. As noted above on the continuum between the market and the state, Corporate Europe is close to the market whereas Fortress Europe is close to the state. Both Corporate Europe and the state are major sources of employment.

POLITICAL STRUCTURES AND BLACK AGENCY

There are still questions that have not been answered and may never be answered. One is what the relationship is between substance and appearance. Political or artistic visibility and exposure in public life does not tell us much about the general position and status of groups in society. National visibility gives rise to EU-wide visibility. The overrepresentation and visibility of black Europe and the African diaspora on France's national football team can be contrasted with the overrepresentation and invisibility of the same in France's prisons. In the same vein, the overexposure of the Somali-born and former Netherlands parliamentarian Ayaan Hirsi Ali can be contrasted with the underexposure of high unemployment rate among Somalis in the Netherlands. Perhaps Ayaan Hirsi Ali gained attention in the media, and thus entered public life, through her Muslim bashing. This coincided with the revival of nativism in much of Europe as well as a call by some women in the center-right liberal party, of which Ayaan Hirsi Ali became a member, to increase the number of women in the party, and the call by some people to increase the number of blacks in the party. Ayaan Hirsi Ali could represent all the three, namely, Muslim basher, woman, and black. But her high-profile status and excessive media exposure does not change the underprivileged status and position of Somalis in the Netherlands.

The rise of Hirsi Ali to public prominence is also an illustration of the difference in black politics in EU, which in turn is a reflection of different political cultures in the EU member states. Black politics in certain EU member states, such as the UK, requires a clearly identifiable constituency, such as a district; black politics in the Netherlands does not require a clearly identifiable constituency. It only requires the political party to place a candidate on a list.

We shall return to this below. For the moment suffice it to say that the enlargement of the EU went hand in hand with the transfer in policy formulation from member states upwards to the EU level. According to the authors of *Europe Inc.*, this

> tends to shift the balance of power between corporate and other societal interests within individual member states. Wealthy corporations and their lobby groups have the means to set up well-staffed offices in Brussels and to hire external consultants and PR agencies. This enables them to keep track of the details of relevant EU policies and to position lobbyists to best influence decision making.
>
> By contrast, European-level umbrella NGOs are often underdeveloped, disconnected and lacking in resources. Social movements are organized primarily on the local and national levels, and the political debates in which they are engaged usually unfold within a national context where European questions receive little attention. (Balanya et al. 2003, 178)

From the point of view of stakeholders, black Europe belongs to the last category, namely, "underdeveloped, disconnected and lacking in resources."

This effect is compounded by the fact that citizenship remains a state project. Thus despite the fact that increasingly, laws governing European states originate from the EU, there is no European citizenship. The position and status of individuals, including Black Europeans and the African diaspora in Europe, derive from EU member states.

Like all social formations, things do change. The position and status of blacks in Europe is no exception. As we noted above, back in the 1960s, Sivanandan had to lecture the "Other" British world about the history of emigration, immigration, and migration by reminding those who objected to the presence of Black Britain that Blacks were in Britain to stay. Sivanandan couched his words in specific historical periods in British history, namely, the history of British colonialism: "blacks were there because whites were there." In his own world, however, Enoch Powell, a Conservative member of parliament who became the symbol of British nativism, warned white Britons in April 1968 that because of (Black) immigrants "their wives [were] unable to obtain hospital beds on childbirth, their children unable to obtain school-places, their homes and neighborhoods changed beyond recognition" (quoted in Sivanandan 1976, 361–62). At that moment both Sivanandan and Enoch Powell were referring to Blacks as immigrants, namely, those who were born elsewhere in the (former) British colonies but had traveled to Britain to continue their lives. When and how did Black immigrants become Black British, and, for that matter, Black Europeans?

In the early 1970s, Mullard reminded his readers that there is something like Black Britain; that is, those who were born of immigrant parents but did not know any other country than Britain. This observation was confirmed by the British government in 1976 when it noted in a white paper that "Ten years ago, less than a quarter of the colored population had been born here: more than three out of every four colored persons then were immigrants to this country . . . About two out of every five of the colored people in this country now were born here and the time is not far off when the majority of the colored population will be British born" (White Paper 1976; quoted from Sivanandan 1976, 366).

The assumption was that there would be a shift from an emphasis on migrants to citizenship and color. Small has described the situation with regard to Blacks of Caribbean origin in Britain (Small 1983). However, as we shall see below, this has not been the case for all Blacks; in terms of ratio or percentage, due to ongoing migration from Africa and elsewhere to Britain, not much has changed. For example, in the 1990s, twenty years later, 36 percent (or about two out of every five) of Africans living in UK were born there (Chikezie, ADF 2001, 4). It is worth noting that the progression from exclusive focus on migrants to Black

Britain went hand in hand with changes in policy and discourse. According to Sivanandan, "The strategy of the state in relation to the Asians had been to turn cultural antagonism into cultural pluralism—in relation to the West Indians, to turn political antagonism into political pluralism" (Sivanandan 1976, 365). In other words, the state approached Asians as a "cultural group" whereas it approached the Afro-Caribbeans as a "racial group."

The notion of Black Britain solves the problem of citizenship, but it does not address the problem of nativism and cannot solve the problem of color. In fact, emphasis on difference and cultural diversity also leaves sufficient room for nativism. Nativism derives from periodization and serves as a powerful force in the policing and the regulating of race and ethnic relations. Whereas citizenship "guarantees" equal legal rights in relation to nationality within the state, nativism becomes a conscious or unconscious attempt by groups and individuals considered to be native Europeans to replace overt rights derived from citizenship by covert rights derived from history and color. On this score, nativism is the structural and ideological attempt by individuals and/or groups to enforce subordination by emphasizing difference and ethnic hierarchy or *etharchy* where biology-informed racism, culture-informed ethnicism, and legal-informed citizenship for the same has failed.

Let us clarify this by stating what nativism is not. Unlike racism, nativism is not based on notions of superiority and inferiority; thus nativism cannot be legislated for or against. What then is it? Nativism is based on notions of inherent historical rights, national identity, and national interest; this makes nativism a powerful ally of national identity and national interest. While under certain conditions class can neutralize racism, class cannot neutralize nativism because the latter appeals to history, belonging, national identity, and national interest. However, like racism, from the point of view of nativism, equality poses more problems than inequality. In other words, both racism and nativism thrive on inequality; but unlike racism, which cannot be defended formally, nativism can be defended formally, in the name of "national identity" and "national interest." This may go some way to explain why in much of Europe there was less resistance to the recruitment of "guest workers" to some European countries in the 1950s and 1960s. It can be recalled that the guest workers were recruited to do low-status jobs that reinforced subordination; this turned into resentment when the former guest workers became unemployed or sought better employment for themselves and their children, based on equal legal rights.

Nativism is the everyday commonsense reminder to Black Europe that they are the "Other," and that there is a formal Europe, namely, white Europe. Part of informal Europe is psychological and cultural. At the psychological level, it is common for ordinary white citizens to ask their fellow Black citizens where they come from. In some cases, it is not enough for the Black to mention which city or town he or she comes from; one also has to mention where one's parents originally came from. It is not existence of color per se that becomes the issue; it is the awareness of both Blacks and whites about the advantages and disadvantages attached to color. The cultural form of nativism finds its expression in "cultural censorship" and self-censorship; that is, attempts by ordinary white citizens to demand or enforce cultural assimilation or subordination of Blacks and migrants or resort to white flight from neighborhoods when it fails, and the awareness of blacks of the same.

We noted above that as part of the EU project, Fortress Europe sets the formal parameters of nativism, which finds its extreme expression in the formation of anti-black, anti-migrant, and anti-immigrant political parties, which in turn express themselves in racism, ethnicism, and xenophobia. In response to this, on the political continuum from right to left, Black Europeans generally vote for or join center-left political parties. For instance, in a recent local council election (March 7, 2006) in the Netherlands, 80 percent of those classified as nonnatives voted for left-wing parties. In the city of Amsterdam, 94 percent of those classified as nonnatives voted for three left-wing parties, namely, Labor Party (80 percent), Green Party (7 percent), and Socialist Party (6 percent). In the city of Rotterdam, 94 percent of those classified as nonnatives voted for three left-wing parties, namely, Labor Party (86 percent), Green Party (6 percent), and Socialist Party (2 percent) (*Volkskrant,* March 8, 2006). One suspects that 80 percent of the so-called nonnatives are not left-wing in their political ideology. However, nativism closes the doors for even socially conservative people of color to join conservative whites in political parties, which brings us to the issue of national interest.

In a much more subtle way, nativism can find its expression in official sponsored research on black Europe, especially when research work on Black Europe becomes part of immigration studies or when immigration studies becomes synonymous with minorities studies; the *insider-outsider paradigm—we* versus *them*—becomes the order of the day. Mainstream white researchers consider themselves as insiders (natives) and their object of research, namely, Blacks and nonwhite migrants, as outsiders (nonnatives). As an illustration, let us use the development of policy and research in the Netherlands as a case.

A decade after British home secretary Roy Jenkins had defined integration as "not a flattering process of assimilation but equal opportunity accompanied by cultural diversity in an atmosphere of mutual tolerance," a Dutch Labor Party member of the parliament, Henk Molleman, attempted to introduce in the late 1970s in the Netherlands the notion of "ethnic minorities" along the lines of the British Race Relations Act (Miles and Phizacklea 1984). He pleaded for a coherent ethnic minorities' policy in the Netherlands in response to the

Moluccan revolt and the ensuing debate around the revolt. In his speech to the parliament, Molleman noted, "The Netherlands society has become a multiracial society where (members of) minorities, as groups and individuals, must be able to participate and emancipate themselves without giving up their own cultural identity and the reciprocal preparedness to dialogue" (quoted in Essed and Nimako 2006).

A ministerial approval of Molleman's motion led to the establishment of the Department of Ethnic Minority Affairs with the Ministry of Home Affairs, which set in motion the formation of a coherent ethnic minority policy program. In the tradition of progressive control, the ethnic minorities policy focused on people from former Dutch colonies and those classified as guest workers, especially Moroccans and Turks. However, in less than a decade, a government-appointed scientific council that was to review the ethnic minorities policy revolted against the concept of "ethnic minorities" and replaced it with the concept of "aliens" (Essed and Nimako 2006). Not only did this "revolt" constitute a revolt against the British model, but it was in response to assumptions rather than data. The general assumption was that ethnic minorities or migrants are demographically very small groups. However around 1985 (two years after the parliamentary adoption of the minorities policy document), demographers observed an "immigration surplus"; partly due to family reunification of immigrants in particular from so-called Third World countries, for the first time since World War II there were more people immigrating to, than emigrating from, the Netherlands. Following this, the official minority policy document of 1983 was replaced in 1989 by another policy report entitled "Allochtonenbeleid" (policy for nonnatives). Since then, anyone with traces of "color" other than "white" is classified as *allochtonen,* a Dutch word for "nonnative" or "alien," irrespective of citizenship. This constitutes the institutionalization of nativism.

The concept of *allochtonen* is not only a qualitative expression of nativism, but it inflates the notion of aliens because it does not distinguish between nationalities, birthplace, and citizenship. On this score, the notion of black Europe has no relevance to Dutch official discourse. Take the case of the Surinamese in the Netherlands as an example. Formally, there are approximately 25,000 Surinamese by nationality or citizenship residing in the Netherlands.The number of people who are classified as Surinamese by birth with Dutch citizenship is 159,000; a further 92,000 are classified as Surinamese born in the Netherlands. This means that there are 251,000 people of Surinamese heritage who are also citizens of the Netherlands; thus approximately 91 percent of Surinamese residents in the Netherlands are formally and legally Dutch citizens (Eurostat 1996; see Mullard et al.). However, from the point of view of *allochtonen,* there are more than 300,000 Surinamese aliens in the Netherlands.

Though many Blacks in the Netherlands object to the use of the term *allochtonen,* it has become so entrenched in official usage and implanted in popular consciousness that it has become difficult to eradicate. In recent years, a group of Surinamese have been defining themselves as Afro-Surinamese, but this has not gained popular usage even among Surinamese. Some object to any reference to their African descent. In a separate development, under the pressure of some Afro-Surinamese, one district council, Amsterdam Southeast, formally abolished the use of the term *allochtonen,* but this has not had any major effect yet. The district of Amsterdam Southeast is one of the Black Europe enclaves where 70 percent of the population is officially classified as *allochtonen* (Nimako 1999).

In other words, the attempt to import the British race relations model to the Netherlands failed; but whether Dutch nativism is an alternative model is another matter. What can be observed is that there are some advantages and disadvantages to notions of natives and nonnatives. We noted above that from the point of view of nativism, equality poses more problems than inequality. This is partly because there is a thin line between nativism and national interest. Underneath the notion of nativism is the notion of national interests and the assumption that the former serves the latter better. There is an inherent tension between nativism and citizenship: decisions to preserve national identity and protect national interest can overlap with the protection of natives and can therefore not be made with or in the presence of nonnatives. This in turn affects division of labor and the selection of people for certain occupations in society, thus reinforcing institutional racism and discrimination.

How do notions and concepts of Black Europe, African diaspora, citizenship, nativism, ethnicity, and etharchy translate into concrete social positions and status of groups in Europe? Let us take a quick glance at the unemployment trends during the past ten years in the Netherlands as an example. At least we can observe eight classifications or categories of unemployed by groups from the Dutch Central Bureau of Statistics, namely, general, gender, natives (or *autochtonen*), nonnatives (or *allochtonen*), nonnatives from western countries, nonnatives from non-western countries, ethnicity, and other non-westerners (including Africans). For the sake of space, and our current subject matter, let us limit ourselves to four categories. First, the general national unemployment rate was 8.1 percent in 1995, dropped to 3.8 percent in 2000, increased to 5.3 percent in 2003, and to 6.4 percent in 2004. Second, national unemployment rate for natives was lower than the average; it was 6.7 percent in 1995, dropped to 3.0 percent in 2000, increased to 4.2 percent in 2003, and to 5.2 percent in 2004. Third, national unemployment rate for western nonnatives was 11.0 percent in 1995, dropped to 5.0 percent in 2000, increased to 6.9 percent in 2003, and to 8.3 percent in 2004. This was lower, however, than the national unemployment rate for non-western nonnatives (including black Europeans and African diaspora) which stood at 26.3 percent in 1995, dropped to 11.0 percent in 2000, increased to 14.4 percent in 2003, and then to 16.0 percent in 2004 (CBS Nederland 2006). Viewed in this context, there are clear advantages and disadvantages associated with being native or nonnative. This pattern is common in EU member states.

We noted above that Enoch Powell became the symbol of nativism in Britain in the 1960s, but compared to the right-wing political parties that emerged in Europe in the 1980s, Powell was a moderate. In Germany and other European countries that did not have or were historically denied colonies, nativism was not even questioned because immigrants and noncitizens were synonymous; every black was by definition an alien and thus knew his/her position in society. However, the proliferation of racist political parties prompted the European Commission and the European Parliament to set up a Committee of Inquiry into the Rise of Fascism-Racism in Europe in 1985; this was followed by a Committee of Inquiry into Racism and Xenophobia in 1990.

Despite these actions, a 1992 study commissioned by the European Commission to study legal instruments to combat racism and xenophobia in EU member states concluded, "Most legal texts do not define racism, racial discrimination or xenophobia. In fact, most legal texts do not mention xenophobia. Defining the scope of the problem is as difficult as regulating it, in part because racism and xenophobia are beliefs or attitudes. In general, efforts are made in law to prohibit manifestations of hatred or preference based on race, color, descent, or national or ethnic origin. Positive measures may also be taken to promote tolerance or integration. States are split over the issue of recognizing group rights, while nearly all have taken or are considering taking measures to restrict immigration and the influx of aliens" (EC 1993, quoted in Mullard et al. 1997). The political irony is that around the same time as blacks in the Netherlands were being declared aliens, German nativism was on the rise from an unexpected quarter. After the fall of the Berlin Wall in 1989, Frank observed the emergence of a new German identity and noted, "This sudden rediscovery of 'our German identity' is not limited to West and East Germany. In Poland, Czechoslovakia, Romania, Hungry, and the Soviet Union all sorts of people, many of whom can hardly speak German, are now finding it economically attractive to rediscover their German identity" (Frank 1990, 20).

We must add that as the economic crisis in Latin America intensifies, some Latin Americans of Spanish and Italian descent are also finding it economically attractive to "rediscover" their Spanish and Italian identity. Whether this is also a consequence of the rise of nativism in Latin America, especially, Bolivia, Peru, and Venezuela, is another matter. What is relevant here is that Latin Americans of Spanish and Italian decent are more welcome in Spain and Italy than Africans.

In conclusion, resistance to notions of assimilation and clamor for cultural diversity by Blacks may also create space for nativism; the problem is that in Europe nativism is tied to national interest and national identity. Nativism becomes the belief that a European is white, or a Black person cannot be a good European.

African Diaspora, Transnationality, and Xenophobia

African diasporic communities have historically been formed through forced or voluntary migration. Historically, forced migration is associated with the transatlantic slave trade and slavery whereas "voluntary" migration is associated with colonialism. At the turn of the twentieth century, "African diaspora" referred only to people of African descent who ended up in the Americas between the fifteenth and the twentieth centuries as a result of the European-initiated transatlantic slave trade and European-led slavery in the Caribbean and the Americas. Part of the formation of African diaspora that emerged from this experience was formulated by Edmondson: "Africa's racial and cultural presence throughout Latin America and the Caribbean is a permanent reminder of the deep-seated historical contacts between the African continent and these African diasporas, of the traumatic conditions of the trans-Atlantic slave trade from which these diasporas were created, and of the racial/cultural ties which have underpinned a sense of trans-continental pan-Africanism" (Edmondson 1993, 854).

Since the beginning of the twentieth century, migration of continental Africans to North America and Europe has given rise to a second category of African diaspora, namely, those whose encounter with, and migration to, Europe and North America was a consequence of European colonialism. Ali Mazrui was thus stating the obvious when, with regard to the United States, he noted two types of diaspora have emerged, namely, African Americans (that is, the first category) and American Africans (the second category). However, he argued that there is also a transition from American Africans to African Americans; the children of American Africans born in the United States generally become African Americans (Mazrui 2005). This can of course be extended to people of African descent from Latin America and the Caribbean who have migrated to the United States. If we take Mazrui's analysis to its logical conclusion, it means that "the African American" is not a static concept; rather "the African American" is what one becomes.

It is not clear why Mazrui did not extend his analysis to the postcolonial period in Africa, an analysis that would be interesting since more Africans have migrated to Europe and North America in the postcolonial period than during the colonial period. In either case, in the long term, the African American and the American African fused to become African America. As we shall argue below, postcolonial migration is a consequence of both *dependence* (of AU states on EU and U.S. "aid") and *freedom* (to travel).

BLACK EUROPE AND THE AFRICAN DISAPORA: CLASSIFICATION AND CLARIFICATION

Even if we limit ourselves to the African diaspora in Europe, critical observation indicates that the broadened notion now covers four types of African diasporas, namely, (1) Black Europeans of African descent, (2) the Afro-Caribbean in Europe, (3) continental African diaspora in Europe, and (4) African Union diaspora in Europe. This gives rise to several considerations. From the perspective of citizenship, by definition, Black Europeans (which now form a little over 30 percent of the Black population) are citizens of member states of the European Union (Mullard et al.). Many, if not most, continental African diasporans in Europe are citizens of different European states. Although their numbers are small, 60 percent of the Ghanaians residing in the Netherlands are legally Dutch citizens; the figure is higher in the United Kingdom (Nimako 2000; Mullard et al.). For the sake of comparison and simplification, let us say that all African Americans are American born and all Black Europeans are born in a European country. As we argued above and will demonstrate below, whereas Black Europeans have been preoccupied with struggles against racism and for social mobility and social justice within Europe, at the broader level of generalization, the African Union diaspora has been preoccupied with economic and political development in Africa.

Even if we limit ourselves to a post-twentieth-century notion of African diaspora, this gives rise to the emergences of two types of African diaspora, namely, continental Africa diaspora and African Union citizens. We shall return to this below. For the moment suffice it to say that some of the African diaspora groups, such as African Foundation for Development (AFFORD) and AfricaRecruit in Britain and Foundation for Democracy in Africa in the United States have responded to the calls of the African Union. Among the African diaspora organizations that have been endorsed by the African Union is AfricaRecruit. One of the objectives of AfricaRecruit is to recruit African diaspora professionals and skilled people to work in different African countries. President Olusegun Obasanjo of Nigeria, then the chairman of the African Union, stated in 2004, "NEPAD as a program of the African Union, recognizes the importance of re-attracting to Africa skills that were lost in the days of instability, uncertainty, and economic downturn. With the new enthusiasm in the continent for transparency, good governance, social justice, accountability and mutually rewarding local and global partnerships for development, we believe that all hands should, and must be on deck to build a virile and vibrant future for our peoples." (AfricaRecruit Web site, accessed February 2006).

President Obasanjo continued, "The *African community* in Diaspora has a major role to play in the new task of transforming, reconstruction and regeneration. Their experiences, values, knowledge, and creativity are very much required to join with home-based efforts to ensure the overall improvement in the African condition. Rebuilding Africa is a collective challenge that must be addressed and this is not the time for *unnecessary theories or excuses*" (emphasis added; AfricaRecruit ibid).

President Obasanjo's letter suggests that African political leaders are struggling with the concept of African diaspora. According to Mr. Gadio, the foreign minister of Senegal, the African diaspora "cannot be solely based on the racial criterion, but also on the African origin and one's feeling of hailing from that origin, both factors which naturally entail *the will to be useful to the continent*" (emphasis added; see Panapress, February 8, 2006). Clearly this institutionalized pan-Africanism is different from early forms of pan-Africanism. Institutionalized pan-Africanism, of which Nkrumah became one of the champions, now finds its expression in African Union, NEPAD, and regionalism devoted to economic development of Africa. The form of pan-Africanism that took shape at the turn of the twentieth century, of which W.E.B. Du Bois is the best-known representative, was a social movement devoted to freedom of Africans worldwide and the self-determination of Africa. As a social movement and ideological expression of African identity, pan-Africanism is one of the most successful movements in modern history because it achieved its aim of freedom and self-determination of African peoples worldwide; people of Africa and African descent worldwide now recognize a shared history. However, as an institutionalized project to foster economic development in Africa, pan-Africanism is less successful (Nimako 2006). The African Union's renewed interest in pan-Africanism should be applauded but the declaration of the African diaspora by the African Union as the latter's sixth region is inadequate, deficient, and contradictory because it does not capture the complexity and diversity of African diaspora. This definition is not intended to reinforce and reinvent pan-Africanism; rather it is a consequence of Africa's economic decline, political implosion, and marginalization in the global economy.

This is also the point at which we could analyze the objectives of AfricaRecruit (in Britain) and the response of the African Union. But the position of organizations such as AfricaRecruit in relation to the African Union's notion of African diaspora poses two problems. First, the above letter suggests that only recently migrated Africans with skills and professions are counted as useful to Africa; the assumption is that there has been a brain drain that has to be reversed. This makes the African Union's notion of African diasporic tradition selective and exclusive and subject to the "development aid" trap. Skills and knowledge are on sale; much of the skill that AfricaRecruit can attract cannot be paid for by African Union member states and has to be paid for through development aid. It was against this backdrop that the West African Regional Consultation, which supported Tony Blair's Commission for Africa initiative, requested the G8 to provide the International Organization of Migration (IOM), the UNDP, and the African Union/Diaspora in Europe "with a fund designed to finance international cooperation programs to allow young executives from the Diaspora to get employment contracts for a set period of time in their parents' homeland." The assumption is that the diaspora is better off than residents of the home countries, whereas in reality, many people of the African diaspora are leading marginal existences in European states. One of the often-cited contributions of the African diaspora to African development is remittance. Even if we consider remittance as contributing to African development, we have to consider two effects. First, Africans abroad do not remit because they have plenty of money, but because they must. Second, despite remittance, emigration from Africa continues, which suggests that it is not making an economic development impact. On this score African economic and political problems affect the identity formation of African diaspora.

The African Union's sixth region initiative does make it possible for the African diaspora to send recognized delegations to African Union meetings and activities. However, the renewed interest of the African Union in its diaspora does not tell us what the African Union and its member states can do for the African diaspora in Europe and elsewhere; the diaspora is expected to do something for Africa. Let us put this into perspective. If we take the first pan-African conference in London in 1900 as the start of formal African diaspora involvement in African development, then we have a one-way traffic.

Even if we limit ourselves to the EU, how can the AU reconcile its sixth region initiative with its dependence on the EU for so-called development aid? Which side will the African Union choose when the demands of the African diaspora are incompatible with the African Union's aid dependence? For instance, when the apartments of West African migrants from predominantly Ivory Coast and Mali were burned in Paris, we did not hear any protest from the African Union and its member states, but when civil strife broke out in the Ivory Coast, France sent troops to protect its citizens. This suggests that the African economic crisis and political implosion have had a negative impact on the African diaspora and on antiracist struggle in Europe. In fact, there are those who argue that Africans in diaspora should be happy that they were forced "out of Africa"; otherwise they would have faced the fate of starving Africans and victims of wars and deprivation.

THE AFRICAN DIASPORA AND CITIZENSHIP

Conflicts of interest with the AU are compounded by that fact that African diaspora interest should not come in conflict with national interests of European Union member states. Apart from citizenship, continental African diaspora migrants are not a homogeneous group due to their legal and social status in the EU and in Africa. This is because people do not just migrate; people migrate for specific purposes. Undocumented migrants aside, the category of African migrants that could be classified as African Union diaspora can be distinguished into four legal and social groups, namely, cultural migrants, economic migrants, social migrants, and political migrants (Nimako 2000).

The first category, *cultural migrants,* refers to those who came to various European countries to study on the basis of "development aid" or cultural exchange agreements between African states and European states but did not return to their native countries after their studies. Cultural migrants live predominantly in former colonial countries. This is the category the African Union refers to as its sixth region. By *economic migrants,* we mean those who came to Europe to work, legally or undocumented. It is worth noting that the EU and its member states do not have regulations that allow immigration for people seeking jobs. Thus with the exception of nationals of Cape Verde who were invited to work as "guest workers" in Rotterdam harbors and Luxembourg in the 1960s, most ACP African migrants regulated their status as workers after they entered the European countries in which they reside; hence the distinction between legal and illegal/undocumented workers and migrants. *Social migrants* refer to those who joined spouses or parents in the context of family reunification, whereas *political migrants* refer to refugees.

Of the four categories, it is the economic and social migrants who tend to form a community (Nimako 2000). Cultural migrants depend on their countries of birth for emigration papers and the European host country for their training, and refugee migrants depend on the European host state for their subsistence. However, economic and social migrants depend on the solidarity among themselves for their survival. This also explains why the African Union notion of African diaspora is selective and thus reflects on the status and position of cultural migrants. Equally important to note is that, at the broader level, the "push" and "pull" factors of migration give rise to different outcomes. The "push" factor gives rise to xenophobia in Europe whereas the "pull" factor gives rise to "new nationalism" in Africa. Not only does emigration give rise to diaspora formation, but economic emigration and politically engineered emigration (such as refugee flow) generate different responses from the diaspora community towards the country of origin. Economic migrants tend to be preoccupied with economic issues in their countries of birth whereas refugees tend to be preoccupied with political issues. In a comparative study of Ghana and Suriname, one of us argued that the consequences of diaspora protest against military rule on the military rulers in both countries were threefold, namely, (1) restrictions on the freedom of movement of the military rulers, (2) democratization of politics, and (3) the rise of new nationalism in both countries (Nimako and Willemsen 2004, 13).

First, in both countries, diaspora political protest restricted the freedom of movement of the coup leaders. This is particularly the case for countries with a sizable diaspora population, namely, Ghanaians in the United Kingdom, and Surinamese in the Netherlands. It made it difficult for Britain and the Netherlands to have warm diplomatic relations with Ghana and Suriname. Thus despite the Western world's formal approval of the economic policies of the Rawlings regime in the context of Structural Adjustment Programs (SAP), Rawlings did not enjoy official visits to Western capitals. It was only after the return to democratic rule that he was officially able to visit Britain. Secondly, protests by the Ghana and Suriname diaspora, resistance to repression from society, and protests against military rule in both countries increased the pressure for the return to civilian rule and democratization of society. Thus a combination of external pressures and internal resistance obliged both Bouterse and Rawlings to transform their military regimes to civilian regimes at the turn of the 1990s. Thirdly, in both Ghana and Suriname, massive migration in the 1970s was interpreted by the left-wing elements in society, especially state employees, as an unpatriotic act on the part of those who chose to migrate. Reinforced by diaspora protests against military rule, by the 1980s this worldview (of a lack of patriotism) had given rise to a new and subtle form of nationalism directed at the Ghanaian and Surinamese diaspora. This is partly because diaspora protest against military rule from abroad was viewed as unpatriotic. The unanticipated consequence of these developments is that this new nationalism transcended the left-wing politics and military rule of the 1980s and became institutionalized in the 1990s. Unlike the old nationalism, which opposed colonialism and fostered pan-Africanism, the enemies of new nationalism are (former) Ghanaian and Surinamese nationals who now live in Europe and North America. These new enemies are not only viewed as living in relative comfort abroad but also as armchair critics of governments and society; this view undermines pan-Africanism.

THE AFRICAN DIASPORA AND XENOPHOBIA

As the example above demonstrates, unlike the business community and civil society, which welcomes diaspora political and economic engagement, state actors do not. Civil society welcomed the role of diaspora because its protest from outside was less risky than open opposition from within. Not only is remittance from the diaspora population to families at home good for business, but it increases the influence of the diaspora on their families at home. It also makes family members at home less dependent on the state and more critical of the same. However, new nationalism has prevented the diaspora from playing a structural political and economic role in both countries.

Thus from the point of view of the African Union, only "cultural migrants," or diaspora members with skills, will be useful to the African Union-NEPAD project. In short, with the exception of cultural migrants, all African migrants or would-be migrants to Europe are subject to the Fortress Europe project; not only does this reinforce xenophobia in Europe but it gives rise to new nationalism in some African countries. It must be added, however, that the status and position of cultural migrants is also a reflection of dependency; it indicates that African states do not have the infrastructure to educate their populations. In practice, this means that amid the widening financial, technological, information, and/or development gap between Africa and Europe, some people succeed to escape poverty, war, and dictatorship in Africa through migration only to be confronted with xenophobia, prejudice, racism, and discrimination in the North. Economic decline and political crisis pushes Africans to emigrate and thus swells the numbers of the African diaspora demographically, but this does not automatically translate into the social mobility of African diaspora in Europe. What then is the proper way to integrate the African Union's institutionalized pan-Africanism into African diaspora pan-Africanism discourse? Let us answer this question in the conclusion.

Conclusion: Some Notes

Let us end on three notes. First, whichever perspective one takes, the black experience in Europe is tied to periodization (migration) and subordination (low social status). This cannot be circumvented. Even where integration has been the professed objective of state policy, it has come with the condition of controlling further black immigration into Europe. In other words, all European states that have attempted to circumvent the issue of subordination by introducing integration policies have also attempted to slow or reverse the flow of immigration of Africans at the same time: fewer is better. This constitutes institutionalized nativism and xenophobia. On the one hand, this has been reinforced by developments in the material world through the ongoing migration of Africans to Europe, which has gone hand in hand with the impoverishment of much of continental Africa. The majority of the African diaspora in Europe that "pulls" the immigrants is impoverished, like their countries that "push" them to emigrate. On the other hand, constant migration from Africa to Europe holds the balance between Black Europeans and the new African diaspora in check and makes the diaspora diverse without helping either of them escape subordination.

The second note brings us back to a narrow definition of the black community that has been common since the 1980s, partly due to official state classifications for policy making and the practice of *self-identification* by Black Europe. Britain is the first country where Black politics and something close to Black scholarship took shape in Europe. However, other countries in Europe do not share the same concepts with regard to the African diaspora. Three variants of race and ethnic relations can be delineated, namely, the British variant, based on citizenship and antiracism; the French model, based on citizenship and color blindness; and the (Dutch/German) continental variant based on nativism. Thus the notion of the Black community, and flowing from that, Black Europe, never gained broader usage in continental Europe. For instance, the notion of *black* is rejected in official discourse in the Netherlands; the concept of *allochtonen* or nonnatives is preferred. Thus one can observe a Black presence in Europe, but one cannot use the European Union as unit of analysis because a European citizen does not exist. Equally, Black European citizenship does not exist because black Europeans belong to EU member states. Citizenship confers power and powerlessness; African diaspora formation is associated with powerlessness. The space of Black Europe depends on developments in the European Union member state in which one lives but not on the European Union project; Black European struggle (if there is such a thing) is thus national not European.

The third and final note is this: the African Union's renewed interest in pan-Africanism should be applauded but the declaration by the African Union of the African diaspora as Africa's sixth region is inadequate, deficient, and contradictory for three reasons. First, the African Union's notion of African diaspora is selective and exclusive because it refers to African diasporans with skills and capital only. Secondly, the majority of African diasporans are citizens of other countries, so the African Union has no jurisdiction over them. Thirdly, the African Union's notion of its diaspora is informed by development aid; it is formulated in terms of what the diaspora can do for Africa but not what the African Union and the diaspora can do for each other. There should be a better way to integrate institutionalized pan-Africanism, which is what the African Union is, and the African diaspora as civil society and social movement. As a start, the more than 100 million African diasporans worldwide can be more useful to the African Union if the African Union considers the African diaspora as a market and consumers of products made in Africa rather than as a forum to appeal for development aid. Continental Africa has the land, the natural resources, and the international legal framework to effect the desired changes. Africans in the diaspora are separated by citizenship but united by history, memory, and race; market and cultural forces can transcend citizenship. This is all the more relevant since history, memory, and culture without production or material base are empty.

References

ACP-EEC Joint Assembly Resolutions: OJ No. C27, 4.2.1991; Doc. ACP-EEC 367/91/fin.

Balanya, B., et al., eds. *Europe Inc.: Regional and Global Restructuring and the Rise of Corporate Power.* Pluto Press: London, 2003.

Chikezie, C. "Supporting Africa's Regional Integration: The African Diaspora—Prototype Pan-Africanists or Village-Aiders?" (African Development Forum 2001; uneca.org/aknf/aknf2001; Apr. 4, 2006).

EEC. *Legal Instruments to Combat Racism and Xenophobia.* Luxembourg, 1993.

———. Lome Convention (Various): But see Lome IV Convention (1992) and Agreement Amending the Fourth ACP-EC Convention of Lome. Luxembourg and the Courier. 155 (January-February 1996), Brussels.

Edmondson, L. "Africa and the Developing Regions." In A. Mazrui and C. Wondji, eds. *Africa Since 1935.* Paris: UNESCO, 1993, 829–70.

Essed, P., and K. Nimako. "Designs and (Co)Incidents: Cultures of Scholarship and Public Policy on Immigrants/Minorities in the Netherlands." In *International Journal of Comparative Sociology* 47, no. 3–4 (2006): 281–312.

Eurostat. Rapid Reports: *Population and Social Condition,* "Non-nationals Make Up Less Than 5% of the Total Population of the European Union on 1.1.1993/1996." Luxembourg.

FitzGerald, M. *Black People and Party Politics in Britain.* London: The Runnymede Trust London, 1987.

Frank, A.G. "No End to History! History to No End?" *Social Justice* 17, no. 4 (December 1990): 7–29.

Hall, S. "What is This 'Black' in Black Popular Culture?" In J. Bobo, C. Hudley, and C. Michel eds. *The Black Studies Reader.* New York: Routledge, 2004, 255–263.

———. "Race and Moral Panics in Post-War Britain." In CRE ed. *Five Views of Multi-Racial Britain.* London: CRE, 1978.

International Centre for Migration Policy Development (ICMPD). *Comparative Study on Country of Origin Information Systems: Study on COI Systems in Ten European Countries and the Potential for Further Improvement of COI Co-operation.* Vienna: ICMPD, 2006.

Mazrui, A. "Pan-Africanism and the Intellectuals: Rise, Decline and Revival." In T. Mkandawire ed. *African Intellectuals: Rethinking Politics, Language, Gender, and Development.* London: Zed Books, 2005, 56–77.

Miles, R., and A. Phizacklea. *White Man's Country. Racism in British Politics.* London: Pluto Press, 1984.

Mullard, C., K. Nimako, and N. Murray. *Demographic and Legal Status of ACP Migrants in Europe: ACP General Guide Book, Volume 1.* Wiltshire, UK: Focus Consultancy, 1997.

Mullard, C. "Racism, Ethnicism and Etharchy or Not? The Principles of Progressive Control and Transformative Change." In T. Skutnabb-Kangas and J. Cummins eds. *Minority Education: From Shame to Struggle.* Clevedon: UK; Phildelphia: PA Multilingual Matters, 1988.

———. *Race, Power and Resistance.* London: Routledge & Kegan Paul, 1985.

———. *Racism in Society and Schools: History, Policy and Practice* (Occasional Paper No.1; Center for Multicultural Education, University of London Institute of Education), 1980.

———. *Black Britain.* London: Allen & Unwin, 1973.

Nimako, K. "African Regional Groupings and Emerging Chinese Conglomerates." In *Big Business and Economic Development: Conglomerates and Economic Groups in Developing Countries and Transition Economies under Globalization.* Barbara Hoogenboom and Alex E. Fernandez Jilberto eds. London: Routledge, 2006.

———. "Labor and Ghana's Debt Burden: The Democratization of Dependency." In *Labor Relations in Development,* ed. Alex E. Fernandez Jilberto et.al., London: Routledge, 2002.

———. "Repositioning Social Policy: North-South dialogue in the context of donor-recipient relation." In *Bridging the Gaps: Essays on Economic, Social and Cultural Opportunities at Global and Local Levels.* Ultrecht: NIZW International Centre, 2002.

———. "The Struggle for Social and Physical Space." In *De Bijlmer Vernieuwt.* Amsterdam: Rooilijn, 6 (June 2002).

———. "De Ghanese gemeenschap in Nederland: van migranten tot etnische minderheid?" (The Ghanaian Community in the Netherlands: From Migrants to Ethnic Minority?). In I. van Kessel and N. Tellegen eds. *Afrikanen in Nederland.* Koninklijk Instituut voor de Tropen, Amsterdam and Afrika-Studiecentrum, Leiden, 2000.

———. *Voorbij Multiculturalisatie: Amsterdam Zuidoost als strategische locatie* (Beyond Multiculturalization: Amsterdam Southeast as Strategic Location). Amsterdam, 1999.

Nimako, K., and G. Willemsen. "Democratic Transitions in Ghana and Suriname, 1980–2000." (Paper presented at the international conference on Globalization, Diaspora and Identity Formation, Feb. 26–29, 2004. Organized by the University of Suriname, Paramaribo).

Obradovic, D. "Civil Society and the Social Dialogue in European Governance." In *Yearbook of European Law* (24). Eds. Eeckhout, P. and Tridimas, T. Oxford University Press, 2005, 261–327.

Runneymede Trust and the Radical Statistics Race Group. *Britain's Black Population.* London: Heinemann Educational Books, 1980.

Sivanandan, A. "Challenging Racism: Strategies for the 1980s." In *Race and Class* vol. 25, no. 2 (1983):1–11.

———. *A Different Hunger: Writings on Black Resistance.* London: Pluto Press, 1982.

———. "Race, Class, and the State: The Black Experience in Britain." In *Race and Class* vol. 27 (1976): 347–68.

Small, S. *Police and People in London II: A Group of Young Black People.* London: Policy Studies Institute, 1983.

UNECA (2001) The New Partnership for Africa's Development (NEPAD) (www.uneca.org/nepad; see also African Union 6th Region Initiative Web site).

Western Hemisphere Africa Diaspora Network (Press Release Mar. 8, 2006; see also the Web site of Foundation for Democracy in Africa, Nov. 18, 2002; see also Panapress, Aug. 2, 2006; see also Angel Tabe, VOA News- Descendants of Africa Unite for the Roots, Washington, D.C., Dec. 18, 2006).

13

The Audacious Josephine Baker: Stardom, Cinema, and Paris

TERRI FRANCIS

Josephine Baker starred in a 1928 silent-era film called *Siren of the Tropics*. In many ways, this French production was an instrument of transformation for Baker. She went from a live phenomenon to a recorded one; from a figure in ambiguously low culture to one in ambiguously less low culture, as film struggled in some cases for legitimacy as a high art and in other cases sought mass appeal; from a Parisian pleasure to an international phenomenon; and from a physically expressive dancer to a potentially emotionally expressive actress, even if the mode was musical-romantic comedy. Elsewhere I have written that Baker updated colonialist fantasy, and as a Black American performer in Paris, she permitted references to Primitivist perceptions of "Africa" and to the American dream, bypassing actual French colonization. *The Fireman of the Folies Bergères* (1927), *Siren of the Tropics* (1927), *Zou Zou* (1934), *Princesse Tam Tam* (1935), and to a lesser extent the postwar film *The French Way* (1945) are all significant engines of Baker's own modernizing process and which she facilitated as parallel trends in African American identity formation and French ideas about racial difference and assimilation. In all of these films, Baker is a witness to or conduit of a romance between white characters while she remains alone on stage. Baker's films, though, are too often consulted as a transparent source of her performances, without sufficient attention to how they are cinematic or what their relationships might be to wider histories of and conceptual approaches to the medium.

The film screen can be described as a window. This metaphor implies a neutral portal through which a scene or various scenes can be observed. However, the window is a framing device. As it delimits space in four directions, it designs our vision of what is being shown within its borders by obscuring all that is outside them—in fact, making us forget about what we do not see, including the frame itself. The cinema is not just the movies, the stories they tell, the actors, and how we feel about them. It is a structured set of meaningful though illusory relationships among films, audiences, critics, producers, performers, and, most significantly, between reality and illusion. The observable movement in motion pictures is an illusion that arises from a collaboration between the viewer's physiological reaction to seeing images projected at 24 frames per second, her imaginative submissions to the narrative's continuity, and the whole apparatus of projection, editing, and performance. These elements create a seamless, seemingly transparent world, centered on the viewer's orientation. The cinematic world is composed of pieces made to feel whole—thousands of little pictures filmed at different times in different locations that are joined together to create the appearance of continuities in space, time, and action. The cinema is also composed of arranged looks—the audience looking at the screen, the camera's (window) view on the scene, and the looks and glances of and between characters that direct our attention, show the relationships between characters and ultimately form our relationship to the characters. All of this seems to unfold in linear, real time. Most narrative films, like *Siren of the Tropics,* aim to make these structures invisible in order to enhance the viewer's pleasure as absorption in the story and the film's capacity for spectatorial dazzlement.

Josephine Baker is a cinematic phenomenon. Before her appearance in films, Baker was known primarily as a live performer and a dancer. And although she created bold contrasts between her onstage and offstage personas through her clothing choices (couture suits and gowns offstage, couture bananas and raffia onstage), resulting in one version of a Primitivist modernism, her dancing and erotic exoticism were seen as natural—not artifice. In a sense, she did not get acting credit for her performances. Her appearance in movies supposedly demonstrated her acting skills despite the fact that her film characters were based on her stage personas (associations with the French Empire) and as she said, her life's story. Baker's films represented a kind of upgrade. Although audiences did not actually hear her voice, Baker's movie roles associated her with speech and writing. The center of Baker's performance remained her dancing body, but dance combined with acting potentially widened the audience's views to include the Black Venus' capacities for thought, language, and emotional expression. That Baker appeared in films was an example of the traditional ways that early cinema drew upon vaudeville and a range of popular live entertainment forms, while she gained an association with the literariness linked with the silent-era cinema's sources in theater. Cinema updated Baker, giving her a modern context, lending her its own status as modernity's medium. It lent her not only its status but also its form, its lexical structures of communication. Baker and cinema were both phenomena of motion, and it makes sense to theorize them together from that standpoint. Further, from a pragmatic perspective, the visualized figure of

Baker cannot exist for today's audiences except as a cinematic phenomenon, a filmic dance text, and, when not in motion, as a still photograph.

As a dancer on film, Baker raises formalist issues for film studies, but she raises historical and conceptual ones as well. What does it mean that an African American actress stars in a French film production, playing a Caribbean role in 1927? Is Baker singular, or does her work indicate or exemplify a wider phenomenon—who were the other black American women in film and what kinds of roles did they play? Who are Baker's peers? We know that Baker is transnational and performative, and I wonder whether there is a link between these two. Does transnationality require performativity? And is this relationship gendered—or rather how is it gendered and raced?

Siren of the Tropics relied on Baker's dancing and featured it at several climactic moments. In the story, Papitou (Baker) falls in love with an engineer who has come to the island where she lives for a surveying project. When he leaves the island, Papitou follows him by stowing away on the ship. In Paris, Papitou takes a job looking after children. While entertaining them, she is discovered by two producers and put into their music hall show. However, she refuses to perform unless they find her a love interest. They find him and bring him to the theater, but instead of bearing a declaration of love, he has news of his engagement to another woman. Baker's solo dance performance occurs after Papitou has found out that her cherished Frenchman does not love her. The plot's trajectory is not toward romance but toward occasions for Baker's dancing: following the engineer was a device for getting her to Paris where she would be discovered and placed in a show. Importantly, Papitou does not have any expressed ambition to be in a music hall show. Her desire is for love and attention, which she audaciously demands as a condition of her performance.

The intertitles that introduce the performance read, "And that night, as she dances for the last time in Paris, as she pretends to be gay, she mourns her lost love, her illusions, all the sweetness of her youth." Papitou's sad emotions are contrasted with her supposedly happy dancing. This characterization transforms her work into play. A shot of the audience shows the accolades Papitou receives. Instead of intimacy and romantic love, Papitou gets public applause. Rather than becoming part of French society through a partnership with the engineer, she has been assigned a role on stage as the entertainment. These are the basic codes of Baker's screen characters.

This dance sequence shows the main principles of Baker's dancing: the speed, angularity, and the way her costume creates more spheres of motion by having parts that move independently of her and reflect light. The excerpt is an example of the way that the story provides context and creates meaning around Baker through her film character. The theatrical context in *Siren* is a reference to Baker's real performance career, and indeed she dances not as Papitou but as herself, doing her signature movements that she had performed on stage and would perform in later films. Baker's dancing in *Siren* tends to be filmed theatrically with tableau shots that show her from head to toe on a stage or a makeshift stage. Cinematic dancing today generally includes perspectives that are not accessible to the live audience such as close-ups on the feet or face, slow motion, or freeze frame. In Baker's context, theatrical framing can refer to the setting, which is often a theatre, but also to the wide perspective that frames the stage. The camera's look imitates the view a live audience member might have. Significantly, however, Baker's dancing is full of cuts and edits—quick changes and an illusory continuity. The world in the film and the world beyond it are layered over each other when Baker dances in the film. We can see the performance—what she actually does—while the story provided a constructed layer of meaning for Baker's performativity.

Baker creates a stage persona, which is then translated through film, but this does not mean that her stage persona is left behind. Baker's performativity is a dense mesh of meanings in which we can tease out the particularities of her performance style and the spectatorial possibilities inherent to cinema. In other words, the figure of Baker is a sign that contains signs. But what is performativity? Why is the term performance insufficient? And what does it mean to think about Baker in this way?

In many ways "performance" adequately describes what Baker does. Baker acts, dances, and sings for an audience. Her mode is entertainment, whether it is comic or musical—usually combined—both of which are tinted with an appeal that depends on sexual and exoticist perceptions of womanhood and blackness, particularly perceptions projected on to a dancing black woman. But performance presumes, and is in many ways limited to, speculations about Baker's subjectivity, biography, and actual personhood. True that Baker must first be understood in concrete terms. For what is unique about Baker is the way she combines angularity, speed, frequent changes, and dances from multiple sources. But on an abstract level, her performance becomes meaningful to a range of discussions on race, racism, and representations when it is understood as constructed within a dense cultural matrix, shaped around her dancing, singing, and films.

Baker's performativity is complicated by her performances in films. Across the films, Baker played characters from Africa and the Caribbean. Both in film and on stage, Baker performed what I call an elastic ethnicity, in which she was in turn represented as Caribbean, African, and American. Baker's performance blended entertainment with ethnological display. She is made an example of a group, but she plays with her roles by being many kinds of ethnicities, obscuring her own origins in the process. Baker intervened in a history of black stereotyping in Hollywood and limited roles for Black women by establishing her career not just outside Los Angeles but outside the United States. Like so many African Americans who established their entertainment or artistic careers outside of the United States, she provided a point of recognition and representation for Black people at home. As a point of success, recognition, and representation, Baker was also a case for the vindication of Black talent.

However, Baker's success functioned beyond the dilemma of the Black image. In her poem "The Josephine Baker Museum," Elizabeth Alexander sets out the broader cultural problematic of Baker's cinematic image. She writes, "In the cinema Mammy hands Scarlett / White underthings to cover her white skin. I am both of them and neither, tall / Tan, terrific, soaking in my tub of milk."[1] Because the poem is set in Baker's house, Alexander's describing it as a museum via the title blurs the conventional line between public and private spaces. This metaphor allows Baker to speak from a radicalized and formalized personal space, and in the lines quoted here, Baker, through Alexander's use of a collective first-person voice, speaks in a critical voice about her own image. In the poem, the figure of Baker describes her unique position between the cinematic white woman and the cinematic Black woman. She implies that while her role is fixed in many ways, similar to the stereotypes of Mammy and Scarlett, perhaps what is of greater importance is the relationship between them—their fundamental simultaneity. This move suggests that Baker is not a simple blend but a "third," as if the Mammy and Scarlett images were superimposed rather than side by side. The question here is how to account for the racialized and gendered construction of Baker's image and how she negotiated her own representation within it.

Josephine Baker's film career from 1925 to 1935 foregrounds the dilemmas of representation that attended black women's creativity at the height of the Harlem Renaissance and European Primitivism, "when the Negro was in vogue," as Langston Hughes put it.[2] Moving beyond the significance of Baker's biography, her multiple self-representations in her performances are the result of what I call the actor's curatorial practice. Baker's trajectory from obscurity and poverty in the United States to fame and wealth in France, the mythic haven for Black Americans, has been discussed by her in coauthored autobiographies, by her biographers, and by other scholars in works such as *Jazz Cleopatra: Josephine Baker in Her Time* by Phyllis Rose, while her movie roles have been examined in contexts that include transatlantic Black modernism, colonialist cinema, Black women's film roles, and writing by Black women.[3]

Baker's success certainly functioned as part of a vindicating uplift narrative that the stories of Black American expatriates permitted, and the work itself engaged issues of Black movie audiences.[4] If seen by African American audiences in the United States, films like *Zou Zou* and *Princess Tam Tam* allowed Black folk to see themselves on screen, beyond the hermetic world of the typical Black-cast race film, in an integrated environment. Baker's films portrayed assimilation and relative acceptance by whites. However, while the films seemed to propose a diegetic world in which the Black viewer could see him or herself moving freely in a white world, the plot usually withdrew the invitation to assimilation and social equality. In Paris, Baker avoided what she disparaged as "mammy roles," reflecting African Americans' own desires to see their lives portrayed in dramatic and serious representations.[5] Baker's goal of being in the movies in a certain way sprang from the same set of representational circumstances that Black moviegoers responded to when they were frustrated by not seeing Black performers on film at all or not seeing them in pleasing roles.

As Richard Dyer has written of the star phenomenon, "stars matter because they act out aspects of life that matter to us."[6] Dyer's analysis helps establish certain facets of the terrain and methodology of this essay: stardom, how it was made, and what it expressed. However, Baker's media production is not sufficient for understanding the historical context of her image. As Dyer says, "The complexity of representation lies then in its embeddedness in cultural forms, its unequal but not monolithic relations of production and reception, its tense and unfinished, unfinishable relation to the reality to which it refers and which it affects."[7] Baker's film roles are examples of the actress's embodiment of the core desires of black spectatorship and the hopes of black modernism, which were legible in the literature and performance of the Harlem Renaissance. With the term "hopes," I refer to a range of intangible ideals such as authenticity, respectability, validation, and progress.

As the first international Black actress to star in films, Baker served as a vindication of Black cultural potential and her success in France provided counter examples to the restrictions on Black life, especially Black success, in the United States. But her performances were not entirely free of the codes of Black minstrelsy even as they embodied a new combination of glamour, drawn from the music hall, and physical comedy that was residual from her American performance style. The films Baker appeared in recalled her stage career and so feature a kind of theatricality that is similar to silent-era films. In her films, Baker is the attraction, and the simple trajectory of the plot is driven by her moments of exhibition but not always moments of reflection, ambition, or initiative. Baker was a star as well as an "ethnographic" exhibit. The making and meaning of her stardom drew on the sexual and the ethnic in order to articulate what Dyer called "ideas of personhood" that were supposedly lost to industrialized society.[8] What is complicated by Baker as the star is that the French embraced her not as representing their French personhood but Otherness as a means to a more modern identity. Using Dyer's vocabulary, they saw her as a private, sincere, and approachable, somewhat folksy individual; however, she was manufactured simultaneously as a Parisianized, glamorous, and eventually unreachable icon. Her films narrativize this transformation. Baker's unreachability, however, sometimes reads like exclusion. The Jazz Empress had the fortitude to capitalize on her Otherness. Baker represented ultimate authenticity, and as a dancer she was all body. But this is only part of her stardom—part of how she was locked in iconicity. Particularly through her films, Baker pushes the boundaries of her initial stardom through film roles that had her moving from country to city, physical expressions to mental ones and back again.

Star images are made, as Dyer observed, and in this respect Baker differed little from other stars. She was produced through her films, public appearances, and coauthored autobiographies, among other materials. As she began to record her songs, Baker's film roles and records were understood through each other. I have focused on Baker's films. The colonialist screen roles through which Baker channeled her performance and authorship mirror the off-screen limitations on her agency as a Black woman in the white male-dominated public sphere, illuminating the shared circumstances of black female protagonists and actors in film, literature, museum-like displays, and theater. Perhaps examining the films of an actress who was bound in many ways by both European and American misconstructions of Black women, who always coauthored her writing, and who played to the fantasies of her audiences in order to find her reflections on black women's creativity might seem to go against the feminist grain. Clearly, the representations of early Black women entertainers drew upon preexisting narratives and images from the unnatural museum[9] of racist and sexist depictions in literature and film. But Baker is more complicated than her peers in this regard: reflecting her double incarnations as "sauvage" and "artiste," Baker has been "decried by some as an agent of minstrelsy and a toady to whites" and celebrated "as a Black heroine and the first modern international star."[10] Her multiple incarnations arise from her curatorial practice of her persona, which drew on a range of aesthetics, dance moves, and costuming within the bounds of her industry and the times in which she lived.

By comparison with Baker, the signification of other black women actors is less sustained for a variety of reasons. They appeared in one or two film roles, such as Nina Mae McKinney; they played the same characters repeatedly, such as Hattie McDaniel; or they made a clear break from one type to another with no ongoing reference point, such as Ethel Waters who went from glamorous secular songstress to matriarchal religiously-oriented vocalist. Baker's dichotomies and contradictions occurred over ten years and her acting roles constantly referenced the complexity of her persona. It is precisely through embodying the Black Venus caricature in its many forms that Baker reflects on and makes visible the underlying conundrums of her creativity and her peers by extension. Baker is exemplary. The actor starred in her films, which were vehicles created especially to showcase her music, dancing, and recently achieved command of the French language, but her characters, all colonialism-derived types, were anti-protagonists in narratives they did not control and could not propel forward. Baker's characters competed against white female supporting characters that were idealized for their whiteness and looked very similar to the sauvage image Baker's presence in the film was directed at countering. *Les Hallucinations d'un Pompier* shows a dancing Baker in contrast to nude white women; *Princesse Tam Tam* contrasts her to Lucie de Mirecourt (the wife of the man she fancies); *Zou Zou* contrasts her to the aptly named Claire (her friend and girlfriend of the man she fancies).

In contrast to Baker, film stars such as Marlene Dietrich performed an ethereal, cool, unreachable beauty. Idealized with light reflecting from her hair and skin, Dietrich's whiteness, angular facial features, and husky voice and exotic accent made her into an icy, inaccessible movie goddess. Although, like Baker, Dietrich performed musical numbers, her movements were characterized by moving one part of the body at a time and moving at a relatively slow speed compared to Baker's polyrhythmic, high-speed dancing. Their dancing personas collided weirdly in Dietrich's memorable musical number in *Blonde Venus* (Josef von Sternberg, 1932). In the sequence, Dietrich takes the stage in a gorilla costume, which she eventually discards, going on to perform in an blonde Afro wig, surrounded by supposedly African-ish dancers. Otherwise, Dietrich and Baker both performed in top hat and tails, sharing a fancy for androgyny and playing with expected gender roles. Finally, the mode of Baker's stardom was different from Dietrich's: Baker extended accessibility to her audiences through products (dolls made in her likeness, a hair pomade for recreating her signature hairstyle at home, and her magazine). The figure of Baker was consumable through a variety of media and commodity outlets and became part of daily life as Other.

The fact that Baker's films were produced in France would seem to put her outside the immediate concerns of the Harlem Renaissance and African American cinema, but indeed as current scholarship on the era foregrounds the rubrics of diaspora and migration, Baker's French films are part of the same "Harlem" cultural matrix as Oscar Micheaux's race films and Bessie Smith's race records. Transatlantic black modernism is the underlying ethos of the Harlem Renaissance. The literature itself takes on themes of travel, specifically travel to Europe, such as in Jessie Fauset's *Plum Bun* and Nella Larsen's *Quicksand*. The wandering that Angela and Helga embarked upon is a metaphor of the modern Black condition. In order to address the theoretical experience and position of Black Americans in modernity, in their novels Fauset and Larsen investigate the dissatisfaction, indeed the alienation, which they believed modernity brought to New Negroes, particularly women, who struggled against patriarchal as well as racist conventions to express and inhabit themselves without the condition

W. E. B. Du Bois described as "double-consciousness: looking at oneself through the eyes of others."[11] Significantly, Baker's work in France was reported in the American Black press, making her story available as a trope in a larger conversation about a better elsewhere for African Americans.

The travels of African Americans, especially performers, writers, scholars, and artists, between New York and Paris during the 1920s and 1930s marked out the international dimensions of the so-called Harlem Renaissance. Neither Harlem nor its rebirth (because it was the continuation of cultural trends begun in Reconstruction and before), the early-twentieth-century cultural movement encompassed southern cities such as Memphis as well as Chicago and the far West. While the Great Migration is characterized as an American movement from south to north, significant numbers of migrating New Negroes crossed the Atlantic for military service in France and other foreign locations, African Americans with means traveled to Europe as tourists, and many returned to Africa as missionaries.[12] Through military bands, such as the one led by James Reese Europe and the general spectacle that black soldiers created for French villagers who had never seen a Black person, African American troops followed in the internationally touring footsteps of choral groups such as the Fisk Jubilee Singers and paved the way for the phenomenal success of Black jazz musicians, Broadway-style productions such as *La Revue nègre,* and the girl from St. Louis, Josephine Baker.[13] Word of the beautiful music, crazy jazz rhythms, and sheer physical energy of black Americans had preceded Baker.

Although French journalists and other observers did not seem to connect them overtly, the performances of African American entertainers in Paris serve as a bridge between the African shows of the late nineteenth century and Baker's Africanist shows of the early twentieth century from an historical standpoint. Black American performers debuted in Paris during the summer of 1914 when jazz drummer Louis Mitchell toured Europe with the band and Broadway dancers Vernon and Irene Castle. But the 1918 success of Europe's 369th Infantry Regiment band's tour through Nantes, Angers, Tours, and Aix-les-Bains is credited with creating a jazz audience in France. Later that same year, Europe's group debuted at the Théâtre des Champs-Élysées with the president of France in attendance. Other regiments had touring jazz bands and black American performers traveled to France to give concerts during the war as well.[14] Some spectators were incredulous, saying that the speed and rhythms of jazz were simply impossible. Reportedly, a few wanted to look at the instruments close up or into their machinery to see how they operated. Black American soldiers brought their cultural wares to France and shared them with the population, thus laying the foundation for the popularity of *La Revue nègre.* At the same time, the great majority of Black soldiers were not jazz musicians. They unloaded cargo in the shipyards, where they were known for their "superhuman feats" and beautiful singing. One observer is quoted as saying, "They are the finest workers you ever saw. One Negro can do four times as much work as any other man, and have fun doing it. The French stevedores stand by and watch with amazement at my hustling gangs. The way they handle a 100–pound crate makes the Frenchman's eyes bulge."[15] These are instances when blacks—even dockworkers who were not performers in the conventional sense—were cast as players in a spectacle. They were spectacularized by the tales that had come before and the delight in seeing "a real one" up close—close enough to touch them.

While accounts of African American experience in Paris generally offer a celebratory narrative of African American success, vindication, absence of racism, and a life beyond the existential dilemmas of blackness, black folks' mythic liberation in Paris was undercut by France's climate of racial curiosity and the simultaneous process of colonization in Africa and elsewhere. There was and remains a clear distinction between *un noir américain* and *un africain,* but in the term *les nègres,* "race, ethnicity, and cultural distinctions are collapsed into one black/nègre stereotyped abyss."[16] What this meant in terms of the larger cultural meaning of Black success in Paris was that Black Americans occupied the place of Africans and profited from the colonial dynamic. We know what France did for African Americans, but what did African Americans do for the French? Why were Black American performers so apparently beloved at the particular times that they were? Black Americans may have been somewhat freed from American racial politics, particularly its more violent manifestations, but their public presence in Paris involved in the cultural politics of the imagination and representation of Africans in French society.

Yet Paris became a focal point for African Americans.[17] "That Paris rather than New York, London or Berlin should be the city where these notions, such as negrophilia, Black liberation, et cetera, were played out is understandable, if not predictable," writes art historian Petrine Archer-Straw. "Paris' modernity was characterized by its openness to Black culture and jazz in particular, the improvised and anarchic musical form that seemed to sum up the unpredictability and anxieties of a new age." She writes that Black Americans were "reflected" and rarely "depicted," but they are evoked as an "invisible presence in a multitude of negrophiliac images and tests from the era."[18] These observations support my contention that African Americans faced a dilemma of visibility and invisibility in Paris, much like they had done in the United States. The crucial difference was that the French racial unconscious of Baker's era involved not a two-way relationship but a three-way one, involving the Empire, France, and black America.

The protagonists of Baker's films and the novels *Quicksand* and *Plum Bun* share the utopian hope of finding aesthetic and personal freedom, really sides of the same goal, in Europe. I have described Baker's characters as not being in control of their destinations, but I must note that, like Helga and Angela, Zou Zou, Papitou, and Alwina are self-aware characters who exhibit ambition for their personal lives, which they imagine can only be fulfilled in Paris. Baker's films and these novels fictionalize Black women's struggle to express their creativity in terms of their personal aesthetics rather than the narrow parameters dictated by propaganda on behalf of the race problem or the caricatures delineated in D. W. Griffith's unnatural museum, *Birth of a Nation.*[19] In fact, as expressions of Black women's creativity, Black female performance functions as a trope for Black women's liberation and personal power to act; however, a crucial part of my story is invisibility—the set of dilemmas and racial, gendered, and economic conditions that render black women hypervisible in terms of their physicality but nearly silent as literal authors and creators of the roles they play. Because Black women in the entertainment industry like Baker tended to be isolated from their families, raised in poverty, poorly educated, and rootless from life as traveling performers, they tended to be vulnerable to the restrictions and sometimes degrading conditions of their job situation because they had few options.

Paul Robeson and Baker clearly moved in the same orbit. A comparison of their films shows that they played similar colonialist characters; however, Robeson's roles were closer to the paradigm of Black male leadership, representing Black insurgency as masculine. Baker's characters moved in the sphere of fantasy, spectacle, and the unconscious—the music hall—rather than politics. Robeson's body and singing were clearly spectacularized in his movies, but its contexts included leadership roles.

Nevertheless, the colonial women Baker portrayed were politically charged by colonialism and American racism. Though Baker learned to speak French fluently, her formal education does not compare to that of her male counterpart, Robeson. Consequently, in public life, Robeson performed a combination of Sambo's docility and Shaka Zulu's power tinged with barely restrained violence, while Baker blended the white feminine ideal of soft sophistication with a stereotypical naïve, sexy savage girl. Robeson played men while Baker played childlike women.[20]

Still, the Primitivist-modern duality Baker uniquely displayed as she parodied and created her film roles can be seen as a destabilizing joke on the insistent gaze of her audiences, directors, and managers. While I have introduced Baker's persona in terms of a split between two opposites, a more nuanced reading of Baker's expansive meaning is to be done, for Baker's was an elastic kinesthetic ethnicity. To the extent that her dancing drew on the chorus line, Baker moved like a machine gone rubbery. The speed remained while her limbs seemed pliable. It eventually came to encompass movements of many Othernesses, whether Arab, Asian, African, or American. Baker could be feminine or masculine as well as androgynous. In playing all these parts, Baker became invisible, in an affirmative rather than a negative way, within a variety of roles, thus generating a powerful sensation-creating, audacious presence. Baker relied on her imagination, and fueled by her boundless energy and nerve, she shimmied her ideas into an unavoidable spectacle and expected to be adored, and she was—that's audacious.

Acknowledged as an important figure in the history of Black dance and performance, Baker was first known for her role in *Shuffle Along*, the first Black musical to hit Broadway.[21] If she is considered alongside her contemporaries in the world of diaspora dance, Zora Hurston and the anthropologist and choreographer Katherine Dunham on the black American scholarly side and Isadora Duncan on the white American experimental art side, Baker seems far more commercial and even compromised than these women. Baker certainly possessed a distinct personal movement vocabulary, however, she lacked the formal apparatuses these women had for linking their work to academic structures. Thus in existing dance scholarship, Baker's fame is acknowledged, but it seems that lacking the scholarly or artistic credentials of her university-affiliated contemporaries (Duncan and Dunham both founded schools to teach their dance practices), she is viewed as a pawn in a cultural system that held ultimate power over particularly her during the 1920s. Hurston and Dunham's relationship to knowledge production is clear while Baker's is more tenuous—maybe even suspicious.[22] But Baker's personal power was her body-authorship or how she curated herself. Her audaciousness was her best accessory and only necessary credential in a world where Black women's bodies were burdened and subject to drudgeries and violences. Baker re-created her ordinary body as a figurative site of pleasure through the apparatuses of cinema and music hall production. There is the phenomenon of *Paris noir*. Black Europe is a social phenomenon as well. And then there is Josephine Baker. A phenomenon of one.

Baker curated herself. Objectified, she mobilized the power of objects in the mise-en-scène of her films and the staging of her live performances to represent her ideas about herself and the world. In Baker's films, for which she provided the basic ideas, she tells the story of the mythic Black Venus, the image or essence of Black female energy as her own story. Baker's films, writings, and live performances all contained automythographical tones; her characters follow a trajectory from obscurity to the music hall stage. The films are perhaps the greatest example of Baker's automythographical self-presentation. In them, her characters' revelations on the stage were basically cinematic versions of Baker's music hall productions. Biographer Rose quotes Baker as saying, "In all the shows I've done, films included, I've insisted that the different stages of my life be represented. Each time . . . there is just a hint of a reminder of the past, for the sake of contrast."[23] In this sense, Baker authored her own persona and sought to authenticate her performances with the story of her life. But this works in the reverse as well: Baker cast her own life into the realm of fantasy, myth, and art.

A second crucial aspect of Baker's self-presentation can be called autoethnography, in which an individual tells her story as the story of her ethnic group. For example, the written narrative that prefaces one of Baker's early concert films, *Josephine Baker, Star of the Folies Bergère,* describes her supposed rise from the cotton fields of the American South to achieve fame in Paris. In fact, Baker was born in St. Louis, Missouri, in 1906 and worked there as a domestic and a performer, not a field hand. The conflicts between Baker's biography and her ethnobiography underline the constructed, larger-than-life nature of Baker's persona. It reveals the ways in which Baker represented the black American story in general, while seeming to be a part, her own phenomenon.

Baker's tendency to generalize her persona as not merely a part of a cultural movement but as the movement itself makes her almost a fictional character in the story of her life, making it difficult to distinguish her film roles from the actual woman. Baker's film roles can stand on their own as theories of her performance style. They show how her persona absorbs and generates relationships between older forms of ethnographic display and performance and her own work in the music hall, blackness and the French avant-garde, and the uncanny, that is, the dissonance of Baker's beauty and foreignness. The films represent Paris of the 1920s and 1930s as Baker's world.

Baker and Black dance itself present a complex relationship between performance and text around the question of technology. Unsurprisingly, dance scholars debate the effect of film on performance.[24] The deeper issues are about dance scholarship's place within the academy and whether it can speak to other disciplines without a proper text. But these tensions manifest as a dichotomy between practitioners or former practitioners who want to preserve the integrity of liveness and the original performance and scholars in other disciplines who are less interested in either liveness or the origins of particular gestures, per se. Purists argue that the context and even the content of dances can be reconstructed through archival research and that this kind of reconstitution, presumably absent the intervention of filmmakers, is the primary contribution of the dance historian. The role of the medium is de-emphasized.

But there is another side to this debate that asserts that the film of a dance is a new text. The filmic dance text is viewed as a self-contained object in a constellation of histories. What is important about this is noting that the various ways that dance appears on film, in newsreels, curiosity or attraction films, concert footage, or in the context of narrative films open up the possibility of thinking about dance in a wider cultural context. Baker's curation of the histories of black female visibility, from the blues to Broadway to French music hall moves in her performance, urges scholars past the traditional split between performance and text and ushers in performance *as* text.

Baker's cinematic performances intersect with two film genres: colonial cinema and musicals. However, she is a minor if not invisible figure in the film histories of colonial cinema by Susan Hayward and David Henry Slavin.[25] This predicament is attributable partly to the impasse between studies of race and ethnicity and studies of cinema. As a Black female entertainer, Baker was "the other of the other," to use Michele Wallace's oft-quoted expression. The French entertainment press called her Ebony Venus, Black Venus, Jazz Empress, and other luminous appellations. The names show that the American-born dancer was seen as the epitome of the Black female form. Black women were perceived as the embodiments of the mythical natural, frenzied, and savage energy that people of African descent supposedly brought to an overly rational, dangerously mechanized European culture. Baker's dances seemed to embody the essence of mythical Black female performance. It is important to remember, however, that when Baker debuted in Paris in 1925, she walked into a preexisting role that had been previously "interpreted" by Sartjee Baartman on stage as "La Vénus hottentote," Laura as the black female figure in Edouard Manet's 1863 painting *Olympia* and Baudelaire's writings inspired by his Creole mistress, Jeanne Duval—as well as the American jazz bands and other performers that date back to the nineteenth century. Baker's legend is about the history of Black female roles in the public imagination or what T. Denean Sharpley-Whiting calls "the black Venus narrative."[26] Baker played roles that represented the variety of the French empire, including a Tunisian shepherd, a Caribbean laundress living in Paris, an Indochinese woman, and vague "tropical" personas. Thus, Baker's version of the legend of black natural and savage energy became a legend as large as the empire.

Baker's screen persona curiously breaks away from and connects her to her earlier days performing in blackface and the history of minstrel theater. Baker's characters were both hypersexualized and childlike, drawing on the Topsy stereotype from plantation pastorals. Baker's uncanny off-screen public embodiment is spelled out in her films: she is both homegrown and exotic to French audiences because she has undergone a "Parisianization" process. This term describes her personal as well as professional development in Paris and the transformation her characters undergo in the films. Unpacking Baker's cinematic performances opens routes to bridging scholarly divisions: the impasse between analyzing race and analyzing film form and the opposition of performance and text. Reading Baker's film roles reveals her position as a prism that embodies and contingently resolves these oppositions partly because of the interdisciplinary nature of cinema, but more so because of Baker's own embeddedness with trends in dance, art, autobiography, and ethnology and the ways her performance functions in the films. Baker brought a "multilingual" dance vocabulary to the colonialist musical comedies in which she appeared.

Baker's film roles constitute a dense layering of associations: her dancing in these films was an "exotic" blend of Black American, African, Latin, and other non-European movements. This elastic ethnicity in the movies, which stretched to include dances from a variety of cultures, mirrored that of her off-screen persona; in the French press, Baker was referred to as Creole, American, and "nègre" or "black." Moreover, while Baker's identity was partly produced in French cinema, the content of her performance drew on Black dance and her American origins. Such internationalism was typical of Harlem Renaissance figures, and the perception of Baker and other Black Americans as the ideal blend of Primitive and modern was absorbed into her public persona.

As a multimedia entertainer, Baker's performances are preserved on film or video, audio recordings, and a variety of reproduced images, including advertisements, studio portraits, and drawings.[27] The clear link among them is Baker's presence. But more importantly they share a larger cultural matrix that includes the cosmopolitan aspects of the Harlem Renaissance, translations of Black American dance vocabularies, and colonialist images in French cinema. Existing scholarship tends to address Baker as one example or even a symptom of these larger cultural trends. However, I argue Baker's performances and their reception make the relationships among these trends visible. Baker made the Black female body the medium of translation between the Harlem Renaissance and European Primitivism by blending Black American and "African" dances in her performance and aggrandizing it for an international audience on film. In this essay, I have sought to reverse the tendency to look through Baker's films as if they were mere windows and present Baker's performance not as an example of a larger idea but as the large idea. Baker was the generative force behind her myth.

Baker's aesthetic totality is expressed through her film roles, presenting the performer as not just a case of a cultural trend but as the trend itself. Baker's performances are displays of her absorption and interpretation of the perceptions of the exotic, the primitive, and the Black body that were emergent in her era rather than as an object under their manipulation. On first glance, Baker can seem to be a screen for the projection of what Rose categorized as "European male fantasy."[28] In this paradigm, Baker's achievements seem to rest mainly upon her biographical trajectory from poverty to wealth and her status as a star of the French music hall. It is doubtful that she would have experienced the same level of success in the United States, and I do not disagree with Rose's premise. Still, we need to expand the scope of inquiry on Baker and emphasize her creativity without diminishing the importance of Baker's life. For Baker's success lifted her out of poverty and in some ways protected her from the brutalities of life for Black women in the United States at that time. However, going back to

Rose's insight, reading Baker's career carries deep political resonance in criticizing the colonialist agenda that helped to fuel her success. Baker is a creative subject working within the colonialist agenda. Primitivism, a set of perceptions Europeans held about the colonial world, did not create Baker, but it did make her a star. Baker walked into a preexisting narrative and forwarded her own notion of these perceptions through her embodiment. Baker's film roles uniquely reveal the ways in which film form absorbed the history of racialized popular entertainment, such as ethnological museums, circus displays, and live dioramas. Examples can be found in Baker's films where they serve to present introductory samples meant to whet the audience's appetite for Baker. In *Zou Zou,* we see a young Zou Zou performing at the circus, then an older woman miming to entertain a child, and finally a woman dancing in a Bakeresque raffia skirt. These moments are opening acts for Baker's big production number but they also offer scenes of Baker's career.

Like motion pictures, Baker expressed her creativity through assemblage. As a curator of black performance, she authored a new understanding of the African American history of stage gestures, black visibility, and female visibility in a white male public sphere. Baker did not stop at gathering these pieces into her roles; she blended them with the aesthetics of European interests in Africa and colonial materials in general.

Notes

1. The expression "tall, tan, and terrific" was an advertising slogan for the chorus line at Harlem's segregated Cotton Club during the 1920s.

2. Hughes emphasizes the role of the body in ushering in the Harlem Renaissance and calling attention to black writers and the worlds they wrote about in their work. *Shuffle Along* was a visual, performative text that acted on the body. Langston Hughes, "When the Negro Was in Vogue," in *The Big Sea* (New York: Hill and Wang, 1993), 223–32.

3. Scholarship on Baker generally views media perceptions of her as symptomatic of the audiences' needs for a return to the so-called primitive essences of themselves. I am not disagreeing with these observations. What I am attempting to do is look at these perceptions from the perspective of the performer, arguing that she engages and embodies the anxieties of her era while reflecting them. See Wendy Martin, "'Remembering the Jungle': Josephine Baker and Modernist Parody," in *Prehistories of the Future: The Primitivist Project and the Culture of Modernism,* eds. Elazar Barkan and Ronald Bush (Stanford: Stanford University Press, 1996), 310–25; Nancy Nenno, "Femininity, the Primitive, and Modern Urban Space: Josephine Baker in Berlin," in *Women in the Metropolis: Gender and Modernity in Weimar Culture,* ed. Katharina von Ankum (Berkeley: University of California Press, 1997), 145–61; Elizabeth Coffman, "Uncanny Performances in Colonial Narratives: Josephine Baker in *Princess Tam Tam,*" *Paradoxa: Studies in World Literary Genres* 3, no. 3–4 (1997): 379–94. A recent publication by Bennetta Jules-Rosette maintains skepticism toward Baker's early banana days, but her

assessment of Baker's later years as savvy and politically innovative is refreshing. Other biographies have left Baker's postwar years blurry or characterized as folly and disappointment. See Bennetta Jules-Rosette, *Josephine Baker in Art and Life: The Icon and the Image* (Urbana: University of Illinois Press, 2007).

4. But the press was not a constant friend of Baker's. They defended her in 1931 when she performed at the Folies, claiming that white audiences were not ready for her sophistication. They ridiculed her when they felt betrayed by her false report of having married a count. The so-called count was Baker's manager and eventually her husband, but her relationship with him did not make her royalty.

5. Lynne Haney, *Naked at the Feast: A Biography of Josephine Baker* (London: Robson Books, 1981), 138.

6. Richard Dyer, "Monroe and Sexuality," in *Heavenly Bodies: Film Stars and Society* (New York: St. Martin's Press: 1986), 19. See also Christine Gledhill, *Stardom: Industry of Desire* (London: British Film Institute), 1991.

7. Richard Dyer, introduction to *The Matter of Images: Essays on Representations* (London: Routledge), 1993.

8. Dyer, *Heavenly Bodies,* 10.

9. The term "unnatural museum" is taken from Zora Neale Hurston, "What White Publishers Won't Print," in *I Love Myself When I'm Laughing,* ed. Alice Walker (New York: Feminist Press, 1979), 169–73. "The question naturally arises as to the why of this indifference, not to say skepticism, to the internal life of educated minorities. The answer lies in what we may call the American Museum of Un-Natural History. . . . It is assumed that all non-Anglo-Saxons are uncomplicated stereotypes. Everybody knows all about them. . . . The whole museum is dedicated to the convenient 'typical.'"

10. Fatimah Tobing Rony, *The Third Eye: Race, Cinema, and Ethnographic Spectacle* (Durham, N.C.: Duke University Press, 1996), 199.

11. W.E.B. Du Bois, "Of Our Spiritual Strivings," in *The Souls of Black Folk* (1903; reprint, New York: Signet, 2003), 43–53.

12. Farah J. Griffin and Cheryl J. Fish, eds., *A Stranger in the Village: Two Centuries of African-American Travel Writing* (Boston: Beacon Press, 1998); Florette Henri, *Black Migration: The Movement North, 1900–1920* (Garden City: Anchor, 1976).

13. See Tyler Stovall, *Paris Noir: African Americans in the City of Light* (Boston: Houghton Mifflin, 1996); Michel Fabre, *From Harlem to Paris: Black American Writers in France, 1840–1980* (Urbana: University of Illinois Press, 1991). For a recent take on cultural exchanges between black American and French jazz musicians, see Jeffrey Jackson, *Making Jazz French: Music and Modern Life in Interwar Paris* (Durham, N.C.: Duke University Press, 2003).

14. Stovall, *Paris Noir,* 20–21.

15. Quoted in ibid., 8.

16. Sharpley-Whiting, *Black Venus,* 8. See also Sue Peabody et al., eds., *The Color of Liberty: Histories of Race in France* (Durham, N.C.: Duke University Press, 2003).

17. See Michel Fabre, "International Beacons of African-American Memory: Alexandre Dumas Père, Henry O. Tanner, and Josephine Baker as Examples of Recognition," in *History and Memory in African-American Culture,* ed. Geneviève Fabre and Robert O'Meally (New York: Oxford University Press, 1994), 122–29.

18. Despite being persuaded by Archer-Straw's analysis of racial dynamics between black Americans and the French, I take issue with her seeming dependence on readers' ability to locate and pin down what she calls "the aspirations and conditions of 'real' negroes." It seems unproductive to base reading Black invisibility as a question of real and accurate representation, for if in the United States performers confronted double consciousness, in France colonialism and the rhetorical presence of Africans added another dimension that was equally as complex. What is crucial to understand about the relationship between the Harlem Renaissance and European Primitivism is the degree to which both movements laid claim to their own notions of "the aspirations and conditions of 'real' negroes" even as they abstracted, distorted, and celebrated different versions of black being. See Petrine Archer-Straw, *Negrophilia: Avant-garde Paris and Black Culture in the 1920s* (New York: Thames and Hudson, 2000), 18–20.

19. For a recent analysis of the racial and aesthetic grammar of Griffith's notorious film, see Michele Wallace, "The Good Lynching and *Birth of a Nation:* The Discourse and Aesthetics of Jim Crow," *Cinema Journal* 43, no. 1 (Fall 2003): 85–104.

20. I am thinking of *The Emperor Jones* (1933), *Sanders of the River* (1935), and *Jericho* (1937); Paul Robeson played cunning adventurers in the first two films and an idealist in the third. However, his roles in *Emperor Jones* and *Sanders of the River* held limitations and suffered from caricature.

21. See Lynne Emery, *Black Dance in the United States from 1619 to 1970* (Palo Alto, Calif.: National Press Books, 1972); Katrina Hazzard-Gordon, *Jookin': The Rise of Social Dance Formations in African-American Culture* (Philadelphia: Temple University Press, 1990); Brenda Dixon Gottschild, *Digging the Africanist Presence in American Performance: Dance and Other Contexts* (Westport, Conn.: Greenwood Press, 1996). Gottschild's work, cited earlier, is especially notable for her attention to the *three-way* influence of Africans, Europeans, and Americans. She moves beyond the black (American) versus white paradigm.

22. Baker's scholarly counterparts Katherine Dunham and Zora Neale Hurston wrote about Africanisms in black American culture based on their field research in the Caribbean and Africa: Katherine Dunham, *Dances of Haiti* (Los Angeles: Center for Afro-American Studies, University of California, Los Angeles, 1983); Katherine Dunham, *Island Possessed* (Chicago: University of Chicago Press, 1994); Katherine Dunham, *Katherine Dunham's Journey to Accompong* (New York: H. Holt, 1946). Hurston also published the results of fieldwork in territory that overlapped with Dunham: *Tell My Horse: Voodoo and Life in Haiti and Jamaica* (New York: J. B. Lippincott, 1938).

23. Phyllis Rose, *Jazz Cleopatra: Josephine Baker in Her Time* (New York: Vintage Books, 1991), 165.

24. Susan Manning, "Performance as History/Method: What Is Our Evidence? What Is Our Vocabulary?" (paper presented at the inaugural meeting of the Chicago Forum on Performance, Chicago, Ill., April 2002).

25. See David Henry Slavin, *Colonial Cinema and Imperial France, 1919–1939: White Blind Spots, Male Fantasies, Settler Myths* (Baltimore: Johns Hopkins University Press, 2001); Susan Hayward, *French National Cinema* (New York: Routledge, 1993).

26. Sharpley-Whiting contextualizes Baker in the history of black female images in French literature. The writer does not offer a detailed formal analysis of more than one

of Baker's performances that would enable the work to speak to Baker's invisibility in studies of French film. However, she does provide other useful terms and concepts, blending insights from literary, black feminist, postcolonial, and cinematic studies; keeping black female iconicity at the center of the analysis rather than using it to discuss masculinity or white womanhood, and the simultaneity of being seen and not being seen that constitutes black female invisibility.

27. Maurice Dekobra, *Sirène des Tropiques* (France, 1927), filmstrip; unknown director, *Les Hallucinations d'un Pompier* (France, 1927); Marc Allégret, *Zou Zou* (France, 1934); Edmond Gréville, *Princesse Tam Tam* (France 1935); and Jacques de Baroncelli, *Fausse Alerte* (France, 1945).

28. When it was published, Phyllis Rose's biography of Baker, cited earlier, provided a significant push away from thinking of Baker merely as a Parisian success story. Rose points out that Baker was a "locus for theorizing blackness." This insight opened up questions that I address in my work. Where I depart from the biography is rather than explain Baker's work in terms of cultural context, I use her aesthetic context of the museum as a concept for describing her performance practice as curatorial.

References

Abraham, John Kirby. *In Search of Josephine Baker.* London: Minerva Press, 2001.

Adams, Rachel. *Sideshow U.S.A: Freaks and the American Cultural Imagination.* Chicago: University of Chicago Press, 2001.

Alexander, Elizabeth. "Josephine Baker Museum." In *Body of Life.* Chicago: Tia Chua Press, 1996.

Allégret, Marc. *Zou Zou.* France. 1934.

Anderson, Lisa M. *Mammies No More: The Changing Image of Black Women on Stage and Screen.* Lanham, Md.: Rowman and Littlefield, 1997.

Archer-Straw, Petrine. *Negrophilia: Avant-Garde Paris and Black Culture in the 1920s.* London: Thames and Hudson, 2000.

Baker, Jean-Claude. *Josephine: The Hungry Heart.* New York: Random House, 1993.

Baker, Josephine. *Josephine.* Trans. Mariana Fitzpatrick. New York: Harper and Row, 1977.

———. Clippings File, 1925–1936. Auguste Rondel Collection. Bibliothèque Arsenal.

———. *Voyages et aventures de Joséphine Baker* (Travels and Adventures of Josephine Baker). Paris: M. Seheur, 1931.

Baker, Josephine, and Marcel Sauvage. *Les mémoires de Joséphine Baker* (Memoir of Josephine Baker). Avec 30 dessins inédits de Paul Colin. Paris: Kra, 1927.

Bennett, Michael, ed. *Recovering the Black Female Body: Self-Representations by African American Women.* New Brunswick, N.J.: Rutgers University Press, 2001.

Blanchard, Pascal, and Nicolas Bancel. "Le Zoo Humain." *De L'Indigène à l'immigré* (From the Indigenous to the Immigrant). Paris: Series Découverts Gallimard, 1998.

Bogle, Donald. *Brown Sugar: 80 Years of America's Black Female Superstars.* New York: Da Capo Press, 1990.

Bonini, Emmanuel. *La véritable Joséphine Baker* (The True Josephine Baker). Paris: Pygmalion/G. Watelet, 2000.

Borshuk, Michael. "An Intelligence of the Body: Disruptive Parody through Dance in the Early Performances of Josephine Baker." In *EmBODYing Liberation: The Black Body in American Dance,* edited by Dorothea Fischer-Hornung and Alison D. Goeller. Hamburg, Germany: LIT, 2001.

Coffman, Elizabeth. "Uncanny Performances in Colonial Narratives: Josephine Baker in *Princess Tam Tam.*" *Paradoxa: Studies in World Literary Genres* 3, no. 3–4 (1997): 379–94.

Colin, Paul. *Josephine Baker and La Revue nègre: Paul Colin's Lithographs of Le tumulte noir in Paris, 1927.* Introduction by Henry Louis Gates, Jr., and Karen C. C. Dalton. New York: H. N. Abrams, 1998.

"Colored Frenchmen and American Meteques." *Literary Digest* (Sept. 1, 1923): 41–44.

Cook, Mercer. "The Race Problem in the West Indies." *Journal of Negro Education* 8, no. 4 (Oct. 1939): 673–80.

———. "Booker T. Washington and the French." *Journal of Negro History* 40 (1955): 318–40.

Cullen, Countee. "Countee Cullen on French Courtesy." *Crisis* (June 1929): 193.

———. "Countee Cullen to His Friends." *Crisis* (Apr. 1929): 119.

———. "Letter from Paris." *Opportunity* (Sept. 1928): 271–73.

Dodds, Sherril. *Dance on Screen: Genres and Media from Hollywood to Experimental Art.* Hampshire, UK: Palgrave, 2001.

Dunham, Katherine. *Dances of Haiti.* Los Angeles: Center for Afro-American Studies, University of California, 1983.

———. *Island Possessed.* Chicago: University of Chicago Press, 1994.

———. *Katherine Dunham's Journey to Accompong.* New York: H. Holt, 1946.

Dyer, Richard. *The Matter of Images: Essays on Representations.* London: Routledge, 1993.

———. *Heavenly Bodies: Film Stars and Society.* New York: St. Martin's Press, 1989.

Edwards, Brent Hayes. *The Practice of Diaspora: Literature, Translation, and the Rise of Black Internationalism.* Cambridge, Mass.: Harvard University Press, 2003.

Ezra, Elizabeth. *The Colonial Unconscious: Race and Culture in Interwar France.* Ithaca: Cornell University Press, 2000.

Fabre, Michel. "International Beacons of African-American Memory: Alexandre Dumas père, Henry O. Tanner, and Josephine Baker as Examples of Recognition." In *History and Memory in African-American Culture,* edited by Geneviève Fabre and Robert O'Meally. New York: Oxford University Press, 1994.

———. *From Harlem to Paris: Black American Writers in France, 1840–1980.* Urbana: University of Illinois Press, 1991.

Fauset, Jessie. *Plum Bun: A Novel without a Moral.* 1929. Black Women Writers Series. Reprint with an introduction by Deborah McDowell. Boston: Beacon, 1990.

Gates, Henry Louis, Jr., and Anthony Barthelemy. "An Interview with Josephine Baker and James Baldwin." *Southern Review* 21, no. 3 (Summer 1985): 594–602.

Gilman, Sander. "Black Bodies, White Bodies: Toward an Iconography of Female Sexuality in Late-Nineteenth Century Art, Medicine and Literature." In *Race, Writing, and Difference.* Edited by Henry Louis Gates Jr. Chicago: University of Chicago Press, 1986.

Gilroy, Paul. *The Black Atlantic: Modernity and Double-Consciousness.* Cambridge, Mass.: Harvard University Press, 1993.

Gledhill, Christine. *Stardom: Industry of Desire.* London: British Film Institute, 1991.

Gottschild, Brenda Dixon. *Digging the Africanist Presence in American Performance: Dance and Other Contexts.* Westport, Conn.: Greenwood Press, 1996.

Gréville, Edmond T. *Princess Tam-Tam.* France. 1935.

Griffin, Farah J., and Cheryl J. Fish, ed. *A Stranger in the Village: Two Centuries of African-American Travel Writing.* Boston: Beacon Press, 1998.

Griffiths, Alison. *Wondrous Difference: Cinema, Anthropology, and Turn-of-the-Century Visual Culture.* New York: Columbia University Press, 2002.

Hallucinations d'un Pompier /Le Pompier des Folies-Bergères. France. 1928.

Hammond, Bryan. *Josephine Baker.* London: Cape, 1988.

Haney, Lynn. *Naked at the Feast: A Biography of Josephine Baker.* New York: Robson, 1981.

Hazzard-Gordon, Katrina. *Jookin': The Rise of Social Dance Formations in African American Culture.* Philadelphia: Temple University Press, 1990.

Hurston, Zora Neale. *Tell My Horse: Voodoo and Life in Haiti and Jamaica.* New York: J. B. Lippincott, 1938.

Jewell, Sue K. *From Mammy to Miss America and Beyond: Cultural Images and the Shaping of U.S. Social Policy.* London: Routledge, 1993.

Johnson, James Weldon, *The Auto-biography of an Ex-Coloured Man.* 1912. Reprint with new introduction by Henry Louis Gates, Jr.; New York: Vintage, 1989.

Jules-Rosette, Bennetta. *Josephine Baker in Art and Life: The Icon and the Image.* Urbana: University of Illinois Press, 2007.

———.*Black Paris: The African Writers' Landscape.* Urbana: University of Illinois Press, 1998.

Kalinak, Kathryn. "Disciplining Josephine Baker: Gender, Race, and the Limits of Disciplinarity." In *Music and Cinema,* edited by James Buhler, Caryl Flinn, and David Nuemeyer. Hanover, N.H.: University Presses of New England, 2000.

Karp, Ivan, and Steven D. Lavine, ed. *Exhibiting Cultures: The Poetics and Politics of Museum Display.* Washington: Smithsonian Institution Press, 1991.

La Camera, Félix. *Mon sang dans tes veines: Roman d'après une idée de Joséphine Baker* (My Blood in Your Veins: A Novel Inspired by Josephine Baker's Ideas). Illustrations by G. de Pogédaïeff. Paris: Éditions Isis, 1931.

Larsen, Nella. *Quicksand.* 1928. In *An Intimation of Things Distant: The Collected Fiction of Nella Larsen.* Reprint with an introduction by Charles R. Larson and a foreword by Marita Golden. New York: Anchor Books, 1992.

Lindfors, Bernth. *Africans on Stage: Studies in Ethnological Show Business.* Indianapolis: Indiana University Press, 1999.

Locke, Alain, ed. *The New Negro: Voices of the Harlem Renaissance.* 1925. Reprint with an introduction by Arnold Rampersad. New York: Atheneum, 1992.

Martin, Wendy. "'Remembering the Jungle': Josephine Baker and Modernist Parody." In *Prehistories of the Future: The Primitivist Project and the Culture of Modernism,* edited by Elazar Barkan and Ronald Bush. Stanford: Stanford University Press, 1996.

McCarren, Felicia M. "Submitting to the Machine." In *Dancing Machines: Choreographies of the Age of Mechanical Reproduction.* Stanford: Stanford University Press, 2003.

McKay, Claude. *Banjo: A Story without a Plot.* 1929. Reprint, New York: Harcourt Brace, 1957.

Negra, Diane. *Off-White Hollywood: American Culture and Ethnic Female Stardom.* London: Routledge, 2001.

Nenno, Nancy. "Femininity, the Primitive, and Modern Urban Space: Josephine Baker in Berlin." In *Women in the Metropolis: Gender and Modernity in Weimar Culture,* edited by Katharina von Ankum. Berkeley: University of California Press, 1997.

Papich, Stephen. *Remembering Josephine.* Indianapolis: Bobbs-Merrill, 1976.

Parker, Andrew, and Eve Sedgwick, ed. *Performativity and Performance: Essays from the English Institute.* London: Routledge, 1995.

Powell, Richard Jr., ed. *Rhapsodies in Black: Art of the Harlem Renaissance.* Berkeley: University of California Press, 1997.

Ramsay, Burt. "'Savage' Dancer: Tout Paris Goes to See Josephine Baker." In *Alien Bodies: Representations of Modernity, "Race," and Nation in Modern Dance.* London: Routledge, 1998.

Regester, Charlene. "The Construction of an Image and the Deconstruction of a Star: Josephine Baker Racialized, Sexualized, and Politicized in the African American Press, the Mainstream Press, and FBI Files." *Popular Music and Society* 24, no. 1 (Spring 2000): 31–84.

Rose, Phyllis. *Jazz Cleopatra: Josephine Baker in Her Time.* New York: Vintage Books, 1991.

Sharpley-Whiting, T. Denean. *Black Venus: Sexualized Savages, Primal Fears, and Primitive Narratives in French.* Durham, N.C.: Duke University Press, 1999.

Slavin, David Henry. *Colonial Cinema and Imperial France, 1919–1939: White Blind Spots, Male Fantasies, Settler Myths.* Baltimore: Johns Hopkins University Press, 2001.

Smith, Shawn Michelle. "Photographing the 'American Negro': Nation, Race, and Photography at the Paris Exposition of 1900." In *American Archives: Gender, Race, and Class in Visual Culture.* Princeton, N.J.: Princeton University Press, 1999.

Stovall, Tyler. *Paris Noir: African Americans in the City of Light.* Boston: Houghton Mifflin, 1996.

Tobing Rony, Fatimah. *The Third Eye: Race, Cinema, and Ethnographic Spectacle.* Durham, N.C.: Duke University Press, 1996.

Torgonovnick, Marianna. *Gone Primitive: Savage Intellects, Modern Lives.* Chicago: University of Chicago Press, 1990.

Wall, Cheryl. *Women of the Harlem Renaissance.* Bloomington: Indiana University Press, 1995.

Wallace, Michele Faith. "The Good Lynching and *The Birth of a Nation:* Discourses and Aesthetics of Jim Crow." *Cinema Journal* 43, no. 1 (Fall 2003): 85–104.

Willis, Deborah, and Carla Williams. *The Black Female Body: A Photographic History.* Philadelphia: Temple University Press, 2002.

Wood, Ean. *The Josephine Baker Story.* London: Sanctuary, 2000.

Young, Lola. *Fear of the Dark: "Race," Gender, and Sexuality in the Cinema.* London: Routledge, 1996.

14

Pale by Comparison: Black Liberal Humanism and the Postwar Era in the African Diaspora

MICHELLE M. WRIGHT

"Black Liberal Humanism" and the African Diaspora

Perhaps more than any other time since the Middle Passage, Africans and peoples of African descent are encountering one another in profound and complex ways as the former, mostly arriving as immigrants to the West, encounter the latter, whose ancestors were part of the Middle Passage. Within Black studies departments and some other parts of the humanities, African diaspora studies is increasing in popularity and visibility, yet "blackness," as it functions in the vast majority of this new scholarship, rarely encounters itself: it just is. As Hegel might characterize it—and this is not a random reference, as it is Hegel's formulation of the Black and Western civilization with which all those who identify as Black must most likely struggle—blackness seems to be produced as *das Ding an sich,* the thing unto itself.

While Hegel would be horrified that I have taken so lowly a thing as blackness and attached it to so august a concept as a self-referential Absolute, his central dynamic that drives progress and thus creates history, his own formulations of blackness in fact point to this conclusion. In his *Philosophy of History,* wittingly or unwittingly, Hegel anchored blackness as the intimate anti-correspondent to the ultimate *Ding an sich,* Reason, which then conflates, for all intents and purposes, with whiteness or, rather, the Aryan. Indeed, whiteness is so reliant upon blackness in Hegel's formulation that a bizarre formula we are all familiar with emerges: rhetorically, whiteness is displayed as the superior quality, but its definition hinges on its relationship to its direct inferior, meaning blackness emerges as the defining and therefore more central quality. Without blackness, whiteness disappears. And what about blackness, should whiteness disappear? According to Hegel, blackness has long existed in its own primitive solipsism, enjoying its own ignorant self-referentiality. In other words, blackness would do quite well.

Hegel was wrong, of course, as blackness did not exist before it was created by those Western scientists and philosophers like Kant, Jefferson, Hume, and de Buffon, who first accorded "the Negro" a frightening (and yet sometimes enviable) homogeneity, the missing link between humans and apes—unable to resist its blood lust and (depending on which of the above you are reading) incapable or perhaps one day capable of evolving into a human being. In looking at much of the scholarship now emerging on Blacks and blackness in the African diaspora, it seems that this homogeneity has surpassed the self-aware limits of strategic essentialism and become an article of faith. While, admittedly, there are many tempting securities and finalities suggested by the idea of a Black collective, I want to argue that its methodology, what I term Black liberal humanism, both in its roots and its outcomes, would disable rather than enable a variety of forms of African diaspora studies. More specifically, the ways in which this methodology both assumes and practices a hierarchy of blackness demotes those Black identities that supposedly threaten the well-being of the imagined collective, thus suggesting that some Africans and peoples of African descent are "less Black" and therefore less valuable to the collective. As a result, their terrors and travails, compared to the pain suffered by those at the top of the hierarchy, are rendered "pale by comparison." The first part of this essay will explore recent publications that exemplify this "pale by comparison" approach, then move to examples of the type of scholarship that enable a wider variety of "blacknesses." The second part of the essay will focus on the broader frameworks of knowledge production in dominant Black discourses on the African diaspora, arguing that they must be reexamined and reimagined in order to accommodate the necessary diversity of the African diaspora.

Most recently, Tommie Shelby has written a treatise on Black solidarity in which he proposes a "version of pragmatic nationalism" (10), one that distinguishes itself from "classic black nationalism" because it does not "underestimate . . . the sociopolitical significance of class and status stratification within the black population; and doesn't fail to appreciate and respect differences within the group—for instance, along the lines of gender, sexuality, national origin, multiraciality, generation, region, religion, cultural affiliation, and political ideology" (10). Shelby goes on to argue that this is feasible through a separation of previously conflated concerns and intriguingly writes, "I contend that we should separate the need for an emancipatory Black solidarity from the demand for a common black identity." The latter, he argues, "is a legacy of black nationalist thought that African Americans do better to abandon" (11).

In the face of those established scholars who either pay superficial lip service to, ignore, or explicitly dismiss feminist and queer critiques of Black nationalist ideologies and heteropatriarchal definitions of blackness, Shelby's assertion that "until greater strides are made against (black) male hegemony, a shared and progressive view of what it means to be black is unlikely to develop" (227) is a breath of fresh air. Yet while Shelby elaborates frequently on Black male hegemony, he never explains what type of feminism and/or queer politics he is embracing, and he does not reference any of the Black feminist theorists and/or queer theorists who have already broken significant theoretical ground on this issue (such as May Ayim, Hazel Carby, Angela Davis, Philomena Essed, Rod Ferguson, Phillip Brian Harper, bell hooks, Audre Lorde, Jean-Paul Rocchi, Hortense Spillers, Claudia Tate, Michele Wallace, or Gloria Wekker, to name just a few). This is significant: although the vast majority of African American intellectuals would (or do) condemn white liberal "antiracist" projects that are designed and deployed without consulting the community they target, that outrage does not seem to transfer to the body of African American scholarship that explicitly condemns misogyny and homophobia yet fails to engage with Black feminist and Black queer theorists.

This is key: the anchor to Shelby's argument is a fluid concept of blackness, one that is never homogenous ("the basis of black political unity should not be a shared black identity," 244), and he spends the bulk of his argument examining how to respect difference even in unity. Yet his invocation of feminism and Black queer ideologies are as "shared identities" because he never explains these differences outside their broadest terms. If, as Shelby insists throughout the book, Black nationalisms are diverse and these differences are crucial, why aren't feminisms and queer ideologies understood to be just as complex, just as defiant to stereotyping and simplistic theorization?

Shelby pays lip service to the importance of these considerations, but the absence of any of their contributions performs the depressingly familiar logic of liberal humanist ideology: there are certain bodies of knowledge that one need not know to advocate because there is nothing to know. I would argue that this is the largest point of connection between (white) liberal humanism and Black liberal humanism—an explicit call for diversity and equal access that goes no further than the period at the end of the sentence. This is because both liberal humanisms automatically script out minority identities on the logic that to be unspoken is to be included—the only characteristic that dominant and minority groups roughly share in the discourse. In (white) liberal humanism, one can speak of "Western philosophy," for example, and only enumerate and explore the contributions of white men without ever uttering either "white" or "men"; therefore, the logic goes, failing to utter "Black" or "female" (which, in liberal humanist discourse, are most often synonyms for "race" and "gender") actually embraces inclusivity. In Black liberal humanism, the grammatical rules are, however, slightly different: as in Shelby, "Black" must be spoken, but "male" need not be. (The justification for the exclusion of other Black identities, however, is almost exactly the same: just as "male" remains unspoken in Black liberal humanist discourse, so, too, can/must "female/feminist/feminism" remain briefly uttered or entirely unspoken in the interest of retaining solidarity.)

The grammar rules differ because Black liberal humanism is a counterdiscourse, one that is not a recent invention but in the past two decades, ironically, has been deployed increasingly to subvert (white) liberal humanist discourse—more specifically, the latter's assertions that equality can only be achieved through the silencing of race as a signifier, much less a discursive category. Nor is Black liberal humanism solely an American phenomenon: Paul Gilroy's *There Ain't No Black in the Union Jack* (1991) memorably demonstrates the inevitable conclusion of liberal humanist logic in his critique of Thatcherism, where a Conservative Party campaign ad asserts its right to ignore—perhaps even deny—race in the name of racial tolerance. Gilroy then deployed the very same "Thatcherite" logic in his two following books—more subtly in *The Black Atlantic: Modernity and Double Consciousness* (1992) and then (to the consternation of many African American scholars, pundits, and public intellectuals), more explicitly in *Against Race: Imagining Political Culture Beyond the Color Line* (2000). I would argue that the few who noticed the liberal humanist logic that exclusion signifies inclusion were those scholars who questioned Gilroy's heavy reliance on heteronormative African American men as the full range of exemplars of diverse yet united culture of what he famously named the "Black Atlantic." Strictly in terms of how race, gender, class, and sexuality are deployed, the only difference between *The Black Atlantic* and *Against Race* is the move from a Black liberal humanism to a (white) liberal humanism.

Setting out with roughly the same agenda as *We Who Are Dark, The Black Atlantic* also explores the basis for a Black collective identity that is not essentialist. Through an engagement with both Enlightenment philosophy and Black modernity—arguments that went on to invigorate interest in a Black studies that went through and beyond African American and/or African foci—Gilroy argues that the paradoxical experience of slavery through modernity by those Africans who underwent the Middle Passage fostered the basis of a diverse yet unified Black Atlantic "nation" of sorts. In *Against Race,* Gilroy critiques Black (again, focusing mainly on straight African American men) culture and politics as too "masculinist," too fascist, and, simply put, too racist. Paraphrasing the argument first made by Gloria T. Hull, Patricia Bell Scott, and Barbara Smith in *But Some of Us Are Brave* that—as far as issues of blackness are concerned—"all the Blacks are men" (also part of the title), Gilroy then argues that the whole concept of "Blackness" (here, synonymous with race, another problematic synecdoche often missed) can never be wrested from its fascist roots and simply needs to be jettisoned. In other words, the greater the exclusion, the greater the inclusion.

While politely distinguishing himself from Paul Gilroy's enormously unpopular political agenda (noting that Gilroy's anti-essentialism screed *The Black Atlantic* asserts the form of a shared Black culture whereas Shelby is interested in a shared Black polis), Shelby practices very much the same methodology, a methodology, I might add, that is familiar to all of us who produce and create and study different types of Black identities, cultures, philosophies, and histories—and believe it or not, here we can also blame Hegel. In brief, the methodology is this: diversity is reconciled with universalism through declaration rather than performance. Just as liberal humanism tautologically argues that all difference will be reviewed equally under its eyes because its view is always already objective, so do Gilroy, Shelby, and others declare that objectivity has been achieved through their methodology because it is objective.

More specifically, they do what Hegel does. By claiming that his methodology is wholly and inherently objective, Hegel objectively determines Western European civilization to be the only civilization of note in all of world history and, even more objectively, that Germany is the most civilized of all geographic areas on the Continent. Under Hegel (and then seconded on the discursive level by Frantz Fanon in *Black Skin, White Masks*), blackness becomes that which any white person can speak about because it is inherently empty—and it is inherently empty because it is entirely self-referential. Blackness is unable to develop because it has nothing to struggle against. As such, blackness joined the new group of "hypo-identities" being created in the West during the Scientific Revolution and Enlightenment: "hypo" because they are identities created by outsiders rather than members of the group that supposedly occupy them but, unlike "Others," they are not constructed as antithetical to subject status. Instead, hypo-identities are what liberal humanisms create in order to establish themselves as always already contingent upon human suffrage (everyone is a subject)—which then gives them the freedom to speak for "everyone" without ever enunciating any other logic or position than their own. Liberal humanist discourse is the anti-dialogic, insisting that one voice can and should speak for many because that voice is transcendent, rising above the meaningless array of minority differences and providing an "objective," "universal" view. Born from the Scientific Revolution and the Enlightenment, liberal humanist logic still pervades many Western disciplines whose telos is a unifying theory and/or methodology, whether it be string, structuralist, or even, in many cases, myself included, poststructuralist.

The African diaspora, contrary to what many would assert, lacks the material, institutional, governmental, and private support necessary to become a "discipline," but it too possesses discourses that take logic from its name—it is a scattering of Africans who, therefore, should be reunited and/or rediscover their common underlying identity (Molefi Asante), possibly shared culture (Gilroy) or a necessary shared politics (Shelby). As such, the battle over who and what Blackness will represent in the African diaspora is now in full swing, and one of the battlegrounds is how that blackness is imagined and constructed through time and space—that is, what the dominant epistemology of African diaspora studies is/will be.

The necessary infrastructure to any intellectual agenda, epistemologies are the arrangement of time and space so that they coincide with their "protagonist"—and here I take a page from Bakhtin and his reading of "simplest time chronotope" produced by the epic. In his own monologic epic of world history, Hegel arranges time and space to coincide with the emergence of the Aryan and his corresponding civilization, and it is this epistemology from whence all others spring. In college courses, academic lectures, journals, and books, reading about the African diaspora is most often a reading through the same logic that constructs dominant African American epistemologies.

These epistemologies, while sensitive to the manifold ways in which dominant American epistemologies attempt to erase, denigrate, and distort blackness in its history, also have blind spots, including the failure to incorporate truly diasporic moments in its history. Anchored in the Middle Passage and masculinist in their orientation, dominant African American epistemologies necessarily struggle to truly incorporate "other" (for example, non-Middle Passage) Black identities, leading theorists such as Shelby and Gilroy to paradoxically call for the silencing/erasure of difference in order to establish diversity. By diversifying our epistemologies first (and here I give the example of greater attention to the world wars and their aftermath), we can begin to engage with difference outside of the hierarchical logic liberal humanisms dictate.

The Middle Passage as Über Trope

In *Becoming Black*, I argue blackness is not simply a white European and American creation; in fact, it is now largely shaped, imagined, and created by Blacks themselves—although one should not doubt that the Black Other is alive and well in many mainstream political, social (entertainment), and scientific discourses. One of the ways in which a relatively progressive view of Black American identity is maintained in both the United States and even in Black communities abroad is through dominant epistemologies—conscious collective constructions that directly contravene some of the United States' most cherished myths about itself and its relationship to peoples of African descent.

In dominant African American epistemologies, the Middle Passage is the trope par excellence, serving many functions at once. First, it subverts the United States' most outrageous self-styling as the world's oldest living democracy. By underscoring our arrival as slaves, and by framing the Middle Passage as no small event but one of forced mass migration to feed an insatiable economic and psychological hunger on the part of whites, this etiological trope of almost all African American epistemologies signals, from the outset, that to understand how Black Americans came to be one must reject or at least radically qualify the explicit or implicit sociopolitical definitions that emerge in television, movies, newspapers, and political discourses.

The Middle Passage also establishes ancestral origin—a cornerstone for establishing Black Americans as equal to their white counterparts. Subject to the whims of official legal discourse, which first declared us property, then, at various stages of "no longer property" (by failing to mark its earlier declaration as simply wrong, the Constitution maintains its right to give or take away our humanity depending on the social, economic, and political fortunes of the moment), African American epistemologies must also direct their counterdiscourse (for that is what it is, after all) to the very heart of American discourse—the Declaration of Independence and the Constitution.

The images that often accompany introductions to the Middle Passage in textbooks (for example, cross-sections of a slave boat crammed with neatly inert Black bodies, the diagram of a muzzle on a slave's head) and documentaries seek to reverse this status by displaying their brutal methods; the slave traders themselves become the objects of our scorn and incomprehension, their former cargo the suffering subjects of *inhumane* treatment. As the site of this inhumane treatment, the Middle Passage points to a moment "before" when we were "Africans" and not cargo—but it is in the imagining of this originary moment where some of the problems of this trope emerge.

Discursively, then, the Middle Passage rejects a central assertion in the United States' self-imagining as a self-determined realm of freedom that has always attracted (never forcibly carried over) equally freedom-loving peoples. Yet one could argue that when we are specific about the signifieds attached to these signifiers such as *self-determination, democracy,* and *freedom,* the Middle Passage does not in fact stage much of a challenge. At the time of its inception, the Founding Fathers were eager to present their new nation as the culmination of the Enlightenment and, whether explicitly stated (Kant, Hegel, Hume) or heavily implied (Jefferson), these were not philosophers operating in an objective bubble but products of their time and therefore subjective in their definitions, methodologies, and goals. Freedom, self-determination, and democracy then were the sole province of property-owning white men (with a few exceptions).

So there is another aspect to our rhetoric that the Middle Passage seeks to flush into the open: that the Founding Fathers did not intend—at least in their own era—to extend "life, liberty, and the pursuit of happiness" to anyone who wasn't exactly like themselves. 1776 is for white men—the rest of us have to wait for incremental gains in 1862, 1865, 1928, 1956, and 1966 (and some of us are still waiting) as we are less important, our freedom largely inconsequential (after all, it did not found a nation!).

This is the point at which African American epistemologies split, depending on which subjects are creating it, and this becomes clear in the way in which the "pre-Middle Passage" moment is scripted. In many cases, Africa is rendered whole (to the point where a less educated reader would be misled by the rhetoric to believe it is a country rather than a diverse continent) and the assumption of a peaceful heteropatriarchal or heteromatriarchal community is imagined. Most often, as Natasha Tinsley in "Black Atlantic, Queer Atlantic: An International Framework for Black Queer Studies" has pointed out, this romanticized past (the province, we should note, of all national narratives, both sovereign and beset) is marked by the ways in which the tragedies and cruelties of the Middle Passage are defined and framed—that is, in the rape of Black women (significant because it points to the loss of Black masculine control over female bodies) and the destruction of a "normative" family—that is, a patriarchal one.

By focusing on the loss of Black patriarchal control, the Middle Passage begins to hierarchize Black subjects much in the same way that the dominant American epistemology it seeks to control does. Just as all Americans are encouraged to celebrate the enfranchisement of property-owning white men on July 4 (and American Indians encouraged to celebrate the beginning of the end of their own sovereignty on Columbus Day), the Middle Passage has been and continues to be used by some dominant epistemologies to produce a new equation: antiblack racism = the emasculation of Black men (heterosexuality is implied here, as the stereotype of gay men argues they have no masculinity to rob). According to the epistemologies that enable this equation, consciously or not, those who are female, queer, or otherwise abnormative, are deemed less important. Black nationalist thought became the culmination of this in charging the goal of the collective to be the recuperation of heterosexual Black masculinity and the disciplining, condemnation, or expulsion of those members (most often determined to be Black feminist and/or queer activists) who failed to adopt this goal (see Dubey, Harper).

Just as dominant white American epistemologies deploy seemingly neutral terms like freedom and democracy to mask a thousand sins of human disenfranchisement, so can the Middle Passage still operate to erase the explicit structure of this hierarchy—one that extends beyond U.S. borders to implicate everyone in diaspora. In signaling and protesting the enslavement of West and East Africans by the so-called Western "democracies," the Middle Passage, when deployed as the de facto "origin" of established Black populations in the West, effectively (re)creates the illusion of all Blacks in the West as always already disempowered. While largely true in the heyday of the slave trade, the radically different circumstances that inform the lives of Colin Powell versus Tawana Brawley end up simplifying blackness to gross distortion, preventing us from truly engaging with all of the other factors that intersect with race and also hierarchize us—economic status being the one that intersects most, I would argue.

While Shelby speaks to economic difference in *We Who Are Dark,* I would argue his construction of blackness is nonetheless based in the assumption of the "Middle Passage" epistemology in which all blackness is always already disempowered. While certainly true for the vast majority of slaves, the economic booms the United States has enjoyed over the twentieth and twenty-first centuries have produced radically different types of Black power and Black disempowerment. Shelby argues that a shared Black politic should be rooted in the principle that "the group's self-conception should be grounded in anti-racist politics and the commitment to racial justice . . . Blacks know . . . that they all want to live in a society where being (regarded as) Black is not a disadvantage" (247). Yet different Blacks suffer differently according to their socioeconomic status—indeed, more than a few would argue that they do not suffer at all. The central definition of blackness brought about by the "Middle Passage epistemology" is defunct because we are not all arriving on the same boat, either metaphorically or literally. Some of us are paddling an inflatable raft from Haiti; others of us arrive in the corporate jet.

The refusal to see these differences does not erase them—witness the desperate logic of the colonial powers in the postwar years as they (with increasing volume to drown out the background noise of "native unrest") insisted that "the natives" *liked* being ruled. These differences are becoming ever more prominent as the African Americanists located in the United States enable, become aware of, malign (deliberately and not), and align with Africans and peoples of African descent in Europe and North America (most of whom did *not,* it should be noted, come through the Middle Passage). Protests by academics who work in Black European studies, such as Gloria Wekker, Vanessa Agard-Jones, Victoria B. Robinson, and Andrés Nader, about the relatively large socioeconomic capital enjoyed and leveraged by many U.S.-based African Americanists has been met, in some quarters, with disbelief—it is the first time many of us have heard "African American" and "hegemony" modifying one another rather than in tension.

Part of this is relative: we U.S.-based scholars who work in Black studies still deal with quotidian humiliations, insults, attacks, and violence, and it therefore hurts to hear a fellow traveler, as it were, point the finger so clearly in our direction for wrongs about which we are sourly unsure. Yet no finger is really being pointed—instead, the freeing effects of our success are being called to our attention, the ways in which many white liberal Europeans prefer to read about African Americans and ignore their own Black populations, not to mention the ways in which some of us attempt to map these varying creations of Black identity onto an African American epistemology.

Having lived for some three centuries under the "one drop" rule, many African Americans strategically essentialize by deploying a deliberate slippage of belonging between themselves and "other" Blacks. As the logic goes, what we have in common—battling and triumphing over racism—is far more immediate and important than that which makes us different from one another. As a result, that which other Black populations understand specifically as "African American" to us is simply "Black"—and, almost inevitably, the African American epistemology becomes normative, and therefore automatically mapped on to other Black populations. The intent can be well-meaning—*we are linked in struggle*—but the effect is, at best disquieting, as a more Hegelian-cum-Fanonian interpretation of Black epistemologies—the progress narrative—emerges. In *Black Skin, White Masks,* Fanon argues that African Americans are "further" along than their Caribbean counterparts because they have undergone the necessary *Aufhebung* or upheaval that drives progress—we have fought for and won our freedom whereas the latter, according to Fanon, had their freedom handed to them, thus foreclosing for the moment the ability for true self-determination.

Through this anchoring of the Middle Passage as the origin of African American epistemologies, then, the "power asymmetries" as Tina Campt has termed them in *Other Germans,* become ignored and the material advantages enjoyed by many Black scholars in the United States relative to Black Europeans (of whom there are very few in academic positions, much less economic and political ones) become a sign of our "natural superiority." This function shouldn't shock us—indeed, it should strike us as familiar because it has been deployed for centuries against African Americans—the concrete material gains enjoyed by many whites become erased at the beginning of the comparison so they can be deployed at the end under the "results" column as "natural advantage" (see *Illiberal Education, The Closing of the American Mind, Losing the Race,* and *The Bell Curve,* but start with Jefferson's section on "Property" in *Notes on Virginia* and then go to the Moynihan Report).

This is not to argue that the Middle Passage must therefore be expunged from African American epistemologies—I would argue that is impossible, given all that it establishes for African American individual and collective identity. At the same time, I do want to signal solidarity with those scholars such as Natasha Tinsley who call attention to the ways in which, uninterrogated, the Middle Passage can distort our past, present, and future both within the United States and the African diaspora as a whole, assuming and asserting hierarchies of Blackness that the majority of us, I believe, eschew. Instead, I want to argue that we can become more aware of the cultural/historical/political specificities of our epistemologies and "retool" some of them to accommodate the very real and wonderful fact of diasporic intersections occurring with ever-greater frequency. In short, I want us to consider another trope in our epistemologies, one that is hardly a panacea (in fact, I will speak to its shortcomings later) but offers greater possibility, flexibility, and a frame that allows both for Black differences and alliances.

In their books *Sable Hands and National Arms: Toward a Theory of the African American Literature of War* and *Private Politics and Public Voices: Black Women's Activism From World War I to the New Deal,* Jennifer James and Nikki Brown respectively direct us towards new and productive ways of engaging with the African diaspora via African American studies. James challenges us to ask (as I did, borrowing the question from her above), why it is that World War II receives so little attention in our classrooms and epistemologies given its profound effect on our postwar lives. While James seeks answers to speak to the African American literary and pedagogical tradition specifically, I want to pose her question within these issues of normative epistemologies and the relationship between African American and Black European studies.

As I mentioned earlier, our dominant African American epistemologies often arrange themselves in a way first asserted by Hegel in his *Philosophy of History* and later revamped by Fanon in *Black Skin, White Masks:* as a progressive narrative in which a collective (and the individual) comes into being by overcoming those obstacles in their path. Figured as struggle, this epistemology is always already masculinized—Frederick Douglass versus Harriet Jacobs, one might say, and indeed when one takes a closer look at how the "heroes" of the African American experience are totemized, this gendering becomes clear: we celebrate Frederick Douglass, W.E.B. Du Bois, Malcolm X, Huey P. Newton, and Stokely Carmichael for "standing up" for their rights. We celebrate Harriet Wilson for lying prone, Harriet Tubman for working in the shadow of night, and Rosa Parks for sitting down, whereas those female figures who are resistant to being troped in this manner such as Angela Davis, Assatta Shakur, and Elaine Brown are situated as secondary to Black nationalism, and often praised (often incorrectly) for standing behind their men like good women.

Our epistemology, then, becomes marked by events and heroes in a very gendered way, in which an assertive, heteronormative Black masculinity is linked to liberation, and the rest are often accorded "special mention" as helpmates—Black liberationists, to be sure, but pale by comparison. This ideological chronotoping makes other events difficult to incorporate outside of very specific circumstances, World War I through to World War II specifically. We need to bring these events back in, I would argue, not only to broaden and enrich all African American epistemologies, but to intersect more productively with Black

European and African epistemologies—and subvert recent and increasing European and American attempts to deploy World War II and the postwar years as a means towards erasing past, present, and future "power asymmetries."

As Sabine Broeck noted in her keynote address at the second annual Black European Studies (BEST) conference in Berlin in 2006, the European Union is hardly a passive entity simply seeking alliance in the face of an increasing hegemonic aggression espoused and practiced by the United States. Some will be familiar with the phrase "Fortress Europe," which refers to an explicit attempt to ahistoricize Europe as a "whites-only" enclave that must now protect itself against the "invasion" of nonwhite hordes. In like kind, in his forward to the in-depth and diverse volume *"Unsere Opfern Zählen Nicht": Die Dritte Welt im Zweiten Weltkrieg* ("Our Victims Do Not Count": The Third World in the Second World War), Kum'a Ndumbe III and the authors of the volume, Birgit Morgenrath and Karl Rössel, note the ways in which the historiography produced by the Axis powers identifies more closely with their former Allied enemies rather than with the colonial subjects who served them. These, Ndumbe argues, are studiously ignored or constantly erased despite their widespread exploitation as soldiers, slave laborers, and prostitutes:

> The history of the Second World War proves itself to be, like all histories, a history of the victors—but also as that of the occupiers and the well-to-do. Germany and Japan, in spite of their military defeat in the written history, belong to the victors; even when both these countries must undertake a critical inquiry and rectification of the historiography, they nonetheless undertake to understand their status as selfsame as that of victors to be wholly correct. The true losers are those who were forgotten in the aftermath of the war, forgotten as if they had never existed throughout its duration; they must, with their children, relearn the history in its written form, a form in which they will never come across their own deeds. Even today, hundreds of million of people and their descendants in Africa, Asia, Latin America, in Australia and in the Pacific Rim still live defeated and voiceless.[1]

As Broeck, Ndumbe, Morgenrath, and Rössel point out, the reasons for this seemingly counterintuitive identification between the former Axis and Allied powers lies in their mutual investment in framing and deploying World War II as the conflict that ended fascism, leaving only democracy in its wake. Through the enactment of this astonishing myth, the human massacres, economic exploitation, and brutal suppression of liberties of the nineteenth and twentieth centuries that occurred in what now largely comprises the "Third World" becomes a tangent, erased of its significance.

In doing this, the United States, Britain, Germany, Japan, Italy, France, Norway (yes, Norway!), Denmark, Sweden, Spain, and Portugal[2] seek to deny their enrichment through the slave trade and colonialism, expunging the latter and transforming the former into some grand gesture of altruism (and paternalism) in which the always already Third World imperfectly receives the altruistic gifts of advanced democratic nations.[3] The new colonization—that is, Western capitalism, spoken to and criticized by a vast range of leftist intellectuals since the postwar years—becomes nothing more than "economic protection" by and for the G8. In addition, "Christian" Europe's centuries-old Islamophobia can be reintroduced as anti-terrorist measures.

This is perhaps where Gilroy's argument in *Against Race* is most troubling (and ahistorical): his invocation of "fascism" is exactly the way in which it is increasingly being invoked by the European Union to disguise and deny so many horrid racist crimes of the past, present, and future. If we do as Gilroy enjoins and label any and all minority ideologies that embrace an essentialist notion of race "fascist," we are allowing the Western invention of Blackness and our long history of both challenging and subverting that invention to disappear. Blackness becomes sucked into the false claim of World War II, eradicating "fascism" and therefore racism. We need to take a page from Gilroy and return to World War II, but not under the liberal humanist resignification of that conflict now so popular among European governments. Instead, we need to return to that era and maintain the striking difference between fascisms and racisms, pointing out, as Tina M. Campt and Clarence Lusane have (*Other Germans* and *Hitler's Black Victims* respectively), that some Black men served in Hitler's S.A. while others were deported to death camps, and that the Allies, the "good guys," treated German POWs better than their own Black servicemen. This was not a conflict between Western democracies and totalitarian regimes, but a conflict between nations long embroiled in oppressing, exploiting, and liquidating other minorities—and justifying it.

Back to Fascism

It is not as if the study of World War II is the panacea to all of our "ills"—heteropatriarchy, nationalism, liberal humanism (Black or white)—it can easily be used to propagate these ideas, and has been. Yet as more scholars—from undergraduates to full professors—seek to integrate their own interests, projects, departments, or disciplines with African diaspora studies, World War II as a shaping trope offers a far broader and more immediate set of connections than the Middle Passage and allows us to explore a variety of Black identities that intersect as they differ.

In his collection of essays *Notes of a Native Son* (1955), James Baldwin pursues the changing and hypostatic nature of Black and white American (albeit only male) identities in the postwar years, tellingly using the trope of the Middle Passage (most obviously evoked in the famous phrase "many thousands gone") as a faint but ever present shadow causing shame and embarrassment—a reminder of its unpopularity as a antiracist strategic device before Black nationalism. Yet it is not as if the postwar years offer an "answer" to this question of identity, as Baldwin puts it in one piece—it is simply the juxtaposition of race and space that endlessly pose this.

In one of his most striking essays, "Encounter on the Seine: Black Meets Brown," Baldwin gives us the image of an African American and a "French African" squared off by the Eiffel Tower, and in doing so neatly evokes and provokes the question of difference in the African diaspora and the central role played by Europe. Here, France exists both as an antifascist and colonialist power, one defeated by Aryans and "liberated" with the help of its own African colonial troops as well as African American ones. The two Black men (and, I should note, this essay, like almost all in the collection, fails miserably in the arena of gender) are both subjects and abject because the forces that brought them there testify both to their vulnerability and their resolute strength. While prone to disastrous stereotyping, Baldwin nonetheless dares to pursue this complex intersection of diasporic epistemologies in ways we have rarely seen since:

> The [American] Negro is forced to say "Yes" to many a difficult question, and yet to deny the conclusion to which his answers seem to point. His past, he now realizes, has not been simply a series of ropes and bonfires and humiliations, but something vastly more complex, which, as he thinks painfully, "It was much worse that that," was also, he irrationally feels, something much better. As it is useless to excoriate his countrymen, it is galling now to be pitied as a victim, to accept this ready sympathy which is limited only by its failure to accept him as an American. He finds himself involved, in another language, in the same old battle: the battle for his own identity. To accept the reality of his being an American becomes a matter involving his integrity and his greatest hopes, for only by accepting this reality can he hope to make articulate to himself or to others the uniqueness of his experience, and to set free the spirit so long anonymous and caged.
>
> The ambivalence of his status is thrown into relief by his encounters with the Negro students from France's colonies who live in Paris. The French African comes from a region and a way of life that—at least from the American point of view—is exceedingly primitive, and where exploitation takes more naked forms. In Paris, the African Negro's status, conspicuous and subtly inconvenient, is that of a colonial; and he leads here the intangibly precarious life of someone abruptly and recently uprooted. His bitterness is unlike that of his American kinsman in that it is not so treacherously likely to be turned against himself. He has, not so very many miles away, a homeland to which his relationship, no less than his responsibility, is overwhelmingly clear: His country must be given—or it must seize—its freedom. This bitter ambition is shared by his fellow colonials, with

> whom he has a common language, and whom he has no wish to avoid; without whose sustenance, indeed, he would be almost altogether lost in Paris. They live in groups together, in the same neighborhoods, in student hotels and under conditions that cannot fail to impress the American as almost unendurable.
>
> Yet what the American is seeing is not simply the poverty of the student but the enormous gap between the European and American standards of living. *All* of the students in the Latin Quarter live in the ageless, sinister-looking hotel; they are all forced continually to choose between cigarettes and cheese at lunch (120–22).

From the product of "ropes and bonfires and humiliations," Baldwin transforms his abject African American into "the American" who acts not unlike a naïve millionaire upon spotting the Latin Quarter, summing up the many contradictions that go into the African American identity, and here Baldwin summons up the largest and most painfully enraging—to be both the continuing victim of a slavocracy and the beneficiary of it. He does this, significantly, through epistemologies, creating each of his characters through his understanding of their histories, that which now makes them "Negro."

Handed a doomed hand by the *philosophes* from the start, "Blackness" has nonetheless survived and even in some cases flourished in the West. The deployment of Black counterdiscourses rather than the denigrating stereotypes of origin has become its central definition. Dominant African American epistemologies have in many ways led the way in the successful subversion of dominant (white) American epistemologies, the latter guided by a liberal humanist logic that seeks to erase difference under the guise of supporting it. Yet the rising power of a unified and increasingly intolerant European Union, a more aggressive United States in foreign affairs, and the postwar facts of diaspora—the greater frequency of intersection between different Black communities, citizens, individuals, writers, scholars, activists, and artists and the expanded reach of global capitalism—require our epistemologies to change so that we can speak to difference without attempting to erase or hierarchize it ourselves. No one need be pale by comparison.

Notes

1. The original text is as follows: "Die Geschichte des Zweiten Weltkriegs erweist sich, wie jede Geschichte, als der Sieger, aber auch als die Besitzenden und Wohlhabenden. Deutschland und Japan gehören trotz ihrer militärischen Niederlage in der Geschichtsschreibung zu den Siegern, denn auch wenn die Historiographie in den beiden Ländern eine kritische Befragung und Korrekturen hinnehmen musste, werden sie als Menschen gleichen Ranges wahrgenommen. Diejenigen aber, die nach dem Krieg vergessen wurden, als ob sie während des Krieges gar nicht existiert hätten, die mit ihren eigenen Kindern die Geschichte neu erlernen müssen, ohne eigene Taten in dieser Ge-

schichtsschreibung wiederzufinden, gehören zu den eigentlichen Verlieren. Verlierer und ohne Stimme, so leben bis heute noch Hunderte Millionen Menschen mit ihren Nachkommen in Afrika, Asien, Lateinamerika, in Australien und in der Pazifikregion" (9).

2. As Tony Judt notes in *Postwar: A History of Europe since 1945*, Spain and Portugal actually remained fascist dictatorships until the 1970s; nonetheless, they also enjoyed the fruits of colonization (see chapter 16, "A Time of Transition").

3. For the European state, facts must be sacrificed to self-regard; in 2006, the French government announced they were expunging the ugly details of their colonialist history from school curricula in favor of a fiction that produced them as civilizers of savagery. The reason, they claimed, was out of concern for the *amor patria* that every French schoolgirl and boy needed to develop.

References

Agard-Jones, Vanessa. "Speaking Plainly About Power: Privilege and the Development of Black European Studies." Paper delivered at 2nd Annual Black European Studies Conference, Free University of Berlin, July 17–30, 2006.

Asante, Molefi. *Afrocentricity: The Theory of Social Change*. Trenton, N.J.: Africa World Press, 1988.

Baldwin, James. *Notes of a Native Son*. 1955. Boston, Mass.: Beacon Press, 1984.

Broeck, Sabine. "Rethinking Europe: Slavery and the Constitution of White Modern Europe." Keynote Address, 2nd International Black European Studies (BEST) Conference: "Black European Studies in Transnational Perspective." Berlin, Germany, July 2006.

Brown, Nikki. *Private Politics and Public Voices: Black Women's Activism from World War I to the New Deal*. Bloomington: Indiana University Press, 2007.

Campt, Tina M. *Other Germans: Black Germans and the Politics of Race, Gender, and Memory in the Third Reich* (Social History, Popular Culture, and Politics in Germany). Ann Arbor: University of Michigan Press, 2005.

Dubey, Madhu. *Black Women Novelists and the Nationalist Aesthetic*. Bloomington: Indiana University Press, 1994.

Fanon, Frantz. *Black Skin, White Masks*. 1980. Berkeley, Calif.: Grove Press; Reissue edition, 1991.

Gilroy, Paul. *Against Race: Imagining Political Culture Beyond the Color Line*. Cambridge, Mass.: Belknap Press, 2000.

———. *The Black Atlantic*. 1992. Cambridge, Mass.: Harvard University Press; Reissue edition, 2005.

———. *There Ain't No Black in the Union Jack*. Chicago: University of Chicago Press; Reprint edition, 1991.

Harper, Philip Brian. *Are We Not Men? Masculine Anxiety and the Problem of African-American Identity*. New York: Oxford University Press, 1996.

Hegel, Georg Wilhelm Friedrich. *Philosophy of History*. Whitefish, Mt.: Kessinger Publishing, 2004.

Hull, Gloria T., Patricia Bell Scott, and Barbara Smith. *But Some of Us Are Brave: All the Women Are White, All the Blacks Are Men: Black Women's Studies*. New York: Feminist Press at CUNY, 1982.

James, Jennifer. *Sable Hands and National Arms: Toward a Theory of the African American Literature of War*. Chapel Hill: University of North Carolina Press, 2007.

Jefferson, Thomas. *The Portable Thomas Jefferson*. Ed. Merrill D. Peterson. New York: Viking Press, 1977.

Judt, Tony. *Postwar: A History of Europe since 1945*. New York: Penguin, 2005.

Lusane, Clarence. *Hitler's Black Victims: The Historical Experiences of Afro-Germans, European Blacks, Africans, and African Americans in the Nazi Era*. New York: Routledge, 2003.

Morgenrath, Birgit, and Karl Rössel. *"Unsere Opfer Zählen Nicht": Die Dritte Welt im Zweiten Weltkrieg*. Berlin: Rheinisches JournalistInnenbüro, Heraugegeben von Recherche International, e.V.: 2005.

Nader, Andrés. "Thinking the Colorlines Across the Atlantic." Paper delivered at 2nd Annual Black European Studies Conference, Free University of Berlin, July 17–30, 2006.

Robinson, Victoria B. "BLACKprint: The Referencing of Black America in Afro-German Cultural Productions." Paper delivered at 2nd Annual Black European Studies Conference, Free University of Berlin, July 17–30, 2006.

Shelby, Tommie. *We Who Are Dark: The Philosophical Foundations of Black Solidarity*. Cambridge, Mass.: Belknap Press, 2005.

Tinsley, Natasha. "Black Atlantic, Queer Atlantic: An International Framework for Black Queer Studies." Keynote Address, Black Queer Studies Conference, Northwestern University, Evanston, Illinois, January 2006.

15

Another Dream of a Common Language: Imagining Black Europe . . .

GLORIA WEKKER

> No one sleeps in this room without the dream
> of a common language.
> —Adrienne Rich, 1978

With "Another Dream of a Common Language," I am borrowing the words of poet Adrienne Rich from her acclaimed collection of poetry *A Dream of a Common Language.*[1] In a courageous reversal that was groundbreaking in the 1970s, Rich's work was driven by the understanding that women are one another's sources of power. In *A Dream,* she addresses a generic Woman who is not marked by any characteristics other than gender. The poet dreams of a language liberated from patriarchal conventions by which all women will be able to understand each other and change the world. In her later work, chastised by the criticism of especially women of color, she realizes that the hegemonic whiteness of the imagined woman is barely masked and that the dream of a common language is an essentializing and totalizing gesture. As Lynda Buntzen notes, "*The* woman has ceased to exist, and with her, perhaps, Rich's dream of a common language," because "it ignores so many voices, languages, gestures, actions."[2]

Yet, in many ways, while remaining mindful of the lurking epistemological dangers, Rich's metaphor is still useful as a starting point for this essay and the project of imagining Black Europe. Rich's imagery calls up the isolation that those of us located in the European academy, and interested in exploring issues of Black diaspora, work to overcome. By invoking "a common language," we are pointed to the reality of multiple languages circulating in the Black diaspora, to the incommensurate positioning of English and other languages, and to the necessity of translation, with all its attendant difficulties.[3] The metaphor invites us to address general, not only linguistic, issues of power and disempowerment in the Black diaspora. In addition, Rich's trajectory teaches us to be cognizant of the many differences characterizing Black European populations, both within and between national borders. These differences should be taken into account from the inception of such a project. Her metaphor prods us to ask difficult questions; for example, following Stuart Hall, we should be concerned with what "this *black* in black Europe is,"[4] while the concept of *Europe* likewise needs to be interrogated. The metaphor appropriately expresses the complexity of the work that awaits us with respect to Black Europe.

In this essay, I want to sketch some contours and contexts of the project of imagining Black Europe. Together, my reflections point to the simultaneous desirability and impossibility of being a Black European.[5] I do not think that the notion of Black Europe or of being a Black European has blossomed in many contexts within Europe itself yet; it is a desire, as Jacqueline Nassy Brown put it in her contribution to the conference; a discourse that is subjugated, I would add, and one that is unevenly spread across the continent and internally variable. It is a potentiality that has yet to come to fruition. In my experience, as well as in Stephen Small's, the only time when I am called a European is in an American context. This should alert us to an important aspect of the situatedness of the concept.

Using Clifford Geertz's well-known image of stripping an onion, I will offer some considerations on Black Europe that in my opinion are vital to a trans- and intercontinental conversation and a successful collaborative endeavor, both in an academic and a political sense. This conversation should keep that nascent but elusive category of Black Europeans in the forefront. The layers of the onion are an analytical lens, and within each orbit, phenomena of the other spheres protrude and impinge. First, it is important to be aware of the wider geopolitical and power dynamics in which the project of imagining Black Europe takes off. Thus, the outer layer of the onion will focus on the main global settings of diaspora—Africa, African America, the African Caribbean, and Black Europe—and explore which relationships exist within Black diaspora globally. Throughout, my main focus will be on the academy. To do so, also by way of illustrating the impingement of the different spheres, I will situate my reflection in a specific, local, Black diasporic setting. Second, I will focus on some powerful contradictions within Europe, that other meaningful context, in which an estimated 18 million Black Europeans seek to come to self-realization.[6] Which conceptualization of the project of Europe, as it is currently underway with its twenty-seven members and associated members, is most enabling for *Black* Europeans and other Others? The third layer, the kernel of the onion, contains the Netherlands, which is a main location in my own positioning. Here I will explore the forms that "racial Europeanization" (Goldberg 2006) taken in a Dutch context. In order to do so, I will describe three characteristics of dominant Dutch self-representation and what those characteristics tell us about the collective imaginary that is operative in the Netherlands with respect to "race." This narrative is but one illustration of the complexity of European race configurations.

A Global View of Black Diaspora

I will start this section with two vignettes taken from everyday life. However inadequate, these vignettes allow me a takeoff point for my reflections on power differentials in the Black diaspora. Both are about being on my way home. One concerns my daily return home, which is set in the southeast of Amsterdam, a neighborhood called De Bijlmer, a seriously economically depressed part of town that has a bad name in the rest of Amsterdam and the Netherlands. This is not unrelated to its having an 85 percent Black population. People are predominantly from the former Dutch colony of Suriname, from the Dutch Antilles, which still form part of the Dutch-speaking cultural ecumene, and from various African nations. The other vignette captures my walking to the hotel from the campus in Evanston, Illinois, where I spent about five days attending the conference "Black Europe and the African Diaspora" in April 2006.

A description of the latter includes the following observations. On this short distance of about seven minutes, I am greeted frequently by unknown Blacks, especially men. When I lived in L.A., at the end of the 1980s and early 1990s, this gesture always struck me as pleasant, as my being acknowledged as a member of an "imagined community," and it still does. I have not systematically studied the phenomenon, but I have noticed that it is both younger and older men who greet me. Men who wear their hair in dreadlocks, as I do, are especially friendly, with beaming smiles. I do not know whether Black American men greet other—unknown—Black men, outside of a sexual context. Neither do I know why Black women greet me less often than Black men. I understand this greeting tradition as one of the ways in which African Americans express and create a sense of community, and it would be interesting to flesh out the gendered and heterosexualizing patterns that are operative in it.

In the Netherlands, Blacks generally do not greet each other on the street if they do not know each other. When I go home from my work in Utrecht, I take the train to Duivendrecht station and from there I take a so-called *snorder,* an unofficial livery cab that takes me home for €2.50. Such cabs are unique to the southeast of Amsterdam, part of a gendered grey economy that in its female compartments includes sewing African fashion, Black hairdressing, other personal services, and catering. *Snorren* is a favorite way for drivers, 99 percent of whom are Black men, to generate additional income. They often do this work in addition to a regular job.

From my conversations with the snorders, I have noted that there is a strong antagonism between Surinamese and African cabdrivers, mostly Nigerians, Ghanaians, Togolese, and Somalians. Stereotypes about each other abound. The Africans state that the Surinamese are lazy, depending on social security, and that men and women have brittle unions, are usually not living together, and do not raise their children jointly. The Surinamese are of the opinion that the Africans are unmannered, that they are thugs and do not think twice about conning their non-African customers, and that I, as a Surinamese woman, should not ride with them. Since I take the first snorder that is in line and do not choose a driver on the basis of nation (or continent), this has caused me some problems with Surinamese drivers in the past. I feel compelled to juxtapose these microlevel, daily experiences with the—sometimes—"high theory" notions of Black Europe, which are far removed from daily, on-the-ground realities. This is Black Europe, too, and I doubt that the protagonists consider themselves as fellow Black Europeans or Black diasporeans.

These vignettes present us with an interesting field for further research, but I now want to proceed in a direction that strikes closer to the academic, diasporic power relations that I want to get at. If I were to bet on where such a proposal on the interactions between different Black diasporic population groups in a European capitol, the mutual representations and micro-economics and -politics, would get funded, I would place my bet on an (African) American rather than a European funding source.[7] This is tantamount to stating the obvious: it does make a difference where one is located for one's chances to do research on African diasporic issues.

We urgently need to address the differential geopolitical, national, and academic spaces that we inhabit within the Black diaspora, where relations are shot through with power differentials, which place Africa-America, by virtue of its being part of the most "powerful nation on earth" at the apex, with Black Europe, the Caribbean, and Africa occupying less powerful, relatively marginalized positions. The emergence of the United States as a world power in the course of the last centuries has had consequences for the displacement of Europe as the global center of academic production and circulation (cf. Hall 1992).[8] Each of the other nodes in the global diaspora is plagued by other complex constraining factors where academic production on the diaspora is concerned. Positioning within the global South often means lack of sufficient funding to do research, a general infrastructure that does not allow easy access to keep up to date in one's discipline, and relations of dependency on the North. Positioning within (Western) Europe has to contend with the widespread aversion to acknowledge "race"/ethnicity at all.

I acknowledge the disenfranchisement of African American researchers within the context of the United States, and I am deeply aware of the struggles that have had to be and still are being waged, from which we, Black diasporeans elsewhere, too, have benefited. In interaction between African American researchers and researchers on the Black diaspora elsewhere, however, there is always a power differential operative, if only in terms of a "race cognizant discourse" (Frankenberg 1993) that is operative in broader sections of U.S. society. While Black scholars started working on a knowledge base from the nineteenth century on and even earlier, this discourse has, since the late 1960s, resulted in larger cultural capital for U.S. Blacks, for example, the existence of Black studies departments, which offer curricula at different levels, degrees, and teaching/research positions; and a variety of funding sources to which one can apply for research. In short, although there has been great pain, often high personal costs, and institutional cutbacks, an infrastructure for knowledge production on black matters has been erected in the United States, with publication outlets, museums, and websites for collaboration and dissemination, that has no parallels in other parts of Black diaspora.

Other scholars have remarked upon the overdetermination of Black diaspora with African Americana.[9] Tina Campt has noted that Black America functions "as a signifier that is always already in the room when blackness gets put on the table." I fully agree with her that, within the context of scholarly discourse on the African diaspora, a relationship of hegemony exists.[10] To name just three expressions of this state of affairs: first, the particular, local definition and understandings of what it means to be Black in the United States has had the tendency to travel elsewhere and to myopically swallow other, sometimes nascent, configurations. The U.S.- inflected understanding of *Black* in Black diaspora treats the category as given and entirely transparent. As Stuart Hall remarks, "The moment the signifier 'black' is torn from its historical, cultural and political embedding and lodged in a biologically constituted racial category, we valorize, by inversion, the very ground of racism we are trying to deconstruct. In addition, as always happens when we naturalize historical categories (think about gender and sexuality), we fix that signifier outside of history, outside of change, outside of political intervention."[11]

The unreflected use of the term *Black* undermines and distorts local understandings and configurations of what it means to be Black. A U.S.-inspired gaze has led to solipsistic attention to population groups who conform to American definitions of blackness, whereas in the Netherlands and Germany, for instance, youths of various ethnic groups, Surinamese, Antilleans, but also Moroccans, tend to form their own new configurations and understandings of "race"/ethnicity. Moreover, the hybrid forms that have always already been in place are not taken into account. As W.E.B. Du Bois reminded us, wherever Black folks find themselves, they importantly take on characteristics of the surrounding society. In order to survive, they need to develop "double consciousness" (1903). Thus, Dutch Blacks—who have been in the Netherlands since the 1950s, but in significant numbers since the middle of the 1970s—are, to a significant extent, shaped by Dutch mores, ways of being in the world, ways of expressing themselves. In order to succeed, they need to partake in the dominant cultural modes of negotiating, of reaching consensus.

Second, the trope of the Middle Passage has come to stand for *the* foundational moment in diasporic history and societies, thereby marginalizing other histories and genealogies that do not foreground "Black Atlantic" travelings. Many European Blacks, for example, Afro-Germans, Afro-French, and Afro-Russians, relate to other periodizations than the "classical" model and are able to trace their origins to some identifiable place in Africa, without interjection of a "New" World setting. As a consequence, slavery does not occupy the same foundational position in various Black European memories and cultural imaginaries.

Third, as I have argued elsewhere,[12] in the study of slavery, the United States has come to occupy the privileged status of the normative, standard model, setting the tone of this body of research, that is, determining which questions are worth asking. One of the regrettable consequences of this state of affairs has been that sexuality during slavery has remained a black box, the great unknown. While we gradually have come to know about the music, verbal arts, aesthetic preferences, and family patterns of the enslaved, about their religious belief systems, about food intake and the bodily stresses and diseases that they suffered from, we know little about how the enslaved saw themselves as sexual subjects in the world. The exploration of sexuality, diasporically, has suffered from the "sex negativity"[13] that has attached itself to the theme in an American context, and this may a fortiori be the case in an African American setting. In other words, I am making a plea for us no longer to be innocent about and oblivious to the power relations that run through the discipline as it has evolved and is evolving, and, by implication, also through this conference. Speaking from an Afro-Dutch location, I see the preponderance of African American researchers studying Black Europe today both as a blessing—precisely because of the power relations that will make the topic more salonfähig in Europe—but also a source of great anxiety to me, if there is no acknowledgment of the different conditions and relative privileges that we are laboring under.

These reflections should not be mistaken either as a lack of recognition of the painstaking and indispensable work that has been done by African American scholars. Nor should it be misconstrued as a plea for epistemological apartheid but, bringing Rich back into the picture, as an urgent call to all of us to practice a "politics of location"[14] so that important and difficult questions can be addressed with epistemological rigor and intellectual integrity. The tasks ahead of us, which entail, in Edward Said's words, "nothing less than the reintegration of all those people and cultures, once confined and reduced to peripheral status, with the rest of the human race,"[15] are pressing enough.

Some Considerations on Europe

> "Europe" is morally, spiritually indefensible.
> —Aimé Césaire, 1972

According to Aimé Césaire, writing shortly after World War II, there are two problems that European civilization has not been capable of solving: the problem of the proletariat and the colonial problem.[16] Now, at the beginning of the twenty-first century, his analysis has only gained in urgency. Césaire's courageous indictment of Europe is well worth repeating: "What am I driving at? At this idea: that no one colonizes innocently, that no one colonizes with impunity either; that a nation which colonizes, that a civilization which justifies colonization—and therefore force—is already a sick civilization, a civilization that is morally diseased, that irresistibly, progressing from one consequence to another, one repudiation to another, calls for its Hitler, I mean its punishment."[17]

Césaire draws intimate connections between the racist methods used in the colonies to discipline the "natives"—the Arabs in Algeria, the coolies of India, and the Blacks of Africa—and the Nazi methods later used and perfected against the Jews and other Others in Europe. The idea of the Holocaust as *the* epitome and model of racist transgression in Europe erases the crimes that were perpetrated against the colonized over four centuries. This excision coincides with the representation that the history and reality of Europe is located on the continent and that what happened in the colonies is no constitutive part of it. At the same time, this regime of truth enables Europe to indulge in the myth of racial purity, as homogeneously white.

Until the middle of the twentieth century, the principal meaning of the term "European" centered on groups of colonizers in the colonized regions of the world. Thus, the construction of the European self and its Others took place in the force fields of "conquest, colonization, empire formation, permanent settlement by Europeans of other parts of the globe, nationalist struggles by the colonized, and selective decolonization."[18] Contemporary constructions of "us," those constructed as belonging to Europe, and "them," those constructed as not belonging, though the specific groups targeted vary over time, keep following that basic Manichean logic. This entails the fundamental impossibility to be both European, constructed to mean being white and Christian, and being Black/Muslim/migrant/refugee. In a return of the repressed, the protracted negotiations of the European Union with Turkey, which has been an "associate nation" since 1963, bring up parts of the European cultural archive, which have constructed Turkey as the barbaric Other.

Given this conceptual expulsion of Blacks from Europe and the simultaneous presence of an estimated 18 million Blacks in the heart of Europe, how do we conceptualize Europe in a way that is enabling? Césaire states that "the great good fortune of Europe is to have been a crossroads, and that because it was the locus of all ideas, the receptacle of all philosophies, the meeting place of all sentiments, it was the best center for the redistribution of energies."[19] He is echoed by Etienne Balibar, who proposes thinking of Europe in terms of "cross-over" patterns. This model insists on the idea "that in the very heart of Europe all languages, religions, cultures, are coexisting and mixing, with origins and connections all over the world."[20] He sees the openness of all regions of Europe to influences from outside as potential, for ethnic and religious conflicts but also for hybridity and cultural invention. This "cross-over" model, of course, is consonant with Europe's antique history, as rewritten in Bernal's *Black Athena,* which convincingly shows the presence of Black culture at the cradle of Europe and the ways in which that presence has been systematically erased.

Notwithstanding the difficulties involved in imagining and inventing ourselves as Black Europeans, there are, to my situated knowledge, two concrete projects that have taken off in the late 1990s and the early years of the twenty-first century. First, there is the Afro-European women's movement, Sophie-Dela, which has its main seat in the Netherlands. This organization was key in the institutionalization of a (so-called static) national monument to commemorate slavery in Amsterdam, in 2000, and it also contributed to the establishment of another (dynamic) monument, called NINSEE, the Dutch National Institute for the Study of the Slavery Past and its Heritage. These two monuments were made possible in a period when the Social Democrats were in office in the Netherlands.

The other initiative concerns BEST, Black European Studies, which has been located at the Johannes Gutenberg Universität in Mainz since 2003 with Peggy Piesche and Fatima El-Tayeb as central figures. BEST is an interdisciplinary, academic project that wants to study the Black presence in Europe from the Enlightenment to today. Although the initiative was taken in Germany, the project collaborates with Blacks in Sweden, Russia, France, the Nordic countries, Spain, Italy, and the Netherlands.

The Netherlands and Racial Europeanization

On September 28, 2006, during Dutch parliamentary debates in which the budget for the coming year was defended by the sitting coalition of CDA, the Christian Democrats, and VVD, the Conservative Democrats, the CDA prime minister, Jan Peter Balkenende, was in an excellent mood. Using the debates as an occasion to favorably position his party for the impending elections in November,[21] he insisted on having all political parties acknowledge the economic prosperity his coalition had brought about: after the sour, it was now time to taste the sweet, as he put it. When the opposition contested his representation of reality and pointed out global economic developments from which the Netherlands now finally profited, Balkenende, an uptight Reformed Christian, repeatedly and gaily threw up his hands in the air and invited everyone to "be happy; why can't you rejoice with us and are you being so sour? We need another mentality in this country. We need a VOC mentality." By referring to the VOC,[22] Balkenende invoked the United East India Company, the main body through which the eastern part of the Dutch colonial empire, the Dutch Indies and South Africa, was managed for four centuries. His statement is a perfect example of "Innocence Unlimited,"[23] the denial and erasure of Empire that is the dominant Dutch discourse towards its colonial and racial history. That history can be invoked because it is clear to everyone that he is only referencing the metropolitan Dutch golden age, not the colonial regime that made it possible.

David Theo Goldberg suggests that different regions of the world have their own "mappings or models" of race, "each one with its own material and intellectual history, its prior conditions and typical modes of articulation."[24] Although these articulations are interactive historically, and are in the habit of traveling, it remains important to delineate them separately, as "the force of race assumes its power in and from the thick contexts of the different if related political regions in which it is embedded."[25] Characteristic of racial Europeanization is that it "has rendered race unmentionable, unspeakable if not as reference to an Anti-Semitism of the past."[26]

In the final section of this paper, I will explore the forms that racial Europeanization take in a Dutch context. The Netherlands has in the past five years, after the murders of Pim Fortuijn and Theo van Gogh, within a European and global context, come to occupy a new position. Its new claim to fame is no longer its proverbial tolerance and hospitality to foreigners and refugees, however contested that notion always already was in circles of Black, migrants, and refugees themselves. Recently, the Netherlands has received much international attention as an example of the failed dream of multiculturalism. Nowadays the Netherlands serves as a deterrent to other European nations for trying out models of multiculturalism, of living together under some semblance of egalitarianism. The subtext is that if even the Netherlands, this paragon of ethnic egalitarianism, has been so unsuccessful at accomplishing multiculturalism, why should *we* even bother? In the current politically revisionist mood sweeping across Europe, multiculturalism within the former metropoles has been pronounced dead while simultaneously, the nostalgia for Empire is played out by engaging in neocolonial and imperial projects.[27] The dominant mapping of race in the Netherlands, as Prime Minister Balkenende's statement illustrates, importantly contains a denial of the Dutch role in Empire, color- and power evasiveness (Frankenberg 1993) and a denial of race as a social and symbolical "grammar of difference."

Dominant and cherished Dutch self-representation is characterized by a series of paradoxes, of which I will name three, which should be taken into account when we want to consider the general Dutch climate with regard to race. The Netherlands is a multiethnic society, and in its self-image it prides itself on being color-blind.

A first interesting paradox is that the majority of the Dutch do not want to be identified with migrants, although one in every six Dutch has migrant ancestry. Whether it is Huguenots, Belgians, Spanish and Portuguese Jews, Hungarians, Indonesians, Surinamers, Antilleans, or Turks and Moroccans, the Netherlands is a nation of (descendants of) migrants. That is, however, not the dominant self-image that circulates. Whereas in the private sphere stories may be woven about a great-grandmother who came from Poland, in the public sphere such stories do not add to one's public persona; they are, rather, curiosities. Belonging to the Dutch nation demands that those features that the collective imaginary considers non-Dutch—that is, language, "exotic" dress and convictions, non-Christian religions, the memory of oppression—are shed as fast as possible and that one tries to assimilate. In the public sphere, the assimilation model of mono-ethnicism and monoculturalism is so thorough that all signs of being from elsewhere are erased. Of course, those who can phenotypically "pass for" Dutch, that is, who are white, are in an advantageous position. It is migrants with dark skin color who do not succeed in enforcing their claim on Dutchness or have it accepted as legitimate. There are no models to deal with ethnic/"racial" difference other than assimilation, and those who cannot or will not be assimilated are segregated.

A second interesting paradox in dominant Dutch self-representation involves the recent past. The dominant self-image is that of innocent victim of German occupation during World War II. That the Netherlands was a perpetrator of excessive violence against the jewel in the Dutch imperial crown, Indonesia, which was fighting for its independence in roughly the same period, does not form part of the Dutch self-image. The euphemistic term "police actions," meaning a dirty war, speaks volumes about a self-image that embraces innocence, being a small but just and ethical guiding nation, internationally: Innocence Unlimited.

The third, overriding paradox involves the more distant past: there is the juxtaposition between the Dutch imperial presence in the world, since the sixteenth century, and its almost total absence in the Dutch educational curriculum, from grade school to university level, and in self-representations, for example, monuments, literature, and debates about Dutch identity. This started to change in 2007, when a national canon committee acknowledged slavery as one of the fifty key events in Dutch history. Knowledge about Dutch overseas expansion in the academy is—not incidentally—still in quarantine in a separate specialization of the discipline of history; it is not considered part of the Dutch cultural archive that needs to be transmitted to future generations.

We are still a long way away from understanding the complex relationships between the Dutch global, imperial role and the internal erasure of this role on the one hand, and the current revulsion against multiculturalism on the other. The past forms a massive blind spot, which barely hides a structure of superiority with regard to people of color. As long as the Dutch colonial past does not form part of the "common," general store of knowledge that society has at its disposal, as long as general knowledge about the exclusionary processes involved in producing the Dutch nation is not circulating more widely, multiculturalism cannot be realized, either.

Forgetting, glossing over, assumed color blindness, an inherent and "natural" superiority regarding people of color, assimilating: those are, broadly speaking, the main Dutch models that are and have been in operation where interaction with "racial" Others is concerned. An innocent, fragile, emancipated white Dutch self is constructed versus a guilty, uncivilized, barbaric Other, which in the past decades has been symbolized mostly by the Islamic Other, but at different times in the recent past has been occupied by Blacks. This dominant context has, with the exception of the 1970s and 1980s, when feminist and antiracist/decolonizing movements were active, not given Black communities much impetus to embrace the label "Black." Black Dutch people (and other ethnic Others) are confronted with an enormous paradox. The implicit and infernal message, the double bind, we get presented with is: "if you want to be equal to us, then don't talk about differences; but, if you are different from us, then you are not equal" (Prins 2000).

In this paper, I have undertaken to sketch some important contexts and contours of the incipient project of Black Europe, with a special focus on the Netherlands. I hope that the complexity, the internal variability, and the wrenching paradoxes that this exercise has shown, precariously held together by the concept of "racial Europeanization," can point us to work towards the possibilities of "a partially shared common language . . . to which strangers can bring their own heartbeat, memories, images of strangers."[28]

Notes

1. Rich, *The Dream of a Common Language.*
2. Buntzen, "Adrienne Rich's Identity Poetics: A Partly Common Language," 332, 333.
3. Agard, "Grammars of Blackness"; Edwards, *The Practice of Diaspora.*

4. Hall, "What Is This 'Black' in Black Popular Culture?" 21.

5. I borrow this phrase from Paul Gilroy's presentation for the Goethe Institute, "On the Necessity and Impossibility of Being a Black European," Munich, March 2006.

6. BEST Web site, http://www.best.uni-mainz.de.

7. I speak from experience because I have twice tried to get funding for a project like this in a Dutch setting. My research on the constructions of female Afro-Surinamese sexual subjectivity also got funded by American sources (Wekker, "I am Gold Money").

8. Hall, "What Is This 'Black' in Black Popular Culture?" 21.

9. E.g., Gilroy, *Between Camps;* Brown, *Dropping Anchor, Setting Sail;* and Campt, *Other Germans.*

10. Campt, *Other Germans,* 178. In the field of popular culture, this hegemony may even be more influential and detrimental. The violence of the gendered and heterosexualized images of men and women that are packaged for global consumption in rap and hip-hop, are but one site where this hegemony is manifest.

11. Hall, "What Is This 'Black' in Black Popular Culture?" 29–30.

12. In my "Sexual Subjectivity in Surinamese Slave Society and its Aftermaths," and *The Politics of Passion.*

13. Rubin, "Thinking Sex."

14. Rich, "Notes toward a Politics of Location," in *Blood, Bread, and Poetry,* 210–31.

15. Said, "The Politics of Knowledge," 379.

16. Césaire, *Discourse on Colonialism,* 9.

17. Ibid., 20.

18. Brah, *Cartographies of Diaspora,* 152.

19. Césaire, *Discourse on Colonialism,* 11.

20. Balibar, "Europe as Borderland," 12.

21. The new elections became necessary after the cabinet Balkenende-II fell in June 2006 because the third coalition partner, D 66, Democrats 66, withdrew its support from the coalition over VVD Minister Rita Verdonk, of Foreigner Policy and Integration Affairs, taking VVD member of Parliament Ayaan Hirsi Ali's Dutch passport away.

22. Vereenigde Oost Indische Compagnie.

23. Title of a presentation I gave at UC-Santa Cruz, 2001.

24. Goldberg, "Racial Europeanization," 333.

25. Ibid., 332.

26. Ibid., 339.

27. Gilroy, "On the Necessity and Impossibility of Being a Black European."

28. Rich, *What Is Found There,* 85.

References

Agard, Vanessa. "Grammars of Blackness: Translation, 'Black' Studies and Diasporic Interventions." Draft article, 2006.

Balibar, Etienne. "Europe as Borderland." Alexander von Humboldt Lecture in Human Geography. University of Nijmegen. November 10, 2004.

Brah, Avtar. *Cartographies of Diaspora: Contesting Identities.* London: Routledge, 1996.

Brown, Jacqueline Nassy. *Dropping Anchor, Setting Sail: Geographies of Race in Black Liverpool.* Princeton, N.J.: Princeton University Press, 2005.

Buntzen, Lynda K. "Adrienne Rich's Identity Poetics: A Partly Common Language." In *Women's Studies* 27 (1998): 331–45.

Campt, Tina. *Other Germans: Black Germans and the Politics of Race, Gender, Memory in the Third Reich.* Ann Arbor: University of Michigan Press, 2004.

Césaire, Aimé. *Discourse on Colonialism.* New York: Monthly Review, 1972.

Edwards, Brent. *The Practice of Diaspora: Literature, Translation and the Rise of Black Internationalism.* Cambridge, Mass.: Harvard University Press, 2003.

Frankenberg, Ruth. *White Women, Race Matters: The Social Construction of Whiteness.* Minneapolis: University of Minnesota Press, 1993.

Gilroy, Paul. *Between Camps: Nations, Cultures, and the Allure of Race.* London: Penguin Books, 2000.

———. "On the Necessity and Impossibility of Being a Black European." Paper presented at the symposium "Territorium and kulturelle Identität—Schwarze Diaspora in den Amerikas und in Europa." Goethe-Forum, München, March 11, 2006.

Goldberg, David Theo. "Racial Europeanization." In: *Ethnic and Racial Studies* 29, no. 2 (March 2006): 331–64.

Hall, Stuart. "What Is This 'Black' in Black Popular Culture?" In Dent, G. ed., *Black Popular Culture.* Seattle: Bay Press, 1992, 21–36.

Prins, Baukje. *Voorbij de Onschuld: Het Debat over de multiculturele Samenleving.* Amsterdam: van Gennep, 2000.

Rich, Adrienne. *The Dream of a Common Language: Poems 1974–1977.* New York: W. W. Norton, 1978.

———. "Notes toward a Politics of Location." In *Blood, Bread, and Poetry: Selected Prose 1979–1985.* New York: W. W. Norton, 1986.

———. *What Is Found There: Notebooks on Poetry and Politics.* New York: W. W. Norton, 1993.

Rubin, Gayle. "Thinking Sex: Notes for a Radical Theory of the Politics of Sexuality." In Vance, C. ed., *Pleasure and Danger: Exploring Female Sexuality.* Boston and London: Routledge and Kegan Paul, 1984, 267–319.

Said, Edward. "The Politics of Knowledge." In *Reflections on Exile and other Essays.* Cambridge, Mass.: Harvard University Press, 2004, 372–85.

Wekker, Gloria. "I Am Gold Money: The Construction of Selves, Gender, and Sexualities in a Female, Working-Class, Afro-Surinamese Setting." PhD diss. UCLA, 1992.

———. "Innocence Unltd: Gender, Race and Nation in the Netherlands." Paper presented at the conference "Remapping Black Europe—New Cartographies of Race, Gender, and Nation." UCSC, October 20, 2001.

———. *The Politics of Passion: Women's Sexual Culture in the Afro-Surinamese Diaspora.* New York: Columbia University Press, 2006.

———. "Sexual Subjectivity in Surinamese Slave Society and Its Aftermaths: The Long and Broad Shadows of the Past." Paper presented at the "Slavery from Within" conference, Middelburg, the Netherlands, June 24, 2005.

AFTERWORD

Black Europe's Undecidability

BARNOR HESSE

Europe is literally the creation of the Third World.
—Frantz Fanon

The stimulating collection of papers in this volume demonstrates, inter alia, how the possible meanings of "Black Europe" both extend and exceed the geographies of the European continent. Comprising neither a conventional spatiality nor a familiar representation, it is located at the intersections of *non-Europe/Europe, outside/inside, other/same, immigrant/citizen, coloniality/post-coloniality.* Its formations are also constitutively entangled in national affinities, diasporic alignments, and their racially convulsive histories. This suggests that Black Europe is rhetorically unsettling for the official map of Europe. As a not yet sedimented signifier, Black Europe exposes the tracks of well-traveled human geographies of displacement and disavowed liberal-colonial assemblages of race, traditionally obscured under the historical imprint "Europe." Invocations of Black Europe oblige us to account for the cultural ambiguities and racial equivocations in our contemporary postcoloniality. So what in this contested multicultural landscape is the imprint of Europe today?

Any contemporary understanding of Europe must take into account a recent historical series of dislocations in its meaning generically. Since the early 1990s' creation of the single European market and the European Union, increasingly strident expressions of renewed white European racial anxieties have begun to connect its disparate national formations. Fueled by nationalist fears of apparently unremitting "non-European" immigration and transatlantic insecurities from the chimerical "war against terror," Europe's postcolonial ethnic differences and urban multiculturalisms are now accused of transforming its major cities into geographies of strangeness, cultural unfamiliarity, and national risk. Mobilizations of cultural racism in various European vernaculars have found their racial profiles embodied literally and figuratively in the resented and violated comportments of economic migrants, refugees, asylum seekers, Muslims, and disaffected ethnic minorities. Across the European Union, different nationalist discourses, largely stimulated by *populist* movements, aided and abetted by the social panics of the *popular* press, have articulated racially exclusive associations between citizenship, secularism, democracy, western civilization, and an often unstated but emotive European whiteness. Whether French, British, or Dutch, these discourses have come to symbolize and demonize the unsettled multiculturalisms of Europe, reframing a protracted postcolonial crisis of national representations in terms of an urban clash of civilizations. The latter is routinely portrayed as inevitable, staged between racially tolerant, authentic, indigenous citizens and racially unassimilated, refractory, immigrant citizens. It would appear that Black Europe is now inescapably part of this context and conjuncture.

Although the idea of diaspora permeates the concept of Black Europe, its permutations still need to engage the unresolved and largely neglected relation between nation and city configurations of blackness, whether Black Britain (London), Black France (Paris), Black Germany (Berlin), or Black Holland (Amsterdam). Since unavoidably these western configurations of the transnational, the national, and the city, bring "Europeanized" and "non-Europeanized" (that is, African, Caribbean, African-American) structures of feeling face to face, at various scales of popular and political cultures. Each fused encounter entangles contemporary nationalisms and postcolonialities, juxtaposing racisms disavowed and racisms exposed and always renarrating western democracies and western imperialisms in their historical entwining, even though each continues to be represented separately in conventionally European discourses. Insufficiently traditional, these kinds of social interruptions of national articulations have been routinely absent from hegemonic accounts of the contemporary meaning of European culture in journalism, government discourses, academic texts, television documentaries, or cinematic treatments. Generally well-resourced by a normative white amnesia, signifiers of contemporary Europe continually avert the possibilities of an ethics of postcolonial memory (Hesse 2002), thereby avoiding the indictment of ostensibly previous racial-liberal colonialities in the production of the national-racial-democratic present. This averting seems to conjure a recurrent political and cultural problem for postcolonial Black populations dispersed throughout the different nations of Europe. Stratified by their racial lineages in the histories of Atlantic slavery and/or formerly colonized countries, economic migrations, and socioeconomically oppressed communities, they are routinely expected to demonstrate national allegiances while living with unreliable citizenship rights and recognition, and subject to the ever-present risks of institutional racism. Through all these travails, they remain marked by their social constitution as the racial other, impaled on the horns of a racially nationalistic dilemma: How might Black communities overcome racial conditions of subordination, marginalization, and silencing, particularly where these have become conventionally associated with their national assimilation?

Although varying in articulation from nation to nation, this particular idea of European assimilation has come to sediment a colonial/racial inheritance in the celebrated postcolonial landscape of liberal democracies. Manifestly it obliges a voluntary commitment to appropriate and absorb a prescribed national culture, in terms of language, history, identity, and politics, yet at the same time, while latently a logic of compulsion, it requires subscription to the culture of racial dominance, the hegemony of Europeanness and whiteness as national representation. Unless sanctioned by the commodifications, celebrations, or exoticisms of popular culture, critical forms of Black political and cultural representation can only emerge in critique of the European public sphere, often through protracted forms of civic and national struggle. Confronting or evading the challenge to expose disavowals and formations of racism, even to expand the meaning of diversity and equality, defines Black Europe's conditions of possibility as much as national pressures to pursue assimilation, though always subject to circumvention, in negotiating terms of social congeniality and social solidarities. If ethnographically Black Europe can be located at this juncture, between the social logics of confrontation/evasion and assimilation/circumvention, we should not overlook the conceptuality of that juncture since it is the locus of different representations of Europe and the undecidability of what that could possibly mean for its mapping.

"Europe"

> The discourse of European identity is a symptom of anxiety about "Non-Europeans."
>
> —Talal Asad

Who are "we" that can speak of Europe? I am reminded of this combined question of authorship and authority by a political incident that took place in June 2002. The British prime minister Tony Blair had proposed to a meeting of the European Council of Ministers in Madrid that "non-European" countries identified as sources of illegal immigration be penalized with cuts in their development aid. Although the proposal was rejected and criticized by Anders Fogh Rasmussen, the president of the European Union, as contravening Europe's human rights tradition, nevertheless, it fleetingly exposed what recurrently expresses itself as the problem of defining a postcolonial Europe. The Blair initiative, the ministerial discussion that followed and even the formal rejection all seemed to combine in disinterring something still unresolved in the dominant European imaginary.

The focus on politically regulating and economically punishing "non-Europeans" from the "non-West" suggested that the European Union's cosmopolitan representations were compromised not only by the familiar reflexes of western imperialism, but also the chimera of a European heritage of liberalism uncontaminated by the history of a European colonialism to which it had never applied itself. Significantly, the EU discussion was not concerned with the old immigration of "non-Europe" in Europe during the three decades following World War II, when arrivals from the former colonies in the Caribbean, Africa, and Asia were both economically procured and racially resented by various strata of European populations and socially managed within national race relations. If that was a problem of race and nationalism, this was now a problem of nationalism and multiculturalism. The newer immigration concern had arisen as a by-product of the neoliberal economics accelerated and globalized by deregulated European national markets since the late 1980s, and after 1992 the removal of internal border controls within the European Union for nationals of member states. One of the most striking demographic features of this multicultural symptom of globalization has been the rise of "world cities," "global cities," and "regional cities" almost semidetached from the nations in which they are formally embedded, with the consequences that in attracting focused migrations, "western"/"European" and "non-western"/"non-European" relationships between places, people, identities, cultures, and discourses are being recast in unsettling and unfamiliar ways at rapid historical speed, all of which are proving to be both destabilizing and intoxicating (Hall 2000; Hesse 2000).

These gestations of fungible, unsettled multiculturalisms now characteristic of the European city are increasingly structured and synthesized by formations of race, ethnicity, religion, and diaspora and their various contestations. It has been suggested that some global cities (for example, Paris, London) are now the sites of new claims on the meaning of citizenship, raising the awkward yet fascinating cultural and political question, "Whose city is it?" (Sassen 1998). The economic logic of globalization, which assimilates labor to capital in drawing western cities into concentrations of both economic disparities and cultural diversities (Sassen 1998, 2000), seems to be unwittingly underwriting the emergence of a "multicultural European city" (Rogers 2000). According to Alisdair Rogers, the incorporation of European nations into the legal sovereignty of the European Union raises novel questions about the national allegiances of its cities. This is because European cities are no longer tightly bound into rigid national territorial units. They are, rather, closely connected to the "supranational, cross-national and sub-national territories" in which the European Union is situated. When this is combined with the range of "non-national" territories that connects the EU to other parts of the world through the various impacts of immigration and settlement, it becomes possible to envisage the "multicultural European city" dislocating the self-evident idea of Europe as a tapestry of discrete, parochial, self-contained nations (Rogers 2000).

Unlike Rogers, however, we should not overlook the other side of multiculturalism, the socially estranged race relations of a European cosmopolitan sociality, which remain frozen in the postcolonialities of regulating the social being and cultural comportments of the "non-European," "nonwhite" racial other. Not only have contemporary patterns and predicaments of the new immigration and its control in Europe reactivated anti-immigrant discourses of exclusion and contamination from the early postcolonial years, they have exhumed and reanimated the remains of colonial and racist dimensions of governance in European democratic culture. Stephen Castles offers a salutary assessment where he observes that racism "does not contradict democracy" because it assists in reinforcing "the boundaries of democratic polities by defining who do not belong and can therefore be excluded from universalistic principles," thereby establishing the conditions in which "the nation-state finds it so hard to accept the principle of multicultural belonging" (Castles 2000, 14). It would appear therefore that the contingencies of institutional racisms and unsettled multiculturalisms within Europe provide it with a much different signature than that which celebratedly underwrites the European Union.

The political antagonisms of contemporary European postcoloniality double up and overlap in profound ways. Antagonisms between multiculturalisms and racisms often resemble and complicate those between migrations and nationalisms. This particular European ambience, if not voluntarily open to critique, is certainly mired in being opened up to the possibility of its "provincialization" (Chakrabarty 2000). Although since the eighteenth-century Enlightenment era, Europe's self-recognition as a distinctive secular, economic, cultural formation has become a recognizable global brand, Europe as a spatial reference has remained a "highly unstable term" (Pagden 2002). Since historically only the Atlantic and Mediterranean have provided "obvious and natural boundaries" (Pagden 2002), the definition of "Europe" has always incorporated uncertainty about its geographic frontiers, with the case for grouping particular territories and peoples together as "European" varying from period to period (Bartlett 1993). Indeed, because Europe is the only continent with no basis in physical geography, its self-exclusion from what is otherwise the continent of Eurasia has historically not been established through geography but through coloniality. Consequently, it is the impact and effects of its coloniality that require interpretation and provincialization.

According to Dipesh Chakrabarty, if Europe as a representational discourse or institution were to encounter its own provincialization, it would experience being challenged and revised at the site of two inheritances in the idea of European domination. The first would be "historicism," which presents "Europe" in political and academic discourse as a discrete geographical entity unfolding from an autonomous, internal history, exhibiting itself as a universal model for humanity. The challenge to European historicism would entail at the very least making "visible, within the very structure of its narrative forms, its own repressive strategies and practices, the part it plays in collusion with the narratives of citizenship in assimilating to the projects of the modern state all other possibilities of human solidarity" (Chakrabarty 2000, 45). In these terms, marking Europe's historical and colonial entanglements with "non-European" ("nonwhite") histories would mean reformulating the European idea, shifting the explanatory resonance of its modernity from racial ethicality and presumptive universality to postcolonial accountability and contested hegemony.

The second site of provincialization would concern the European ideal of "the political." This conventionally represents "Europe" as providing responsible adjudication and supervision of the secular capacity "non-Europeans" ("nonwhites") are deemed to have in governing and regulating themselves (hence their ascribed status of "waiting" for European recognition) or in developing their own criteria of politics (hence the attribution of "nonpolitical," "cultural," or "religious" to non-European/nonwhite social movements). Any revision to the European ideal of the political would involve questioning the primacy of secularism (Asad 2005) that occludes how the meaning of "being human" evokes a synthesis of spiritual, religious, and secular questions as well as passionate attachments to particular forms of non-European representation. Critical revision would need to emphasize that "Europe appears different when seen from the experiences of colonization or inferiorization in specific parts of the world," since these "different geographies of colonialism" speak of "different Europes" (Chakrabarty 2000, 16).

In this way, we may begin to think of the European political as always already "Creolized" in the precise sense that Edouard Glissant (1988) gives to that term. It suggests that the identities of these various Europes and non-Europes as entities were not constituted prior to contacts of political, economic, and colonial entanglements and ensuing racial formations, imbrications, and antagonisms, that is, their Creolization. If critically revising the political heritage of Europe can reveal these various inheritances of Creolization as alternative inscriptions of its heritage, then it presages conditions of possibility for its contested appropriation by all who live in Europe's cities: those who are identified with and affected by its nations and who may well be compelled to transform or defend its imaginary in terms of their own particular memories and desires.

In the politics of its unsettled multiculturalisms, contemporary Europe is currently encountering its reconfiguration as a protracted site of postcolonial undecidability. Jacques Derrida's idea of undecidability suggests the meaning of contested and questioned experiences has no fixed inheritance or self-evident designation. Consequently, despite Europe's reliance on a "metaphysics of presence" (Derrida 1973) for the modernity of its universal representations, the irrepressible intrusions of racial/colonial modernities also inscribe it in the impossibility of deriving a settled contemporary meaning for Europe from any conventionally established rule of adjudication or fixed criteria of heritage. For example, undecidability arises when we are confronted by the prospect that a European culture of human rights or tradition of liberalism cannot be rendered distinctly separable from a European culture of colonialism or a tradition of racism (see Goldberg 2000; Metha 2000). It requires us to ask what is European about a Europe in which non-European immigration and nonwhite settlement is simultaneously accommodated as the economic rule, celebrated as cultural diversity, and derided as racialized excess? What is European about a Europe that inherits and inhabits institutional formations of race, ethnicity, diaspora, and globalization that can be valorized as valuable resources for developing cosmopolitan democracy and readily trivialized as cultural exoticism or social contamination? Whatever Europe now means, in this exposure, its presumed copyright of modernity's emancipatory traditions can no longer serve as an exclusive guide, since those emancipations were also predicated on the rule and exploitation of a non-Europe that always resided symbolically and territorially within it, yet was always disavowed. Consequently, in the absence of any established algorithm that accounts for the meaning of Europe, faced with the historical indivisibility of Europe's liberal and racial signifiers and the convergence of its democratic and colonial revolutions (Hesse, forthcoming), very different and new conceptual *decisions* need now to be taken about the significance of Europe. Undecidability compels a decision that marks a radical departure from conventional formula. A decision must be taken on the idea and symbolization of Europe, where issues of representation arise in the face of competing, contested and alternative possibilities. This undecidability is what impregnates Europe when the colonialities, migrations, settlements, and racializations that signify the incubation of Black Europe can no longer be aborted from Europe's representations of its progeny. It invites us to engage Black Europe's disavowed histories and geographies, which now translate as unsettling multiculturalisms, vibrating between racial assemblages of "Europeaness" and "non-Europeaness." Through the rites of European undecidability, we need to reimagine the meaning of the signified *Europe* in the signifiers "Europe," "non-Europe" and "Black Europe," where each implies the other and is encountered in each other's racial configuration.

"Non-Europe"

> In the beginning, there was no Europe.
>
> —Norman Davies

Where is "non-Europe"? If we understand it as Europe's anterior, absence, or antithesis, it is only because it was historically insinuated into ontological form by the colonial constitution of Europe in the Americas, Asia, the Pacific, and Africa. As this is hardly the map of a self-evident or natural human geography, it might be said that non-Europe is wherever the European relation of coloniality has been enacted and sustained. Of course, it needs emphasizing that this modern colonial line, not entirely explained though powerfully symbolized by the whiteness/nonwhiteness of the color line, traditionally divides non-Europeanness from Europeanness and is constitutive of the social relation inherited and known as race. If, as Max Weber once suggested, the symbol of modernity accrues from the progressive disenchantment of the world, we should note that historically it was accompanied by the discursive invention of Europe in relative secular autonomy from Christendom (Davies 1996), a history that also propelled economic and Christian worldly desires whose disenchantment was compensated for by the fantasies of material enrichment, empire, and religious conversions in overseas colonizations (Wolf 1982; Mignolo 1995).

In the history of Europe, this and later colonial history has become the history of non-Europe as the elsewhere and the otherwise. Though intellectually disavowed, it nevertheless accumulates as the unexamined cultural inheritance of familiar western philosophical and sociological discourses on transitions to modernity that routinely esteem the universality of European values in scientific rationality, capitalism, secularism, liberalism, and historiography (Hesse 2007). Such epistemological conceit, in erasing the significance of coloniality in constituting both Europe and non-Europe in relation, has underwritten a widely disseminated western intellectual tradition, a social theory known as *Eurocentrism.* This suffuses and reproduces the generic idea of a non-Europeaness, arrested in development, exterior to progress, weighed down by tradition, that naturally explains why modernity is written into a normative idiom, comprised of hegemonic projects of governance and universalism, principally valorized as European cultures of universal representation, the aesthetics of European corporeality and the sovereignty of European geography (Said 1979; Amin 1988; Mudimbe 1988; Blaut 1993; Sayyid 2002). Non Europeanness in these inflections finds its traditional modern designation as the subaltern of an *onto-colonial power* (see Hesse, forthcoming), fixed in exotic cultures, inferior corporealities, friendly or hostile geographies and western-read histories. This is the non-Europe incorporated into and expelled from the regimen of Europeanness in Europe, the Americas, African, Asia, and the Pacific, always positioned by the relational institution of race.

Contemporary discussions of essentialism and social constructionism that usually surround the designation of race have tended to neglect the historicity of its pragmatic colonial imposition, discursively and materially engraved in a protracted and complex intellectual and institutional process that endured from the late fifteenth century to the eighteenth century (cf. Boxill 2001). What emerged as the colonial distinctions assembled between non-Europeanness and Europeanness, across and within the metropole and colony, remains the basis of contemporary popular, social, and pseudo-scientific racial classifications. In other words, beyond its institutional modalities, race is inherited as a modern imaginary that consecrates the difference between a distinctive Europeaness and the regulation of its designated non-Europeanness, providing both with a colonial rather than a biological ancestry. The importance of this imaginary lies in its provision of a "horizon" that "structures" the social "field of intelligibility" (Laclau 1990), facilitating and limiting the conceptual conditions under which it becomes possible to perceive, think, and feel things and relations in particular ways and not others. It signifies what is in excess of institutional designation, in the case of non-Europe, its designation according to the historical institution of Europe's earlier socio-theological formation.

We should not forget that the colonial idea of non-Europe emerged conceptually over the course of modern time (Mignolo 1995); even by 1500 the term "Europe" was hardly in general use and the geographical terrain with which its inhabitants associated themselves was more a spiritual and theological construction than a secular and historical one. Instead, it was known as *Christendom* (Bartlett 1993; Davies 1996). Nevertheless, the social processes comprising that formation do bequeath a significant heritage. According to Robert Bartlett (1993), the Latinized establishment of Christendom between 1050 and 1500 had three significant dimensions for the subsequent emergence of the European idea in what was otherwise the western extremity of the Asian continent. The first was the "ethnicization of Christianity" in which "credal difference and ethnic identity became inextricably entwined." Being born a Christian in Christendom underwrote universal Christian identity in parochial cultural terms. Secondly, there was a "racializing trend" where Christians were defined against "alien peoples" using metaphors of race and blood to signify an acclaimed unique descent as one corporeal people. Thirdly, Christianity was territorialized, which represented it as a spiritual geographic location: Christendom (Bartlett 1993, 252–53). What each of these social processes exemplifies are forms of social embodiment that became fused in Christendom's logic of equivalence between culture, corporeality and geography.

From 1492 onwards, that logic of equivalence was inherited, elaborated, and represented as race in the modern/colonial distinctions instituted and imagined between Europe and non-Europe. Not even the Enlightenment's eighteenth-century codifications of race in philosophical and anthropological discourses questioned this logic of equivalence. It was generally assumed and expanded in the modern/colonial European synthesis of bodies, territories, cultures, histories, dispositions, climates, and sociality, which continue to underwrite what we understand as race (Hesse 2007). Such a formation and formulation of race was and remains modernity's colonial distinction between Europeanness and non-Europeanness. Though often symbolized as whiteness and nonwhiteness, its various interpretations are still carried out within that haunting grid of coloniality, albeit the latter is disavowed. Consequently any tabulation of racial categories has always been established on the basis of a singular white/European category reconstituting that grid through its gaze, initially separating itself from a plurality of nonwhite/non-European categories, which it surveys and regulates, and then including itself in the tabulation of races that it also defines and ranks within the same grid. Despite popular and scholarly fixations on race as the summary of comparative anatomies or visually embodied differences, the meaning of race, which represents non-Europe for Europe, has always been extra-corporeal. Positioned and embodied by Europe's cultural, political, historical, ecological, and religious assemblages of the historically colonial relation, this racial difference constituted by a designated non-Europeanness always poses the social question of its accommodation or regulation by whatever assembles itself as European. We can see this problematization in contemporary political and cultural dislocations of Europe, where diverse settlements and penetrations of non-Europe have radically disrupted the hegemonic colonial equivalence between culture, corporeality, and geography, unraveling the old certainties of these racial moorings in any figuration of its emblematic cities and most prominent nations as unmistakably and unremarkably white. Though not without its enduring racial antagonisms, the postcolonial settlements and unsettled multicultural sociality associated with the end of the European empires, migrations from non-Europe and their generations of communities within Europe, are variously, and sometimes seamlessly, urban, national, and global. Consequently, they routinely resist being translated into the reductive terms non-Europe.

"Black Europe"

> I wanted to create an Antillean French, a black French that while still being French, had a black character.
>
> —Aimé Césaire

Most European nations, particularly the former colonial front line in western, southern, and northern Europe (Spain, Portugal, Holland, Sweden, Denmark, France, Britain, Belgium, Germany, and Italy), have responded to the historical infusions of Black populations from Africa and the Caribbean and their Black European descendents with varying mixes of exclusionary racism, social mainstreaming, and compulsory assimilation. Yet despite the long modern history of Black populations in Europe, particularly given the complexity of that history after the second world war, "Europe" and "European" remain so articulated with assumptions of whiteness, disavowals of its coloniality, and hallucinations of ethical universalism, that to posit even the idea of Black Europe seems heretical, if not perverse. Where the question of racism is officially acknowledged in Europe, with the possible exception of the UK, it is largely understood in Eurocentric terms, derived from the western liberal reaction to the Nazi genocide of Jewish populations in the heartlands of Europe during the second world war (Hesse 2004a). Racism construed as individual race discrimination, race hatred, and racially legislative exclusions is understood to have arisen from and to be found lingering in states of exception (cf. Schmitt 2005; Agamben 2005), contrary to the civilized rule of western culture in Europe (Hesse 2004b). This has even prompted one historian of postwar Europe to write recently, "Holocaust recognition is our contemporary European entry ticket" (Judt 2005). The significance of Black Europe's formations through Atlantic racial slavery, Western imperialism, and postcolonial racisms is almost invisible by comparison.

It is perhaps understandable why Paul Gilroy declared over a decade ago in the opening line of *The Black Atlantic,* "Striving to be European and black requires some specific forms of double consciousnesses." He suggested that "racist," "nationalist," or "ethnically absolutist" discourses had so dominated political representations as to make "European" and "black" "appear to be mutually exclusive." Consequently, this meant the theoretical and political task now became "occupying the space between them or trying to demonstrate their continuity" (Gilroy 1993, 1). Yet this idea of the "between" or "continuity" seems to sustain the polarization Gilroy wants to criticize; it assumes the conceptual objective is to reconcile or negotiate these two aspects of a duality made available by racist discourses. But this forgoes the critique of that racial duality, namely that Black Europe is both, neither, and more. The complexities of thinking through figurations of Black Europe arise from its being irreducible to the fixed terms of either Europe or non-Europe in the classical metropole and colony schema. Its emergent identifications can be seen more acutely as a territorial imbrication of Europe and non-Europe undergoing radical revision by Black political and cultural spaces of representation. Here blackness may be said to signify African, Caribbean, and even African American entanglements in urban, national, and diasporic trajectories within an undecidable Europe obliged to search for new postcolonial forms of representation. This, however, says very little about the imaginaries of Black Europe that might analytically be thought to bear out this process.

I want to suggest that here finally we might (re)turn for guidance to one of the most sustained configurations of Black Europe as an imaginary during the twentieth century, which occurred almost incidentally as part of the fermentations of the much maligned negritude movement during the 1930s to 1960s that was centered in Paris (see Wilder 2005). Although not traditionally seen in these terms, negritude symbolized the political idea of Black Europe in a number of significant ways, particularly if read through the formulations of Aimé Césaire. Firstly, it underlined the resistance to the coloniality and racism of Europe as the social terrain of African- and Caribbean-derived cultures in forging dialogical Black representations within shared European idioms. Secondly, it emphasized the problem of racial alienation within Europe where Black populations are either exoticized or demonized and the historical values of Black cultures are repressed while the universal credentials of European culture imposed. Thirdly, it embodied the critique of assimilation to the racial rule of European culture within Europe, registering its own aesthetic, intellectual, and political terms of engagement. Fourthly, its poetic innovations within the French language, through efforts to purge it of its rhetorical whiteness and develop the semantic possibilities of critical Black representations, demonstrated the capacity of Black cultural interventions to transform European culture without it ceasing to be European in the process of becoming self-critically European. Negritude symbolized the Black European experience of the African diaspora, where Europe became the site for meetings between diverse ethnicities from Africa, the Caribbean, and Europe, as well as the horizon of cultural networks developing awareness of the issues raised by Black populations in other parts of the world, particularly the United States. If we sanction this analytical distinction between the critical European politics of Negritude and its pan-Africanist poetics, then it becomes possible to see in its configuration of Black Europe, the imbrication of Europe, non-Europe, and the situated excess of the African diaspora. It remains symbolically the most insightful way of characterizing the cultural and political resources of Black Europe, particularly at the moment of its most recent intellectual discovery in African American studies, where its undecidability is often overlooked.

Acknowledgments

My thanks to Richard Iton and Stephanie Y. Evans.

References

Agamben, G. *State of Exception.* Chicago: University of Chicago Press, 2005.

Amin, S. *Eurocentrism.* London: Zed Books, 1988.

Asad, T. *Formations of the Secular: Christianity, Islam, Modernity.* Stanford: Stanford University Press, 2005.

Bartlett, R. *The Making of Europe: Conquest, Colonization and Cultural Change, 950–1350.* London: Penguin Books, 1993.

Blaut, J. M. *The Colonizer's Model of the World: Geographical Diffusionism and Eurocentric History.* New York: Guildford Press, 1993.

Boxill, B., ed. *Race and Racism.* Oxford: Oxford University Press, 2001.

Castles, S. *Ethnicity and Globalization.* London: Sage, 2000.

Césaire, A. *Discourse on Colonialism.* New York: Monthly Review Press, 1972.

Chakrabarty, D. *Provincializing Europe.* Princeton, N.J.: Princeton University Press, 2000.

Davies, N. *Europe: A History.* London: Pimlico Books, 1996.

Derrida, J. *Speech and Phenomena.* Evanston: Northwestern University Press, 1973.

Fanon, F. *Wretched of the Earth.* London: Penguin, 1963.

Gilroy, P. *The Black Atlantic.* London: Verso, 1993.

Glissant, E. *Caribbean Discourse: Selected Essays.* Charlottesville: University of Virginia Press, 1988.

Goldberg, D. T. *The Racial State.* Oxford: Blackwell, 2000.

Hall, S. "The Multicultural Question." In B. Hesse, ed., *Un/Settled Multiculturalisms: Diasporas, Entanglements, Transruptions.* London: Zed Press, 2000.

Hesse, B. *Creolizing the Political: A Genealogy of the African Diaspora.* Durham: Duke University Press, 2008.

———. "Racialized Modernity: An Analytics of White Mythologies." *Ethnic and Racial Studies* 30, no. 4 (July 2007): 643–63.

———. "Im/Plausible Deniability: Racism's Conceptual Double Bind." *Social Identities* 10, no. 1 (January 2004a): 9–29.

———. "Discourse on Institutional Racism: The Genealogy of a Concept." In I. Law, D. Phillips, and L. Turner, eds., *Institutional Racism in Higher Education.* London: Trentham Books, 2004b. 131–48.

———. "Forgotten Like a Bad Dream: Atlantic Slavery and the Ethics of Postcolonial Memory." In D. Goldberg and A. Quayson, eds., *Relocating Postcolonialism.* Oxford; Malden, MA: Blackwell, 2002. 143–73.

Hesse, B. ed. *Un/Settled Multiculturalisms: Diasporas, Entanglements, Transruptions.* London: Zed Press, 2000.

Judt, T. *Postwar: A History of Europe since 1945.* New York: Penguin Press, 2005.

Laclau, E. *New Reflections on the Revolution of Our Time.* London: Verso, 1990.

Metha, U. S. *Liberalism and Empire.* Chicago: University of Chicago Press, 2000.

Mignolo W. *The Darker Side of the Renaissance.* Ann Arbor: University of Michigan Press, 1995

Mudimbe, V. Y. *The Invention of Africa: Gnosis, Philosophy, and the Order of Knowledge.* Bloomington: Indiana University Press, 1988.

Pagden, A. *The Idea of Europe: From Antiquity to the European Union.* New York: Cambridge University Press, 2002.

Rogers, A. "Citizenship, Multiculturalism and the European City." In *A Companion to the City.* Ed. G. Bridge and S. Watson. Oxford: Blackwell, 2001. 282–91.

Said, E. *Orientalism.* New York: Vintage Books, 1979.

Sassen, S. *Globalization and Its Discontents.* New York: New Press, 1998.

———. *Guests and Aliens.* New York: New Press, 2000.

Sayyid, S. *A Fundamental Fear: Eurocentrism and the Emergence of Islamism.* London: Zed Books, 2002.

Schmitt, C. *Political Theology.* Chicago: University of Chicago Press, 2005.

Wilder, G. *The French Imperial State: Negritude and Colonial Humanism between the Two World Wars.* Chicago: University of Chicago Press, 2005.

Wolf. E. *Europe and the Peoples without History.* Berkeley: University of California Press, 1982.

CONTRIBUTORS

DARLENE CLARK HINE is Board of Trustees Professor of African American Studies and Professor of History at Northwestern University. She was the founding director of the Center for African American History that sponsored the Black Europe symposium. She is the co-editor (with Jacqueline McLeod) of *Crossing Boundaries: Comparative History of Black People in Diaspora*, and (with David Barry Gaspar) of *More Than Chattel: Black Women and Slavery in the Americas* and *Beyond Bondage: Free Women of Color in the Americas*. She is past-President of the Organization of American Historians and of The Southern Historical Association. Hine is a member of the National Academy of Arts and Sciences.

TRICA DANIELLE KEATON is an Associate Professor of African American and Diasporic Studies at Vanderbilt University. She has been a visiting scholar at the École des Hautes Études en Sciences Sociales in Paris where she was a Chateaubriand Fellow, and she is also an Associate of the W. E. B. Du Bois Institute for African and African American Research at Harvard University. She is the author of *Muslim Girls and the Other France: Race, Identity Politics, and Social Exclusion*, articles on race and identity politics in France, and coeditor of this anthology and a forthcoming anthology on the Black presence in France.

STEPHEN SMALL is Associate Professor and Chair of the Department of African American Studies at the University of California at Berkeley where he earned a doctorate in sociology. He teaches courses in the comparative historical sociology of Africans throughout the diaspora, with particular focus on the United States, England, and the Caribbean. He also teaches qualitative methods. He was director of the study center of the University of California's Education

Abroad Program in France (Bordeaux and Toulouse), 2002–2004; and he has been director of UC-Berkeley's summer program in Brazil (Salvador and Rio de Janeiro) each summer since 2001. His recent publications include *Representations of Slavery, Race, and Ideology in Southern Plantation Museums* (cowritten with Jennifer Eichstedt), and *Race and Power: Global Racism in the Twenty-first Century* (cowritten with Gargi Bhattacharyya and John Gabriel).

ALLISON BLAKELY is Professor of European and Comparative History at Boston University since 2001, having formerly taught for thirty years at Howard University. He received his BA from the University of Oregon, and his MA and PhD from the University of California, Berkeley. He is the author of *Blacks in the Dutch World: The Evolution of Racial Imagery in a Modern Society*, American Book Award winner *Russia and the Negro: Blacks in Russian History and Thought*, several articles on Russian populism, and others on various European aspects of the Black Diaspora. His interest in comparative history has centered on comparative populism and on the historical evolution of color prejudice. His current main project is an overview of the history of Blacks in modern Europe. Among the awards he has received are Woodrow Wilson, Mellon, Fulbright-Hays, and Ford Foundation fellowships. He has served as President of the Phi Beta Kappa Society (2006–2009) and as consulting editor of its journal, *The American Scholar*.

JACQUELINE NASSY BROWN is Associate Professor of Anthropology at Hunter College of the City University of New York and the Graduate Center of the City University of New York. She is the author of *Dropping Anchor, Setting Sail: Geographies of Race in Black Liverpool*.

TINA M. CAMPT is Associate Professor of Women's Studies, History, and German at Duke University. Campt is a historian of modern Germany history, feminist theorist, oral historian, and ethnographer whose work focuses on issues of gender, memory, and racial formation among African diasporic communities in Europe, and Germany in particular. She is the author of *Other Germans: Black Germans and the Politics of Race, Gender, and Memory in the Third Reich*. She is coeditor with Michelle M. Wright of a special issue of the journal *Callaloo* on the Black German experience, and together with Paul Gilroy coedited the volume *Der Black Atlantik*, a collection of essays emerging out of her work as a guest curator of the multimedia cultural project "The Black Atlantic: Traveling Cultures, Counter-History and Networked Identities" at the House of World Cultures in Berlin. Together with Deborah Thomas, Campt is co-convener of the multiyear scholarly and curricular project "Diasporic Hegemonies: Gendering the Diaspora and Racing the Transnational" and coeditor of a special issue of *Feminist Review* of the same title. She is completing her second monograph, *Image Matters: Archive, Photography, and the African Diaspora in Europe*, a study of how two different Black European communities—Black Britons and Black Germans—used photography as an expressive cultural practice to create forms of identification and community in the first half of the twentieth century in Germany and the UK.

FRED CONSTANT is Professor of Political Science at the University of Antilles and Guyane (France), former provost of the International Francophone University of Alexandria (Egypt), visiting scholar at New York University, and currently on leave from the French Ministry for Foreign Affairs. He is the author of several books and articles on the issues of citizenship, ethnicity, equality, membership in postcolonial France, and the Caribbean. His latest study, "Aimé Césaire in Politics: Seven Lessons of Leadership," will appear in the journal *French Politics, Culture, and Society.*

ALESSANDRA DI MAIO teaches at the University of Palermo and is visiting Professor at the University of California at Los Angeles. Her area of specialization includes black, diasporic, migratory, and postcolonial studies with a particular attention to the formation of transnational cultural identities. Among her publications are *Tutuola at the University: The Italian Voice of a Yoruba Ancestor*, the collection *An African Renaissance*, and *Wor(l)ds in Progress: A Study of Contemporary Migrant Writings*. She is the Italian translator of Nuruddin Farah and Wole Soyinka.

PHILOMENA ESSED is a Professor of Critical Race, Gender, and Leadership Studies at the Leadership and Change Program at Antioch University. She is also an affiliated researcher at Utrecht University in the Netherlands in graduate gender studies. Her books include *Understanding Everyday Racism*; *Diversity: Gender, Color, and Culture*; *Race Critical Theories*; *Refugees and the Transformation of Societies*; and *A Companion to Gender Studies* (selected as an outstanding academic reference by the American Librarian Association).

TERRI FRANCIS teaches in the Film Studies program and the Department of African American Studies at Yale University. Her first book, *The Audacious Josephine Baker: Blackness, Power and the Cinematic Body,* is forthcoming.

BARNOR HESSE is an Associate Professor of African American Studies at Northwestern University. He is author of *Creolizing the Political: A Genealogy of the African Diaspora* (forthcoming).

DIENKE HONDIUS is an Associate Professor of History and Sociology at Vrije Universiteit in Amsterdam and at the Anne Frank House. She published extensively on the history of anti-Semitism and race relations in the Netherlands. Among her books are a study of post-Holocaust anti-Semitism, a study of the acceptance of ethnic, religious, and racial intermarriage, a book about the segregation of Jewish schoolchildren in Amsterdam during the Nazi occupation, and articles on race and racism. The chapter in this volume derives from research for her new book, *Race in European History: The Persistence of Paternalism.*

EILEEN JULIEN is Professor of French and Comparative Literature at Indiana University in Bloomington, where she teaches twentieth-century literature and culture with a focus on Africa, the Americas, and Europe in their relationships to one another. She is the author of *African Novels and the Question of Orality*; a memoir, *Travels with Mae: Scenes from a New Orleans Girlhood*; and co-editor of the forthcoming *Locations and Dislocations of African Literature: Humanists and Social Scientists in Dialogue.* Julien was the founding director of the West African Research Center in Dakar, Senegal (1993–95).

KWAME NIMAKO is President of OBEE Consultancy and teaches International Relations at the University of Amsterdam. He is a member of the Scientific Council of the National Institute of Dutch Slavery and Its Legacy (NiNsee) and the author/coauthor of some thirty books, reports, and guide books on economic development, ethnic relations, social policy, urban renewal, and migration. His recent publications include "African Regional Groupings and Emerging Chinese Conglomerates" in *Big Business and Economic Development: Conglomerates and Economic Groups in Developing Countries and Transition Economies under Globalisation,* edited by Alex E. Fernandez Jilberto and Barbara Hogenboom; and he is coauthor with Philomena Essed of "Designs and (Co)incidents: Cultures of Scholarship and Public Policy on Immigrants/Minorities in the Netherlands," in the *International Journal of Comparative Sociology.*

TIFFANY RUBY PATTERSON is Associate Professor of African American and Diaspora Studies at Vanderbilt University, where she teaches African American and black Atlantic history. She has published *Zora Neale Hurston and a History of Southern Life* and is associate editor of *Black Women in United States History.* She is author of "Diaspora and Beyond: The Promise and Limitations of Black Transnational Studies in the United States," in *Les diasporas dans le monde contemporain: Un état des lieux,* edited by W. Berthomiere and C. Chivallon, and coauthor with Robin D. G. Kelley of "Unfinished Migrations: Reflections on the African Diaspora and the Making of the Modern World," in the *African Studies Review.* She is currently working on *A Question of Color,* a volume in the Schomburg Black Experience in the Western World series, and a history of color consciousness in the United States and Jamaica.

T. DENEAN SHARPLEY-WHITING is a Professor of African American and Diaspora Studies and French, and director of the program in African American and Diaspora Studies at the W. T. Bandy Center for Baudelaire and Modern French Studies at Vanderbilt University. Her books include *Negritude Women; Black Venus: Sexualized Savages, Primal Fears, and Primitive Narratives in French;* and *Frantz Fanon: Conflicts and Feminisms*. She has coedited three volumes, the latest of which is *The Black Feminist Reader*. She has recently completed a book on young Black women and hip-hop culture, *Pimps Up, Ho's Down: Hip Hop's Hold on Young Black Women*.

TYLER STOVALL is a Professor of French History at the University of California, Berkeley. He is the author of numerous articles. His books include *The Rise of the Paris Red Belt* and *Paris Noir: African Americans in the City of Light*. He is currently working on a study of Caribbean migration to France.

ALEXANDER G. WEHELIYE is Associate Professor of African American Studies and English at Northwestern University, where he teaches African American and Afro-diasporic literature and culture, critical theory, and popular culture. He is the author of *Phonographies: Grooves in Sonic Afro-Modernity*, which was awarded the Modern Language Association's William Sanders Scarborough Prize for Outstanding Scholarly Study of Black American Literature or Culture. Currently, he is working on the vexed category of the human in modernity as it pertains to Afro-diasporic culture and how W.E.B. Du Bois and Walter Benjamin imagine the marginal as central to the workings of modern civilization.

GLORIA WEKKER is a Professor of Social and Cultural Anthropology specializing in women's studies, African American studies, and Caribbean studies. She holds the IIAV chair in gender and ethnicity in the faculty of the arts at Utrecht University in the Netherlands and is the director of GEM, the Center of Expertise on Gender, Ethnicity, and Multiculturalism in Higher Education at the same university. Her most recent publication is "The Politics of Passion: Women's Sexual Culture in the Afro-Surinamese Diaspora," for which she won the Ruth Benedict prize of the Society of Lesbian and Gay Anthropologists of American Anthropological Association.

MICHELLE M. WRIGHT is an Associate Professor of African American Studies at Northwestern University. She served as the Fulbright senior lecturer and scholar in the Amerika Institut at Ludwig-Maximilians Universität in 2006–7. She is the author of *Becoming Black: Creating Identity in the African Diaspora* and the editor of several volumes on race, gender, sexuality, and identity in the African diaspora including *Reading the Black German Experience*, a special issue of the journal *Callaloo* edited with Tina M. Campt; *Domain Errors! A Cyberfeminist Handbook* with Faith Wilding and Maria Fernandez; and *Blackness and Sexualities* with Antje Schuhmann. She is the author of several articles published in the United States and Europe and a contributor to the award-winning volume *James Baldwin Now*. Her next project looks at the epistemological constructions of Black collective identities in the African diaspora and is tentatively titled "The Physics of Blackness: Reconsidering the African Diaspora in the Postwar Era."

INDEX

Page numbers in *italics* refer to illustrations.

THE NEW BLACK STUDIES SERIES

Beyond Bondage: Free Women of Color in the Americas *Edited by David Barry Gaspar and Darlene Clark Hine*

The Early Black History Movement, Carter G. Woodson, and Lorenzo Johnston Greene *Pero Gaglo Dagbovie*

"Baad Bitches" and Sassy Supermamas: Black Power Action Films *Stephane Dunn*

Black Maverick: T. R. M. Howard's Fight for Civil Rights and Economic Power *David T. Beito and Linda Royster Beito*

Beyond the Black Lady: Sexuality and the New African American Middle Class *Lisa B. Thompson*

Extending the Diaspora: New Histories of Black People *Edited by Dawne Y. Curry, Eric D. Duke, and Marshanda A. Smith*

Activist Sentiments: Reading Black Women in the Nineteenth Century *P. Gabrielle Foreman*

Black Europe and the African Diaspora *Edited by Darlene Clark Hine, Trica Danielle Keaton, and Stephen Small*

The University of Illinois Press
is a founding member of the
Association of American University Presses.

Composed in 10.5/13 Adobe Minion Pro
with FF Meta and Berthold Akzidenz Grotesk display
at the University of Illinois Press
Manufactured by Sheridan Books, Inc.

University of Illinois Press
1325 South Oak Street
Champaign, IL 61820-6903
www.press.uillinois.edu